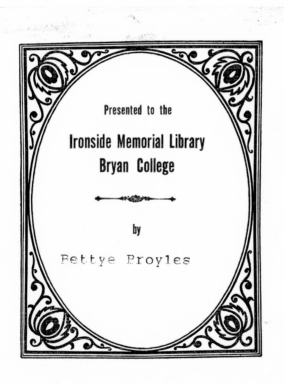

Grit-Tempered

THE RIPLEY P. BULLEN SERIES

Bettye J. Broyles

GRIT-TEMPERED

Early Women Archaeologists in
the Southeastern United States

Edited by Nancy Marie White,
Lynne P. Sullivan,
and Rochelle A. Marrinan

FOREWORD BY JERALD T. MILANICH, SERIES EDITOR

University Press of Florida
Gainesville · Tallahassee · Tampa · Boca Raton
Pensacola · Orlando · Miami · Jacksonville

138273

04 03 02 01 00 99 6 5 4 3 2 1

LIBRARY OF CONGRESS CATALOGING-IN-PUBLICATION DATA
Grit-tempered: early women archaeologists in the southeastern United States /
edited by Nancy Marie White, Lynne P. Sullivan, and Rochelle A. Marrinan;
foreword by Jerald T. Milanich.
p. cm. — (Ripley P. Bullen series)
Includes bibliographical references (p.) and index.
ISBN 0-8130-1686-X (alk. paper)
1. Women archaeologists—Southern States—Biography. 2. Archaeology—
Southern States—History—20th century. 3. Southern States—Biography.
4. Southern States—Antiquities. 5. Indians of North America—Southern
States—Antiquities. I. White, Nancy Marie. II. Sullivan, Lynne P. III. Marrinan,
Rochelle A. IV. Series.
CC110.G75   1999
930.1'092'275—dc21   98-50942

The University Press of Florida is the scholarly publishing agency for the State
University System of Florida, comprising Florida A&M University, Florida
Atlantic University, Florida International University, Florida State University,
University of Central Florida, University of Florida, University of North Florida,
University of South Florida, and University of West Florida.

University Press of Florida
15 Northwest 15th Street
Gainesville, FL 32611-2079
http://www.upf.com

CONTENTS

FIGURES AND TABLES

FOREWORD

Engendering archaeology is an issue that has drawn widespread attention as our discipline has grown. Inquiries into the past no longer ignore the roles women played as leaders, food producers and processors, and craft makers. If females composed 50 percent of past populations, it is only good science to study them along with the other 50 percent.

Engendering archaeology also has brought renewed emphasis on the roles of women in the history of our discipline. Women have contributed a great deal to southeastern archaeology, although that fact has not always been recognized. And it is no overstatement to say that in the past, women archaeologists sometimes faced opposition from men. Today, however, women archaeologists are everywhere, from chairing academic departments to running cultural resource firms, from serving as presidents of the Southeastern Archaeological Conference to directing excavations in the riverine swamps of the Florida panhandle.

These modern successes are due in large part to the accomplishments of women such as those whose careers are highlighted in this volume, women who blazed the trails in what traditionally has been viewed as a male-dominated field. Those pioneers serve as role models for today's women archaeology students, who no longer are told they cannot participate in an archaeological field school because there are not enough bathrooms, nor are they shunted off to the laboratory while the guys grab the shovels. Things are not what they were, thanks to the early women in southeastern United States archaeology.

The remarkable histories of many of those trailblazing women archaeologists are presented here in what, at least for the southeast United States, is itself a pioneering effort. Assembled by Rochelle Marrinan, Lynne Sullivan, and Nancy White, three dynamic scholars who continue to make important contributions to their discipline, *Grit-Tempered: Early Women Archaeologists in the Southeastern United States* is a thoroughly enjoyable and informative book. In my judgment it is the very best of the volumes focusing on women in anthropology, and I am pleased it has been published in the Ripley P. Bullen series.

Jerald T. Milanich, Series Editor

PREFACE

PATTY JO WATSON

This is a remarkable book about ten remarkable archaeologists who made significant contributions to their discipline during a time when that discipline was structured to exclude their kind (female). In addition, the reader will discover what little is known of the mostly anonymous crews of black women who shoveled and toted dirt at Irene and other southeastern sites during the depression years.

Feminist revisions of scholarly preserves have become almost the norm these days. Although overtly feminist perspectives have been slow to appear in North American archaeology, they became prominent in the 1980s, and there is now a respectable literature of publications exemplifying various aspects of feminist approaches to archaeology. This book differs from its predecessors by its focus on the Southeast region of the United States and by its combination of autobiographical with biographical treatment of some amazing women who carried out some amazing work in a wide variety of archaeological venues. Several of the biographees created relatively high-profile careers and were still pursuing their work when this volume was written, while others labored and died in obscurity, emerging from the shadows of archaeological history only because of persistent work by the editors and authors of *Grit-Tempered*. Archaeological readers cannot fail to be deeply impressed by the achievements highlighted in the chapters of this volume, whereas those without specialist concern for the Southeast will be drawn into these life narratives by their intrinsic human interest. Potential readers who find the feminist agenda—and, indeed, feminist anything—

unappealing will discover in this book a wealth of information and local color about the Southeast just before and after World War II, and about the history of archaeology. In fact, very few of the women whose lives are the subjects of chapters here thought of themselves as anything but archaeological scholars engaged in pursuit of knowledge about times and places that fascinated them. Not one of them was or is a self-styled feminist or a self-conscious role model, and virtually none of them would be called aggressive, strident, or pushy by even a totally unreconstructed male chauvinist. Yet they are all, without exception, strong and determined women who overcame substantial obstacles to get access to work they wanted very badly to do and—once granted access—did that work extremely well. That is perhaps the most important theme that emerges from these accounts of their lives, brought together and seen through the press by three younger but equally determined women archaeologists: Nancy Marie White, Lynne P. Sullivan, and Rochelle A. Marrinan. The authors and editors have assembled an important and compelling document about women in archaeology and about archaeology in the Southeast. Read it!

ACKNOWLEDGMENTS

We are grateful to many who helped in the preparation of this book. Most important are the women themselves—Bettye Broyles, Hester Davis, Yulee Lazarus, Carol Mason, Martha Rolingson, Liz Wing, and the late Madeline Kneberg Lewis, as well as Patty Jo Watson—who answered written questionnaires, allowed interviews on numerous occasions, provided advice, sentences, and photographs, helped us correct various problems, read and reread chapters, and never tired!

The University of South Florida (USF) provided White with a Research and Creative Scholarship Grant that permitted travel, taping interviews, and photographic reproduction. Archaeology student Karen Mayo of USF helped with audio- and videotaping during the Arkansas interviews, and students Lou Groh and Jennifer Berke of Florida State University (FSU) joined us during interviewing Bettye Broyles in Tennessee. Many people provided documentary materials and gave advice and leads. They include archaeologists Jim Bradley, Chad Braley, Jeff Chapman, Ann Early, Mike Fowler, Pat Galloway, Bennett Graham, Bill Haag, Mary Ann Levine, Ed Lyon, Bob Mainfort, Jerry Milanich, Brian Robinson, Mike Rodeffer, Frankie Snow, Chris Trowell, Jack Walker, Gordon Willey, and the late Jimmy Griffin and Jesse Jennings. Others who assisted with information and manuscript needs in Tallahassee are Gregory K. Toole, Maria Chavez-Hernandez, Joan Byrd, Anna Campbell, Kathleen Fawcett, Jane Feehan, Georgia Henry, Bryan Johnson, Ann Spangler, Gregory Heide, and Audrey Trauner. Marianne Bell at USF transcribed some thirty hours of interview tape recordings. Andrew and Marion Whiteford provided information on their friend Madeline Kneberg Lewis, and newspaper reporter Leslie Peacock helped with interpretations of Arkansas archaeology. Bill Landry, of WBIR TV in Knoxville, assisted with interviews of Madeline and graciously gave us copies of his professionally made videotape. Archaeologist/artist Scott Mitchell interpreted our Mississippian bird woman. Gail Whalen helped with information on black women at Irene Mound. Miles Wright, photographer at the Frank H. McClung Museum, made the prints for the chapter on Madeline Kneberg Lewis. Susan Rossi-Wilcox and Mary

Gaudet at the Harvard Botanical Museum provided additional data on Margaret Ashley. Staff at the Indian Temple Mound Museum in Fort Walton Beach, Florida, provided materials on Yulee Lazarus, and Jimmy Moses helped videotape her. People who read portions or offered insights, information, comments, and encouragement are Ann Early, Patricia Griffin, Lee Hutchinson-Neff, Bonnie McEwan, Bob McGimsey, and Ray Williams. Thanks also to John P. Sullivan for helping mom check the compiled reference list against the text, and to Tony White for helping mom host editorial sessions at his home.

The designs on the first page of each chapter were drawn by Bettye Broyles (1968) from Swift Creek Complicated-Stamped ceramics found at sites in Georgia, Florida, Alabama, and Tennessee. They are reprinted with the permission of the Southeastern Archaeological Conference, which also gave permission to reprint Cheryl Claassen's article in chapter 5, which was originally published in *Southeastern Archaeology* 12, no. 2 (Winter 1993).

My interest is not in where the soul goes,
but in what the soul leaves behind.

Margaret E. Ashley (Towle), 1928

1

Women in Southeastern U.S. Archaeology

Nancy Marie White

Archaeology is catching up with the rest of anthropology in examining two of the hottest subject areas lately: the history of the discipline and gender issues. After a few early efforts (Williams 1981; Conkey and Spector 1984; Kramer and Stark 1988), there is now much more exploration of gender, both in the archaeological record and in the recovery, analysis, and interpretation of it. It has been a long wait. In *Engendering Archaeology*, Gero and Conkey (1991: Preface) express their amazement that by the late 1980s such topics as gender dynamics in prehistory and sexism in archaeology were not commonplace, given their emphases in other social sciences. Recognition that it was time to see women in the whole field of anthropology came earlier (for example, Rosaldo and Lamphere 1974; Friedl 1975; Kessler 1976; Morgen 1989; Gacs et al. 1989; Levine 1991; diLeonardo 1991; Ortner 1996). Perhaps the situation is analogous to that in the natural and physical sciences, where a slow trickle of early work (for example, Mozans 1913 [1974]) has been followed in the 1990s by an explosion of studies (among the best are Bleier 1984; Fausto-Sterling 1985; Harding and O'Barr 1987; Haraway 1989; Schiebinger 1989; Stolte-Heiskanen 1991; Kass-Simon and Farnes 1990; Brush 1991; McGrayne 1993; *Professional Geographer* 1994; Rossiter 1995 and 1982; Sonnert 1995; Pycior et al. 1996; Wylie 1997;

Eisenhart and Finkel 1998; and *Science*'s 1992, 1993, and later "Women/ Gender in Science" section and responses). The postmodern/postprocessual concern with critical theory and the viewpoint and circumstances of the investigator have become increasingly of wider interest than just in obscure biographies after the scientist dies (though postprocessual archaeology has really paid less attention to women and gender than is claimed; see Engelstad 1991).

Gender in Southeastern Archaeology

Conferences on gender in archaeology have included at least four held in the southeastern United States, including one in which we offered a preliminary description of the research in this volume (White, Marrinan, and Davis 1994; Sullivan 1994; see also Gero and Conkey 1991; Claassen 1992; Claassen and Joyce 1997). Other important conferences/compilations include Walde and Willows 1991; Siefert 1991; Bacus et al. 1993; duCros and Smith 1993; Nelson, Nelson, and Wylie 1994; Balme and Beck 1995; Wright 1996; Hays-Gilpin and Whitley 1998. Only a few papers in these volumes pertain to southeastern U.S. archaeology, however. Other, much-needed works on women in the field (for example, Irwin-Williams 1990; Bender and Parezo 1994; Conkey and Gero 1997) do not deal with the region in proportion to its importance in the history of archaeology; only one mentions a few southeastern U.S. studies (Nelson 1997, citing Bridges 1989; Claassen 1991). Yet the Southeast, with its many ethnographic examples of matrilineal and matrilocal societies, elaborate ceremonialism, sports and warfare, powerful chiefly politics, and prehistoric socioeconomic stratification, not to mention its role as an early center for archaeological theory, should be prime archaeological territory for exploration of material correlates of gender and of the gender roles of the people who explore them.

Southeastern archaeology has been viewed as lagging behind in theoretical development recently (Dunnell 1990; Peebles 1990; Johnson 1993), even though the Southeast was originally an area of major advances such as the first regional culture history syntheses. From a materialist/cultural ecological perspective, one might say that much of the data-oriented nature of archaeology in the Southeast may be because of the emphasis on fieldwork. The climate permits more of it, and fieldwork was emphasized during the early decades of this century because of public works projects (Willey and Sabloff 1993; Lyon 1996; Fagette 1996). It continues to be important with the Sunbelt development boom that necessitates so much cultural resources management (CRM). The good-old-boy tradition could be said to encourage physical, outdoor (not to mention male-oriented) activity such as fieldwork, which, if done often, leaves less time for theorizing. Even outsiders, "carpetbaggers" (Johnson 1993:212) who have ended up doing southeastern archaeology, have been bewitched by this tradition. Its advantage (Watson 1986, 1990; Dunnell 1990; Peebles 1990; Johnson 1993; White 1995) is that it has allowed us to stay out of the fray a bit (whether New archaeology vs. Old, processual vs. postprocessual, scientific vs. humanistic), not worry about the torturous prose of postprocessual theorizing (the "cabalistic code that can be deciphered only by the fully initiated" [Watson 1991: 274]), and get a lot of good work done. As Sabloff has noted (1992:267), most American archaeologists are really still doing culture history anyway.

None of this implies that there is no appreciation in the Southeast of major trends in our discipline, including critical or Marxist or symbolic archaeology and gender studies; there has been renewed interest in theory-building lately, and some exploration therein of gender (for example, Claassen 1997:68–71). One example is Sassaman's (1992) work on early fiber-tempered ceramics, with implications for women's and men's roles (though such gender hypotheses are just as impossible to test [so far] in southeastern prehistory as elsewhere). Claassen's studies of Archaic shell mounds also address the possibilities of changes in labor by gender at the end of the Pleistocene epoch, as well as symbolism in connection with male and female activity areas (Claassen 1991, 1996).

Southeastern Archaeological Conference (SEAC) programs now include symposia on gender, beginning with one organized in 1991 by Kathleen Marie Bolen and Ruth Troccoli (much impetus for this study has come from graduate students). The 1991 symposium included Pat Galloway's crowd-pleaser, "Where Have All the Menstrual Huts Gone?" which noted the male establishment's squeamishness in recognizing archaeological traces of what was doubtless a common building at many native settlements. Galloway's slides portrayed that squeamishness with scenes from sanitary products commercials in which *blue* liquid is poured over absorbent pads, and beautiful women are pictured wearing *white*. Her paper (Galloway 1997) emphasized ideological and social concepts about prehistory that we should be more interested in investigating.

Blood symbolism, biological/calendrical cycles, red pigment, and comparative female and male power are anthropological topics now drawing enormous interest among sociocultural theorists (for example, Buckley and Gottlieb 1988; Knight 1991), and occasionally material evidence for things such as menstrual huts is indeed being sought (Crown and Fish 1996). One study suggests that women's synchronous monthly cycles and accompanying beliefs were the very bases for scheduling Native American subsistence behavior among hunter-gatherers (Buckley 1988).

Among settled agriculturalists, "simple" farmers and horticulturalists have high rates of matrilineality and consequent female equality of power or status (for example, Lepowsky 1994); the shift to (supposed) male dominance comes when intensive mechanized (plow) agriculture takes over (for example, Boserup 1970; Martin and Voorhies 1975; Sherratt 1981; Ember 1983; a good example of an archaeological test of this model is Robb 1994). But in the Southeast and elsewhere in the New World there was no shift to mechanized farming. Is this why matrilineality and the retention of women's status was possible? (And what happens with the emergence of male-dominated states based on non-plow agriculture in the rest of the New World?) The stereotypical example of simple but intensive agriculture is always the Iroquois, thanks to Louis Henry Morgan (1877) and his supposed confirmation of that matriarchal stage in the human past first proposed by Bachofen (1861; Martin and Voorhies 1975:146–55). Standard gender-in-anthropological-perspective textbooks do *not* mention aboriginal southeastern U.S. societies, which were presumably more complex than northeastern ones (such as the Iroquois) and which were classic examples of (matrilineal) chiefdoms based on intensive but nonmechanical agriculture (Hudson 1976).

These are not just questions of idle interest. Matrilineal, matrilocal societies with "simple" agriculture (without domestic animals or plows) are thought to be *politically* very different, more peaceful, or at least having greater internal political stability because of the breakup of related males as they marry out into other households (Martin and Voorhies 1975:220–29). Furthermore, as anthropologists are putting to rest the notion of universal male dominance among human cultures (Leacock 1981; Mukhopadhyay and Higgins 1988; Higgins 1989), many gender systems, especially in matrilineal societies, can be understood not in terms of dominance and subordinance but of duality and complementarity, even in the physical, material record (Spain 1992:59).

The new striving to see the individual in prehistory making adaptational choices has inspired work such as that of Watson and Kennedy (1991), who object to the notion (from Smith 1987) that plants "domesticated themselves" in the eastern United States. They suggest that, if divisions of labor during Archaic times *did* resemble those of much later historic groups (a big "if" and not yet testable), women's familiarity with plants led directly to their increased control over them. Some theorists have entertained such ideas for years, but others cannot accept them. At the 1983 SEAC meeting, Lewis Binford's keynote address, on the origins of food production in the Southeast, went right from models of men controlling hunting to men controlling food production (tied somehow into his ethnoarchaeological research with the Nunamiut in the Arctic). I asked the obvious question, phrased as "What about the place of woman the gatherer in this model?" His incongruous answer was that, being a man, he had not been able to observe women's roles among the Nunamiut. This is interesting because an absence of empirical data has not prevented him lately from speculating on Neanderthal women's and men's roles, and how their separation (and women's use of different, simpler tools) led directly to their conquest by incoming modern *Homo sapiens* (Shreeve 1995:159–66, 330–31; Fischman 1992).

Recent research on biological evidence of sex in the archaeological record, including skeletal remains (for example, Bridges 1989; Armelagos and Hill 1990; Cohen and Bennett 1993) and beyond (in coprolites: Sobolik, Gremillion, Whitten, and Watson 1996; Sobolik 1996) promises exciting data for testing gender hypotheses concerning diet, health, nutrition, and divisions of labor. Yet when it comes to exploring southeastern prehistoric socioeconomic stratification, political economy, and even ideology, in all the latest works (for example, Dye and Cox 1990; Barker and Pauketat 1992; Pauketat 1994; Scarry 1996; Muller 1997), ideas of gender or even political implications of matrilineal kinship or matrilocal residence are invisible (exceptions are Widmer 1994; Galloway 1995), even though there is conservative to wild speculation about everything else.

This lack of a gendered perspective is noteworthy because matrilineality, matrilocality, and control of production are all contexts in which women are likely to be particularly politically influential (for example, Mukhopadhyay and Higgins 1988; Stone 1997). When theorists "discuss power in archaeology, class not gender is their concern" (Engelstad 1991), even though gender is the most ubiquitous basis for stratification/differentiation throughout human cultures. Even a couple of male archaeological theorists have recently admitted that "[g]ender may be the central structuring principle of human social and cultural life, the ground upon which everything else is built" (Preucel and Hodder 1996:418).

While we do not intend this volume to be a rabid radical feminist polemic (though those are occasionally healthy for any science), we do wish to bring up, in the context of the lives of the women described, ideas for serious consideration in southeastern archaeology. Many now realize "that, more than any other approach within the human sciences, feminism does fundamental damage to the established traditions of working within archaeology" (Thomas 1992). But so did the "New" archaeology, and other major paradigm shifts, and we are none the worse off for the danger.

Research Background

The lumping of two potentially disparate issues—gender in the archaeological record and women in archaeology—could be seen as inappropriate. (Indeed, it is disappointing to note that so many publications on gender address only women's roles. There is at least one other gender and often more out there, especially in native America [Callender and Kochems 1983; Williams 1986; Roscoe 1991; Herdt 1994; Jacobs, Thomas, and Lang 1997; Kehoe 1998], and finally someone is looking for "two-spirits" or berdaches [third and fourth genders] in the archaeological record [Hollimon 1997].) The two issues—women doing archaeology and looking for gender in the past—are inseparable because one's gender (the cultural role only loosely based on biological sex) is a major part of the enculturation process and cannot help but influence how one does science, whether in choice of issues to investigate or interpretation of results. Just as with social class, ethnicity, and political orientation (Patterson 1995), most aspects of one's career are affected by gender; it does not take a Foucault or critical theorist to understand that the personal is political is professional. This makes biography a crucial part of the history of archaeology.

Thus the chronicle and inspirations of this research should be related. Several years ago, Hester Davis visited the University of South Florida for a presentation on public archaeology and later spoke about her early career experiences. When she mentioned that she was told to go on Luther Cressman's field school at the University of Oregon to do archaeology because he would take women, and that she was often part of a dig as the official cook, I exclaimed that she ought to write that stuff down because it was fascinating history. Her response was to suggest that I write it down, and later, that I should get going because Madeline Kneberg Lewis was retired, in her eighties, and living near Tampa. At the 1991 SEAC meeting in Jackson, Mississippi, keynote speaker Jesse Jennings, describing changes in the profession over the last fifty years, said that the greatest change was that there were more women in the field. He predicted that one day a crew of all women would be digging a site somewhere. By 1991 of course this scenario was already common.

That SEAC meeting got many archaeologists talking. Rochelle Marrinan, sitting next to me during one well-known senior archaeologist's presentation, noted dryly that his typical traditional slides of gorgeous artifacts were taken on a terribly wrinkled blue cloth. (Would a woman have remembered the iron?) As the idea of researching early women in the Southeast gained momentum and Hester and I roped in Rochelle, we garnered anecdotes from people who remembered notable women from decades ago. One story from the fifties concerned male field-workers' reluctance to hold a stadia rod for Bettye Broyles as she ran the transit, since this apparently meant acquiescence in a situation where a woman was in charge.

Addresses were collected, and plans were made to begin with Madeline Kneberg Lewis. Lynne Sullivan, independently researching Madeline as part of producing the Chickamauga project, left unfinished by the Lewises (Lewis, Lewis, and Sullivan 1995), called to ask about joining us for an interview. We had contacted Madeline, who was happy to meet with Rochelle and me in March 1992. We spent many hours at her home in Winter Haven, Florida. She warned us she might tire quickly, then proceeded to answer questions for many hours, demonstrating her new electric scooter, discussing early hominids, world archaeology, art, her painting and orchid-raising, her late husband, the old anthropology crowd at the University of Chicago in the 1930s, and other fascinating stuff. We recorded this interview on audiotape and planned another interview in April that we would video-tape, with Lynne joining us. But then at the last minute, Madeline fell and broke a bone and was unable to meet with us (Lynne and family at least got to Disney World). In fall of 1992, while I spent the semester teaching in Florence, Italy (and also trying to track down Madeline's 1920s residence along the Arno river), Hester, Rochelle, and Lynne presented our work at SEAC and also at Cheryl Claassen's gender and archaeology conference in North Carolina (Claassen 1994).

Madeline and I stayed in touch by phone. When a Knoxville television station called about interviewing her for their "Heartland" series, she was well again. Show host Bill Landry, his crew, and I, warned again about how she might tire easily, were warmly welcomed for several hours of videotaping. Though they reduced it to a four-minute spot (shown on Knoxville television in spring 1994), they gave us the entire video session for future use, as well as a videotape version of a 1940s Tennessee archaeology film from Madeline that they were able to salvage.

Meanwhile we made up a questionnaire for the women we were to interview and got nice responses. We put a call for information in many newsletters, and Carol Mason responded from Wisconsin. In summer 1993 I interviewed Yulee Lazarus in northwest Florida and also later, when she was visiting her daughter in Tampa. Conversations at SEAC meetings led to including Margaret Ashley, Isabel Patterson, and others. We collected references, addresses, and stories. For example, Hester heard (from Bill Haag of Louisiana and Ray Thompson of Arizona) that Major Webb faced a situation in the 1930s in some parts of Kentucky where all the unemployed men were already hired, so he asked to hire African-American women for crew members. The WPA said no, it was against their rules for women to push wheelbarrows. But some of the women asked if they could "tote" the backdirt instead. This was acceptable to the WPA brass, so they were hired. Another story concerned an early 1970s SEAC board meeting, before elections were formalized, where a prominent archaeologist responded to the nomination of a woman for office by saying "This goddam women's lib has got to stop!" Some younger archaeologists remembered from their earliest experiences at SEAC that Bettye Broyles was a commanding female presence. But some noted that older, prominent male archaeologists, even those who would be teachers and mentors of women, occasionally expressed disdain for Broyles on the level of a peer, especially because she did not have a Ph.D., much less a master's degree.

We planned to interview Bettye Broyles in May 1994, and I had driven north as far as Rochelle's in Tallahassee when we got news that Broyles had been hospitalized for what proved to be, luckily, a brief illness. We rescheduled for fall, after the SEAC meeting. All four of us (Hester, Lynne, Rochelle, and I) went to Chattanooga, along with Rochelle's graduate students Lou Groh and Jennifer Berke, and interviewed Bettye in her magnificent house that she and her eighty-something father built. Warning us that she might tire early (!), she enthusiastically shared scrapbooks, Chinese food, historic quilts, and wonderful memories for many hours on into the night. Hester later revisited her for more documents, photos, and good stories.

In October 1995, student Karen Mayo and I traveled with two video cameras and a tape recorder to Arkansas, where we interviewed Hester and Martha Rolingson. We were joined by Ann Early, herself in Arkansas since 1973, and Patty Jo Watson, of Washington University, whom we invited to be a commentator/interviewer/partial interviewee, all with the backdrop of the spectacular Toltec Mounds clothed in autumn foliage (fig. 1.1). In November 1995 the SEAC awarded Madeline Kneberg Lewis and Bettye Broyles its highest honor, the Distinguished Service Award, in only the second year since its creation. Bettye came to Knoxville to receive it in person, and we showed the "Heartland" show video of Madeline.

Many connections became apparent during the course of our work. My colleague at USF, medical anthropologist Linda Whiteford, is the daughter of anthropologist Andrew "Bud" Whiteford, who worked for Madeline

Fig. 1.1. Martha Rolingson, Patty Jo Watson, and Hester Davis being interviewed at Toltec Mounds Archaeological State Park, October 1995. Mound A is in the background and Mound Pond is off the picture to the right; view facing southwest.

Kneberg and Tom Lewis in Tennessee in the 1940s. Linda taped an interview with her dad, and Andrew and his wife, Marion, have graciously answered more of my questions. Jerald Ledbetter's research in Georgia archaeology demonstrated that Margaret Ashley, Isabel Patterson, and Bettye Broyles all worked at different times at the Bull Creek site in the Chattahoochee Valley (and I have worked farther downriver in this valley). Broyles told us that, growing up in Tennessee archaeology, she was very aware of Kneberg. Lynne Sullivan grew up in Bradley County, Tennessee, just across the river from Rhea County where Broyles grew up. Carol Mason published on historic Yuchi pottery, debunking the postulated connections with the Mouse Creek phase in Tennessee suggested by Lewis and Kneberg; Mouse Creek was later researched by Sullivan. Mason was at FSU during the time that Yulee Lazarus was getting FSU professors to travel to Fort Walton Beach to assist avocational archaeology. Rochelle Marrinan also trained as a nurse, as Madeline Kneberg did, and worked at the hospital in Winter Haven near Madeline's Florida home. Hester Davis got her undergraduate college training in Florida at Rollins College, in Orlando, the city where Yulee Lazarus was born.

Of course everyone in a profession, particularly those working in the same geographical region, or in a field as relatively small as archaeology, has connections of differing kinds and degrees. We could even note the earliest

Fig. 1.2. Researchers and subjects at Brennan's for breakfast, New Orleans, Society for American Archaeology meeting, 1996. *Left to right:* Nancy White, Carol Mason, Rochelle Marrinan, Lynne Sullivan, Hester Davis.

interests many of our women had in common, such as music, art, church activity, southwestern U.S. archaeology, or the satisfaction with tedious lab work. Doubtless any volume of biographies in a profession will find many links among the subjects. As members of a minority in their profession, two of our subjects themselves have written about women in archaeology (Davis 1989; Rolingson 1997).

In January 1996 we met in Tampa to outline this volume and assign tasks. We met Mason in New Orleans at the 1996 SAA meeting (at Brennan's for breakfast; fig. 1.2), and progress continued. Some setbacks occurred, such as the lack of response to a questionnaire about women in archaeology sent out to anthropology departments in the Southeast. We also failed to get the story of Sheila Kelly Caldwell, daughter of A. R. Kelly and wife of Joseph Caldwell. For many other women there was insufficient information. Among these were Rowena Kelly (Sheila's mother), who was said to have run the lab for A. R. Kelly in Georgia and worked for years on various projects such as a classification for Swift Creek Complicated-Stamped design motifs (Walker 1994), and Catherine McCann, who coauthored with Joseph Caldwell the Irene Mound report (1941). We heard of others who had done southeastern work but whom we could not include, such as Elizabeth Garland, now retired from Western Michigan, who researched the Obion site in western Tennessee (Garland 1992), and Florence Hawley (Ellis Senter), a pioneer in dendrochronology in the Southeast (fig. 1.3; Frisbie 1974). There were two similar women from Alabama: Marion L. Dunlevy Heimlich, who published *Guntersville Basin Pottery* in 1952, and Julie (or Christine) Adcock (later Christine A. Wimberly), who was university-trained and hired because she was thought to be an appropriate supervisor for a crew of African-American women (Fagette 1996:113). There must be so many other women, lab workers and field-workers of the past, whose names we will never know (fig. 1.4). Also in 1996 Madeline Kneberg Lewis suffered a stroke from which she did not recover. She died on July 4, but she had a copy of the book with the first articles we published (White, Marrinan, and Davis 1994; Sullivan 1994), about which she was very pleased, and she had received her SEAC award.

Researchers' Background

We each come from very different backgrounds and training, which has made the project all the more interesting. I grew up in the big city (Cleveland) where the nearest thing to a wilderness experience was reading jungle adven-

Fig. 1.3. Florence Hawley (Ellis Senter) researching tree rings in the Norris Basin, Tennessee, 1930s. (Photo courtesy of the Frank H. McClung Museum.)

Fig. 1.4. Lab worker at the National Park Service Southeastern Archeological Center, Macon, Georgia, 1940s, name unknown. (Photo courtesy of the National Park Service Southeast Archeological Center, Tallahassee.)

ture novels and exploring vacant lots, so southeastern archaeology was extremely attractive. A graduate student in the 1970s, I faced no real discrimination at my midwestern university. Amid the fervor of newly erupted feminism, it was hard not to notice sexism in archaeology, however. Two incidents made a lasting impression. One occurred during the visit of eastern U.S. archaeology legend James B. Griffin. After his lecture, during discussion with the students, I asked him why he kept referring to the flintknapper as "he." Griffin replied, "See this tie?" He held out what I think was a blue tie with light-colored pigs on it and said something like, "These are male chauvinist pigs and that's what I am!"

Another time, during a conference on hunter-gatherers at the State University of New York at Binghamton, as a visiting student I was privileged to lunch with the assembled scholars. Meg Conkey and her students had organized the conference, and one speaker was Paleolithic specialist Leslie Freeman. At lunch around the big table I asked Freeman, who had similarly referred to all past humans using male generic pronouns, how he could tell that the flintknappers were men. He replied with something like, well, that's an interesting question because we found this one area of the site where the lithic artifacts were particularly crude, and we thought that was the women's and children's activity area. After this, I am sure I remember Conkey elbowing him in the ribs, though I believed he was answering in complete seriousness. This is another question open for debate: which is worse, continuing lack of awareness at the end of the twentieth century, or continuing refusal to entertain an enlightened view despite having been made aware?

Lynne encountered quite a different experience in her training. After wanting to be an archaeologist since the age of six, she was told as a freshman anthropology major at the University of Tennessee in 1971 not to apply for a summer field crew job because females were not hired (and this was the home institution of Madeline Kneberg). The reasons were all typical: the work was too physically demanding, the field camp was too spartan, and it would be too difficult to arrange separate bathrooms. These "reasons" were hard to take for someone who loved camping and the out-of-doors, had taught backpacking, and spent every summer since she was twelve living in a tent. Women's experiences at that university fortunately have changed considerably since then.

Rochelle grew up in central Florida and spent lots of time, beginning about age seven, walking through orange groves picking up artifacts. She read the books of Ann Axtell Morris and decided she did not want just to accompany an archaeologist husband. She was also inspired by reading Margaret Mead, whose work provided a quiet kind of knowledge that women could succeed at nontraditional occupations (she finally did get to meet Mead much later and have her autograph a well-worn copy of *Coming of Age in Samoa*). At age thirteen she wrote to William Sears, then at the Florida State Museum (now the Florida Museum of Natural History), about his excavation at the MacKenzie Mound in Lake Weir, got a good response, and did a science project on the subject that made it to the state fair. Faced with the prospect of going to nursing school, Rochelle got her Girl Scout Council executive to write to the Florida State Museum about a career in archaeology. Ripley Bullen replied, not optimistically. After nursing school, registry, and working for two years, she went back to junior college, then transferred to the University of Florida, had a field school with Charles Fairbanks, and entered a new career, becoming especially interested in faunal analysis after studying with Liz Wing. Fairbanks and Jerry Milanich offered her the shell rings on St. Simons Island as a dissertation topic.

Hester's story is in chapter 10. It includes expectable conditions from an earlier generation. She is the most unusual of us in this volume, wherein she is both interviewer and interviewee, bringing both emic and etic views to the research (though of course etic is just someone else's emic). In the end, Hester decided not to be an official editor, though she has done enough work on the project to be one. Emic and etic are further blurred in this book, as we asked our subjects to review the chapters about them and correct mistakes or express their wishes about how things were portrayed. Chapters were written using the subject's own words and ideas as often as possible, and all have concepts, sentences, and references from all of us.

We all have our own ideas about how to do archaeology, our own best field, lab, and conference stories, and our own pride in southeastern archaeology. Is it harder to do fieldwork here? Probably, since it is hotter and buggier, and perhaps it requires more physical labor because of deeper, richer cultural deposits. I am inspired by Pat Watson's comments after the end of the videotaping, when she said there were so many more issues for women in archaeology that we had not had time to address, such as what a pain it is to have your period in the field. Of course we must talk about such things too. Lately I have discovered several colleagues who hate fieldwork and find it uncomfortable. So far these have all been men (though Madeline Kneberg Lewis also said she was not interested in it—too hot!). So much depends upon one's physical fitness and personal ecology, not to mention the place of outdoor experience in one's socialization and upbringing, and the experience of one's first fieldwork. Perhaps I was lucky to have a professor who did not confine women students to the screens or lab while men held the shovels, though it often worked out that way as individuals drifted toward what they were comfortable with. In my own field schools I assign equal amounts of shoveling and lab work to all, including myself, and expect people to ask for help or a change if they need it.

It could be argued that the way women are traditionally socialized in our society makes them well suited for field and lab management (White and Essenpreis 1989; Kelley 1992:88), with better skills in scheduling, health and safety, and attention to tiny details of forms, tables, microflakes, or palynology. The presence of more women generally in anthropology has resulted in a greater concern for safety, I believe (for example, Howell 1990), though the archaeologist I have seen most dangerously unconcerned about crew accidents and health was a woman.

Other studies (for example, Gero 1985, 1991) have noted the female tendency to prefer/excel in perceived tedious tasks such as sorting lithic debitage, while males prefer analysis of big things thought to be more important, such as whole points, or concentration of their efforts upon fieldwork.

The lives portrayed in this volume defy these stereotypes, however, as in Martha Rolingson's study of Paleo points and sites in Kentucky, or Rolingson's and Broyles's conducting survey by themselves (something we would usually not do today, for other reasons, such as those health and safety considerations). Rolingson finds numbering artifacts a boring chore, but Hester Davis recounts her pleasure and relaxation in doing this as being similar to that of doing fine needlework. My best lab students report similar satisfaction with detail work, but they are both men and women. Indeed, the SAA's recent survey of the profession indicates proportionately more men than women prefer lab work (Zeder 1997:65). So perhaps soon we can get away from the silly markedness (Shapiro 1982) in the label of "woman archaeologist," and pointedly train everyone in as many areas as possible of our multifaceted profession.

To direct fieldwork you need training in it, and clearly women have sometimes been prohibited. When I was a graduate student in Cleveland, it was common knowledge that paleoanthropologist Donald Johanson would not take women into the field in east Africa, except perhaps single ones, and Lynne recounts a similar attitude in Tennessee and Alabama archaeology in the 1970s. Illumination of this male attitude is eloquently documented for a related field profession in Laurence Walker's (1991:202) description of his ruling, as dean of a forestry school, that a young woman could not attend a three-week field trip unless she got some other female to accompany her. When she was unable to find one, she sent her mother to plead with him and ask why there must be two girls. He said, "to protect the professor." When she asked, who is this professor you cannot trust, he said, "It is I."

Things are getting easier for field archaeologists, men and women, and not only because of changing attitudes and technology. For example, rather than take the women aside and explain ways of coping with periods or bathroom issues in the forest, we can hand the whole crew the hilarious book *How to Shit in the Woods* (Meyer 1989), which has a chapter for women entitled, "How not to pee on your boots." Similarly, since sexual harassment is no longer a hidden issue, one can explain that the buddy system is not just for physical safety reasons, but to prevent anyone, male or female, from being hassled by a lecherous farmer, for instance.

Changing technology has probably had equal effects for men and women doing fieldwork. Inadequate amounts of fixit knowledge can be compensated for with duct tape and superglue, and pumps and boats are easier to operate with electric starters. The field experience need be no more physically taxing for men than for women. There also looms the debate concerning the need to do fieldwork at all to be an archaeologist. While many groups of professionals are thinking about this issue, from the feminist Internet discussion groups to professional societies (see such works as Gero 1985; Preucel and Joyce 1993), the issue is real and will become more urgent as more of the world is covered in concrete, and archaeologists dig into libraries and museum collections instead of soil.

Another recent trend is for many more women to have come into archaeology via cultural resources management (CRM) and historic archaeology, because those niches have only recently opened, and they have grown at a time when women's interest and ability to get into archaeology have also grown (Zeder 1997). It has also not hurt that woman-owned firms sometimes have advantages such as preferential treatment in bidding on contracts. By comparison, the percentages of women in traditional (academic, museum) prehistoric archaeology have changed to a lesser degree. But the CRM expansion has allowed some women to occupy powerful positions in government agencies and private firms; in many of the former, affirmative action guidelines have been important. All this cannot help but affect the profession. For example, the cooperative atmosphere of professional archaeology in Florida (as compared with rivalries and cutthroat business practices I hear about in other states) may be due in part to the large proportion of Florida archaeologists who are women (more than one-third of the members of the Florida Archaeological Council, the professional organization, including several past presidents). It is probably also due (as Donna Ruhl has reminded me) to the kinds of men who trained the current generation of Florida archaeologists, humanitarians such as Charles Fairbanks and Ray Williams, who encouraged many women and emphasized sharing data.

There will always be battles to fight. Discrimination based on sex or gender (or presumed gender behavior or even sexual orientation) is taking some curious turns. One contract archaeology program in Florida ends up with de facto discrimination by sending out field crews to do shovel tests individually instead of in pairs, with each digger carrying both shovel and legless box screen. In addition to the safety factor of one excavator alone on a shovel test two hundred meters away from the next one, the logistics require one to cease shoveling and lift a heavy screen filled with soil, hold it up, and shake it from side to side. Besides damaging anyone's back, this technique is sure to be even harder for women, who on the average have less upper body strength than men. When I asked during a visit why there were no women on the crew, the answer was, well, we had one but she quit (no surprise).

Another weird situation I have witnessed recently in contract archaeology is dictated, I suspect, mostly by general greed instead of sexism. This is the requirement that a field crew be all men, or else all women, so that they can be doubled up in motel rooms and cost the company less money. Apparently the assumption is that it is less threatening to room with a person of the same sex than of the opposite sex. This leads logically to the interesting assumption that gay individuals either do not exist on field crews or are not as threatening in a bedroom situation as are straight folks, legendary aphrodisiac powers of the field situation notwithstanding.

Summary Comments on This Volume

As with any work by multiple authors, there is unevenness from chapter to chapter here, with each woman's life presented in a slightly different manner. Though this might be considered detrimental to the book's quality, we very much wanted different voices to show the diversity among the women profiled and also the different authors' viewpoints. Much scholarship is situated within relations of power and subordination in the contemporaneous intellectual climate. "The anthropologist's own positionality is multidimensional and changing, depending upon context and historical circumstance" (Lamphere et al. 1997:5). Some outrageous statements in this work might seem tame in the future; some moderate statements might later seem outrageous.

Our research on the women presented in this book is perhaps late in coming compared to similar biographies of women in other archaeological regions, but it perhaps will permit more overview, comparison, and synthesis. For example, the conditions, accomplishments, and types of women in southwestern U.S. archaeology (Babcock and Parezo 1988; Parezo 1993; Cordell 1993) would be fascinating to compare, given the wide open spaces, harsh climate, ethnic and socioeconomic composition of the population, literary and artistic frontier atmosphere, and intellectual climate of the Southwest. In the Southeast we have a very different economic base, the depression days and WPA, the rural but deeply forested, more hidden, wet landscape, the conservative educational and social traditions. A great deal of work on early women in Old World and classical archaeology as well as in other regions of the New World is now becoming available (for example, Williams 1981; Leakey 1984; Irwin-Williams 1990; Allsebrook 1992; Cordell 1993; Claassen 1994; Lister 1997; Diaz-Andreu and Sorensen 1998). They are seen as everything from prominent husbands' helpmates and efficient lab directors to writers who could synthesize or Indiana Jones types in their own right (or various combinations of all of these). Many were wealthy patrons who did active excavation as well. This tradition may have begun with Queen Caroline Murat (sister of Napoleon Bonaparte; her son is buried in Tallahassee) at Pompeii (Mozans 1913:311–17) and continued through recent times, as in the southwestern United States, and is seen in this volume with Isabel Patterson. We wish to add this volume to the collections of all these fascinating stories.

Role models of all kinds are never out of fashion, of course, nor are female role models in archaeology just for young women embarking on such careers. We hope in this book to show some of the evolution of the place of women in archaeology in the Southeast and in general. The roles of these women are sometimes less than prominent. Despite the fact that most either did not marry or married an archaeologist who may have overshadowed them, did not have children, did not become famous, and made contributions that are still sorely undervalued (some factual data are tabulated below), the women in this book have been extremely satisfied with their career choices and their work. This seems to be a pattern, in archaeology, anthropology (Gacs et al. 1989), and science in general. Gould's 1993 essay "The Invisible Woman" is subtitled "In the past, even great female naturalists gained little more than a passing nod in a preface." Other writers such as Irwin-Williams (1990) and Parezo (1993a) use the same term, "invisible," for women in archaeology. Bonta's summary data on twenty-five pioneering women field naturalists (1991:xiii) noted that most had enlightened and independent parents, all liked men but nearly half never married, most were childless, many were associated with or married to supportive males in similar fields, and all seemed to feel little or no rivalry but only appreciation for the powerful men in their fields because they believed that the work was all that mattered. This is remarkably similar to the general profile of the women we describe in southeastern archaeology (though our sample size is smaller by over half). In fact it is similar to the profiles now being assembled of women scholars and scientists of many disciplines, with emphasis on the love of the work. Keller's (1983) pioneering study of Nobel laureate Barbara McClintock documented well her "feeling for the organism" and immense pleasure in the lonely and for so long unrewarded and unrecognized work on the genetics of maize. McGrayne (1993:5) notes among Nobel Prize-winning women a passion for discovery: "First, they adored science. They triumphed because they were having a wonderful time."

Table 1. Summary data on the women in this volume

Name	Birth/death dates	Geographic origins	Years of archaeological work	Years of SE work	Married?	Husband	Children?	Degrees
Ashley	1902–85	Georgia	1926(?)–30, 1944–85	1926(?)–30	Yes	Gerald Towle, archaeologist	No	A.B, Oglethorpe College, 1924 Grad work, Columbia, 1920s, Ph.D., 1958
Patterson	1894–1955	Georgia	1934–55	1934–55	Yes	Wayne Patterson, lawyer	No	B.A., Hollins College
Kneberg Lewis	1903–96	Illinois	1932–61	1938–61	Yes, at age 58	Thomas Lewis, archaeologist	No	M.A., Chicago, 1936
Broyles	1928	Tennessee	1951–84	1951–84	Yes, twice	Musician, mail carrier	No	B.A., Chattanooga, 1955
Bullen	1908–87	Massachusetts	1942–80	1950–80	Yes, twice	Ripley P. Bullen, archaeologist, Kenneth Bullen, retired businessman	2	A.B, Radcliffe, 1943; grad work, Harvard
Lazarus	1914	Florida	1953–present	1953–present	Yes	Bill Lazarus, avocational archaeologist	2	B.A., Fla. State College for Women, 1936
Mason	1934	Florida	1958–present	1955–58	Yes	Ronald Mason, archaeologist	2	B.A., FSU, 1956; M.A., Ph.D., Michigan, 1957, 1963
Davis	1930	Massachusetts	1957–present	1959–present	No		No	B.A., Rollins Coll., 1952; M.A., Haverford, 1955; MA, UNC, 1957
Rolingson	1935	Kansas, Oklahoma, Colorado	1958–present	1958–present	No		No	B.A., U. Denver, 1957; M.A., Kentucky, 1960; Ph.D., Michigan, 1967
Wing	1932	Massachusetts	1962–present	1962–present	Yes	James Wing, ceramic artist	2	B.A., Mt. Holyoke, 1955; M.A., Ph.D., Florida, 1957, 1962
Watson	1932	Iowa, Nebraska	1954–present	1960s–present	Yes	Richard Watson, philosopher	1	Ph.D, Chicago, 1959

We must be careful not to use personal statistics about the women to draw any specific conclusions. Yes, some long-awaited new studies show particular career patterns among women in archaeology (Nelson, Nelson, and Wylie 1994; Zeder 1997), with documentation of all the disadvantages, and many other studies also now provide quantitative data on circumstances and career choices (for example, Zuckerman 1991; Davis et al. 1996). But there is too much argument over correlation vs. causation, and statistics can be suspect. Xie (1996) notes conflicting evidence for female engineering students as being more likely to have no brothers and having just as many brothers as anyone else. Cole and Singer (1991) note women's lower productivity in science, assumed to be because of family and other typical issues, but they cite data showing that women with children are just as scientifically prolific as women with no children. Zeder (1997) describes American women archaeologists as being generally less productive and obtaining less funding support than men and continuing to make greater personal sacrifices in their family lives to pursue archaeology careers. But producing a baby and a monograph or a field project in the same year is not uncommon for many women in archaeology, since the turn of the century example of Harriet Boyd Hawes (Allsebrook 1992:133–35); it just takes careful planning.

Dena Dincauze (1992:132–33) did note that, though she is the third woman president of the Society for American Archaeology, she is the first presidential mother and grandmother. But she cautions that exploration of career styles in archaeology would contribute more than pages of statistics. Perhaps women must develop a greater diversity of career styles given the circumstances they are put into or shut out of (cf. Eisenhart and Finkel 1998). Paleoanthropologist Pat Shipman (1995) has documented the subtle but powerful gender discrimination that led to her choice of the nontraditional career of freelance scientist, a role in which she embraces for herself the character of a provocative trickster. And we now know that women receive proportionately fewer grants, especially for field research, than do men (Gero 1985; Stark 1991, 1992; Zeder 1997) and have many other barriers to breach (nicely outlined in Parezo 1993a) to make a career equal to that of the average man. Indeed we are not the first to point out how much better than the average man a woman has to be to succeed. By documenting the careers of what must therefore have been among the very best of archaeologists, we hope to improve the way for any who come after. As Bella Abzug has said (Stephens 1993), "Our struggle today is not to have a female

Einstein get appointed as an assistant professor. It is for a woman schlemiel to get as quickly promoted as a male schlemiel."

Our sample of women in southeastern archaeology shows a wide range of career styles. Several women excelled at fieldwork. Many labored with archaeologist husbands, though that, as with other sciences, may "more frequently [have] enhanced a woman's prospects for carrying on significant research than for securing credit for that research" (Pycior et al. 1996:8). Most leaned toward the arts, drawing or music. All associated the life of archaeology with something exciting and joyful, and many worked with avocational archaeologists and collectors. Enormously notable in terms of current trends (Sabloff 1996; Jameson 1997), all seem to have recognized very early the importance of public archaeology and contributed toward it in major ways. All our women were essentially (or seemingly) in charge of their situations, and none indicated any major sexism that hampered her career. Andrew Whiteford said Madeline Kneberg encountered no discrimination directing the Tennessee lab during the WPA days because "she ran the place." However Kehoe (1995:1601) notes that, during research on women anthropologists in the Southwest, Parezo (1993b) admitted that "getting [the women interviewed] even to admit that they had experienced any form of discrimination was like pulling teeth."

We at first thought that it was possible that the early women in the Southeast had few problems doing archaeology because there were just so few of them, and that discriminatory practices came later, whether after World War II when men returned to their jobs, or in the 1960s and 1970s when there were so many women entering the field that perhaps a threat was perceived. This seems to be wrong. There were lots more women in all areas of archaeology than we imagined, even though many—most?—of their names, life stories, and contributions remain unknown. Most of the women in this book, for example, noted many other women in their field schools, often a predominance of women, not only as fellow students but also as helpmate wives, cooks, and lab assistants. Because of the undervaluing of their contributions, or perhaps shorter duration in the field because they then took up more traditional women's roles, there surely are far more such "invisible women" than we think.

The traditional wisdom is that there were few women in the sciences. On the history of entomology, for example, a recent reviewer notes the "detailed accounts of the lives of the real-life men (and very occasional women) who basically founded the discipline" (Berenbaum 1995:2035). It now seems simply that there were many women in all these other disciplines too, but few of them were *visible*. Morse's (1995:10) study of physical/natural sciences notes "There are far more women scientists in history than one would imagine if one relied on the scant handful of well-known figures that appear in most textbooks." Hubbard (for example, 1988:13–14) reminds us of the enormous role of women in the production of science in general, as wives, sisters, secretaries, technicians, and students. Kastner (1993:78) answers Gould's notion of invisible women naturalists in a review of Vera Norwood's (1993) *Made from This Earth: American Women and Nature,* which documents the abundance of women in the diverse areas of natural history, from science to big game hunting, and the special relationship of women to nature (shades of the Sherry Ortner vs. Claude Lévi-Strauss [Ortner 1974, 1996] debate; see also Stange 1998).

There is no doubt that the case is the same in archaeology. All we have to do is overcome ever lessening resistance and find all those women; even Griffin (1992) could do it. Their invisibility may be just as much because of acceptance of their assumed social roles, past and present, as because of discrimination. Any museum, for example, has a volunteer force usually dominated by women, but representations of women in the exhibits are heavily male-biased (Jones and Pay 1990; Gifford-Gonzales 1995). "The Drudge-on-the-Hide" is the woman in the diorama of ancient life, on her hands and knees in the museum case, scraping hides, or doing whatever task prevents her from looking up, while the "Guy-with-a-Rock" is upright and doing more "important" things (Gifford-Gonzalez 1995:1–3; Wiber 1997); this is not a bad metaphor for the division of labor in many archaeological workplaces.

It is also possible that we recognize more things today as discriminatory that would not have been considered as such earlier, because of cultural values (Cole and Fiorentine 1991). Madeline Kneberg Lewis and Yulee Lazarus, and surely Adelaide Bullen too, adored their husbands, delighted in working for and with them, but outlived them, and continued the archaeological interest. As Carol Mason, herself the wife of an archaeologist, has already pointed out (1992:97), there were many more women than we realize in archaeology, accepted as a part of the field but often forgotten: "Most of them were not major theoreticians, areal synthesizers, or even famous archaeologists, but neither are most archaeologists any of these things either. What matters is that they were doing prehistoric research, often local, basic archaeological dog work whose value will endure as part of the cultural historical record." This statement conjures up the image of

Madeline Kneberg Lewis telling us how she slaved over the tables in the books she produced with Tom Lewis; each line of data had to be pasted in by hand, she said. Kehoe (1995:1601) notes that without the contribution of these tedious background details that women have done in archaeology, "The field would be disjointed, like a Constable landscape blank except for cows and a cathedral spire."

Women's names appear in the pages of reports and journals regularly in the Southeast, if in small numbers, throughout the decades. Many were amateurs, many professionals to varying degrees (remember that many early figures in archaeology were actually from other fields: A. R. Kelly of Georgia was a physical anthropologist; William S. Webb of Kentucky was trained in physics). Some may have been students or others working in the shadow of important figures, such as Regina Flannery in South Carolina, who published (1943) on some of Warren K. Moorehead's work, or Lucy B. McIntire, who was noted as a field supervisor at the Bilbo site (Waring 1940:152). Fagette (1996:113–14) notes that women were conspicuous by their absence in New Deal archaeology (though Lyon 1996 mentions many, such as Alice Hendrick, who studied Hiwassee Island pottery) but were more present and influential in positions within the government bureaucracy. Susan Wurtzburg's excellent paper (1994) on women in Louisiana archaeology documents several, such as Caroline Dormon (who is referred to as an ecologist in Bonta 1991:xiii), and shows that most did not have advanced training or hold archaeological positions, consistent with the acceptable Louisiana social context of their times. This is undoubtedly true for other states in the Southeast. A list of the attendees at the 1953 SEAC meeting at Chapel Hill shows eleven of the thirty-nine people were women, including wives of Joffre Coe, John Goggin, John Gillin, B. C. McCary, and Stanley South, all referred to by a "Mrs." in front of their husbands' names, and also Madeline Kneberg and Sheila K. Caldwell. But there are also the following: Ester Araya Hunter, Mrs. John M. Parker III, and Marguerite Van Doorslaer. These women could be traced, but this is less likely for the African-American women hired to dig at famous sites in Georgia and Kentucky, though attempts are being made (chapter 5). Cotter (1993:35) shows a photo of the crew of black women at the Swift Creek site in which A. R. Kelly is presenting one woman with an award; surely some field documents contain these women's names, at least? What did they think of the work? The whole profession?

In presenting the lives and work of some pioneering women in southeastern archaeology, we hope to show the importance of their achievements and contributions. This research should continue, since there are so many more questions to ask. We have mountains of interview transcripts that are useful for researching women and the history of archaeology. Many lives that we were unable to document surely need recording, women in the Southeast whom many readers will realize have been left out. Another future project is editing our ca. thirty hours of videotape into a good production. We are just beginning to recognize our collective professional heritage in southeastern archaeology and the roles in it played by several who are forgotten or less celebrated.

Recent years have seen a spate of good volumes documenting more inside stories in the history of archaeology (for example, Reyman 1992; Christenson 1989; Watson 1985), including biography of famous figures (for example, Willey 1988; Sabloff 1998). In an impassioned letter to anthropologists, Poewe (1991) asks for more vigorous histories of anthropology and considers writing honest, accessible autobiography and biography a duty we must do for our "historically starved students." Christenson (1989:77) has noted that how we present the history of our discipline would change if more women conducted research on the topic. Douglas Givens, in an article entitled "The Role of Biography in Writing the History of Archaeology," notes (1992:55–56), "If the field and laboratory are vital in shaping individual contributions to archaeology, then archaeology must be derived in part from individual effects upon them. . . . Archaeologists bring to their field and laboratory work life experiences that are outside their professional domain" that we should discover, document, and analyze as we endeavor to have our discipline grow and prosper and, of course, be useful. As Madeline Kneberg Lewis said in one phone conversation (May 20, 1994), we must remember that "archaeology can be a tremendous force in the future of the human species."

2

Margaret E. Ashley

Georgia's First Professional Archaeologist

FRANK T. SCHNELL, JR.

At the 1992 Southeastern Archaeological Conference, Margaret Ashley was noted as an early southeastern archaeologist about whom little was known. Even during the 1930s, she was considered among colleagues to have been "Moorehead's assistant at Etowah, but no more than that" (Gordon R. Willey, personal communication, 1993). In fact, Margaret Ashley was far more: not only Georgia's first trained archaeologist but also perhaps the first woman anthropologist in the South (Fitz 1928).

Early Georgia Work, Boas, and Moorehead

Margaret Elizabeth Ashley was born in Atlanta on January 12, 1902. In *A Standard History of Georgia and Georgians* (Knight 1917:1995), fifteen-year-old Margaret Elizabeth was characterized as "a precocious child and in her tastes promises to be literary, like her father showing a preference for history." Her father, Claude Lordawick Ashley, was head of the Atlanta city council and a descendant of William Lordawick Ashley, who had received a land grant near Charleston, South Carolina, from Queen Anne in the early eighteenth century. The Ashley River at Charleston is named for the family. Margaret's grandmother, Fannie Baisden Dunham, of Liberty County, Georgia, was a descendant of the Dunhams who came from England in the same vessel with Georgia colony founder James Edward Oglethorpe in 1733 (ibid.:1994–96). Author Margaret Mitchell was a contemporary of Margaret Ashley and, although there is no known connection between the two, it has been pointed out by Georgia genealogist Kenneth H. Thomas, Jr., that it was quite appropriate for Mitchell to select the name "Ashley Wilkes" for the ultimate aristocratic character in her novel *Gone with the Wind.*

Margaret Ashley's mother, Elizabeth Miller, was a daughter of Captain Hiram Miller, "a veteran of the Federal army, who, during the war between the states, like the late Colonel Ashley of the Confederate army, was severely wounded at the Battle of Chickamauga" (ibid.:1995). Apparently another member of her mother's family interested in archaeology had lived in Georgia. In 1927, Margaret Ashley visited F. W. Miller in East Orange, New Jersey, to inspect "material characteristic of the higher culture found in the southwestern part of Georgia" (Ashley 1928a). F. W. Miller and George B. McKnight had excavated at the Kyle Mound in Muscogee County prior to 1909 (Brannon 1909:195–97). The Miller collection from the Kyle Mound is now in the National Museum of the American Indian.

At some time in her youth, Margaret was apparently stricken with polio, which affected her ability to walk in later years (Mary Gaudet, personal communication, 1993). After overcoming the illness, she graduated with an A.B. degree in English literature and a minor in journalism from Oglethorpe University in 1924. An Oglethorpe graduate of that period informed me that the university did not then offer journalism but allowed journalism courses under a cooperative arrangement at Emory University. It was perhaps the same for Margaret Ashley, and it was at this time that she may have first established her relationship with Emory. After graduating, she entered Columbia University, seeking a graduate degree in anthropology.

Records of her academic career at Columbia have not been examined. In a letter dated March 23, 1994, Jerald T. Milanich states that his inquiries indicated that the anthropology department at Columbia University did not have old student files. Inquiries at the graduate school also were not fruitful. To date, the knowledge of her academic career at Columbia begins in 1926, with a series of letters between Miss Ashley and her major professor Franz Boas. These letters are preserved in the archives of the American Philosophical Society. In this set of sometimes chatty exchanges, Boas and Ashley primarily correspond about her excavations at what was then known as the

Indian Island site (now known as the Shinholser site, 9Bl2) in Baldwin County, Georgia. This project, beginning with her first visit to the site on May 26, 1926, brought about an archaeological baptism by fire. In her letters to Boas, she discusses not only her attempts at obtaining stratigraphic information from her excavations but also her confrontations with the landowner, who was dissatisfied with the cautious pace of work. On June 28, 1926, she wrote to Boas: "So on May 28th we began to trench [the smaller mound] B. I worked carefully and slowly. The rewards were not as spectacular as Mr. Shinholser had expected. They consisted of potsherds in abundance, broken shell, some of which had been worked, bone and charcoal. I was not at all disappointed but I noticed that he was becoming impatient. . . . He suggested the use of tractors and plows."

She solicited in the blind a letter from Boas forbidding her to use the tactics being pressed upon her by the landowner. On July 1, 1926, Boas wrote her two letters, one for Mr. Shinholser to see, stating, "The value of the material obtained from the mounds depends entirely upon the care that is taken in opening the mounds and in recording accurately the location of the specimens," the other advising her to "convince him that slowness will pay him." On July 23, 1926, she wrote and thanked Boas, telling him that his letter had its effect and that their ruse had worked: "During our discussion I showed him your letter and it produced the desired effect, for which I am indeed grateful to you" (letters on file at the American Philosophical Society Library).

It is not known whether she conducted more work there after July 1926, although she had planned to return. A short, general report on her investigations was published by the Museum of the American Indian (Ashley 1927). She discusses only the excavations of Mound B, the stratigraphy, and the materials recovered, with some illustrations. It is clear from the letters that Boas preached careful, meticulous, recording of associations and the importance of all material remains. Ashley was doing in Georgia what Boas's students did: become good anthropologists collecting primary, empirical data and using stratigraphic excavation techniques (Browman and Givens 1996).

On September 1, 1926, she wrote to Boas that she had spent most of her recent time traveling throughout the state visiting sites. In July 1927, she formally began what she called "an archaeological survey of Georgia" (Ashley 1928b), presumably to be her dissertation topic. She reported that "to date, four counties have been thoroughly surveyed and many individual sites investigated. Through public interest, approximately 500 sites

(mounds, villages, etc.) have been reported" (not a bad total for any archaeological survey). An article in the December 25, 1927, issue of the *Atlanta
Journal Magazine* recounts her visit to a petroglyph site near Cumming and
describes her research in the C. C. Jones, Jr., library's notes and manuscripts.
Charles C. Jones, Jr., was a pioneer in southeastern archaeology, author of
Antiquities of the Southern Indians, Particularly of the Georgia Tribes
(1873).

In the September 1 letter, Margaret stated that she met with the president
of Emory University, who asked her to organize a department of archaeology
and also to represent Emory in Warren K. Moorehead's excavations at the
Etowah site (9Br1), in northern Georgia, since a portion of the collection
recovered there was supposed to go to the university. It is thus apparent that
even in the Etowah excavations, her role was much greater than just being one
of Moorehead's assistants, though it has been her only acknowledged work in
southeastern archaeology. Investigations at Etowah began in the winter of
1928. Excavations with spectacular results had already been carried out there
by Cyrus Thomas for the Smithsonian Institution in 1883–84 (Thomas
1887:96–107). The most comprehensive later investigations of the site were
done in the 1950s by A. R. Kelly and Lewis H. Larson, Jr. (Kelly and Larson
1957:60–67), including a map by Bettye Broyles (see chapter 6).

In December 1927 Moorehead wrote to an associate in Maine that
Ashley, who had taken her doctorate at Columbia (though actually she had
not yet finished), would be joining him and his wife at Etowah and would
take over when they departed in the spring. He noted that it was "a great pity
that the people of Georgia do not make arrangements to have such work
carried on in the future, particularly so, now that they have a very competent, trained, and brilliant young woman, who is ready to 'step in'" (quoted
in Robinson 1995:4).

Although Ashley undoubtedly spent some time at the Etowah site working with Moorehead and his principal field assistant Gerald Towle, then a
Harvard graduate student, during the late winter and spring of 1928, it is
apparent that she spent a major portion of her time continuing what she had
been doing, exploring other Georgia sites. "Miss Ashley was given workmen
to assist in preliminary studies of several mounds and village sites some
distance from the central village" (Moorehead 1932:v). As reported in the
Etowah Papers, she visited at least twelve archaeological sites in northern
Georgia and tested several, including the Shellman, Lewis, Mumford, and
Leake mounds, the West Knight and Foster's Bend sites, and sites on
Pumpkinvine and Stileboro Creeks. She may also have participated in the

excavations at Carter's Quarters on the Coosawattee River (Moorehead et al. 1932:151–57). The most extensive work subsequently carried out at any of these sites was at Foster's Bend (renamed the King site, 9Fl5), by Garrow, Hally, and others (Blakely 1988).

After the field excavations, she returned to Andover with Moorehead and Towle, where, Moorehead wrote (1929), "Miss Ashley is studying the pottery of the Etowah culture for Phillips Academy." That study was published as her major contribution to the *Etowah Papers*. In it she describes their (her?) attempts at stratigraphic seriation for the ceramics but records no success, although she does clearly recognize, for instance, the differences between the ceramic stamping motifs of what we now know as Lamar, Wilbanks, and Etowah complicated-stamped types. It is not clear whether Ashley actually conducted any of the excavations at Etowah, although it seems probable. She reports, "The means of finding stratification, used extensively and found to be so satisfactory in the Southwest, were attempted. Test trenches and pits were dug at intervals over the area covered by the village site, but though the pottery from the different levels was kept separately, upon examination there could be found no lines of demarcation. Whether this negative evidence is due to the churning of the earth during high water, or to the original deposition in the site, remains an open question" (Ashley 1932:107). This is not too surprising, since finding stratigraphy in the village area on a site as large and complex as Etowah, with no prior models, and with the limited amount of excavation dedicated to the task, would be a daunting task even today.

Although not explicit in the *Etowah Papers,* it appears that there was at least a mind set of gender segregation among the investigators. Moorehead, Towle, and Willoughby are all noted as the excavators of the burials and ritual paraphernalia, while Ashley is only working on the "ceramic art" (domestic women's work?) at Etowah and subsequently at Carter's Quarters. Moorehead does mention briefly Ashley's work at other sites, but this was testing largely conducted in "domestic" contexts.

By July 1928, Margaret Ashley had returned to Georgia from Massachusetts, conducting an archaeological survey in the vicinity of Columbus. One of the underwriters of the Etowah excavations had been Tom Huston, of Tom's Toasted Peanuts, a snack food manufactured in Columbus, Georgia, and still popular throughout the South. He hired her to investigate sites both in the Columbus area and on the Flint River near Reynolds. Huston hired my father, Frank T. Schnell, Sr., as Margaret Ashley's driver and field assistant. He was a "well known Columbus youth" and president of the Eagle Scouts;

they were assisted by "the spades of negro helpers" (Fitz 1928). Archaeological sites were visited in Harris, Muscogee, and Chattahoochee Counties, and excavations were conducted at several, including the Winfree Mound (9Hs2) on Mulberry Creek (fig. 2.1). In her manuscript, on file at the Columbus Museum, she describes the excavations in a narrative fashion, mentioning the recording of trench cross-sections (Ashley and Schnell 1928:5). No illustrations are included with this narrative. One site they visited was a stone mound complex in Harris County on a mountain ridge overlooking the Chattahoochee River. It consists of two concentric stone circles with a number of stone cairns nearby. Although no excavations were undertaken here, she states that it was "one of the most interesting in the country"

Fig. 2.1. Margaret E. Ashley auger testing to bottom of a stratigraphic trench at the Winfree Mound, 9Hs2, summer 1928. (Photo by F. T. Schnell, Sr., courtesy of the Columbus Museum.)

Fig. 2.2. Margaret E. Ashley with Frank T. Schnell, Sr. (the author's father) near the Flint River, October 1928. (Photo courtesy of the *Columbus Ledger Enquirer.)*

(ibid.:8). It was subsequently named the Ashley site (9Hs6) and has been entered on the National Register of Historic Places. The present owner has made a verbal pledge to protect the site in perpetuity.

Another site visited by Ashley and Schnell in Muscogee County was Upatoi Town, (9Me42), now on Fort Benning and recently the subject of several investigations (Braley and Wood 1982; Elliott et al. 1996; Briuer et al. 1997). Ashley and Schnell (1928:9a) gave an account of the ruins of three log buildings which may have been a part of the community of Upatoi, described by Benjamin Hawkins in 1798 and 1799 (Hawkins 1938:56–57). She considered the possibility that the ruins might have been plantation buildings, since she is careful to note that "No evidence of any European material was found" (Ashley and Schnell 1928:9a). Although Upatoi was a Native American site dating from the eighteenth to early nineteenth century, it is unlikely that extensive European material would have been found. Elliott et al. (1996) do not report a great deal of European material in their much more extensive examination of the area. Ashley and Schnell's visit to the site was exactly one hundred years after the removal of the Native Americans from Muscogee County, so it is entirely possible that what they saw were the ruins of buildings from the community of Upatoi. It would be a direct confirmation that the Creek Indians used log structures during the latter part of their occupation in the Chattahoochee Valley.

Fig. 2.3. Margaret E. Ashley in the southwestern Georgia archaeological survey vehicle, a Model A Ford. (Photo by F. T. Schnell, Sr., courtesy of the Columbus Museum.)

Frank J. Mulvihill (1925) had reported several archaeological sites along Bull Creek in Muscogee County, and Ashley examined these. Although she visited the Bull Creek site (9Me1), it was heavily overgrown and she found few specimens. Not quite ten years later, a WPA excavation led by Frank Lester found much more. This later work was initiated by Isabel Patterson (Patterson 1950; Ledbetter 1995, 1997), who is profiled in the next chapter. It is unknown whether Ashley and Patterson knew or knew of each other.

After spending portions of July, August, and September around Columbus, Ashley and Schnell moved to the Flint River (figs. 2.2, 2.3), and it is at this point that the manuscript ends. For three weeks they excavated at the Lockett Mound, now known as the Neisler site (9Tr1). The top of the platform mound was extensively trenched (fig. 2.4), and two "fire pits" were found. In the village area 250 test units and fourteen burials were excavated. Two burials were removed for further study, and the rest were left *in situ*. When a news reporter asked for a bone as a "souvenir," Ashley firmly declined: "We do have respect for our finds" (Fitz 1928). Excavations of unknown extent were also carried out at the Thornton Mound, now known as the Hartley-Posey site (9Tr12; fig. 2.5). I have several photographs taken by the Columbus newspaper and by my father during these excavations. A Lamar Complicated-Stamped vessel found at the Neisler site is in the collections of the Columbus Museum, where there are other records pertaining to Ashley's work. Another item that showed up later from the Neisler Mound was a negative-painted dog effigy bottle (fig. 2.6), one of only four examples of this type known. It was not directly associated with Ashley's work there but was brought to attention through the later writings of Isabel Patterson, who publicized the Bull Creek site, which produced the other three examples of this unusual vessel type (see next chapter; Schnell 1990:67; Ledbetter 1997:178).

Fig. 2.4. Summit of the Neisler Mound, 9Tr1. Attached note on original photo states, "The top of the mound looking west. Frank took these from a tree in the east slope." (Photo by F. T. Schnell, Sr., courtesy of the Columbus Museum.)

Fig. 2.5. Margaret E. Ashley standing on top the Hartley-Posey Mound, 9Tr12, October 1928. (Photo courtesy of the *Columbus Ledger Enquirer.*)

Fig. 2.6. Negative-painted dog effigy bottle from Neisler Mound, 9Tr1, one of only four known of this type, the other three being from the Bull Creek site (compare fig. 3.4). (Photo courtesy of Jerald Ledbetter.)

According to the *Columbus Ledger Magazine* (Fitz 1928), Emory University was to receive half of the material recovered in Ashley's excavations and the remaining half would go to the "Halawaka Museum," which was Tom Huston's private collection and the foundation for a future museum. The name Halawaka came from his country retreat (fig. 2.7), near Halawaka Creek, north of Columbus. Portions of the material excavated from Etowah had also gone to this "museum," since Tom Huston had been an underwriter of that project as well. When the Columbus Museum was founded in 1953, the bulk of the Halawaka collection was turned over to the new institution, with Ashley's catalog, done in October or November 1928. By this time, she had become well established in anthropology. She was a member of the American Anthropological Association (AAA) Council, apparently having been elected in 1928 along with Carlton Coon, Fannie Bandelier, and others.

Fig. 2.7. Margaret E. Ashley on the steps of "Halawaka," businessman Tom Huston's retreat on the Chattahoochee River. (Photo by F. T. Schnell, Sr., courtesy of the Columbus Museum.)

It is a curious accident that Margaret Ashley's most widely published contribution to archaeology during this period of her life, other than the Etowah ceramic analysis, was a short note in the *American Anthropologist* in 1930. In this note, she explains the technique she used to develop illustrations of ceramic sherds (Ashley 1930). Although perhaps not a significant publication, it is indicative of her all-inclusive interest and willingness to contribute. There is said to be a film at the Andover Academy of or by Ashley documenting various archaeological investigations as well.

During April 1929, Ashley was still in, or had returned to, Georgia, according to documents discovered by C. T. Trowell at the Georgia Historical Society (letter dated July 17, 1993). She was in the Okefenokee Swamp visiting archaeological sites with Marmaduke Floyd and Dolores B. Colquitt of Savannah and others. According to Mrs. Colquitt's diary, Margaret Ashley showed a knowledge of artifact types and styles beyond the state, identifying at least one artifact as being of the "Florida peninsula culture." The diary also indicates that she was a very capable outdoorswoman, knowledgeable in the treatment of snake bites. This did not fit her image later in life.

Abandonment of Archaeology

Between April and October 15, 1929, Margaret assisted Gerald Towle at excavations he was conducting in Maine, under Moorehead's guidance, for the Robert S. Peabody Foundation. They were working at the Overlock Cemetery, in Warren (Brian S. Robinson, personal communication, 1993; Robinson 1995), a Late Archaic "Red Paint" burial site. On October 16, she wrote to my father, stating that she had just returned from Maine and offering to employ him as her assistant for a winter field season beginning in January 1930. After chatting about the recent marriage of my uncle and the wedding present she was sending, she made a jocular remark that would be ironic: "Now don't tell me that you are going to get married for that would spoil all of my plans." By this time, my father was engaged, and within months Margaret Ashley would also be married. She wed Gerald Towle in Atlanta on February 18, 1930. Her marriage to Towle would affect her plans far more drastically than her assistant's marriage.

In less than a year after the letter to my father was written, she abandoned archaeology for some fourteen years—never returning to fieldwork. Why did this happen, in the midst of a full-scale effort of visiting dozens of archaeological sites and recording hundreds? I have uncovered no convincing evidence to explain this drastic turning in her life. She and Gerald may have spent some time in Georgia, but by 1938 they returned to Cambridge, Massachusetts (Robinson 1995:17). Although she was still a member of the AAA in 1931, by 1935 her name disappeared from the membership rolls. It was a time of general reassessment for many anthropologists. Ruth Bunzel was apparently a friend of Ashley's (in Boas's June 25, 1926, letter to Ashley, he tells her that "Bunny" has gone to Zuni). Bunzel wrote, "One can think of the golden age as that bright morning of the world when one could walk freely in the garden of delights with no responsibilities and no care for the morrow. In that sense the golden age of anthropology came to an end in 1930 when the shadows in the world began to lengthen" (Bunzel 1960:576). She referred not only to global politics but probably also economics. The date of Ashley's letter to my father noted above was only eight days prior to the infamous Black Friday, the day the stock market fell, marking the beginning of the Great Depression.

It was certainly a time of reassessment for Warren K. Moorehead, who announced in his *American Anthropologist* report for 1930 that "after consultation with a number of archaeologists, [he] decided to abandon further field operations and concentrate on a study of type distributions in the United States during the next six years" (Moorehead 1931). Whether or not this statement had a direct impact upon Ashley's program, it may well have had a considerably chilling effect. Perhaps another factor was the strain that constant fieldwork had placed on her polio-weakened legs. Some years later, in Cambridge, she was hit by a girl riding a bicycle, aggravating her leg problems to the extent that she was never again able to walk well.

But perhaps the most compelling reason for Margaret Ashley's abandonment of archaeology in 1930 may be that in that year she married Gerald Towle. He was born in 1896, served in the Aviation Section of the Signal Corps during World War I, and graduated from Harvard University in 1920. His biography in the Harvard Class of 1919 Fiftieth Anniversary Report states that "The greater part of his time was spent in looking after his mother's estate and in the study of archeology, a field which he shared with his wife" (Anonymous 1969:561). Depending upon the character of the estate which he managed, it may be that the beginning of the Great Depression was a period of great stress for Gerald Towle. Various accounts do indicate that he and Margaret were probably quite wealthy. They had no children.

Towle appears to have had difficulties with his archaeological work; he is not listed as one of the authors in the Etowah papers. Attempts by

Frederick Johnson to recover information from him about his excavations had been futile, according to Brian Robinson of the University of Maine. Robinson stated that he "recently found several letters from Gerald Towle (mostly 1929–30 but one dated 1938) and there is simply no evidence that either of them were doing archaeology after 1930" (personal communication, August 26, 1993). Ashley may not have shut archaeology completely out of her life, however. By 1941, she was listed in *American Antiquity* as a member of the Society for American Archaeology. The first annual meeting of the Society had been held in conjunction with a meeting of the American Anthropological Association on December 28, 1935, in her husband's hometown of Andover, Massachusetts (Guthe 1936), but it is not known whether either she or her husband attended.

It would be unjust to blame Ashley's marriage to Gerald Towle for her departure at the peak of her development of a program in Georgia archaeology and just as she was becoming an established professional anthropologist. However, after a fourteen-year hiatus, Margaret Ashley Towle returned actively to anthropology and archaeology in 1944, the year in which Gerald Towle died. He reportedly took his own life, in his mother's house.

Some of the origins of her departure from Georgia archaeology may lie in the social mores of that time. As has been expressed to me by every individual interviewed who knew her, Margaret A. Towle was a quiet, genteel, aristocratic southern lady. Gordon Willey viewed her as "very pleasant, very southern, and very much a lady" (personal communication, 1993). Such ladies were not expected to live a rough field life, and especially not expected to "have a job," as it was expressed by someone who knew her. With the end of the golden age of anthropology as defined by Bunzel, perhaps Margaret Ashley Towle felt too bound by her social heritage to compete in the rough-and-tumble world of depression-era field archaeology. We will never know.

Return to Anthropology in Paleoethnobotany

Her return to the profession in 1944 led in a very different direction. In the four years following Gerald Towle's tragic death, she apparently had become a very private person, but she immersed herself as a volunteer at the Harvard Botanical Museum. By the late 1940s, a series of papers began to emerge dealing with the ethnobotany of pre-Columbian Peru (Towle 1948, 1952a, 1952b, 1952c, 1954, 1956, 1957, 1958). At some point, apparently encouraged by Duncan Strong of Columbia and Paul Mangelsdorf of the Botanical

Fig. 2.8. Margaret Ashley
Towle ca. 1960s at the Harvard Botanical Museum.
(Photo courtesy of the Harvard Botanical Museum.)

Museum, Margaret Ashley Towle re-entered the Ph.D. program at Columbia.

In 1958, she submitted her dissertation, entitled "The Ethnobotany of
Pre-Columbian Peru as Evidenced by Archaeological Materials." In 1961,
it was published as Number 30 of the *Viking Fund Publications in Anthropology*. In an *American Antiquity* review, Hugh Cutler (1962) of the Missouri Botanical Garden decries how "botanists and anthropologists pay
relatively little attention to vegetal material from archaeological sites or
living cultures." He says that "Towle's book not only fills a long need for a
summary of useful plants of pre-Columbian Peru, but will aid anyone who
wants to study plants today in fields and markets, wherever Indian cultures
persist, from Mexico to central Chile." Gordon Willey's foreword to the
volume states that the book is for anyone "interested in the story of man and
agriculture" (Willey 1961).

Margaret Towle continued working at Harvard for the remainder of her
life as an associate without stipend. Her picture is on the wall at the Botanical
Museum today (fig. 2.8). She became an AAA Fellow in 1961, and a Fellow
of the Linnaean Society in 1970. She was a continuing support for students

at Harvard and other institutions. Even after the bicycle accident, which caused her to be home-bound, she continued to welcome students into her apartment on Concord Avenue, assisting, supporting, and teaching. Margaret E. Towle, as she signed herself to friends, died on November 2, 1985. Peru lost a pioneering contributor to an understanding of its native peoples in their environment, but Georgia and southeastern archaeology lost even more.

A Legacy in Tragedy

In 1957, the year prior to completion of her dissertation, my father wrote Margaret Towle to re-establish contact and to "introduce" his teenage son who recently had become determined to be an archaeologist. In her response (February 25, 1957), she stated "I shall be glad to write-up a brief account of our work at the Lockett Farm [the Neisler site, 9Tr1], for I think there should be some resumé of the excavations somewhere. I cannot do it at the present time but it will be forthcoming."

In that same letter, however, it was apparent that she was acutely aware of the advances in archaeology since her pioneering work. About the *Etowah Papers* she wrote, "Dr. Moorehead's work is now 'outmoded.' Remember, that was done thirty years ago and much work has been done there and in Georgia archaeology generally, since the twenties." She did remember her era in Georgia with some nostalgia, however, for she wrote: "Over my desk in my little study is a small wall-bookcase in which I keep the more cherished mementos I have collected. On the bottom shelf is a picture of Jerry [Gerald Towle] and Dr. Moorehead taken at the Etowah site when they were digging there. I have placed your model [of an Etowah-inspired figure] by the side of the picture. On the other side is a nice stone ax from Foster's Bend near Rome."

In the time span between her Georgia research and her rekindled interest, much had changed. Rather than recognizing her work for the pathbreaking effort it was, she was apparently embarrassed at the elementary level of her investigations when compared with the ensuing years of research. It is my sense, from the letter she wrote to my father in 1957, and another she wrote to me in 1964, that perhaps her greatest personal regret was in not accomplishing what seems to have been her primary aim in the 1920s: establishing a stratigraphic sequence for Georgia. She tried at Shinholser, at Neisler, and at several sites in the Chattahoochee Valley. Most visibly, she tried at Etowah and at many other sites in north Georgia—all without luck.

But doing this for the first time in any region is a monumental task. Robert S. Neitzel (personal communication, ca. 1959) once told me a perhaps apocryphal tale that the entire Lower Mississippi Valley stratigraphic sequence was based upon one 10 x 10-foot square, and that it was strictly luck which placed that test at the right location. The young Margaret Ashley may have had the misfortune of never placing her tests at the right location. Within ten years of her investigations, working with public relief crews, A. R. Kelly (1938), Robert Wauchope (1948), and Gordon Willey (1939) had accomplished what had always eluded her.

Like so many pioneers, Margaret Towle did not realize her own importance. Like so many women, she considered her work inadequate. In a letter to me in 1964, she said that she had looked again at her notes from the 1920s. Then she wrote what to me is one of the most tragic lines I have ever read in archaeology: "But I was well aware that archaeology in Georgia had gone far beyond what I had done, and so last year I destroyed all the material I had."

It is tempting to end on that dramatic note, but I cannot. Margaret Ashley Towle deserves more. She once said that her concern was not for where the soul went, but for what the soul left behind (Fitz 1928). Despite her statement to me that everything had been destroyed, elements of her work survive, at the Phillips Academy, at Emory University, at the Columbus Museum, at Harvard, and in the hearts and souls of her students and colleagues. I now realize that although I owe much to many, in the deepest psychological sense, I owe a lifetime of devotion to archaeology to that almost mythical heroine of my father's youth, Margaret Elizabeth Ashley.

Selected Bibliography of Margaret Ashley Towle

Ashley, Margaret E.
1927   A Creek Site in Georgia. *Indian Notes* 4:221–26. Museum of the American Indian–Heye Foundation, New York.
1928a   Georgia. In Reports. *American Anthropologist,* n.s 30:504.
1928b   Report on Archaeological Field Work in Georgia. *American Anthropologist* 31:343–44.
1930   On a Method of Making Rubbings. In Discussion and Correspondence. *American Anthropologist* 32:578–79.
1932   A Study of the Ceramic Art of the Etowans. In *Etowah Papers,* edited by W. K. Moorehead et al., pp. 107–36. Yale University Press, New Haven.
Ashley, Margaret E., and Frank T. Schnell, Sr.
1928   Mound and Village Sites in Harris, Muscogee and Chattahoochee Counties, Georgia. Manuscript on file, Columbus Museum, Columbus, Georgia.

Towle, Margaret A.

1948   Report on the Plant Remains from Pachacamac. Manuscript on file at the Harvard Botanical Museum, Cambridge.

1952a   The Pre-Columbian Occurrence of *Lagenaria* Seeds in Coastal Peru. *Botanical Museum Leaflets* 15:171–84. Harvard University, Cambridge.

1952b   Plant Remains from a Peruvian Mummy Bundle. *Botanical Museum Leaflets* 15(9):223–46. Botanical Museum, Harvard University, Cambridge.

1952c   Descriptions and Identifications of the Viru Plant Remains. In *Cultural Stratigraphy in the Viru Valley, Northern Peru, the Formative and Florescent Epochs,* edited by William Duncan Strong and Clifford Evans, Jr., pp. 352–56. Columbia University Press, New York.

1954   Plant Remains. In *Early Ancon and Early Supe Culture,* by Gordon R. Willey and John M. Corbett, pp. 130–38. Columbia University Press, New York.

1956   Descriptions and Identifications of Plant Materials from the South Coast of Peru. Manuscript on file, Harvard Botanical Museum, Cambridge.

1957   Plant Remains from the Site of Chiripa, Bolivia. Manuscript on file, Harvard Botanical Museum, Cambridge.

1958   Plant Remains from Certain Sites in the Rimac Valley, Peru. Manuscript on file, Harvard Botanical Museum, Cambridge.

1961   *The Ethnobotany of Pre-Columbian Peru.* Viking Fund Publications in Anthropology, no. 30. Published for the Wenner-Gren Foundation for Anthropological Research. Quadrangle Books, Aldine, Chicago.

1969   The Ethnobotany of Pre-Columbian Peru as Evidenced by Archaeological Materials. Ph.D. dissertation, Columbia University (1958). University Microfilms, Ann Arbor, Michigan.

3

Isabel Garrard Patterson

Advocate for Georgia Archaeology

R. Jerald Ledbetter

Isabel Patterson was an enthusiastic admirer of archaeology and history whose greatest contributions to these fields were in public education and support for professional archaeology in Georgia. Her work led to the designation of the Ocmulgee National Monument at Macon. She was an ardent promoter of research into the route of Spanish explorer Hernando de Soto through the southeastern U.S. in the early sixteenth century, and she coordinated fieldwork in southwest Georgia around Columbus. A history of that city notes that to her "should go the credit for exciting Columbus residents about their rich Indian heritage" (Kyle 1986:200). Patterson wrote essays for the *Atlanta Constitution* and local Columbus newspapers, as well as more academic contributions relating primarily to the Bull Creek site in Columbus. She was a prominent citizen and amateur archaeologist who, as a result of the emergence of public works archaeology in the 1930s, helped and influenced the careers of many well-known southeastern archaeologists.

Patterson died more than four decades ago. There is scant information on her life beyond the letters and writings that survive her. Fortunately she safeguarded much of this, and it was donated to the Columbus Museum after her death. These files include drafts of her papers; scrapbooks and photograph albums, which are a primary source of information on excavations conducted by A. R. Kelly in the Columbus area; and letters to and from renowned archaeologists and political figures. The files have been utilized to document the previously unpublished WPA-era excavations at the Bull Creek site (Ledbetter 1997). A substantial collection of the correspondence between Patterson and A. R. Kelly from the 1930s through 1950s has also been compiled (Ledbetter 1995).

Georgia Background

Isabel Garrard was born in Columbus at the historic home of Wildwood on December 23, 1894. The house, built in 1831, had been the birthplace in 1835 of Augusta Jane Evans Wilson, a famous nineteenth-century novelist, and was associated with the prominent Urquhart and Garrard families. Isabel was the eighth and youngest child of Louis F. and Anna Foster Leonard Garrard. Louis had a Harvard law degree and was an attorney and politician. He served in the Georgia House of Representatives from 1878–83, becoming Speaker of the House for the last two of those years until he was defeated for reelection in 1894, the year Isabel was born. He was also president of the Columbus Railroad Company and associated with insurance and real estate companies as well. He and his wife both died in 1908.

Isabel (fig. 3.1) attended Lucy Cobb Institute in Athens, Georgia, a well-respected young ladies' school, and graduated from Hollins College. She was a member of Phi Mu sorority and wrote a history of that organization. On June 24, 1915, she married H. Wayne "Pat" Patterson, another prominent Columbus citizen. He had graduated from Georgia Tech, where he had been captain of the football team and an All-Southern tackle for coach John Heisman in 1911. He was an electrical engineer and active in real estate and insurance as well.

Isabel's passionate interest in archaeology and history appeared in her writings as early as 1934. She described the professional excavations going on at Macon, which she visited often (fig. 3.2), and included quotations from archaeological and historical works. Some of her own, often romantic, views of archaeology were also expressed in support of the fledgling efforts in public works archaeology in the state:

> The excellent work [at Macon] . . . seems marvelous and crowds of sightseers have attested their interest—but on April 1 when the new rulings go into effect the money for expert supervision will be canceled. It is unwise to carry on excavations without the direction of expert

archaeologists as much of our pre-history, if not all, would be lost to us forever. The importance of this work done in a careful scientific manner is of unlimited educational value to the state of Georgia. We must have a good archaeologist in charge and it is, of course, preferred to have the one already familiar with this work which has been so ably begun in central Georgia. . . . Now that some effort has been made to ascertain the origin, the culture and the history of the mound builders, it is shameful to have to discontinue scientific excavations and carefully supervised study of every object, pot sherd, and skeleton found. It is, too, unthinkable to admit that there is not some happy solution to this problem so that this excellent work may be carried on—especially at this time when there are hundreds of men of the CWA who need work and with supervision of trained archaeologists can continue to hold jobs and likewise discover the pre-history of Georgia. (Patterson 1934a)

Fig. 3.1. Isabel Garrard Patterson, ca. 1915. (Photo courtesy of the Columbus Museum.)

Fig. 3.2. Isabel Patterson standing on excavated stairway in "Indian mound on Bibb Mills property," Macon, Georgia, today known as Ocmulgee National Monument, 9Bi1. This photo was in the *Atlanta Constitution* on April 15, 1934. (Photo courtesy of the Columbus Museum.)

In this article she went on to note that scholars from the Universities of California, Minnesota, and North Carolina had shown interest in the study of Georgia's archaeology and history by translating Spanish accounts, "but we Georgians have been woefully lacking in our efforts to discover our prehistory." To her credit, she was very interested in the Indian history of the area as well as that of her own Euro-American ancestors, and she read diligently on early migrations of the Creeks. She wrote about Cherokees and others as well, lamenting Indian removal and treatment by whites and praising southern Indians who fought for the Confederacy during the Civil War (1934b, c, d).

Both John R. Swanton and A. R. Kelly instructed Patterson on how she might help archaeology. Kelly wrote to her in August 1934 (Ledbetter

1995:1) that he was proposing to the federal relief agency several research projects, including work at important Lower Creek sites on the Oconee River. Community support and a small sum of money, as well as the labor supply and work relief needs of the area, would be important in consideration of the proposal. He asked her to do some "discreet 'politicing' [*sic*]" and garner backing for a project to explore the historic Coweta town. He mentioned admiring her articles in the *Atlanta Constitution*. In early 1935, Kelly's correspondence with Patterson mentions providing her with photographs and being pleased at receiving from her the first example of a Folsom point he had ever seen, from north Georgia (Ledbetter 1995:4–5).

Patterson's work with Swanton apparently began independently about the same time. Kelly commented in a letter dated April 21, 1935, that he "did not know until a short time ago that you were also getting sherd collections for Dr. Swanton. I fear that we are really working our collaborator too hard; at least I am because my working arrangement with you was probably made later" (Ledbetter 1995:6). Patterson's family connections proved invaluable in obtaining support for both Swanton and Kelly, who got endorsement from Georgia politicians and funds from wealthy individuals.

Patterson also implemented archaeological survey of the Chattahoochee River Valley, although little is recorded about this. Apparently, her goal was to provide large artifact collections to both Kelly and Swanton in order to persuade them to excavate sites in Columbus. She also tried to convince the professionals that an ethnological movie of living Indians should be done (Ledbetter 1995:8–9). Kelly wrote that he would try to obtain for her some assistants, whom she could pay $30 per week (which they would consider adequate), for the survey (Ledbetter 1995:13–14).

The Bull Creek Site and Public Support

Isabel Patterson is best known for her work at the Bull Creek site (9Me1), which she first encountered on that survey. It is a late Mississippian village and cemetery known for several reasons, including the three famous negative-painted dog effigy bottles it produced (figs. 3.3, 3.4), and the note by James B. Griffin that Lewis Binford claimed to have worked on excavating those bottles, even though he would have been only six years old at the time (Griffin 1994:52; Willey 1994:41; Ledbetter 1997). In March 1936, Patterson wrote to Kelly:

> Yesterday afternoon I found the road by the Columbus Air Port was dry enough to get over in my car. It was too muddy and really impass-

able when Frank was here, so I could not show him one of my mainest
(?) treasure finds—*a house in a mound!* There is about a foot of top soil
then a layer of about 2 inches of black dirt. Just below this are *wood*
timbers, which seem to slant a bit; then at intervals of some several feet
are upright wood pieces—In absolute conjunction with this wood are
fragments of pottery sticking out of the bank."

She sent catalogued sherds and maps and asked for help (Ledbetter
1995:14–15).

The Bull Creek site had been noted earlier by Frank J. Mulvihill (1925)
and briefly visited by Margaret Ashley (Ashley and Schnell 1928; Ledbetter
1997:19–21). Kelly's associate Frank Lester, who had been in the Columbus
area previously, was sent to do test excavations over a period of fourteen
months. He doubted that there was enough of the house left to get a complete
floor plan, but Patterson wanted him to try. She had already published one
newspaper story about the site. Kelly liked it because, he wrote to her, it

Fig. 3.3. Isabel Patterson and exhibit of burial with dog pot from Bull Creek site, at
1954 opening of the Columbus Indian Gallery. *Left to right:* Joseph Caldwell, Eugene
Cline (exhibits preparator), Joseph B. Mahan, Jr. (gallery curator), Minnie (Mrs.
Tom) Huston, A. R. Kelly, Patterson. (Photo courtesy of the *Columbus Ledger
Enquirer.*)

Fig. 3.4. Negative-painted dog effigy bottles from the Bull Creek site, 9Me1, in the Chattahoochee Valley. *Top,* from Burial 7; *middle,* Burial 16; *bottom,* Burial 3 (compare fig. 2.6). (Photos courtesy of the Columbus Museum.)

emphasized "scientific methods and technique, rather than ordinary collection" (Ledbetter 1995:18). Lester produced a preliminary report, a typed version of his field notes, but a final report was never published. In 1936, Patterson gave a paper on the site, called "The Archeological Survey of the Chattahoochee Valley" at the second annual meeting of the Society for American Archaeology in Washington. (In a letter to her from Carl E. Guthe [December 3, 1936], he indicates his surprise at her submission of 27 1/2 pages. He advises her to aim for a more scholarly audience and cut her paper to 6–7 pages. In a subsequent letter [January 12, 1937], he congratulates her for a good presentation and slides and apologizes for not being able to visit her room after the session to see the materials she had brought.) Her short published report appeared in the first issue of *Early Georgia* in 1950 under the name "Mrs. Wayne Patterson."

Patterson also gave popular talks and worked on museum exhibits. Much local interest centered upon the burials from Bull Creek. She apparently insisted that the first burial with a dog pot be removed intact in a block of earth, for a more precise exhibit. She wrote:

As the magic spades of archaeology dig up the artifacts of forgotten realities the ancient history of the new world is furnished with material documents of human activities in those misty centuries before Christopher Columbus. . . . Nothing that concerns humanity is alien to archaeology which quickens the twilight world of inanimate things with a vitality that makes the inheritance of the ages a living possession of priceless worth. . . . Today there is no subject more elusive, though probably not one as relentlessly sought, as ancient man in America and his descendants." (Patterson 1937a)

In 1938 Patterson instigated work at the Kasita site (9Ce1), also known as the Lawson Field site, at Fort Benning, in the Chattahoochee Valley (Willey and Sears 1952). She had asked Kelly to see about getting research conducted there and he responded that he would (in the same letter asking for a small loan since he had run out of funds; she sent it right away). Gordon R. Willey was sent to Kasita to direct investigations of this historic Creek town. Willey wrote (letter to N. White, November 1997) that he had been working for Kelly's huge federal relief project at Macon and other locations in 1936, and after that for two years for the WPA, which was under National Park Service auspices. He came to know Isabel Patterson through occasional visits he made with Kelly to Columbus and also her visits to Macon. He remembered well her impressive rambling house, Wildwood, then on the outskirts of Columbus, where she still lived with her husband. She talked about her childhood and her "Old South" upper-class background, and Willey noted that she was petite, vivacious, attractive, dedicated, and full of energy and enthusiasm. He reported that during the two weeks of his Kasita excavations she never missed a day at the dig, and "she became pretty miffed at me when I pulled our crew out after two weeks and returned to Macon." He considered her a very interested amateur and appreciated her research support. She is credited in the report on the site with handling all the local arrangements (Willey and Sears 1952:3).

Much of Patterson's role seems to have been as this kind of facilitator, smoothing the way for the work to proceed. In one letter in August 1937, Kelly asked for her help in obtaining a permit from Georgia Power Company to excavate on their land near Milledgeville (Ledbetter 1995:22). She read reports and offered opinions on archaeological interpretation, apparently, becoming a go-between for Kelly, Swanton, and other professionals. She snagged funds not only for excavation but also for such items as travel to professional meetings. Another of her goals was to formalize a field archaeology program at the University of Georgia (Lyon 1996:112); a chair of archaeology was established by 1938. Patterson also made or had made some movies of the Kasita excavations (film donated by the Columbus Museum to the National Anthropological Archives at the Smithsonian) and the 1939 de Soto celebrations in Florida, Georgia, and Mississippi (films stored at the Columbus Museum).

The de Soto Route and Celebration

Isabel Patterson provided much of the impetus, through the National Society of the Colonial Dames of America, for the creation of the de Soto Commission, the only commission the U.S. Congress had ever established to study a historical event (*Columbus Ledger,* 1955). It is curious that her name does not appear in the official report (Swanton 1939), since other documentation indicates she was an important figure in the entire de Soto phenomenon. Official commission members included Swanton, Walter B. Jones of Alabama, and Louisiana archaeologist Caroline Dormon (Swanton 1939:v; Wurtzburg 1994:125), among others.

Patterson's interest in de Soto may have predated her work in archaeology but was critical to it. As secretary for the de Soto Committee of the Colonial Dames, she was influential for Swanton's research. She had read his work and was eager to help his attempts to trace de Soto's expedition. It is important today, when debate concerning the route and consequences of de Soto remains so great (e.g., Hudson and Hudson 1989; Milanich and Milbrath 1989; Clayton, Knight, and Moore 1993; Milanich and Hudson 1993; Hudson 1993; Ewen and Hann 1998), and our tools for investigating are more sophisticated, to note that Swanton and others were just realizing in the 1930s how meticulous archaeology was needed to supplement history.

In the Columbus Museum files are notes on sites visited by Patterson, including several considered possible locations along de Soto's path. Gordon Willey (letter to N. White, November 1997) related that he accompanied Patterson, Swanton, and others on some of the exploratory trips in which "DeSotoan river crossings, descriptions of hills nearby, etc., were mulled over as they tried to plot the old Spaniard's route. I can remember a couple of occasions when they spotted an Indian site in such a place and felt that this strengthened the case, and I had to pour cold water on the identification by pointing out that the pottery was all of an unfortunately much earlier date."

Isabel channeled substantial energy into the de Soto 400th anniversary celebrations of 1939–40. Her letters as early as November 1937 to important legislators such as Senators Claude Pepper and Kenneth McKellar indicated that the pageant could be greater than any World's Fair yet undertaken. She presented the final commission report before the national meeting of the Colonial Dames in Washington in May 1940, with the goal of bringing great honor to Georgia. The presentation included maps, "5 stunning dioramas" portraying events in the narrative, such as the landing in Florida and the discovery of the Mississippi River, and a display consisting of a large wooden replica of the state of Georgia "showing DeSoto's trail in gold with white lights along it, drawings of noted scenes displayed thereon and approximate locations of the towns visited with the names and dates illuminated by red electric lights," all accompanied by painted wooden figures of Spanish soldiers, priests, and Indians (*Columbus Ledger,* 1940).

As professionals today continue analyzing and reconstructing de Soto, it is important to see how establishment of points along his route was at that time also enormously entwined with local society and politics. In a letter to Patterson dated January 1, 1939, Swanton mentioned some of the details of a particular site location that area residents had disputed, and he said he hoped there would be no "'bataille de dames' or 'de hommes'" over the issue. Swanton's report (1939) differed in some ways from Isabel's previous ideas but she accepted it as the final authority. A letter she sent him dated October 21, 1939, expresses that humility:

I read the Recommendations in your Report to Congress and the Summary of the route of DeSoto through the present state of Georgia. I explained it as well as I could and all were thoroughly impressed. A lady from Ware County, Mrs. J. L. Walker, was really shocked to learn that DeSoto did not cross or even touch the Okefenokee Swamp, as she had believed this for many years. Mrs. Nathaniel B. Stewart of Americus was equally certain that DeSoto had passed through Sumter County at the site of the town now named DeSoto, and Mrs. Lamar C. Rucker of Athens thought that DeSoto had visited Fort Mountain. I told them I understood exactly how they felt and know the sources from which they had found these routes, but in the light of the records from the documents, recent translations, and the Report of the Fact-Finding Committee of the United States DeSoto Expedition, which had the benefit of scientific knowledge, the other writers were mistaken in their conclusions. I told them too that many of my own ideals of the 1540 locations were wrong. . . .

The topography of the country, the distances recorded between places, days spent resting or travelling, the rivers described and the crossings as well as the evidence of Indian sites and the language of the people that DeSoto met must be properly accounted for and the transcription of place names. In other words, besides topography, there were ethnography, anthropology, ethnology, and archaeology to illuminate the documents of Hernando DeSoto's Expedition, and as the State Archeological Survey directed by the University of Georgia expands and reconstructs the aboriginal history the towns De Soto visited may possibly be unearthed. . . .

Please send me the suggestions for Pageants and other observances. . . . I hope to have a number of well-organized groups before 1940 that will execute magnificent celebrations. I want to get a trained group to act as DeSoto and the principal characters to travel from Tallahassee to Bainbridge, and follow the route. . . . In the towns that will arrange for a DeSoto Spectacle and furnish the people to take the remaining parts of the army of DeSoto and the Indians which they encountered, the cost of the trained group of travellers could be met by charging a small admission.

In 1939 festivities began in the Tampa area, where de Soto was thought to have landed in 1539. Sponsored by the Florida State Fair, the "Pan American Hernando de Soto Exposition" ran from January 31 to February 18. A photo on file in the Columbus Museum (fig. 3.5) shows Patterson with

Fig. 3.5. Isabel Patterson *(second from left)* and other (unidentifiable) dignitaries in Tampa at the Hernando de Soto Exposition and 400th anniversary celebration, winter 1939. They are viewing what appears to be a diorama showing a native village with palm trees and (spear-carrying?) Indians (greeting? investigating?) as Spanish ships arrive. (Photo courtesy of the Columbus Museum.)

various dignitaries viewing a diorama showing Spanish ships approaching an Indian village. Local newspaper archives of the time contain many stories of the entire exposition, showing Indian and Spaniard reenactors, along with schedules for agricultural displays, auto races, and stunt daredevil shows. The pageantry was ten years in the making. It is all the more understandable given the psycho-political atmosphere of the time. On the front page of the January 31, 1939, *Tampa Tribune* is a large sketch of a smiling de Soto in helmet and armor, standing in front of the Florida State Fairgrounds, but giant headlines feature Hitler's latest demands. When gloom is on the horizon, one can momentarily forget with historic celebration.

Later Years

With the end of public works archaeology at the beginning of World War II, Isabel Patterson's influence declined somewhat. She remained active in the state archaeological society and Colonial Dames and continued site investi-

Fig. 3.6. Isabel Patterson at Kolomoki Mounds near Mound D, just before its excavation, 1950. (Photo courtesy of the Columbus Museum.)

gations and anthropological correspondence. By 1940, Isabel, who had always written to "My dear Dr. Kelly" and been addressed as "Dear Mrs. Patterson," had become "My dear Mrs. Patterson"; by 1945, it was "Dear Isabel" (Ledbetter 1995). As late as 1950 she was still trying to persuade Columbus city officials to continue excavations at Bull Creek, and Kelly to write a full report on it. She apparently continued to help with the establishment of the Columbus Museum (Ledbetter 1955:52–53), which set aside its "Indian Room" in her honor and exhibited many of her finds (Kyle 1986:200). She stayed connected with professional investigations, such as Sears's excavations at Kolomoki (fig. 3.6), and served on the board of directors of the Historical Society of Columbus, especially their historic markers committee.

We know little of Isabel Patterson's personal life. She and Wayne had no children, and she was certainly active in other areas of public service, such as organizing the first Girl Scout troop in Columbus and serving the Red Cross for more than thirty years. She died at age sixty after a long illness, in January 1955. A. R. Kelly was an honorary pallbearer at her funeral (*Columbus Ledger,* 1955). Her husband, Wayne, outlived her by thirty-two years. His obituary (*Columbus Enquirer,* 1987) mentions a second wife, but not Isabel.

Some thoughts expressed by Swanton (letter to Joseph Caldwell at Ocmulgee National Monument, May 17, 1955), following Isabel's death, portray her impact:

The Spring Number of "Early Georgia" just received contains interesting material but along with it a sad note in recording the death, or
as we are used to saying in my Church, the passage to a higher life, of
Mrs. Patterson who was such a good friend to me and to the entire
cause of Georgia archaeology for so many years. I suppose "Early
Georgia" itself is something of a monument to her.

We of the sterner—and stupider—sex are wont to express amusement at times at the naivty [sic] and, as we choose to call it, the "un-
critical," childlike enthusiasm of women who take up a cause, but we
have to admit that it is after all the women who "get things done," who
prod our slow-wittedness into action. We have, from the French I
think, a rather unsavory statement in any mysterious or unexpected
situation that "there is a woman at the bottom of it." But the cavil
becomes hushed whenever we review the things which have had a
woman at the bottom of them. What would army hospitals be like
today if there had been no Florence Nightengale [sic], or our prisons
if there had been no Elizabeth Fry, or our own social welfare work if
there had been no Jane Addams. And so it goes all down the line when
one undertakes to explore what it was that made such and such a man
or such and such a cause successful and locate "the power behind the
throne."

And so undoubtedly you will miss the dynamism of the little lady
who has gone from among you, but the work in which she was interested will go on and others will come forward and take her place.

Sincerely, John R. Swanton (Formerly head of the Bureau of Ethnology, Smithsonian Institute, now retired).

Patterson was not a professional, and it is possible that Kelly or others did
help her write her articles, though the public perceived her as an expert.
However, her interest, education, wealth, and social background allowed
her to participate in public works archaeology to enormous effect. Her
ability to be a benefactor, but also to question the professionals and absorb
the wealth of discoveries during that era, put her into a position of more than
a sponsor. For a brief time she had a hand in shaping the future of southeastern archaeology.

Bibliography of Isabel Garrard Patterson

1934a   Excavation of Indian Mounds Near Macon Unearths Data of Far-Reaching Importance. *Atlanta Constitution,* April 15.

1934b   De Soto's Route through Georgia Followed Line from Bainbridge to Augusta; Did Not Enter North Georgia according to Records. *Atlanta Constitution,* April 29.

1934c   Georgia Deeply Stirred 100 Years Ago over Question of Removal of Cherokees. *Atlanta Constitution,* May 20.

1934d   Story of How the Indians Gradually Yielded All of Georgia to the White Man. *Atlanta Constitution,* May 22.

1934e   DeSoto's Romance with Princess Cofitachiqui as He Crossed Savannah at Silver Bluff. Introductory Adventure of Following the DeSoto Route. *Atlanta Constitution,* June 24.

1935   Asiatics First "Discovered" America 10,000 Years Ago. *Atlanta Constitution,* September 28.

1936a   Archeological Survey of the Chattahoochee Valley. Paper presented at the second annual meeting of the Society for American Archaeology, Washington, D.C. Manuscript on file, Columbus Museum of Arts and Sciences, Columbus, Georgia.

1936b   Valuable Finds Spur Interest in Archaeological Explorations in Famed Chattahoochee Valley. *Columbus Ledger Enquirer,* April 5.

1936c   Indian Relics to Be Sought in This Area. Jaycees Will Sponsor Archaeological Survey in Bull Creek Section. *Columbus Ledger,* April 24.

1937a   Skeleton of Ancient Indian to Be Exhibited as Georgia Archaeologists Meet Here. *Columbus Ledger-Enquirer,* May 30.

1937b   Indian Trails Study Slated by Archaeological Pilgrims in Valley of Chattahoochee. *Columbus Ledger,* June 10.

1937c   Bull Creek Village. Unpublished manuscript on file, Columbus Museum of Arts and Sciences, Columbus, Georgia.

1950   Notes on the Exploration of the Bull Creek Site, Columbus, Georgia. *Early Georgia* 1 (1):34–40.

4

Madeline D. Kneberg Lewis

Leading Lady of Tennessee Archaeology

Lynne P. Sullivan

It was the summer of 1938, the middle of the Great Depression, and jobs were hard to find. Madeline loaded her mother and oldest sister, Goldie, in a new Ford car bought especially for the trip and drove in the summer heat from Chicago, Illinois, to Knoxville, Tennessee. She had accepted a position as a physical anthropologist on an archaeological project funded by the Works Progress Administration (WPA) and administered through the University of Tennessee. With careful budgeting, her $200 a month salary would be enough to keep the three of them in food and shelter, as well as to send money to her widowed sister Bessie, who had two young daughters, in Minneapolis. Madeline had previously met Tom Lewis, the head of the Tennessee project, at a conference in Columbus, Ohio. He seemed like a bright fellow and was handsome, too. Fay-Cooper Cole, her mentor at the University of Chicago, thought the experience would be good for Madeline, and her friend Bill Krogman also advised her to take the job.

Perhaps with some trepidation on her first day at work, Madeline entered the large room that served as the archaeology laboratory in the engineering building at the University of Tennessee. The study of human bones was not her specialty, nor was archaeology. She was not sure just what to expect, but life up to now had taught her to be flexible and ready to learn new skills. Seated at a table in the lab were a young man and woman. He was using calipers to take careful measurements on a stone tool, then calling the numbers out for her to write down. Surrounding them were stack after stack of large pasteboard boxes filled with pottery, stone and bone tools, and ancient human skeletons, all piled high to the ten-foot ceiling—the results of four years of fieldwork by WPA crews.

Lewis had just received permission to hire a laboratory staff and the lab work was woefully behind the fieldwork. With the construction of Tennessee Valley Authority reservoirs, excavations were ongoing of sites that would forever be lost to archaeology. Truckloads of boxes of artifacts and field notes were arriving weekly at the Knoxville lab. Madeline gasped as she watched the pair of workers continue to make painstakingly slow measurements, and she thought to herself, "How can they focus on such details when they are about to be buried by the boxes? This lab needs organization and priorities set!" With that observation, Madeline Kneberg was on her way to becoming the lab director. She knew her work in the WPA project lab was cut out for her, but she could not know then that the job in Tennessee was not temporary. Years later she would remark, "It lasted the rest of my life!"

Archaeology done in conjunction with the public works projects of Roosevelt's New Deal launched the careers of many southeastern archaeologists. Madeline Kneberg Lewis (fig. 4.1) was one of the few women who became widely recognized as a result of her work on these projects. She was elected a fellow in the American Association for the Advancement of Science and, if not the first, was one of the first women to hold a full professorship in anthropology in the Southeast. She is most famous for her collaborative work with her (future) husband Thomas M. N. Lewis and for her efforts to bring archaeological interpretations to the general public, but her early work in physical anthropology and her pioneering work in what is now known as the field of bioarchaeology are worthy of recognition.

Madeline's career in anthropology was not a planned one. She was a woman of diverse talents and interests, who followed (often of necessity) a winding, but always interesting, path through life. Madeline received support from many influential male colleagues and seems to have been comfortable in and drawn strength from a professional world in which men served as her confidants and mentors, while the women closest to her (her mother and oldest sister) were her dependents. As one colleague commented in regard to the WPA lab, "Madeline didn't have to worry about discrimination. She ran the place!"

Fig. 4.1. Madeline D. Kneberg. (Portrait taken from a brochure about the Oconaluftee Indian Village published by the Tsali Institute, probably in the early 1950s.) (Photo courtesy of the Frank H. McClung Museum.)

The information in this chapter about Madeline Kneberg's career derives mainly from a tape-recorded interview made on March 15, 1992; a video-taped interview made in 1994; and a transcribed interview with both her and Lewis done on December 19, 1972. The 1992 interview was conducted by White and Marrinan, the 1994 interview was done by Bill Landry of WBIR television (Knoxville), and Charles W. Crawford of the Oral History Research Office of Memphis State University conducted the 1972 interview. Telephone calls on August 7, 1992, and August 27, 1993, between Kneberg and White, and Kneberg and Sullivan, respectively, also added information and clarified details.

Growing Up in Moline

Madeline D. Kneberg was born on the banks of the Mississippi River in Moline, Illinois, on January 18, 1903, and was the youngest of three daughters of Charles E. and Anna Anderson Kneberg. Her parents were brought as young children to the United States by her Swedish immigrant grandparents who settled in Moline. There, they were part of a large community of immigrants who maintained Swedish traditions through church and civic groups. Her father's family apparently was well off financially, but in 1892 he began an interior decorating business in downtown Moline. Charles later built a building known as the Kneberg block on the corner of Fifth Avenue and Sixteenth Street. Anna Kneberg also worked as a decorator and helped clients select furniture and oriental rugs.

Madeline was born after her parents had been married twenty-four years and her father was fifty-two years old. Blue-eyed and a strawberry blonde, Madeline was the apple of her father's eye. Unlike with her older sisters, Goldie and Bessie, Charles Kneberg not only encouraged Madeline's athletic abilities (giving her baseball gloves instead of dolls), he taught her to drive a car by the age of thirteen. Madeline recalled, "My father did his best to make a boy out of me." Both parents supported her interests, indulging and nurturing Madeline's independent nature.

Madeline's father also encouraged her to draw. She referred to him as "an artist." Not surprisingly, Madeline's early interests focused on the arts. This thread was to run through her archaeological career in her drawings and paintings for publications and exhibits. Madeline also had a passion for singing. The Scandinavian community in Moline was avidly interested in singing, as is evident in the many notices for songfests, choir rehearsals and performances, and concerts by Swedish opera stars that appeared in the local newspaper. Madeline sang in the church choir, and opera singing was to become her initial career goal.

Her father was killed in a tragic accident in April 1916, two days after his sixty-fifth birthday. As reported in the *Moline Daily News,* April 7, 1916, Mr. Kneberg suffered dizzy spells for several weeks after falling from a ladder. A spell overtook him at a railroad crossing and he fell in front of an oncoming train. The funeral at the Swedish Methodist Church was attended by hundreds of people, as Kneberg was quite well liked. A pastor from Chicago conducted part of the service in Swedish, and there were solo performances by several singers.

Madeline was thirteen and in the eighth grade in the Moline school when her father died. The death of her husband must have been devastating to Madeline's mother as Madeline remembered using the driving skills taught by her father to take her mother on weekly visits to the cemetery. At sixteen years of age, Madeline left Moline to attend boarding school at Southern Seminary in Buena Vista, Virginia, where she completed preparatory school, and then enrolled at Martha Washington College in Fredericksburg for a year. During this time, she coached a girls' basketball team and taught horseback riding.

Opera Singing in Florence

In her later teen years, Madeline became serious about a career as an opera singer. In 1924, at age twenty-one, she went to Florence, Italy, to study opera singing. The teacher, an American, had five female students. Madeline soon found that she did not fit well with the group and cabled her mother to get permission to be on her own. She spoke no Italian but took a class at the University of Florence. Languages evidently were not difficult for her; she had taken French in school and was the only girl in the original group who could communicate in Paris. Madeline found an Italian voice teacher who was more to her liking—Mario Anacona, a retired baritone from the Metropolitan Opera in New York City.

She stayed in Florence for four years, living in a pensione on the Lungarno Serristori along the Arno River. Her mother joined her after the first year. While in Italy, Madeline visited many historic sites and museums. Her recollections of this time were fond ones: "I love Florence. I don't know whether I enjoyed the art or the music more there, but I always went to all free days at the museum."

The years in Italy were a turning point in Madeline's life. Sanitation in Florence during the 1920s was not good. Madeline suffered chronic sinus infections and finally had a tonsillectomy upon her return to the States. Worrying about her health and the implications for her singing career disturbed Madeline. She was uncomfortable being so self-absorbed and decided, after eight years of study, that she did not want to sing professionally. Besides the increased self knowledge she gained, her experience in Italy was eventually a career benefit.

From Nursing to Physical Anthropology at the University of Chicago

After returning to the United States, Madeline sought a new career. An admired friend, a public health nurse, inspired Madeline to go into nursing. Madeline enrolled at Presbyterian Hospital in Chicago and graduated after three years of training. She then decided that she wanted to become a physician, so she enrolled at the University of Chicago in 1931.

Madeline had only one year of college, but she was able to complete a Bachelor of Science degree in one year. She had taken chemistry and bacteriology during her nursing training, and she received credit for three years of Italian study. She majored in sociology with a minor in psychology but also took anthropology and several history classes. Fay-Cooper Cole, who was head of the anthropology department, was interested in Madeline's experience in Italy and her nursing background. He encouraged her to go into physical anthropology. She still wanted to go into medicine, but the financial situation caused by the Depression gave her second thoughts.

In 1932 Cole received a grant from the National Research Council that paid Madeline fifty dollars per month to work on a problem concerning racial differences of human hair. The search for distinct biological differences in human races was a popular research topic of that era. Madeline worked in the histology and microscopic anatomy lab of William Bloom, a well-known histologist. She developed procedures for examining the microscopic anatomy of hair and hair follicles. These tedious procedures created cross-sections of the hair shafts and follicles, allowing their shapes and sizes to be observed.

Her first publication on the project (Kneberg 1935) describes the procedure for sectioning hair shafts and shows photomicrographs of the resulting cross-sections. Kneberg found considerable variation in hair shaft shapes from individual people, and she determined that Martin's (1914) index of hair shaft diameters did not reliably correlate with racial groups. She suspected that the form of the hair shaft related to the structure of the follicle, thus providing a physical basis for a hair's relative curliness or straightness. Kneberg's (1936a, 1936b) second set of publications describes the procedure for creating scalp sections for studying hair follicles and the results of a study of hair weight. The latter study found no correlation between hair weight or size and race. Her work on the hair project became her master's thesis and the topic for her doctoral dissertation.

While working in the microanatomy lab and taking anthropology classes, Madeline met and learned from several well-known anthropologists. The four faculty members who most influenced her training and intellectual development were Franz Weidenreich, A. R. Radcliffe-Brown, Fay-Cooper Cole, and Thorne Deuel. Cole became a lifetime mentor and friend.

Weidenreich, an anatomist and physical anthropologist who reconstructed human fossil remains, also worked in Bloom's lab, where Madeline and he became friends. Weidenreich was then in his sixties and had come to the United States to escape the Nazis. He was working on "Peking man" (now classified as *Homo erectus*). Weidenreich's work profoundly affected the development of human paleontology, especially his "trellis" model of human evolution (Trinkaus 1982:266–67). Through their friendship at the lab, Madeline probably observed and learned some of Weidenreich's techniques for reconstructing human anatomy from fossil bones. Her lecture notes (curated at the McClung Museum) suggest that when she later taught human evolution, she incorporated his views into her lectures.

A. R. Radcliffe-Brown undoubtedly influenced Madeline's view of anthropology as one of her teachers. She also worked with him. Radcliffe-Brown, an Englishman educated at Cambridge, was a major figure in the development of contemporary social anthropology. He viewed anthropology as a natural science of society, based on the comparative analysis of social systems. To him, social life was an adaptive system of interdependent parts, such as religious activities or legal systems. The interconnections between the parts were important in maintaining the social structure and keys to understanding the overall system. Madeline greatly respected Radcliffe-Brown, who, she said, "treated her just like one of the fellows." His view of society likely iniiuenced her work with Tom Lewis as they sought to delineate various "parts" of past cultures (for example, technology, subsistence, and community life), as in their work on the prehistory of the Chickamauga Basin (Lewis and Kneberg 1946; Lewis, Lewis, and Sullivan 1995).

The faculty member who most influenced Madeline's career was Fay-Cooper Cole. Cole was one of a now nearly extinct breed—a general anthropologist. Before coming to the university in the late 1920s, he trained as a physical anthropologist, did research in the Philippines in both physical anthropology and ethnology, and worked at the Field Museum. At Chicago, Cole developed an archaeological research program in Illinois to train anthropology graduate students.

Cole ran archaeological field schools for nearly a decade. Students from all over the country attended these schools as they were the only ones that existed at the time (Fowler 1985:7). Cole's field schools developed techniques for excavating mounds and villages and for keeping systematic records. The Chicago field schools "became famous for their system of horizontal and vertical control of archaeological excavations" (Fowler 1985:7). Cole was thus instrumental in developing modern archaeological field techniques. His emphasis on scientific data collection, including systematic excavation and recording techniques, and his view of archaeology influenced Madeline although there is no evidence that she attended a field school. Jennings (1994:44) states that Cole's graduate students were required to take field school. Why Madeline apparently did not attend is unclear, perhaps because she was training in physical anthropology rather than archaeology. Women did attend the field schools (see Fowler 1985).

The other faculty member interested in archaeology was Thorne Deuel. Cole and Deuel collaborated on publications and were among the first to look systematically at excavated materials with an eye toward interpreting the functional implications of the artifacts (Willey and Sabloff 1977:135). In *Rediscovering Illinois* (Cole and Deuel 1937), they "followed the procedure of listing all of the discovered archaeological traits of any one site component under functional categories such as 'Agriculture and Food-getting' or 'Military and Hunting Complex.' Traits were so classified depending upon their form, appearance, and the contexts in which they were found" (Willey and Sabloff 1977:135–36). This innovation kept the investigators thinking about "activities" rather than just the objects. Their work was compatible with that of their colleague in social anthropology, Radcliffe-Brown, who envisioned society as a system of interrelated parts. Kneberg and Lewis built upon this perspective; they focused not only on various activities but saw the archaeological record as a way to understand past cultures. Their focus was on the past peoples and cultures, not on the artifacts alone. Cole was fond of saying that he and Deuel were developing techniques that would "make the dead past live again" (Fowler 1985:9). Madeline's view of the goal of archaeology was quite similar, although she notably added a strong interpretational vision that made the past "come to life" for the general public as well.

Madeline also met the well-known social anthropologist Robert Redfield, a Chicago graduate who began his career as a lawyer. He helped widen the scope of anthropology from a focus on "primitive" peoples and the comparative study of civilizations to include folk traditions and modern urban culture. Kneberg recalled that Redfield "called archaeologists and physical anthropologists 'ghouls'." He was working in Mexico at Tepotzlan when she first arrived.

Another person Madeline remembered in the anthropology department was the famous modern dancer and anthropologist Katherine Dunham. An evening Madeline recalled was when Dunham took a group of anthropologists and students to a nightclub where there were albino African Americans.

Some of Madeline's classmates at the University of Chicago who went on to careers in anthropology included Jesse Jennings, Charles Fairbanks, Harriet Smith, Fred Eggan, Wilton Krogman, John McGregor, Joseph Caldwell, and Florence Hawley. Jennings and Fairbanks later worked on the WPA projects in Tennessee, as did Andrew Whiteford and J. Joseph Bauxar (a.k.a. Finklestein), two younger Chicago students; Whiteford met Madeline at Beloit College (see p. 65). Hawley also worked on the Tennessee WPA projects as a dendrochronologist (see fig. 1.3) and spent time in Tennessee on the Norris Basin project. Smith and Krogman were close friends of Kneberg's. Madeline later arranged for Smith to be offered a job by Tom Lewis to work in the Knoxville WPA lab (letters are on file at the McClung Museum). Smith, an archaeologist, already had accepted a job in Illinois to supervise WPA excavations of the Murdock Mound at the Cahokia site. Not only were these the first carefully controlled excavations of a mound at this large site (Fowler 1985:8), Smith was one of the few women to supervise fieldwork on WPA projects (see Claassen, chapter 5, this volume). Krogman, a leading forensic anthropologist, wrote in 1962 the classic text, *The Human Skeleton in Forensic Medicine* (Thompson 1982:362). He left Chicago for the University of Pennsylvania, where he later recommended Madeline for the WPA job. After Madeline went to Tennessee, she and Krogman kept in touch (letters are on file at the McClung Museum). She consulted him on problems with the skeletal materials, and when she began teaching, she sought his advice on appropriate texts.

Before leaving Chicago, Madeline continued working for Cole on the hair project and clung to her ambition to become a physician. She took gross anatomy, microscopic anatomy, and physical chemistry. The Great Depression made her financial situation increasingly difficult. To make ends meet, she lived with five nurses in a one-bedroom apartment. Some of the other women worked nights, so they slept in shifts. The rent was only six dollars each per month. Madeline kept up her interest in singing and made five dollars per Sunday singing in the university choir. She finally gave up trying to be a physician; medical education was expensive and her family did not have the money. She decided to continue in anthropology because she enjoyed it and that was the path that seemed to be laid for her.

Madeline completed her thesis on the hair project in 1936 and was awarded a master's degree in anthropology. She took a temporary job at Beloit College in Wisconsin as a substitute for Paul Nesbitt, who was curator of the Logan Museum and head of the anthropology department. Nesbitt was on leave to finish his dissertation under Cole; it is likely that Cole helped Madeline get the Beloit job. She was there for six months, living in a boarding house, looking after the museum, and teaching second semester general anthropology (two sections) and a class on the Pueblo Indian (a newspaper clipping from the Alumni Records Office, Beloit College, notes that Kneberg "attended school in Florida before taking work at Chicago." The reporter must have misunderstood Madeline's stint in Florence and mistakenly reported the location as "Florida"!). The Wisconsin winter of 1936–37 was bitter. One frozen day Madeline skated to the museum in a pair of ice skates borrowed from her landlord's daughter.

Madeline knew Thorne Deuel was interested in the effigy mounds of the upper Midwest. In the spring of 1937, she arranged a collaboration between Beloit College and the University of Chicago to excavate a conical mound near Shireland, Illinois, as a field experience for her students. The mound was the largest of a group of sixteen that included effigy mounds. Deuel brought the field equipment and some student supervisors. The dig lasted only two days (May 21–22) and was Madeline's only field supervisory experience before going to Tennessee. Students who worked on the dig included Lewis Austin, John Bennett, Benjamin Bradley, William Brook, Willard Byers, Robert Clark, Jean Davidson, John DeYoung, Virginia Drew, Lowell Dwinnell, Don Eldredge, William Fischer, Claire Lichtenberg, William McKnight, Beth Smalley, Hale Smith, and Andrew Whiteford. As noted above, Whiteford later would be employed in the laboratory on the Tennessee WPA projects. John Bennett went on in archaeology, worked in northern Illinois, and became a professor at Washington University in St. Louis. Hale Smith became a professor at Florida State University with Charles Fairbanks (see Mason, chapter 9, this volume), although Fairbanks eventually left for a position at the University of Florida. Deuel left Chicago later in 1937 to become director of the Illinois State Museum (Fowler 1985).

After the stint at Beloit, Madeline returned to Chicago to continue work on her Ph.D. She later insisted that she never pretended to be an archaeologist; she was a physical anthropologist. For her dissertation project, Madeline resumed investigating why some people have curly hair, and she worked in the microscopic anatomy laboratory. She took and passed her preliminary examinations. The dissertation was all that was left to complete for the Ph.D.

These circumstances lasted only a short while, however, as Krogman and Cole recommended Madeline to T. M. N. Lewis for the job in Tennessee. Since it was the Depression and money was still a problem, at age thirty-five, Madeline decided to take the job. Her mother, Anna, and sister Goldie were staying with her other sister Bessie, but they came to Chicago and headed to Knoxville with Madeline. At that time the WPA salary "seemed like a fortune," Madeline later remarked. Even though she "never pretended to be an archaeologist," the rest of Madeline's career was destined to make her one.

Thomas McDowell Nelson Lewis

Madeline's story is not complete without mention of her collaborator and eventual spouse, Thomas M. N. Lewis. By all accounts, Tom was a trim, handsome man with polish gained from education at Princeton and service in the Navy (fig. 4.2). He was born in Chambersburg, Pennsylvania, on March 27, 1896, but grew up in Watertown, Wisconsin, where he went to the public schools and collected arrowheads. He attended Northwestern

Fig. 4.2. Thomas M. N. Lewis. (Portrait from the Kneberg papers curated at the Frank H. McClung Museum; probably dates to the 1930s.) (Photo courtesy of the Frank H. McClung Museum.)

College for five years and Lawrenceville Prep School in New Jersey for one year, then entered Princeton University until enlisting in the Navy in May 1917, during World War I. He returned to Princeton after the war, graduated in 1919, and in 1920 started graduate school at the University of Wisconsin, where he took anthropology classes. His schooling was cut short because his father became ill. Tom's father was a manufacturer of masonite and fiberglass and was anxious that Tom work with him at the family firm in Watertown, the G. B. Lewis Co., which was started by Tom's grandfather. Tom did so for over a decade, working up to sales manager with a territory from coast to coast (as reported in a 1961 newspaper clipping in the files of the McClung Museum). During this time he occasionally did archaeological fieldwork with Will McKern, director of the Milwaukee Public Museum.

When archaeology became part of the New Deal projects, there was a need for experienced field supervisors. McKern recommended Tom to William S. Webb for a job on the Norris Basin project in Tennessee. Webb, a physics professor at the University of Kentucky, was avidly interested in archaeology and became the archaeological consultant for the TVA after McKern refused the offer (Lyon 1996:40). (See Jennings 1994:84–86 for an entertaining, informative, and positive portrait of Major Webb.) In late 1933, Webb offered Lewis the job of supervising the Norris excavations. Tom consulted with McKern and accepted the offer after arranging to leave the family business. In 1934, at the age of thirty-eight, and four years before he would hire Madeline Kneberg, Lewis went to Tennessee with his first wife and young daughter.

Tennessee and New Deal Archaeology

Lewis's arrival in Knoxville and confrontation with the job at hand was no less overwhelming than Kneberg's was to be. The project he was to supervise, near LaFollette, Tennessee, began the following week. Waiting for him would be fifty men and two supervisors. The latter were collectors from Dayton, Tennessee, who had no professional training but were familiar with local sites. The next Monday, Lewis found the fifty men sitting on a large mound.

The nature of large southeastern mounds was not completely understood in the early 1930s. It was only suspected that some mounds were substructures for buildings. After finding a line of posts, Tom realized that this mound was not a burial mound like those he had excavated in Wisconsin but did indeed contain evidence of buildings.

Tom had field forms from the Milwaukee Public Museum. Like Cole, McKern used standardized forms for recording burials, structures, and other archaeological features. Tom also had photography experience and taught the field-workers how to get proper light on the archaeological features.

The work force went from fifty to one hundred the next week—eventually there were five hundred men working at sites throughout the Norris Basin. Their pay was one dollar a day via the Federal Emergency Relief Act (FERA). Tom had a car and driver to visit the sites in a four-county area. Sometimes there were too many men and not enough supervision. When this happened, Tom had to tell some of them just to sit down until FERA could assign them elsewhere.

Tom was unemployed after the Norris fieldwork was completed in June 1934. He waited to see if he would be hired for more TVA work. Webb contacted President James D. Hoskins of the University of Tennessee to suggest that Lewis be hired to supervise future work in the TVA reservoir areas. During that summer, Tom continued to live in Knoxville and went out on his own to find sites for future excavations. His surveys were mainly in eastern Tennessee in the Chickamauga Basin, and the Little Tennessee and Hiwassee River valleys.

In August, Tom learned that the Board of Trustees had decided to employ him—even though they had to let a large portion of the faculty go for lack of funds. The board realized the importance of the archaeology being done

Fig. 4.3. WPA field camp in Humphreys County, Tennessee, November 1935. Tom Lewis is leaning on the right side of the sign. Other men pictured (as identified by James B. Griffin) *(left to right),* are O. C. Ogle, Charles H. Nash, Lewis, Georg W. Neumann, and Charles J. S. Parsons. (Photo courtesy of the Frank H. McClung Museum.)

before flooding of the TVA reservoirs, and the huge loss if something was not done. Lewis became the university's archaeologist on September 1, 1934. He was made an associate professor and charged to supervise all archaeological work in the state. The Division of Anthropology was established as a section of the history department.

During 1935, Tom ran small projects in Humphreys and Cheatham counties (Lyon 1996:140–41) and organized the work for the Chickamauga Reservoir near Chattanooga, which began in early 1936. The WPA paid for the labor (fig. 4.3), and the TVA provided photo processing and mapping, and some supplies. Tom hired young archaeologists from several universities as field supervisors, including several University of Chicago students: Jesse Jennings, Stuart Neitzel, Charles Fairbanks, Charles Nash, John Alden, Paul Cooper, and Paul Maynard. Jennings was the main supervisor. Another Chicago student, Chandler Rowe, was employed later on, in 1941–43.

The crew was one hundred out-of-work miners from Soddy, Tennessee. The miners were a troublesome lot (Jennings 1994:86–87). At one point, they threatened to strike for better wages and pooled their money to send a representative to Washington. The man left and was never heard from again. Fieldwork continued in the Chickamauga Basin until 1939. (See also Jennings 1994:87–90, whose account of this project is less than favorable toward Lewis. His descriptions of the field conditions, including the sinking of the houseboats in which the crew lived, and of his relationship with Lewis provide a valuable perspective on the situation.)

Tom set up a lab in Knoxville to catalog materials brought from the field. He was hoping to spend a large sum of TVA funds on this lab, but Webb (still serving as the TVA consultant) did not approve the expenditure. Webb feared that a request for a lot of money would cause the TVA to lose interest in the archaeology, which was not legally required (Lyon 1996:144). Boxes of artifacts piled up in the laboratory and a large backlog of uncataloged and unanalyzed materials developed. Finally in 1938, the WPA program was restructured to support laboratory analysis and publication. Establishment of large, central laboratories was encouraged by the WPA scientific consultant, and Webb was persuaded to allow Tom to develop the Knoxville lab. By this time, the laboratory work was four years behind the fieldwork (Lyon 1996:149–51).

Madeline encountered this situation upon her arrival in Knoxville in June 1938. She immediately recognized that a huge amount of work had to be done even to get to the point where she could analyze the skeletal material, and that priorities would have to be set. She went into "triage mode": she studied field notes, plats, and records; she developed a plan for the information so that it could be preserved and properly organized, and so that a publication could ultimately be produced; and she sent the plan to Lewis in the field at Chickamauga. Lewis came to Knoxville to go over the plan with Madeline. He not only agreed to it, he made Madeline the lab director. Tom took the young man, Earl Loyster, who had been painstakingly measuring stone tools in the shadow of the piles of boxes, back to the field.

Working with Tom, Madeline got the laboratory running. Her goal was to catch the laboratory work up with the fieldwork. She selected WPA workers with clerical or other relevant skills and hired several anthropology graduate students and a few skilled WPA employees as supervisors. The WPA lab workers were from Knoxville and many were professional people, unlike the field-workers who generally were less educated and from rural backgrounds. So many people were hired that the lab was moved from the engineering building to West Strong Hall, an old house with three floors. The lab occupied all three floors. At its peak in 1939–41, there were forty workers and half a dozen supervisors. A draftsman, Herman Strauch, was hired to do artifact illustrations. The WPA also gave Madeline an administrative assistant to help with the paperwork for the employees—there was a lot of it.

The students hired as supervisors were Andrew H. ("Bud") Whiteford, J. Joseph Bauxar (a.k.a. Finklestein), and Alice Hendrick. Madeline hired Whiteford and Bauxar as artifact analyst and project ethnohistorian, respectively. Whiteford had been a student at Beloit College when Madeline taught there and later went on to graduate school at the University of Chicago. Bauxar was a graduate of the University of Oklahoma who went on to graduate school at Chicago. Hendrick was a University of Michigan graduate who supervised the pottery cataloging and classification. She was hired by Lewis before Madeline's arrival (and was the young woman in the lab when Madeline first arrived). Another supervisor was Doc Goins, an ex-pharmacist, who supervised a group of elderly men to clean human bones in the second floor osteology lab.

As laboratory director, Madeline had general oversight of materials preparation, restoration, and cataloging, as well as analysis. Her goal of clearing the lab backlog was met near the end of the Chickamauga work. Under Madeline's direction, the Knoxville lab developed an innovative attribute-based system for artifact classification, a technique for pottery vessel reconstruction, and numerous card files for analytical purposes and collections management. For the Chickamauga project alone, the lab classified more than 360,000 pottery sherds and some 100,000 stone, bone, shell, and copper artifacts. They also reconstructed several hundred pottery vessels and examined all of the nearly 2,000 recovered skeletons for age, sex, and pathologies. When asked about Madeline's contributions, several people who worked with her, or who were active in southeastern archaeology at the time, uniformly described her as the dynamic force in the lab and the source of inspiration for much of the analytical work. Jennings (1994:89–90), who had a low opinion of Lewis, remarked that Kneberg was "a quite capable classmate" and that he always thought Madeline was responsible for the credibility and success of *Hiwassee Island* and *Eva*. He also noted that James B. Griffin's view that Andrew Whiteford was responsible for the quality of the Tennessee reports was "easy to accept"!

Tom and Madeline worked on a manual that described the field and laboratory methods used by the Tennessee projects (Lewis, Lewis, and Sullivan 1995: Appendix C). Both the manual prepared at the University of Alabama lab and the one at Tennessee relied on systems developed by Fay-Cooper Cole's field schools. The Tennessee manual also delineated field techniques developed under Tom's supervision through years of experimentation and explained the complicated catalog and file system that Madeline used in the laboratory.

By the summer of 1939, Madeline clearly was in Tom's confidence and empowered by him to be directly involved in project management. They also were developing a close working and personal relationship, one that was to continue for the rest of their careers and lead to their eventual marriage. As early as 1939, in correspondence to colleagues, Tom and Madeline referred to each other on a first-name basis and, in reference to issues of project management, in terms of "we." About this time, Tom also became divorced (Marion Whiteford, personal communication, 1998).

Madeline sometimes went with Tom to the field. She appears in a film Tom made of the Chickamauga excavations, pointing out the stratigraphy in a mound profile, but Madeline had no inclination to do fieldwork and was happy to manage the lab. She later commented, "I used to go out with my husband and visit the field parties. I can remember in the summer the heat was terrible. I wondered how they could stand it."

During the summer of 1939, the pot also began to boil on several simmering disagreements with Webb. More than fifty years later, Madeline was visibly uncomfortable discussing these problems. Not insignificant factors in the quarrel were the approach taken by the Tennessee projects and the amount of time for report preparation this approach required. The argument mainly was over whether the reports should be comprehensive and analytical as Tom and Madeline wished, or abbreviated and descriptive as Webb requested (see Lyon 1996:146). Another significant issue was the direction of the archaeology in the Kentucky Basin—a reservoir spanning the Kentucky-Tennessee border. Madeline explained that "Webb was a very good amateur archaeologist, but by the time of the Kentucky Basin work, the University of Tennessee had a full-fledged anthropology program. Webb wanted control of the entire Kentucky Basin."

Since the initial quarrels over the lab, Tom differed with Webb on several other occasions. The conduct of the survey in the Chickamauga Basin and the authorship of the report were contentious issues. Lewis was unhappy with the survey Webb designed because the depths of sites were not tested. Furthermore, Webb denied Lewis's request to do a survey that specifically would look for the earliest culture in the area (Lyon 1996:143). Webb was under the impression that he would write the report on the Chickamauga work, as he had done for several other TVA basins, but the University of Tennessee requested that, as their employee, Lewis should write the report. Tom eventually got this responsibility, but the quarrel was not over.

Madeline's and Tom's training from Cole and McKern taught them that archaeology was more than the objects; culture was not just things. Madeline and Tom were interested in bringing the past "to life" and strongly felt that to do so was their professional responsibility. They appealed to McKern, Cole, and Carl Guthe for defense of their position. Guthe, an archaeologist at the University of Michigan, was chairman of the National Research Council's Committee on State Archaeological Surveys and instrumental in the development and oversight of the federal archaeology programs (see Lyon 1996). Madeline was no "shrinking violet" in her convictions, as can be seen in a series of letters between Lewis, Kneberg, McKern, Cole, and Guthe about the situation with Webb. These letters date between July and August of 1939 and are on file at the McClung Museum. In July 1939, Lewis wrote to McKern after a visit by A. R. Kelly (who at the time was working for the National Park Service [see chapter 3]):

We were almost as much perplexed with his state of mind when he left yesterday as we were at the end of our first hour's conversation with him on the preceding day. His close contact with the affairs in Washington seems to have discouraged him to the point where he no longer has any strong convictions about anything. . . . One of the first discussions we had with Kelly had to do with our procedure in connection with the Chickamauga Basin report. He stated his opinion that we ought to do something similar to the Norris Basin report and that floored us for a few moments. . . . He also informed us that Jennings had turned down your request to review the Norris Basin report and that he [Kelly] had taken over the job, since he believed it to be a report of considerable merit. . . . Madeline started to work on him, with an occasional squawk from my corner. I have an idea that we shattered his slightly uncertain convictions quite perceptibly. . . . He did assure us before his departure that our proposed Chickamauga report would be preferable to the Norris Basin type of report.

Madeline found occasion to discuss with him the Gilbertsville [Kentucky] Basin developments and learned that Webb has been dealing with the Head of the National Park Service. . . . The plan is to make a cooperative project out of it, under the direction of the University of Kentucky with the TVA and National Park Service participating. Madeline pointed out all of the dangers contingent to such a plan, and he [Kelly] looked a bit perplexed when he departed yesterday.

Madeline also wrote to McKern: "There is a fundamental disagreement between what we are attempting to do and what Webb considers an adequate treatment of the data. . . . You, Guthe and Cole are in a position to advise us as to the extent of the sacrifices to be made. Everyone on the Tennessee staff will stand behind Tom to the limit and you know that you can count on me as long as I remain here to fight for him."

Despite the problems with Webb, Tom and Madeline managed to keep their WPA funding, the authorship of the Chickamauga report, and oversight of the Kentucky Basin project. To comply with contractual obligations, they submitted a large, draft report of work in the Chickamauga Basin to the WPA in June 1941 (which years later was completed and published as Lewis, Lewis, and Sullivan 1995). They also circulated a mimeographed copy of the first chapter (Lewis and Kneberg 1941), which summarized the findings, as a preliminary report.

The WPA projects continued for another two years with a variety of laboratory arrangements. Before the work at Chickamauga was completed, the University of Tennessee began work on other TVA reservoirs: Watts Bar, Fort Loudoun, Douglas, and Kentucky Lakes. There also were several other smaller projects around the state, including WPA excavations of the Mound Bottom site near Nashville, and of the Chucalissa site in Memphis with Civilian Conservation Corps (CCC) labor. Chapman (1988) estimates that in the six years between 1936 and 1942, University of Tennessee crews excavated 1,577,920 square feet of 62 sites. By 1942, the total cost of federally supported archaeology in Tennessee was about $600,000 (Lewis 1942).

When the field operations shifted to the Kentucky Basin, in northwestern Tennessee—the other end of the state from Knoxville—the distance made it more efficient to set up a field lab there (at Paris, Tennessee). A branch lab was established at Rockwood, Tennessee, for the Watts Bar project. One reason for the field lab arrangements was that in 1940, the university took over Madeline's salary and she had the new duty of teaching anthropology. Human evolution was one of the courses she was to teach. Knoxville is only sixty miles from Dayton, Tennessee, the scene of the infamous 1926 Scopes trial, but Madeline was not too worried about teaching evolution. University President Hoskins told her to teach what she thought she should—the university would back her. Cole offered to testify for her if she got arrested, as he did for Scopes. Madeline's approach was to teach scientific facts; what the students did with the information was up to them.

Madeline tried to keep up with both the lab work and the teaching, but inside of two years, the world drastically changed. Within weeks after the bombing of Pearl Harbor in 1941, the federal government stopped all the fieldwork and disbanded most of the lab. By June 1942, the program ended.

The workers were needed for the war effort; several of the WPA supervisors were drafted. The end of the New Deal projects came so fast that Tom and Madeline personally had to pack up the lab. Archaeology came to a grinding halt during the war, and Tom and Madeline never again had the funds or labor force for large projects. The New Deal era "Golden Age" of southeastern archaeology was over.

In retrospect, Madeline had few regrets about the work she and Tom did and the approach they took: "We tried to sample all the sites we could in which the different prehistoric cultures were represented. . . . We could have excavated and investigated more sites having the same cultures, but that would have been a duplication in a way, so it's very difficult to say how much was actually lost. . . . We only examined possibly . . . in East Tennessee about five percent of the actual sites that are now under water. No one will ever know how much was really lost, but I think that we got most of the story. . . . What I was trying to do in the lab was to preserve the records and the materials for the future because we were limited in what we could accomplish, especially when I was trying to teach." Another development during the WPA years was that Madeline once again shifted her career focus: "I lost interest in physical anthropology to a large extent because archaeology was such a challenge."

World War II

The wartime years were difficult and frustrating ones, both personally and professionally. Madeline's mother was now an invalid, watched by a nurse while Madeline taught all day. Then, Madeline took the night shift. Because of this situation, Madeline was able to teach home nursing for her wartime service obligation as a Red Cross nurse. Her mother died in 1943.

Neither Tom nor Madeline taught anthropology during the war. There were not many students at the university, and faculty had to do whatever was needed to keep a salary. In 1943 and 1944, Madeline taught European history to servicemen from the Air Corps pre-flight training program. Her job was to supply them with a context for the war. Tom was the liaison between the Air Corps and the university. Madeline became curator of the university's art collection when the Air Corps program ended. She and Tom did research at the lab whenever they could find time and managed to prepare the manuscript for the Hiwassee Island report. Madeline later commented that working on the Hiwassee Island report was when she and Tom "really developed their approach toward the work."

Archaeology for the Public, Oconaluftee, and the McClung Museum

After the war, Tom and Madeline realized that a broad-based constituency was needed if archaeological research in the state was to continue. They began a variety of educational programs aimed at the general public. Madeline recalled that, "There were so many pothunters, so many sites being destroyed. We tried to get to the young so that they would grow up to respect the past." They did radio shows about archaeology on a local station and reconstituted the Tennessee Archaeological Society (TAS) to promote archaeology in the state and to teach amateurs proper recording techniques. Founded in 1925 by P. E. Cox, a former Tennessee State Archaeologist (Cox 1926), in 1944 the TAS had only twenty-nine members. By 1945, there were nearly a hundred (membership roster, *Tennessee Archaeologist* 1945:14). The society's publication, the *Tennessee Archaeologist,* was Tom's idea of a way for amateurs to make positive contributions. The first issue appeared in December 1944, with Tom as editor and Madeline as coeditor. She and Tom also began a section entitled "Editors' Notes" in which they reported on various amateur collections, unusual artifacts, and the like.

This pattern of Lewis taking the lead credit for their collaborative work was to continue throughout their careers (Lewis and Kneberg 1941, 1946, 1947, 1954a, b, 1955a, b, 1956, 1957, 1958a, b, 1959; Lewis and Lewis 1961). In regard to their collaborative writing projects, Madeline said, "we battled it out, we battled it out a sentence at a time. I was more for the popular, and he was more academic."

Madeline did publish her own work under her name alone (1945, 1952c, 1953, 1954, 1956, 1957, 1959, 1961, 1962). Her first solo archaeological publication, "The Persistent Potsherd" (Kneberg 1945), was aimed at educating the public about what could be learned about the past from pottery. She also wrote a series of creative, educational essays that were posed as autobiographies of prehistoric Indians at various points in time. These were published anonymously in the *Tennessee Archaeologist* (Kneberg 1951a, b, 1952a, b).

One of Madeline's and Tom's most enduring publications is their coauthored popular book, *Tribes That Slumber* (Lewis and Kneberg 1958a). The title is from a quote by William Cullen Bryant that Madeline found in *Bartlett's Quotations:* "through the still lapse of age all that tread the globe are but a handful to the tribes that slumber." *Tribes* went to a ninth printing and Madeline continued to get royalties up until her death. She acknowledged doing most of the writing, although she did not claim senior authorship. The illustrations for *Tribes* and for *Hiwassee Island* also are Madeline's work.

She did them at night at home. About the popular publications, Madeline explained, "We tried to make [past peoples] seem like real people, to make them easy to visualize. . . . *Tribes* is not geared to any particular age group; we just tried to make the past understandable to the general public."

In later years, Tom's and Madeline's active involvement with amateurs and the TAS became a way to do much of their field research. They supervised amateurs to investigate sites, especially those threatened by development. Before passage of federal and state historic preservation laws in the 1970s, working with amateur groups was one of the few ways to salvage sites slated for destruction. Madeline often accompanied Tom on field trips and they continued this work until their retirement. Sometimes these field experiences could be harrowing, as she recounted in a 1961 newspaper article (in the files of the McClung Museum). In December 1957, they and three amateurs were stranded on an island in the Chickamauga Reservoir when TVA unexpectedly began releasing water from the Watts Bar Reservoir. Their boat was washed away and they were stuck in a driving rainstorm with no shelter and only medium-weight clothing. As night began to fall, they dug into a duck blind for shelter and managed to start a fire from some splintered stumps. The fire led the Coast Guard and a Red Cross search party to rescue them.

A much safer field experience during the 1950s was on the Cherokee reservation in North Carolina. Madeline and Tom helped the Cherokee learn about their past traditions. They became consultants for the Eastern Band of Cherokees, through the Cherokee Historical Association, in developing the Oconaluftee interpretive center (Lewis and Kneberg 1954a). This outdoor museum shows traditional Cherokee lifeways at various time periods and continues as a setting for traditional craftspeople to show their skills and techniques.

Madeline and Tom worked with the Cherokee to design the center because the superintendent of the Cherokee reservation approached them for help with the project. They helped pick the site, worked with the Cherokee people, and made many Cherokee friends. After the center was planned, the National Park Service paid Madeline three hundred dollars to write a manual for the guides. Madeline did the bulk of the work on this project. Her papers now on file at the McClung Museum contain many letters about innumerable details of the reconstruction—everything from the color of wall paint, to costumes for the guides, to interpretive pamphlets for visitors. Even though this is the case, all project correspondence and even the final report reference Madeline as "Miss Kneberg" and Tom as "Dr. Lewis."

Madeline recalled that "It was an exciting project and meant jobs for the

Cherokee. . . . Oconaluftee was the most fun of anything we did." She also noted that "The Cherokee didn't have much self esteem then. . . . They didn't pretend to know much about their old ways. . . . Learning something of their past helped them become proud to be Cherokee." She recalled that at the time, "Tennessee was a 'happy hunting ground' for pothunters [who] dug graves to sell the pots. The Cherokee were concerned about this [looting] then and today are more conscious of their heritage." The strong economic benefits to the Cherokee of the development of Oconaluftee Indian Village and related tourist attractions in the 1950s is noted by Finger (1991:137–38; but see also French 1977). Although Finger (1991) discusses anthropological fieldwork during this time, he apparently was unaware of the involvement of anthropologists, or specifically of Kneberg and Lewis, in the development of Oconaluftee. He does not mention them.

Madeline also was active in a group known as the Tsali Institute for Cherokee Indian Research, which advised the Cherokee Historical Association and also promoted and sought funding for research on the Cherokee. Madeline was the sole female board member, serving as secretary. Several other academics were on the Board of Trustees or otherwise involved, including archaeologists A. R. Kelly, William Sears, Joffre Coe, John Witthoft, and Tom Lewis.

For several summers, Tom and Madeline stayed at the Boundary Tree Inn and spent two or three days at Oconaluftee. Madeline recalled working with the Cherokee women to make pottery in the traditional way. The women had tried to do firing in cooking ovens, but the pots didn't get hard and melted as soon as liquid was put in them. Madeline showed the women how to fire pots in open fires. They discovered that if corn cobs were placed in the pots during firing, the resulting ashes sealed and made the pots waterproof. Tom helped the men with flintknapping, and Madeline used Tom's hands in the flintknapping illustration in *Tribes That Slumber.* She also used some of the Cherokee people at Oconaluftee as models for other drawings in the book. Madeline noted that the Cherokee had not lost their basketmaking tradition. She helped make dyes for cane and kept a collection of several Cherokee baskets as a memento from the Oconaluftee work. Another very special memento (in her papers at the McClung Museum) is a pamphlet with photos of costumed Cherokee interpreters doing activities such as grinding corn, making a canoe, or shooting a bow. The native staff of Oconaluftee autographed Madeline's copy. Madeline and Tom's work was only a minor part in the revival of native crafts among the Cherokee—the major influence

Fig. 4.4. Madeline Kneberg and Thomas Lewis in the offices of the Frank H. McClung Museum. (Photo courtesy of the Frank H. McClung Museum.)

being the programs of the Indian New Deal (Finger 1991:82–83)—but their efforts significantly influenced portrayal of traditional handicrafts at Oconaluftee.

Tom and Madeline also became the primary proponents for a museum in which to care for and interpret the materials collected by the huge Tennessee WPA projects (fig. 4.4). Madeline recalled that Tom was eager that the ultimate objective of the WPA work should be a museum in which to portray the past to the public. He advocated for a museum supported by the State of Tennessee since he was hired by the university (Lewis 1935, 1937, 1942) and worked on several museum projects before the war, hoping to get a series of wayside museums and site interpretive centers established across the state. After the war, Tom and Madeline helped with other such projects, including the exhibits at Lookout Point in Chattanooga (Nyman 1994).

The dream for the museum in Knoxville came to fruition in 1960 with the opening of the Frank H. McClung Museum at the University of Tennessee (fig. 4.5). Tom and Madeline worked with the architect Malcolm Rice to plan the building. They had known since 1955 that funding for a museum was willed to the university by Judge and Mrs. John M. Green (the museum was named for Mrs. Green's father), but by 1959 when the money became available—and Tom was appointed director and Madeline assistant director—Tom felt he did not have the health to do the work of getting the museum up and running. Madeline explained that Tom was happy finally to have gotten the museum and to have assured preservation of the collection for the future. Getting that much done was an accomplishment.

Fig. 4.5. The Frank H. McClung Museum at the University of Tennessee–Knoxville. (Photo courtesy of the Frank H. McClung Museum.)

Scholarly Contributions

The impact of the scholarly accomplishments of Kneberg and Lewis must be evaluated in the context of their time. As Fairbanks (1970) explained, much of what could be called the scholarly "infrastructure" for southeastern archaeology was a byproduct of the large-scale federal projects in the 1930s. Archaeologists working in the Southeast at this time saw their "primary objectives as the definition of complexes, establishment of regional chronologies, and the tracing of inter-areal relationships" (Fairbanks 1970:44). The only existing regional chronology was the one developed by Ford (1935a, b, 1936a, b) for Louisiana. The Midwest Taxonomic Method developed by McKern ("the McKern System") was the major analytical tool available in 1938. This classifactory system, combined with the trait element comparisons advocated by Kroeber (1940, 1942), became strong influences in archaeological interpretation and led to detailed comparisons of trait lists as a method for identifying and differentiating archaeological complexes.

The archaeological complexes associated with any of the historic southeastern tribal groups were unknown, and ethnohistory was a new and unfamiliar word. The direct historical approach, which matched historically recorded cultural attributes with archaeological materials, was just being discussed. Not only were these building blocks of archaeological approaches just being formed, the institutional basis for archaeological research was virtually nonexistent. Webb's operation in Kentucky was the only semblance of a permanent research base for archaeology in the region (Fairbanks 1970).

Madeline and Tom's New Deal work either made or enabled significant contributions to most of these research goals. Although rooted in the WPA work, the majority of these accomplishments came to fruition after World War II. Kneberg and Lewis established the first regional chronology for the Upper Tennessee Valley. The archaeological complexes they defined still form the basic framework for today's refined versions. They also used the most up-to-date approaches available. The trait list comparisons they developed for the Chickamauga Basin (Lewis and Kneberg 1946; Lewis, Lewis, and Sullivan 1995) stand among the most elaborate and thorough use of this analytical method. Hiring a project ethnohistorian and using the Direct Historical Approach were cutting-edge approaches for the time. Their establishment of the department of anthropology and the McClung Museum at the University of Tennessee resulted in a permanent home for archaeological research in the state.

Madeline's primary field of physical anthropology was coming into its own in the 1930s. Not only did the American Association of Physical Anthropologists hold its inaugural meeting in 1930 (Spencer 1982), Hooton's seminal bioarchaeological work on human osteological material from Pecos Pueblo was published in that year. His study was the model for such research from 1925 until the late 1940s (Armelagos et al. 1982). Hooton advocated racial typology as a method for investigating the biological history of a population (Armelagos et al. 1982:309) and pioneered research on disease profiles in prehistoric populations using archaeological samples (Ubelaker 1982).

Madeline's research on human osteology never received much recognition from the scholarly community, probably because she had lost her original interest in this field of investigation and, with the exception of the Hiwassee Island and Eva reports, she did not publish the osteological data or results. Nonetheless, the data collection program she instituted for the WPA osteology lab was comparable to the best work being done in that field of study at the time. Following Hooton's model, she systematically made measurements for typological comparisons and collected data on pathologies. Rather than being oriented toward particular racial groups, her skeletal typologies focused on different Native American occupations of various archaeological sites (see Lewis, Lewis, and Sullivan 1995, volume II). Her reconstructions of facial characteristics of prehistoric individuals were among early efforts to apply forensic techniques (probably developed with advice from Krogman) to archaeological material (fig. 4.6).

Despite her failure to publish the osteological work, Madeline actively published her archaeological research. Soon after the war, she began publishing a variety of scholarly reports and articles. Her first major collaborative publication with Tom was the report of excavations at one of the Chickamauga Basin sites, *Hiwassee Island* (Lewis and Kneberg 1946). For several centuries, this now well-known site was the location of a large prehistoric town with platform mounds, as well as numerous burial mounds and shell deposits associated with earlier cultures, and a historic Cherokee settlement where Sam Houston, the famous politician and military hero, reportedly lived for a time. The WPA team expertly excavated one of the platform mounds, part of the surrounding village, and several of the burial mounds and shell middens. "When we did *Hiwassee Island*," Madeline recalled, "we picked that site particularly because it covered different groups and we decided that was one way we could sort of cover some of the other sites incidentally by doing that." As she did for *Tribes That Slumber*, Madeline made interpretive illustrations for *Hiwassee Island* (fig. 4.7). The illustrations actually were paintings, and one was reproduced in color for the frontispiece of the first edition of *Hiwassee Island*.

Fig. 4.6. Madeline Kneberg sculpting a bust based on her reconstructions of ancient Native American physical characteristics. (Photo courtesy of the Frank H. McClung Museum.)

Fig. 4.7. Reconstruction of the Hiwassee Island site as drawn by Madeline Kneberg (Lewis and Kneberg 1946: frontispiece). (Courtesy of the University of Tennessee Press.)

Madeline said that she and Tom were constantly exchanging ideas and had a continuous conversation about interpretations and what they were trying to do; they "worked as one person" and she never knew "where she stopped and where Tom began." She referred to Tom as the "more practical" of the two, in the sense that she was more able to imagine past peoples' lives in a "popular" sense. Madeline also felt that their work drew criticism at times because it was too popular. She explained that the emphasis in the 1930s was on developing scientific techniques for data collection, not so much on reconstructing the past. Madeline thought that some people were obsessed with scientific technique. Certainly one had to have accurate information on which to base reconstructions, but the point was to interpret the data.

This interpretive approach also drew considerable praise. In a 1949 editorial in the *Pennsylvania Archaeologist* entitled "Let's Put Some Meat on the Bones," Vernon Leslie urged archaeologists to interweave the taxonomy of the McKern System with interpretations based on human relationships and ecology. He pointed to Lewis and Kneberg's work as an example:

Individuals who wish to examine a study which combines to an admirable degree the human approach with the sternly academic are advised to examine *Hiwassee Island* by Lewis and Kneberg. . . . Here we see a successful effort to present the various groups inhabiting a site not only as components of a foci but also as flesh and blood human beings who "lived, felt dawn, saw sunset glow." In particular, Madeline Kneberg's drawings of various aspects of aboriginal life derived from the archaeological evidence are to be instanced. Most remarkable are her reconstructions of physiognomy based on skeletal remains. In this process she has virtually achieved the suggestion contained in the title of this article. (Leslie 1949:2)

Praise for *Hiwassee Island* also came from one of archaeology's most vocal internal critics, Walter Taylor. He described the book as "quite possibly the best archaeological report I have had the occasion to read" (Taylor 1948:9).

The year after *Hiwassee Island* was published, Tom and Madeline began working on the earlier, "pre-pottery" time period and jointly authored a monograph on the Archaic horizon in western Tennessee, based on the Kentucky Lake research (Lewis and Kneberg 1947). This work began a series of publications on the early cultures of the Tennessee Valley (Kneberg 1954; Lewis and Kneberg 1951) and was part of a broader effort during the 1950s to define the eastern Archaic, an effort that only very recently was aided by radiocarbon dating. At a 1955 conference in Bloomington, Indiana, organized by J. Charles Kelly, they presented a paper entitled "The Archaic in Western Tennessee," which may be the only one of their collaborative manuscripts for which Madeline is senior author. All of this work on the Archaic culminated at the end of the 1950s with publication of a synthetic article in *American Antiquity* on the Archaic in the Middle South (Lewis and Kneberg 1959), and of the Eva site report (Lewis and Lewis 1961).

During the 1950s, Madeline produced a number of other publications, including her chapter (Kneberg 1952c) on the Tennessee area in Griffin's *Archaeology of Eastern United States*. One of the best known is her article that establishes the sequential ordering of the various styles of engraved shell gorgets (Kneberg 1959). Two other major articles deal with classification problems of projectile points and chipped stone tools (Kneberg 1956, 1957). Toward the end of the work on the Archaic, she began working on the problems of the many varieties of Woodland pottery (Kneberg 1961, 1962).

Madeline and Tom continued trying to get more of the WPA research published during the 1950s. An outline and partial draft manuscript entitled

"Cultures of the Hiwassee River Valley" is included in Madeline's papers that she willed to the McClung Museum in 1996. The draft provides interpretive summaries of the sites investigated along the Hiwassee River by the WPA Chickamauga Basin project. The manuscript is not dated but must date post-1946, as the Hiwassee Island volume (Lewis and Kneberg 1946) is cited. A detailed outline and copious notes for a volume on Cherokee history and culture also are with her papers and appear to be by-products of her work at Oconaluftee.

In addition, during the 1950s, Madeline became one of the first female full professors in the liberal arts college at the University of Tennessee. She and a historian, Ruth Stevens, were the only female full professors outside of home economics. The title was not, however, accompanied by a pay raise. In regard to her teaching career, Madeline's hope was that she had cultivated young people's interest in archaeology. She found teaching to be a creative process—like music. Some writing efforts during the 1950s also were related to teaching responsibilities. A now little-known manuscript (Lewis and Kneberg 1955b) appears to be a text Madeline and Tom wrote for classes on Tennessee archaeology.

Both Tom and Madeline kept up scholarly contacts through regularly attending conferences, hosting scholarly visitors, and performing service activities at the university. They were members of Sigma Xi and worked on getting a chapter of it, as well as a Phi Beta Kappa chapter, at the University of Tennessee. Even though Madeline had turned her interests more to archaeology than physical anthropology, she still maintained ties to physical anthropology as evidenced by a visit to Knoxville in the spring of 1950 from noted physical anthropologist T. Dale Stewart of the Smithsonian (reported in a newspaper article dated April 11, 1950). Madeline also fondly recalled discussions with archaeologists Robert Wauchope and William Haag. Of the well-known archaeologist James B. Griffin, Madeline related, "we used to argue" (cf. the discussion of pottery typology at the 1959 meeting of the SEAC, Williams 1962).

In 1961, the University of Tennessee Press published the report on the Eva Site, one of the WPA excavations in the Kentucky Reservoir (Lewis and Lewis 1961). This now classic report on the Archaic period in the mid-South was Madeline's and Tom's final collaborative publication as this year also was when they decided to retire, marry, and move to Florida. Madeline did all the statistical work for *Eva,* and remembered that, "[The Eva report] was a pain in the . . . because he [Tom] had gone [to Florida] by that time and I was [in Knoxville] trying to do those tables, an awful lot of tables; you do them by stripping tape on them. I used to work on that at night." Madeline participated in one more publication that appeared in 1965, an edited account of the sixteenth-century expeditions of Juan Pardo through eastern Tennessee. For the first time, she worked on a publication with someone besides Tom (Folmsbee and Lewis 1965).

Of their scholarly contributions, Madeline's only regret was that they did not find or recognize the early sites in eastern Tennessee. It was not until the work for the Tellico Reservoir project in the Little Tennessee River Valley in the 1970s (Chapman 1977, 1978, 1984) that the geomorphology of the Tennessee Valley was better understood and the existence of deeply buried, early sites was known. The circumstances of the WPA work, Madeline explained, were such that, "We were confined to work, because of the financial arrangements that TVA had to make with the property owners, to taking the line of the basins, the high water level . . . so [we were not able to investigate sites above the TVA acquisition line]. . . . We didn't know at the time that back up on those earlier river terraces that there were sites, because the sites were buried. It was only when the waters were impounded and with heavy wave action that much of this was exposed. Then it was too late."

Many of Madeline's and Tom's ideas and interpretations now are outdated or no longer accepted, such as their view that population migrations explain the changes they observed in prehistoric lifeways, or the correlations made between archaeological complexes and historic tribes. Nonetheless, their work was at the innovative edge of archaeological research at its time, and the legacy they left in the form of systematic collections and records is a contribution that will continue to provide fodder for archaeological research for generations to come. It was therefore especially fitting that upon Tom and Madeline's retirement, the University of Tennessee Board of Trustees designated the archaeological collections at the Frank H. McClung Museum as the Lewis and Kneberg Collection.

Marriage and Retirement

In 1961 at sixty-five years of age, Tom Lewis decided to retire. Madeline was fifty-eight. Her big choice was whether or not to marry Lewis and move to Florida. Madeline explained that Tom thought it was not a choice at all, "he just said we're moving there." So, she quit her job in Knoxville and went to Florida where Tom had built them a retirement home. Madeline felt she had used up a lot of energy during the twenty-three years at the University of Tennessee. "You could do just so much in a lifetime. You can undergo just so much stress; it wasn't easy. It wasn't easy to get anything published; it wasn't easy to do anything in those days because there was so little money."

Madeline also termed her relationship with Tom "the longest courtship on record." After twenty-three years of working together, they married in June 1961. Madeline explained that they had not been able to marry earlier due to family responsibilities and nepotism rules at the university that did not allow spouses to work in the same department. Madeline's older sister, Goldie, had continued to live with her and became an invalid due to diabetes. Madeline cared for Goldie until her death in January 1961. Tom's mother also was ill and needed care, and he was putting his daughter from his first marriage through college at Vassar. Despite the lack of formality for their relationship, Madeline recounted that she and Tom "spent more time together than a lot of husbands and wives do because we were together all day long, and then on weekends he always came over to my house [where] he had a big vegetable garden in the back yard. He rented an apartment [but] was [at Madeline's house] all day Sunday."

After their marriage, Tom left in July to finish the retirement house on a lake in Winter Haven, Florida. Madeline explained that Tom chose the location because, "he had a friend, a classmate from Princeton, who lived up the street and [a] lot was for sale [so] he bought it." Madeline stayed in Knoxville until October to finish the Eva report and to help get Alfred ("Ted") Guthe settled in as the new director of the McClung Museum. Ted was an archaeologist with a doctorate from Michigan and museum experience in Rochester, New York. He also was the son of Tom and Madeline's longtime friend, Carl Guthe.

Madeline and Tom brought their library and some notes to Florida and Tom set up a darkroom, thinking they would get some more work done. Madeline kept up her painting after retirement, including painting a portrait of Tom. But, the darkroom soon became a storage room, and fishing and bowling began taking up more of their time. Madeline especially liked to go deep sea fishing. Tom Lewis died after thirteen years of retirement. Madeline termed this time together a "thirteen-year honeymoon."

Although she never had children of her own, Madeline enjoyed time with her step-grandchildren, the children of Tom's daughter. Her step-grandson, whom she said was "just like my own," named his daughter for Madeline.

Madeline rode a bicycle daily until in her eighties. She gave up bowling at age eighty-six and gave up driving at eighty-eight (fig. 4.8). The husband of her African-American household helper (eighty years old himself) drove her to the store where they kidded him about driving "Miss Daisy." Mad-

Fig. 4.8. Madeline D. Kneberg Lewis at home in Winter Haven, Florida, March 1992. (Photo by Nancy White.)

eline remained mentally sharp and active, and she kept up friendships through correspondence with botanist A. J. (Jack) Sharp at the University of Tennessee, and through *Teocentli*, a newsletter originally started by Carl Guthe to maintain personal contacts among a network of archaeologists. She raised orchids and read copiously on new findings in human evolution and current events until her failing eyesight forced her to have someone else read to her.

In 1994, at the age of ninety-one, Madeline was still willing to share archaeology with the public and agreed to be interviewed for television programs about the WPA/TVA archaeology projects in Tennessee and about her own career. In 1995, she was awarded the Southeastern Archaeological Conference's highest honor, the Distinguished Service Award. After suffering a stroke in 1995, Madeline never recovered her health. She died in her sleep on July 4, 1996, at ninety-three years of age.

On Being an Archaeologist and Life in the 1990s

To Madeline Kneberg Lewis, the purpose of archaeology was straightforward: "to reconstruct the past." Somewhat ironically, Madeline did not look back in her own life. She chose to let the past go, not to look at it as a better time, but rather as something that happened. Madeline was, however, concerned with the future and the legacy she and Tom left for archaeology. She repeatedly emphasized that a major objective of their work was to make it possible for people in the future to use the information they had collected. They knew they could never take advantage of the full potential of the vast WPA collections and never expected to do so in their lifetime.

Madeline felt that archaeology has the potential to show the human race its pitfalls and past mistakes. She was concerned that science today tends to ignore the humanities and that more emphasis is on physical sciences. To her, this trend is bad because many of the modern world's problems relate to the humanities and social science. She believed overpopulation is today's greatest problem; she associated overpopulation with competition for space and natural resources, citing the Balkans as an example.

Her advice to young archaeologists was to "try to find something original, whether in an application, interpretation of history, or whatever." She believed that "originality is the key to success" and that "there's too much repetitiveness in [research in] science and history. Something becomes the style or the fad for the day . . . and then everyone does it. It is individuality that carries things forward [and it is individual] people [who] develop ideas and techniques." While she felt that it is important to have purpose, it is equally important "to do it [in] your own way, not to follow anyone else—to be your own monitor."

Madeline was modest about her own accomplishments. She said she simply did what needed to be done on a day-to-day basis. In spite of often assuming the secondary roles to which women traditionally have been relegated when collaborating with men (for example, second author, lab director, coeditor), Madeline never felt overshadowed by Tom. She also recalled seldom feeling discrimination or problems resulting from being a woman, and she felt lucky to have been associated with many great names in anthropology. The fact that Tom consistently was addressed as "Dr. Lewis" and she as "Miss Kneberg" did not seem to bother her despite the fact that she had completed all but the dissertation requirement for the doctorate and Tom had no degree beyond the baccalaureate. Madeline did admit to getting headaches from the smoke-filled rooms at conferences but did not feel strange or isolated due to being female.

Madeline felt that one had to cope with whatever life presented and that the Depression taught many people how to deal with changes. After all, she herself had to change career tracks several times—from music to medicine to anthropology. Nevertheless, Madeline made significant contributions to southeastern archaeology and wielded considerable power both beside and behind her husband's throne. But, as a proper lady of her time, she did not insist on the center stage she earned as the leading lady of Tennessee archaeology.

Selected Bibliography of Madeline D. Kneberg Lewis

Folmsbee, Stanley J., and Madeline Kneberg Lewis, editors
1965   Journals of the Juan Pardo Expeditions, 1566–1567, translated by Gerald W. Wade. *East Tennessee Historical Society's Publications* 37:106–121.
Kneberg, Madeline D.
1935   Improved Technique for Hair Examination. *American Journal of Physical Anthropology* 20:15–67.
1936a   Hair Weight as a Racial Criterion. *American Journal of Physical Anthropology* 21:279–86.
1936b   Scientific Apparatus and Laboratory Methods: Differential Staining of Thick Sections of Tissues. *Science* 83(2):561–62.
1945   The Persistent Potsherd. *Tennessee Archaeologist* 1(4):4–5.
1951a   An Archaic Autobiography. *Tennessee Archaeologist* 7(1):1–5.
1951b   Early Projectile Point Forms and Examples from Tennessee. *Tennessee Archaeologist* 7(1):6–19.
1951c   An Early Woodland Autobiography. *Tennessee Archaeologist* 7(2):31–38.
1952a   The Autobiography of a Memorial Mound Builder. *Tennessee Archaeologist* 8(2):37–41.
1952b   The Autobiography of a "Bone House" Indian. *Tennessee Archaeologist* 8(2):37–41.
1952c   The Tennessee Area. In *Archaeology of Eastern United States*, edited by James B. Griffin, pp. 190–98. University of Chicago Press, Chicago.
1953   The Cherokee "Hothouse." *Tennessee Archaeologist* 9(1):2–5.
1954   The Duration of the Archaic Tradition in the Lower Tennessee Valley. *Southern Indian Studies* 5:40–44.
1956   Some Important Projectile Point Types Found in the Tennessee Area. *Tennessee Archaeologist* 12(1):17–28.
1957   Chipped Stone Artifacts of the Tennessee Valley Area. *Tennessee Archaeologist* 13(1):55–65.
1959   Engraved Shell Gorgets and Their Associations. *Tennessee Archaeologist* 15(1):1–39.
1961   Four Southeastern Limestone-tempered Pottery Complexes. *Southeastern Archaeological Conference Newsletter* 7:3–15.
1962   Woodland Fabric Marked Ceramic System. Proceedings of the Sixteenth Southeastern Archaeological Conference (Macon, Georgia, 1959), *Newsletter* 8:33–40, edited by Stephen Williams.
Kneberg, Madeline, and T. M. N. Lewis
1952   Comparison of Certain Mexican and Tennessee Shell Ornaments. *Tennessee Archaeologist* 8(2):42–46.

Lewis, Thomas M. N., and Madeline D. Kneberg

n.d.   Manual of Field and Laboratory Techniques Employed by the Division of Anthropology, University of Tennessee, Knoxville, Tennessee, in Connection with the Investigation of Archaeological Sites within the TVA Dam Reservoirs. On file, Frank H. McClung Museum, University of Tennessee, Knoxville. (Also: Appendix C. In *The Prehistory of the Chickamauga Basin of Tennessee*, compiled and edited by L. P. Sullivan. University of Tennessee Press, Knoxville, 1995.)

1941   Prehistory of the Chickamauga Basin in Tennessee. University of Tennessee, Division of Anthropology, Tennessee Anthropological Papers, no. 1 (mimeographed).

1946   *Hiwassee Island: An Archaeological Account of Four Tennessee Indian Peoples.* University of Tennessee Press, Knoxville.

1947   *The Archaic Horizon in Western Tennessee.* Tennessee Anthropology Papers, no. 2, University of Tennessee Record, Extension Series, vol. 23, no. 4, Knoxville.

1954a   *Oconaluftee Indian Village: An Interpretation of a Cherokee Community of 1750.* Cherokee Historical Association. Cherokee, North Carolina.

1955a   The A. L. LeCroy Collection. *Tennessee Archaeologist* 11(2):75–82.

1955b   The First Tennesseans: An Interpretation of Tennessee Prehistory. Department of Anthropology, University of Tennessee, Knoxville.

1956   The Paleo-Indian Complex on the LeCroy Site. *Tennessee Archaeologist* 12(1):5–11.

1957   The Camp Creek Site. *Tennessee Archaeologist* 13(1):1–48.

1958a   *Tribes That Slumber: Indians of the Tennessee Region.* University of Tennessee Press, Knoxville.

1958b   The Nuckolls Site. *Tennessee Archaeologist* 14(2):60–79.

1959   The Archaic Culture in the Middle South. *American Antiquity* 25(2):161–83.

Lewis, Thomas M. N., and Madeline D. Kneberg, editors

1954b   *Ten Years of the Tennessee Archaeologist, Selected Subjects.* J. B. Graham, Chattanooga.

Lewis, Thomas M. N., and Madeline Kneberg Lewis

1961   *Eva: An Archaic Site.* University of Tennessee Press, Knoxville.

Lewis, Thomas M. N., Madeline Kneberg Lewis, and Lynne P. Sullivan (comp. and ed.)

1995   *The Prehistory of the Chickamauga Basin in Tennessee*, 2 vols. University of Tennessee Press, Knoxville.

5

Black and White Women
at Irene Mound

CHERYL CLAASSEN

The Irene Mound in Savannah, Georgia, is a key site in Georgia prehistory. It was excavated from October 6, 1937, to January 1940 by a crew of 117 people, who were supervised first by Preston Holder and then by Vladimir Fewkes, Claude Schaeffer, and finally Joseph R. Caldwell. All personnel were employees of the Works Progress Administration (WPA), one of Roosevelt's New Deal programs created to combat the severe unemployment of the 1930s. While women comprised a "surprisingly" large number of the university-trained archaeologists in the 1930s (Fagette 1991), they were not among the "chosen" to direct New Deal archaeological projects (with the notable exception of Dorothy Cross), and they were rarely employed even as staff, despite their efforts to the contrary (see Appendix 1). Women were, however, unquestionably key to the success of the Irene project and did a major part of the work for the report itself. Except for the writing done by Caldwell and physical anthropologist Frederick Hulse, the photography by Leonard Bloom, and ceramic experimentation by Antonio Waring and Fewkes, the final report on Irene was the product of women's labor.

Thirty-two women, probably all white and including the academically trained Catherine McCann, contributed substantially to the project and to our impression of the prehistory of the Georgia coast as seen through Irene. At least eighty-seven black women excavated the site and thus provided the data to be interpreted. In this chapter, I will elaborate on the activities by women at Irene while showing that the experiences for white and black women at the site were very different from each other. Exemplifying that difference, and the level of racism and classism which provided the context for their different experiences, is the fact that we know the names of the thirty-two white women and their specific contributions yet do not know the name of any one of the black women. Rennie Simson (1983:230) has optimistically said that "past efforts to delineate the experience of black women relied very heavily on the pens of empathetic black males and sympathetic whites." The present effort is no exception.

The New Deal

Newspapers of January 1938 such as the *Huntsville Times* of Alabama (all newspaper clippings are on file at the Georgia Historical Society, Savannah, Georgia) reported unemployment in the United States between 7.8 and 10.9 million (*Huntsville Times [HT]*, January 4, 1938). In Georgia, 130,903 people were officially unemployed, while in Alabama the number was 150,145, of whom 51,203 were women (*HT*, January 3, 1938). So severe was the unemployment and so massive was the expenditure of federal funds in the New Deal that, as of April 1939, only three counties in the entire United States had not been the site of a New Deal make-work project (*HT*, April 2, 1939). Federal and state governments were well aware that both men and women, white and nonwhite, were among the unemployed and devoted considerable time and thought to developing "appropriate" relief work projects for those different subsets of the unemployed population. It was particularly difficult, however, to find work appropriate for women. By July 1938 in Madison County, Alabama, ninety enrolled families represented by a female family member sat idle awaiting relief work on a suitable project (*HT*, July 3, 1938).

Suitable Projects for Women

Several New Deal projects awaiting approval in 1938 would employ women in Huntsville (Madison County), Alabama, and several others were operating at the time. One pending project would employ fifty-eight women and nine men to repair toys and furniture for relief families' use. Sewing rooms, employing fifty to sixty women and located throughout the county, to renovate and repair donated clothing and household articles (excepting mattresses), were approved later that July. Another Madison County project used forty women as laborers, three as forewomen, one as a carpenter, one as a timekeeper, and one as a supervisor to clean and renovate public buildings of the city and county (*HT,* May 23, 1938). In Savannah, Georgia, 167 women (including 106 black women) were trained as housekeeping aides to assist in homes where the usual white housekeeper was temporarily disabled. "This course assists them to more efficiently care [for] the sick and the aged, and enables them to give a higher type of service in the homes. . . . This is truly a missionary work. . . . No work is too hard or too menial for them to do" (*Savannah Tribune [ST],* April 14, 1938).

The use of black women in white homes was normalized by the earliest slave owners. It continued to be an appropriate place for them with emancipation. "The so-called Domestic Science Movement of the twenties and thirties elevated proper maintenance and care of the home to preposterous levels of class indulgence" (Aptheker 1982:115). By 1930, 60 percent of domestic workers were black women. Domestic work remained the major source of income for black women through the end of World War II, for they were excluded from most other areas of employment (Aptheker 1982:113–14).

For men of any race, appropriate relief work was construction of buildings and roads, painting, carpentry, ditch digging, writing, photography, and acting. For educated white women, appropriate work was writing, acting, typing, filing, and teaching. For uneducated women of any race, appropriate work was cleaning, tending the sick, housekeeping, cooking in soup kitchens, sewing in sewing rooms, and refurbishing toys. Given that these were the tasks that women "normally" did, they were not considered "labor." Women's WPA projects fell under the jurisdiction of the "Women's and Professional Projects" branch, also known as "non-manual" projects.

County boards of commissioners, city councils, and chambers of commerce worked jointly with representatives of the Public Works Administration to develop and fund projects. Many white men, and some white women, then, were the people responsible for determining the appropriateness of projects and implementing and maintaining notions of useful projects, laboriousness, and women's work. In light of the descriptions of New Deal projects for women, it is somewhat incredible that the outdoor, physical labor of archaeological excavation came to be considered appropriate work for women, "a fact that remains uncelebrated in archaeological texts" (Cotter 1993:30).

How Archaeology Became Suitable for Women

John Cotter (1993:30) credits the New Deal with "the birth of archaeology as a serious American discipline." Archaeological excavations began receiving New Deal support in 1934 (Lyon 1996) through the Civil Works Administration and the Tennessee Valley Authority. However, in Alabama, David DeJarnette, who was in charge of staffing and running the Pickwick Basin and Guntersville Basin projects, found the local WPA officials unsympathetic to archaeology and uninterested (Lyon 1996). Despite federal and state approval of the Guntersville Basin project in 1936, a lack of men qualifying for relief work prevented William S. Webb from starting this project.

Black women and men had been involved in New Deal archaeological laboratory and museum projects in Alabama. In Birmingham, a museum extension program was approved in July 1938 that employed women to make objects, specimens, models, and exhibits. Christine Adcock, with a B.A. in anthropology from the University of Alabama, supervised mixed white and black, female and male laboratory crews at the Alabama Museum of Natural History for many years in the WPA era (Christine Adcock Wimberly, personal communication, 1992). "In a letter to William Webb, David DeJarnette indicated that 'Miss Weber and Dr. Petrullo' exerted pressure to 'sponsor an excavation using Negro women' in the Guntersville Basin. Christine Adcock was named as the potential supervisor" (Fagette 1996). For reasons that Christine Adcock Wimberly no longer remembers, she never did direct such a field crew.

In Georgia, the employment of black women at Swift Creek, Irene, and Macon was possibly the idea of Arthur R. Kelly, under whose supervision black women were first employed in the field. Judging from the dates of fieldwork, it seems that black women were first used as excavators at the Swift Creek site. Kelly and Smith (1975:1–2) wrote in their report on the Swift Creek site that the investigations, which began in March 1936 and continued into the winter of 1937, had been "set up by WPA authorities to employ thirty to forty Negro women as an archaeological field crew under white supervisors trained by A. R. Kelly and J. A. Ford." The project was regarded as a successful experiment. "The results were satisfactory; the archaeological excavations were no more exacting physically than was the farm labor to which most of the workers were accustomed. The trenches and profiles were neat and precise" (Kelly and Smith 1975:2).

Kelly was apparently so impressed with the Swift Creek excavation that he approached other WPA personnel with similar proposals. He also was in charge of the excavation at Macon, which used black women's labor, according to the Swift Creek site report (Kelly and Smith 1975). And, it was Kelly who approached Lucy B. McIntire about a similar arrangement at Irene (see Appendix 2).

White Women and the Irene Mound Project

Of the thirty staff positions that apparently were available at Irene, only one was filled by a trained woman archaeologist. The simultaneous use of untrained black women as laborers and the virtual exclusion of trained white women at Irene, Macon, and Swift Creek is strong evidence that contradictory attitudes about women existed among male archaeologists. Nevertheless, women contributed substantially to the research under way at Irene.

It is highly likely that the mound called Irene would have drawn less attention had it not been for the historical research and writing of Dolores B. Floyd (Mrs. Marmaduke Floyd) of Savannah. Her self-published *New Yamacraw and the Indian Mound Irene* (1936) documented the Moravian building on the mound and Moravian interaction with local Indians. Vladimir Fewkes's first monthly report, nineteen pages in length, contained six verbatim pages from Floyd's manuscript (properly attributed), and Antonio Waring frequently referenced her book in his writing on the mound (Williams 1968). She was praised numerous times by Fewkes, addressed local audiences and the state archaeology society on at least two occasions, and was often part of tours of the mound for visiting dignitaries. We know she joined Margaret Ashley for fieldwork (see chapter 2). Fewkes expressed the hope in one monthly report that she would write the final report.

Lucy B. McIntire, the field supervisor for WPA "non-manual" projects and not an archaeologist, was often praised by Fewkes and the press for her leadership and constant interest in the project. She approved the excavation for WPA sponsorship. The final report is dedicated to her (Caldwell and McCann 1941). Other WPA officials who visited the project were Mrs. Ellen S. Woodward, assistant administrator of the women's and professional division (see Ware 1981), and Mrs. Thomas C. Myers, area supervisor.

Mary Granger, supervisor for the Federal Writers' Project in Savannah, used her workers and resources to research the topographic changes in the site over the previous century. According to Fewkes, "without the aid of Miss Granger and her staff we would have suffered from a pronounced hiatus in so far as the recent topographic history of our site. As it turns out we have the privilege and advantage of using data which have taken a great deal of time and effort to accumulate . . . and will save time and money on our project" [*Savannah Morning News (SMN)*, April 6, 1938].

Adelaide Kendall Bullen, referred to as an architect and sculptor by the local paper but better known as an archaeologist (see chapter 7), spent one week at the site. During this time she constructed a clay model of the mound for display and wrote a poem about the site which she dedicated to Dolores Floyd (*Savannah Evening Press [SEP]*, March 24, 1938).

Fewkes and Caldwell sought a cultural context for the prehistoric record they were uncovering at Irene, and each man made one major sojourn to various sites in the state. Isabel Garrard Patterson (Mrs. Wayne Patterson; see chapter 3) of Columbus took Fewkes to several sites that she had recently explored, and he was most impressed with Kolomoki (*SEP*, March 30, 1938), which she was instrumental in preserving. Her praise of the work at Irene was cause for a newspaper article (*SEP*, April 20, 1938). Bessie M. Lewis of Pine Harbor planned a trip for J. R. Caldwell "and it was through her intimate knowledge of local archaeology Mr. Caldwell was able to visit and survey twenty sites" (*SEP*, April 21, 1938). The site of Shellman's Bluff was surveyed with the "valuable assistance of Gladys Kenner of Darien" in addition to Bessie Lewis (*SEP*, April 21, 1938). Fewkes invited the Society for Georgia Archaeology to have its annual meeting in Savannah and was delighted when he was "loaned a collection of beautiful projectile points most of which were collected at Millhaven by [Mrs. E. T. Comer] and Mrs. H. Wayne Patterson" for display during the meeting (*SEP*, May 5, 1938). Conversations with these women and visitation to sites known by them greatly influenced Fewkes and Caldwell's impressions of cultural particulars, overlaps and distinctions, and consequently, their interpretive remarks about Irene.

The Moravian link to the site attracted the attention of the Moravians of North Carolina. They sent first Adelaide Fries, an archivist from Winston-Salem, and then Dr. Lucy Wenhold, professor of foreign languages at Salem College, Winston-Salem, to examine the site and talk with Dolores Floyd and Vladimir Fewkes (*SMN*, April 114, 1938).

Thousands of mostly women students from area high schools, usually led by women teachers, visited the mound during Fewkes's tenure. Even a class of biology students visiting the excavation consisted of four women and one man.

Catherine McCann, graduate student in anthropology at the University of Pennsylvania, joined the project staff in July 1938 to "study the human ecology of the state of Georgia, a study directed towards the determination

of the natural resources available to and the environmental factors imping-
ing upon the Indian tribes" (*SEP*, July 25,1938; see also *SMN*, July 26,
1938). The work was to result in maps and charts showing the various
physiographic areas, the important climatic factors, and the distribution of
different plants and animals within the state, and it would provide the background for a fuller state-wide archaeological survey. "The ecological approach is still very new in American anthropology, but Miss McCann is well
qualified for a study of this kind, having specialized in this field at the
Universities of Wisconsin and Pennsylvania" (*SEP*, July 25, 1938). She published two articles on the faunal remains (McCann 1939a, 1939b) from
Irene and one on the ceramics (McCann 1941). Catherine McCann also was
the coauthor of the final report (Caldwell and McCann 1941).

Virginia Griffin "supervised the reconstruction of the skulls, made all
observations and many of the measurements, while [Frederick Hulse was]
responsible for the statistical analysis" (Caldwell and McCann 1941:ix).
Hulse was the sole author of the physical anthropology section in the report.
Profiles, views of the mound, and illustrations of artifacts were drawn by
three students of Lila M. Cabaniss of Savannah: Vivian Freund, Dell Smith,
and Alvin Landy (*SMN*, April 8, 1938). The maps and drawings included in
the final report were drawn by Margaret Winkers. Annalou Friedman,
teacher of secretarial classes at the vocational high school, volunteered her
typing students to type all field notes and reports; eleven of her sixteen
students were women (*SEP*, March 16, 1938). The final report was typed by
Mae Royall.

Black Women at Irene: Racism or Opportunity?

In the midst of all the school children, dignitaries, officials, archaeologists,
and townspeople (up to 1,700 some Sundays) were 87 black women cutting
steps, digging squares and trenches, removing logs and brush, excavating
burials and artifacts, using block and tackle, picks, shovels, wheelbarrows,
brushes, and stools, and doing other work once considered inappropriate for
women (figs. 5.1, 5.2, 5.3; see also photos in Williams 1968). Gender and
race prejudice in the first half of this century, the exclusion of women from
science and scientific projects, and men saying "women were absent from
archaeology because the field conditions were too harsh" are known to all
women archaeologists. We also know that black women and men are glar-
ingly absent in our discipline. Our first encounter with these women in their
long white dresses, bent over shovels atop the Irene Mound, brings smiles to

Fig. 5.1. The Irene Mound crew, 1937–40. (From the archives of the Southeast Archeological Center [SEAC No. 02-044-007981]; photo courtesy of the National Park Service.)

many women archaeologists and a sense of a hidden or secret past—a fact, Cotter (1993) says, to be celebrated. Many of us may be able to say exactly when and where we were when we learned that Irene had been dug by black women. But just as we do not yet know the name of a single woman on that crew, we also do not know how any of them viewed this work (see Addendum).

Joffre Coe, who supervised government-sponsored archaeology projects in piedmont North Carolina, reminded me in a phone interview that blacks were absent in North Carolina mountain counties where the Peachtree Mound excavations were located and that mountain mores would not permit the use of women on digs (Joffre Coe, personal communication, 1992). Again, we are reminded of the attitude that excavation work was thought inappropriate for women by white men and women.

There is also evidence that at least some black newspaper men in Savannah believed that archaeological labor was equally inappropriate for black women. Shortly after the excavations began at Irene, the *Savannah Morning News* (with a white publisher) of October 9, 1937, published two photo-

Fig. 5.2. Women shoveling soil into a carrying basket at the Irene Mound, 1937–40. (From the archives of the Southeast Archeological Center; courtesy of the National Park Service.)

Fig. 5.3. Women digging trenches at the Irene Mound, 1937–40. (From the archives of the Southeast Archeological Center; courtesy of the National Park Service.)

graphs of black women at work on the mound. Five days later, the weekly *Savannah Tribune* (with a black publisher) carried this small comment, reproduced in its entirety here:

The excavation of the Irene Mound by Negro women of this city bears investigation. It must not be known by those in authority of the class of work these women are called upon to do. They are forced to pull the block and tackle in removing large logs and stumps, digging ditches, undermining stumps using mattocks, shovels, pitchforks, and rakes. Rattlesnakes and other poisonous reptiles are killed almost daily. The WPA and especially those in charge will be called upon to give these women who are willing to work a lighter class of work. (*ST,* October 14, 1937)

A second comment appeared as an editorial in the *Savannah Tribune* the following week:

A few weeks ago, cuts of the excavation at the Irene Mound in the north sector of the city were shown in the local newspapers. In some of them was noted colored women with hoe and spades doing masculine work. No one with the least consideration would have forced women to perform such laborious tasks. It is true that these women were in need of employ, and want forced them to accept, but in their need there should have been an adherence to the human side. The attention of some of our clergymen were [*sic*] called to the case. A few of them made an investigation with verification. Even worse, there was no shelter to protect the workers in event of rain, such as was had during the past weeks, aside from the dangers of poisonous snakes. It is hoped that the clergymen will see the ones in authority and endeavor to have our women given such employment that the more benefit [*sic*] the sex. (*ST,* October 21, 1937)

Whatever exchanges there were with Preston Holder and Lucy McIntire over this work assignment, black women were used for the next fourteen months. While the white press gave the project weekly coverage during some periods (without mentioning the presence of the women; saying instead that the archaeologists found this or that), the *Savannah Tribune* never again mentioned or alluded to the Irene Mound project. Apparently, if at least middle-class black men had had a voice in the decision, their mores likewise would have precluded the use of black women as archaeological laborers. New Deal administrators no doubt were anxious to find sources of income for the women on their rolls. Since WPA rules specified that no more than one family member could be enrolled, each woman represented the total earning power of her family. It may be that Lucy McIntire's black crew at Irene, advertised through her paper presented to the Society for Georgia Archaeology in 1938 (Appendix 2) and widely known through archaeological meetings and interest in Irene, forged the way for the use of black women on several other excavations in the South, bringing them much needed income. Black women made up part of the crew at Macon in Georgia and participated in some projects in piedmont North Carolina as early as 1938. Black women also were added in November 1939 to the ongoing dig by black men at the Whitesburg Bridge site in Madison County, Alabama. Webb and DeJarnette (1948:10) note that "One unusual feature of the excavation [at Whitesburg Bridge] was the employment for the last seven months of a negro crew made up of both men and women. This was made necessary because of the excess of unemployed negro women on the WPA rolls of Madison County. After slight modifications of the techniques of excavation were made in order to conform to WPA regulations governing the employment of women in the field, the work proceeded in an efficient manner. It was thus demonstrated that a mixed crew properly guided could do satisfactory field excavations."

I find it interesting that while the white newspapers of Savannah made much of the dig at Irene, their counterpart in Huntsville, Alabama, makes absolutely no mention of the project at Whitesburg Bridge. That project clearly did not attract the attention, even from the archaeological community, that Irene did. No doubt this was partly due to the large number of shell middens like Whitesburg Bridge that had been excavated in the Huntsville area in the previous four years, and perhaps also because of the personality of Vladimir Fewkes, who was clearly revered by the Savannah press and welcomed public interest in the project at Irene.

Was Archaeological Work a Welcome Opportunity?

Despite the money temporarily brought into the households of some of Savannah's black women from their work at Irene, there were at least four ways the redefinition of archaeological fieldwork as black women's work may have been viewed by them not as a blessing but a curse: (1) the actual pay received, (2) the public statement on their femininity, (3) their daily isolation with white men, and (4) the employment "dead end" of archaeology.

Claims of racism in WPA projects were raised occasionally. Some southern WPA supervisors were said to be preferentially enrolling and employing whites or requiring black women to accept cotton-picking work at four cents per hundred pounds when non-enrolled cotton pickers earned considerably higher wages. While northern black and white WPA workers were said to receive equal pay for equal work, southern black workers were often paid less than white workers on the same project, and racial work allotments favored whites. Republican Robert Taft pointed out that blacks on WPA rolls were threatened with "economic servitude akin to serfdom" and "that blacks would be better served by government stimulating jobs for them where they would have an opportunity to earn more than a bare existence" (*ST*, April 6, 1939). Perhaps there are records which will allow us to examine the pay received by black women and white men engaged in excavation. Much circumstantial evidence suggests that the women were paid less than either whites or black men by the WPA.

In a world where white middle-class standards of womanliness precluded manual labor of this type and where white middle-class living standards served as the model for success and correctness, was the redefinition of archaeological labor as appropriate for black women yet another systemic means of defining racial difference—a white restatement of black women's unwomanliness that had accompanied their presence in white U.S. society since the beginning of importation? Angela Davis (1971:7) reminds us: "This was one of the supreme ironies of slavery: in order to approach its strategic goal—to extract the greatest possible surplus from the labor of the slaves—the black woman had to be released from the chains of the myth of femininity. . . . In order to function as slave, the black woman had to be annulled as woman, that is, as woman in her historical stance of wardship under the entire male hierarchy. The sheer force of things rendered her equal to her man."

Women's WPA and National Youth Administration projects were supervised by women. The only exceptions were archaeological projects that were supervised by white men at remote locations—a potentially dangerous situation that not even the black press was willing to name and clearly one inappropriate in either white or black society in the South.

The effect of rape on black women by white men, particularly in plantation settings, is a prominent theme in black women's fiction and history in this country, to the point that "nobody was sent out before you was told to be careful of the white man or his sons" (Clark-Lewis, quoted in Collins 1990:176). Bell hooks, no doubt, would explain that the redefinition of excavation as appropriate work for black women was based on this history of rape. "The significance of rape of enslaved black women was not simply that it 'deliberately crushed' their sexual integrity for economic ends but that it led to a devaluation of black womanhood that permeated the psyches of all Americans and shaped the social status of all black women once slavery ended" (hooks 1981:52). Not only did the history of rape of black women lead to a racially based definition of womanhood and femininity that allowed for black women to be employed as excavators, but also the persistent threat of rape made the archaeological field situation one that black women must have entered with trepidation. There were 117 crew members at Irene so there were (in addition to Catherine McCann) apparently 29 men as staff—a ratio of one (white?) man for every three women. Was this situation adding fear to insult?

Archaeological work opportunities were not designed to teach marketable skills. Indeed, few of the WPA projects were so conceived; nevertheless, their result was several years of experience as a road builder, carpenter, electrician, teacher, homemaker aid, painter, writer, artist, or actor. But because there was no market for archaeological laborers in a normal economy, working on an archaeology project was an employment dead end. I propose that white society's notion that black women needed no road out of poverty also led to the redefinition of archaeological work as appropriate work for poor black women, and by 1940, even poor white women. "The most striking fact about American economic history and politics is the brutal and systemic underdevelopment of Black people" (Marable 1983:1). Many scholars and literary writers have pointed out that black women had fewer work opportunities and faced greater job-related discrimination than did black men. Archaeological work produced no black competitors for white jobs while providing temporary income for families.

One point of potential interest suggested by this investigation is the evolution of the mixed crew. It seems that single sex crews were used from 1934 into 1938, that the mixed gender but single race crew was tried next, perhaps first at Whitesburg Bridge in November 1938, and that then the mixed gender, mixed race crew was implemented, perhaps first at Town Creek for the 1940–41 crew.

Joffre Coe has a photo of the Town Creek Mound crew in 1941 showing one white female, one white male, three black males, and four black females, all digging (and cf. Coe 1995, esp. fig. 2-12). About his experiences with labor provided by relief programs, he said (phone interview, July 15, 1992) that many of the WPA-certified people had a physical handicap explaining their unemployment. "We took who we had and let them do what they could. Women weren't too good at wheel-barrows, but liked to shovel which surprised us. They also liked to work in pairs. Shoveling, assisting, about all they could do, couldn't read or write."

The use of black women as archaeological laborers may have scared white women away from fieldwork. Paul Fagette (1996) has pointed out that while white women were well represented in university archaeology programs in the 1930s, their virtual absence in the field might be attributed to the perception that only black women worked on digs and therefore it was, as heavy labor, something that respectable women did not do.

Respectable women were, of course, white women. It appears that for the black editors there was a race-free, class-free definition of womanhood. Both class and race entered into the definition of woman for the white administrator, however. The respect accorded poor white women by WPA administrators varied. An incumbent chairman of the Huntsville, Alabama, city council was criticized for making white women perform manual labor in negro cemetery beautification projects. His defense was that both he and the city council were opposed to any such assignment and "the board never has sponsored a project that required a white woman to wear overalls and work with a pick and shovel" (*HT,* April 15, 1940). (Black women diggers did not wear overalls.) Appalachian mountain mores would not allow white women to labor so, either. However, on the piedmont of North Carolina in 1940, white women were assigned to the excavation of Town Creek Mound.

Discussion

We may never know how typical the level of involvement by white women in the Irene Mound project was in the early excavations of this century. It is striking that we find it in the South, where Wurtzburg (1994) has pointed out the impediments to women's education and where stereotypes about upper-class women would preclude images of them collecting artifacts and surveying sites. It is also curious that many of the men who were much involved in the archaeology of Georgia and Florida during this period would come to see women as so marginal to the activities of archaeology.

There is no certain conclusion to be drawn as to the malevolence or benevolence of black women's inclusion by the WPA as excavators on archaeological projects. White feminists are likely to view the inclusion of black women on archaeological projects in a positive light, while black feminists are likely to see it as race and sex relations as usual. For many of the enrollees, the employment opportunity was no doubt a godsend. For others, it may have been humiliating and, for some, it may have evoked both feelings. With thousands of white visitors present on a weekly basis at Irene, there were, no doubt, jokes at their expense, stereotypical comments about an innate black fear of the dead, comments about primitives digging up primitives and human evolution, and comments about their femininity commensurate with attitudes of the times and with the work they were performing. The photograph of the Swift Creek crew shows a woman receiving an award, indicating that there was some pride associated with the work (Cotter 1993). It remains now to find at least some of their impressions, meanwhile hoping that the community of women working at Irene, Swift Creek, Macon, and Whitesburg Bridge provided each woman some shield from humiliation, a sense of security, and some valued friendships, experiences, and memories.

Addendum to the 1993 Article

A week after returning from the 1996 SEAC meeting, where I had declined the editors' request for an update on the crew at Irene (for lack of ideas on how to get any new material), I got a phone message from Gail Whalen, a graduate student at Armstrong State College in Savannah, telling me that she had gotten access to a box of photos of the excavation at Irene recently given to the Georgia Archaeological Society, Savannah chapter. She was interested in the women's crew and wanted to talk to me about them. When I called back I realized that she did indeed hold the key to unlocking more information about these women. I indicated that she should strive to get names. I would help if I could, and if she found crew members, I wanted to interview them. For the next five months Gail met and rebounded from multiple setbacks in her quest to find the names of these women, demonstrating a remarkable single-mindedness and ingenuity. Only when a local television station aired some photos of crew members during the half-time coverage of a local high school championship basketball game, however, did she have success. She conducted several interviews with kin of these women (Whalen and Price 1998), and I joined her in April 1997 for three of the interviews. The following comments are based on these interviews and my notes.

I wonder now if I and others have not overestimated the number of women who dug at Irene, placed at more than eighty. One photograph shows fourteen women starting a trench into the top of the mound; another shows nine women and one black man sitting by the river, and a third shows ten women and two men, one of whom is clearly black. (Photographs taken by the Floyds appear to cover the beginning and the later stage of the project and typically contain women in them. Official photographs for the project usually do not include workers. The captions to several photos indicate that Marmaduke Floyd viewed some of his subjects as lazy.) Fifteen to sixteen women at one time seems a likely number, as does a total of forty-eight over the course of the three-year project. A ruling that enrollees could work for only eighteen months did not go into effect until 1940, the final month of excavation, so crew turnover may have been low. Perhaps five black men may have been hired as laborers also.

Descendants came forward in 1997 with stories of mothers and neighbors who worked at the Irene Indian mound. The names we have so far are Annie Scott Grant, Mrs. Mattie Smith Thesus, Mrs. Gussie Wright White, Hattie Gamble Coleman, Susie Jones, and Elizabeth Hayward. All of these women had children and either no husband or a disabled husband.

Annie Grant was raising a son and two nieces. She told stories of working with the burials. Mattie Smith smoked a pipe and may be the woman depicted in several photos cleaning profiles with a pipe in her mouth.

J. A. White's mother, Gussie White, frequently spoke of her crew days. He relates that she worked at two other local sites, Bilbo and Deptford. He was thirteen when she worked at Irene, and he remembers her walking to a corner where she caught a ride to the site. She always carried her boots. His father was injured and unable to work. The $2.50 per day the WPA paid her helped satisfy their $11 monthly mortgage payment. In later years she integrated white churches by walking to the front and sitting down, organized the first black PTA in Savannah, and even in death in 1953, left her funeral arrangements to a struggling black mortuary. She died at age sixty-three. All of the prominent whites and blacks of Savannah attended her funeral, including Lucy McIntire.

Hattie Coleman was a domestic worker prior to working at Irene. Her granddaughter, Ethel Hunter of Savannah, thinks she valued the Irene work as the most intellectual stimulation in her adult life. Hunter never heard negative comments about the experience and recalls no injuries or sickness. Mrs. Coleman's husband was dead and her children grown when her employment began. Hunter's mother was ill, so Mrs. Coleman took care of daughter and granddaughter at her home. Hunter remembers her grandmother bringing colored rocks and crab apples home from the site. She recalls being fascinated by the things and hearing her grandmother talk about having to dig just so, about being instructed by a supervisor, about bones. Her grandmother showed her how to use a trowel and the first-grader practiced. Her grandmother was very strict. After the WPA work, Hattie Coleman got involved with Father Divine, a charismatic black religious leader with a white wife who had sugarcane plantations in Florida and Cuba.

Mrs. Coleman made health candy to sell for Father Divine's cause and followed him to Westchester County, New York, where she died in her sixties in 1945.

Mrs. Rebecca Wright was five or six years old when her mother, Susie Jones, worked at Irene; her father was recovering from a bad stroke. Susie Jones told her children how sad she was that they were digging up the bones of the Indians. They should not have been disturbed and should have been treated with more respect. Young Rebecca always imagined that they were digging up graves in a cemetery. Mrs. Jones often came home exhausted because the work was so hard. After laboring all day, she cooked dinner and cared for her husband and the four children. Mrs. Wright remembers that one day her mother collapsed at the site and was brought home very sick. She never returned to the mound after that and was never able to work again.

The workers came from several neighborhoods in Savannah, such as Eastside and Wilmington Island. Churches posted WPA hiring notices. Roosevelt mandated one-hour lunch breaks. During that time and after work awaiting transportation, which may have cost 15 cents each direction, some of the women would fish in the Savannah River. Oscar Williams, a supervisor of a crew of black women paid by the WPA to gather Spanish moss for the mattress factory, says the women carried straight razors and knives for protection from men in general, and that he carried a gun, although WPA rules forbade it. John White said women of those days carried razors, knives, jars of potash (lye) mixed with syrup, or ice picks for protection. Both he and Mrs. Hunter said their relatives would not have worked on the mound if they were afraid, and that neither woman was afraid of any man. On rainy days Mrs. Hunter remembers her grandmother sewing indoors. Larry Meier, an archaeologist in Atlanta, reports that A. R. Kelly rewarded his crews for good attendance, for doing delicate work well, and for other reasons, in an effort to keep their attention and keep them honest. It is not known to what extent Kelly's reward practice was carried out at Irene.

Ethel Hunter never saw Irene Mound. Her school did not have field trips. White schools commonly brought their children to visit, and the visit of at least one black school group was reported in the paper. John White played around the mound. Next to the mound was a black cemetery, which has survived the Georgia Port Authority development, which has claimed the mound and lands owned by black families (Gail Whalen arranged for our visit to the cemetery in April 1997).

No informant had heard of any sexual harassment, racial problems, or misbehavior on the part of the white men associated with the project. No informant reported a woman who disliked or complained about her experience there. Several people interviewed pointed out the excellent pay and the steady work and projected gratitude on the part of the women. It seems that the darker potential I suggested was not realized by these particular women and may not have existed.

In the interim since this article was first published, more has been learned about some of the white women mentioned. Harriet Smith, author of the 1937 letter seeking WPA employment as a field supervisor in Appendix 1, was finally employed to supervise the excavations of Mound 55 (Murdock Mound) at Cahokia, from June 11 to December 14, 1941 (Fowler 1997). She was the first woman in Illinois to direct an excavation. For sixteen seasons she ran the NSF-funded high school excavation opportunity at four Illinois sites. Her career included working for the Illinois State Museum, the Chicago Academy of Science, the Science Division of Coronet Films, and the Field Museum of Natural History, always in the field of education (Pickering 1992). "In 1989, the Illinois Association for the Advancement of Archaeology presented her with their first Professional Service Award" (Dunkerley 1992:3). The cover of *Illinois Antiquity* for December 1992 presents a photo of Smith at work; she died May 18, 1992.

Catherine McCann, the only woman archaeologist with a supervisory position, got an A.B. in Latin from the University of Montana, then an A.M. in Latin at the University of Wisconsin. She studied anthropology at Wisconsin and at the University of Pennsylvania from 1937 to 1938 and worked at the Deptford site in 1940 (Lyon 1996:110–11).

In sum, these women appear to have been largely middle-aged, often in their forties, with dependent husbands and children. Our interviews revealed the use of at least one woman as excavator at two other coastal Georgia sites, Bilbo and Deptford. With a lot of luck and perseverance, this addendum will not be the final word on the women excavators of Irene, Swift Creek, Macon, Whitesburg Bridge, Bilbo, or Deptford.

Appendix 1. Letter Seeking Supervisory Assignment

September 19, 1937
Mr. Vincenzo Petrullo
Consultant in Archaeology for WPA
Walker-Johnson Building
Washington, DC
Dear Dr. Petrullo:
    A friend of mine—engineer on a State Planning Board—advised me to

write to you as the person most immediately in touch with archaeological activity throughout the country.

It may be that you already have my name on file, as I have been told that I was recently recommended by the Department of Anthropology at the University of Chicago with which I have been associated for five years in graduate study and research—in response to a request from Washington, DC for archaeologists. Whether this inquiry came from your office or some other I have been unable to ascertain, as our departmental secretary, chairman, and dean are all out of town this month. It is because I am not familiar with the degree of interrelationship between the various governmental services employing archaeologists and museum and laboratory specialists that I am bothering you. Since openings for women in my field are limited, I am anxious that my application be on file in all departments which might be [word or words are unintelligible] interested in employing me.

At present my name is at the top of the Park Service Civil Service list to be called to the first archaeological position "suitable for a woman"—that is, in a museum or laboratory or as an areal supervisor in the field (since obviously it would be out of the question to call me to lead a labor crew from camp headquarters). However, I might be notified of such an appointment tomorrow or two years from now. I've already been waiting since April, and it has now become imperative that I leave no stone unturned in attempting to establish myself in a position of financial stability.

I assure you my training and qualifications are adequate, and the whole problem hinges on whether my prospective employers are willing to take a chance on a young woman in what, by precedent, is a man's field. An inquiry directed to the Department of Anthropology at the University of Chicago for personal and professional recommendation or to the National Park Service, Department of the Interior regarding my examinations for Junior Park Archaeologist (written on August 23, 1936 and oral in March 1937) will convince you not only of my training and ability, but of my sincere interest in the profession I chose when, as a youngster in seventh grade ... Iver's Last Days of Pompeii became my favorite literature.

I should greatly appreciate any information and advice you can give me either as to specific openings you consider suitable for me or as to any state or governmental departments or institutions you know to be ... engaging in archaeological or museum activity.

That ... is an imposition upon your time and good nature, I'd be most deeply grateful for any attention you may be able to give my problem.

Sincerely yours,
Harriet M. Smith
... Road
Evanston, Illinois
[Note: She did not receive employment until 1941. Thanks to Ed Lyon for sending me a copy of this letter, which he found in WPA project files for Georgia.]

Appendix 2. The Use of Negro Women in WPA Work at Irene Mound, Savannah, by Mrs. Lucy B. McIntire, Field Supervisor, Works Progress Administration, Savannah, Georgia

[Delivered before the Fall Meeting of the Society for Georgia Archaeology, in Athens, Georgia, October 14, 1938. Originally printed in the *Proceedings of the Society for Georgia Archeology* 2(1):23–25, February 1939. Reprinted with permission of the Society for Georgia Archaeology.]

> *Beneath those rugged elms, that yew tree's shade,*
> *Where heaves the turf in many a moldering heap,*
> *Each in his narrow cell forever laid*
> *The rude forefathers of the hamlet sleep.*
> Gray's Elegy

Elms and yew trees do not abound at Irene but their place is taken by moss hung oaks and whispering pines where the sound of cool waters lapping on the shore adds its own note to the strangely aloof and slumbering peace of Irene. It is a peace so real and palpable in atmosphere that even the songs and dark laughter of a hundred Negro women busily at work only accentuate its character. Even without the archaeological evidence that has recently revealed itself there was something about Irene which spoke of a hallowed spot, a sort of sacred isle. As early as in the days of Oglethorpe this atmosphere aroused interest and speculation over the mound which stood there looking out across the water, evidence of man's effort to make tangible and lasting the trail of his occupancy, for the Indians of that day asked Ingham when he built his Mission on top of the mound if he were not afraid to live there as the mound was haunted by spirits.

There is no documentary evidence as to how Irene got its name but it is significant that one of the boats in which the Moravians came to America was called Irene and they were certainly preoccupied with the thought of peace as is evidenced by the fact that they named their settlement in North Carolina Salem, which means peace also. At any rate it is interesting that a spot of such distinctive atmosphere as this site, should be called Irene.

Today any one with imagination who visits Irene has little difficulty in visualizing those days when brown-skinned people erected that mound, for under the same oaks move other dark-skinned figures carrying basket loads of dirt even as these Indian women may have done, and with the same careful deliberateness with which Irene was built it is today being dismantled that its long-buried secrets may be discovered.

Little trace of the daily living of those primitive people has been found at this site. Ceremonial structures and all types of burials, flexed, bundle and urn are all over this place. One fancies in the stillness there is a sense of all these sleepers, whose rest after so long is being disturbed.

Even the Negro women have this feeling and with the reverence of primitive people for the dead they sit on stools gently brushing the earth from some ancient chieftain's bones taking meticulous care not to disturb one detail of the burial.

Of course, to the average citizen the idea of large numbers of Negro women being employed on such a highly scientific project as archaeological research is very humorous, eliciting such remarks as, "What do you use 'em for, local color?" And from the critical, "I suppose they won't go to sleep in a grave yard is the reason you put them on that project." But as a matter of fact from the viewpoint of WPA employment these archaeological projects offer an ideal solution for the placement of the number of unskilled Negro women in need of work assignments, and from the standpoint of archaeology they have proven careful, docile, efficient workers, especially suited to this type of work. By temperament they are undisturbed by monotonous routine and opposed to hurry and bustle; by training they are docile, accustomed to unquestioning obedience; while by religion they have a great respect for the abodes of the dead. They are sturdy and strong and used to work with hoes and spades. One wonders sometimes what goes through their heads as they peel the layers of earth off with obedient care until the first evidence of a burial or some artifact is uncovered. Perhaps their carefulness is accentuated by reluctance to disturb a burying ground of any sort but their interest in everything that is uncovered is keen and intelligent. Some of them have become skillful at identifying pot sherds and even at restoration and none have expressed any superstitious reluctance to do the work.

It is highly interesting to hear one of them boasting of the day's finds and using words with the assurance of familiarity which the average person unfamiliar with archaeology has never heard. Their childlike interest in any kind of treasure hunt is caught and whatever their mental reservations as to the insanity of white people who find bones and broken bits of pots, treasures worth seeking, they enjoy the spirit of the hunt thoroughly and learn quickly the necessity for the utmost care in this work for which they display great deftness.

Mr. Waring said to me once "I want to put some of the women to getting these things out, they can do it so much more skillfully than I can."

Of course an intelligent class of white foremen under the direction of trained archaeologists is used to supervise the activities of each group and record the necessary notes, but all the actual digging and cleaning off of skeletal material and artifacts are done by the women.

It is arresting to the imagination to see them two by two carrying between them white oak baskets, made for the project—which are probably very like the baskets used by the Indians—and swaying to the rhythm of "Ain't Goan' Study War No More" as they uncover the graves of ancient warriors who looked on war as a *sine qua non* of living.

Recent discoveries at the site give evidence that this mystical atmosphere of Irene speaks truly, for in addition to the large burying ground surrounding the mound itself, we have recently uncovered a most interesting structure full of urns and other burials, which appears quite definitely to be an ossuary, contemporaneous with the top mantel of the mound, as all the urns are of Lamar design.

I am going to ask Mr. Claude Schaeffer to go into the scientific details of this discovery, but I want to call attention to the fact that in this little triangle at the juncture of Pipemakers Creek and the Savannah River, possibly at one time a small island, there is a veritable City of the Dead with every evidence of use over a long period of time by various peoples, who must have handed down the tradition of this sacred spot and doubtless came from some distance at times to lay the bones of their dead under the shadow of the moss-hung oaks in a place of dignity and concentration.

The antiquity of the mound, as Mrs. Floyd points out, was indicated by the size of the trees which the Moravians cleared from the top of the mound in order to erect the school house. Like the Negro women and like the true archaeologist as well, I approach Irene with reverence and feel that through it much of the deep beliefs and ceremonial custom of a primitive people may be revealed to us.

The project for the excavation at Irene was drawn up by Dr. A. R. Kelly and submitted through my office on September 16, 1936. Excavations started September 10, 1937, with Preston Holder in charge. Mr. and Mrs. Marmaduke Floyd and Mr. Antonio Waring were the principal movers in the local efforts to get the work at Irene started. The Chamber of Commerce agreed to sponsor the project and raised the necessary local funds for its operation. This society, the Moravian Society, and many interested individuals contributed to this fund.

Mr. Holder was in charge from September 10, 1937, until January 29, 1938. During this time the site was cleared, a small portion of the undisturbed part of the mound exposed with three profiles out on the north side of the mound and checked at five foot intervals which determined three periods of mound construction. Mr. Holder's work also disclosed some evidence of burials and wall structure to the west of the mound which later proved to be the ossuary. Correlation trenches were also dug and some skeletal and pottery material were moved and catalogued.

Dr. Fewkes took charge on January 29, 1938. The outstanding discovery during his regime was the portion of the cellar of the Moravian Mission conforming in location and size to Ingham's description.

Technological studies of pottery made through the cooperation and assistance of research consultants in various institutions reveal that Spanish moss was used as a tempering medium in certain instances.

The continued excavations of the mound proper under Dr. Fewkes tended to establish the function of the mound as being that of a ceremonial edifice, upon the successive mantels of which Indian structures were raised. Further exploration has borne this out. Also additional analysis of pottery found in the different mantels was carried out, although no definite conclusion as to a statistical interpretation was revealed.

Work was also done on the Indian cemetery adjacent to the mound resulting in the discovery of two very interesting cases of cranial deformation and other good skeletal material.

Two arrowheads of flint were found but as a whole very little stone work has been found at this site.

Dr. Fewkes left on June first and Mr. Caldwell continued the work until Mr. Claude Schaeffer arrived to take charge on June 11, 1938. Many interesting developments have taken place under his regime which he will describe in greater detail at this time.

Editors' note: This article is reprinted from *Southeastern Archaeology* 12(2):137–47 with permission of the Southeastern Archaeological Conference. The photos are changed from that printing, end notes are incorporated into the text, and the addendum presents new material. Thanks to Ed Lyon for sending me a copy of this article.

6

The Life and Times of Bettye J. Broyles

"I Did a Man's Work for Thirty Years"

HESTER A. DAVIS

Bettye's house is built into a hill in the northern suburbs of Chattanooga, Tennessee. There are four floors; you enter from the driveway by one series of steps into the first floor, or by more steps onto a landing between the second and third floors, which are the main living area. Bettye built the walls and decking of this house, with the physical aid of her father. The design is similar to one she built when she lived in Morgantown, West Virginia. The large living area is full of bookcases, boxes of papers, African statuary, masks and wall hangings, ashtrays, and comfortable chairs. She settled into her father's old recliner, Classic Coke and cigarette in hand, to talk about her life.

Early Interests and Archaeology

"I was born on August 16, 1928, in Birmingham, Alabama, but that was never home. Within six months, my folks had moved to my father's home in

Rhea County [Tennessee] and my only brother, Jim, was born there nineteen months after I was." Bettye's roots in East Tennessee go back, on both sides of her family, to the last part of the eighteenth century. She has records to prove her genealogy to the satisfaction of the East Tennessee Historical Society, making her family one of the "First Families of Tennessee" (that is, those residing in the state before 1796). Bettye can regale you with tales of generations of the Locke, Howard, and Broyles families, and she has published a 523-page history of the Locke Family, her mother's line. She found that her great-great-great-grandfather, Thomas Locke, was born in St. Albans, Herefordshire, England, in 1750.

As president of the Rhea County Historical Society since 1986, she maintains the same energy and enthusiasm for organizing their records as she did in the 1960s and 1970s with the minutes and publications of the Southeastern Archaeological Conference (SEAC), the Eastern States Archaeological Federation (ESAF), and the West Virginia Archaeological Society. But, we get ahead of our story.

Bettye's first two years were spent in Rhea County, sometimes in the home of her father's parents, as the Depression affected her father's ability to keep a job. Howard Broyles attended business school after graduation from high school in 1918 and was trained as a bookkeeper. He worked with lumber companies all his life, including when, with a partner, he owned a lumber company in Chattanooga. When Bettye was three, the family moved to Dalton, Georgia, because her father got a job with a lumber company there. Just after her seventh birthday, Bettye started school; she had been kept at home during her sixth year so that she and her brother could start school together. The family moved to Chattanooga when she was in the third grade.

She remembers that even in grammar school, she liked to draw, copying things from books in considerably more detail than her teachers asked. She recalls no deprivations during the Depression and assumes that her grandparents, who owned a large tract of land in Rhea County and "one of the first automobiles in the neighborhood," were able to help if there were short times.

Because she started school late, she graduated from high school just before her nineteenth birthday, and that fall she married her high school sweetheart, a young jazz musician who played professionally in the area. Bettye had studied piano for seven years by this time, and appreciation for music was a bond. She is not only handy at graphic arts but is an accomplished seamstress; she made her very traditional wedding dress (with four-foot train) and all the bridesmaids' dresses.

The marriage lasted just over two years, and in 1950 she was divorced. She went to work doing window displays in a department store in Chattanooga. Her spare time was spent studying the area's numerous Civil War battlefields. "Well," her father said, "if you're really interested in history, you might as well go to college." She enrolled at the University of Chattanooga for the fall semester of 1950. She began majoring in history, which most interested her (being surrounded by family heirlooms, portraits, documents, and stories).

In 1951 she joined the Chattanooga chapter of the Tennessee Archaeological Society (TAS), and by 1953 she was its president. Between her freshman and sophomore years, with nothing better to do, she says, she spent the summer in the library writing a manuscript on burial customs around the world. She had no immediate goal for this work, and she later loaned the paper to a friend, but it was never returned. In the summer of 1953, she and her parents took a trip to the Southwest, and her fate was sealed. They visited Chaco Canyon. Pueblo Bonito was the only place available to regular visitors, but excavations were going on at Chetro Ketl, and because of Bettye's interest, they were able to see the dig. "That's what I want to do," she remembers thinking.

That fall at the annual meeting of the TAS, Glenn Black, archaeologist at Indiana University, was the guest speaker. He discussed using students at Angel Mounds, where he had a long-term project. Bettye asked how a student might work for him. He told her the procedure for enrolling in his field school, and in the spring of 1954 she was accepted for that summer's work.

She did not go unprepared. After talking to Black, she returned to college to pursue her interest in archaeology. She was advised to do two things—take a course in engineering surveying, and change her major to sociology (since there then was no anthropology taught at the University of Chattanooga)—which she did. Doing so made a major change in her life; knowledge of the workings of a transit, alidade, and plane table became a mainstay for her career, and switching majors meant a delay in graduation.

The letter from Black saying she was accepted into the field school also said: "I should advise you, perhaps, that this will be a most unusual summer. It is unusual in that a very few students will be attending and those few are all girls." Unusual for Black, perhaps, but Bettye, of course, knew no difference (fig. 6.1). The influences that permeated Bettye's approach to fieldwork were set that summer by Black's example. He went on in his introductory letter: "The girls usually wear jeans or similar slacks on the dig—shorts are not permitted." Indeed, says Bettye, "I never allowed shorts and halters on

Fig. 6.1. The 1954 Angel Mounds field school. *Left to right:* Lily Marchant, Ann Stofer, Joan Popoff, Bettye Broyles. (Photo courtesy of Bettye Broyles.)

any of my digs. You can't sit in the dirt in shorts." At sixty-six, she sat for us on her living room floor with her feet tucked underneath her, demonstrating the position that Black required—never cross-legged or with the feet in front to be in the way of the troweling.

Fresh from her engineering surveying class, Bettye said that one day Black had to go to Bloomington and asked her to teach the others how to use the surveying instruments. She clearly remembers one person who could not get the knack of leveling the transit. This use of her special skill reminded Bettye of the advice that Black gave her (and perhaps others) concerning a career for a woman wishing to be an archaeologist: "Develop some special area of expertise." He did not discourage her but said essentially that being able to bring to her career something "extra" would stand her in specially good stead. That she had one such skill already was evident, and that her artistic talents were to become another was soon to be obvious as well.

This advice is particularly interesting in light of what we can read between the lines in Black's description of what was to happen in the field that summer of 1954: "This matters not to me [that there will be only "girls"] but it will alter normal activities somewhat. This alteration may very well be to your general benefit. There will be an emphasis probably on the working over of materials—classifying, cataloging, photographing, etc., of objects from a variety of sources and less of actual excavation. All phases of field work normally taught here during the summer will be given this year but it will be less intensive. Use of surveying instruments, staking, taking elevations, digging, etc., will all be carried out but there may be more inside work than usual."

Could it be that Black was adjusting his thinking about how much digging he was going to get done that summer because he had an all female crew? Is this a picture of a male archaeologist preparing to teach female archaeologists their appropriate role in the field? Bettye does not recall any more or less emphasis on any part of the archaeological work done; she thinks he may have been referring to the small crew, which would get less digging done. She remembers that they did a little bit of everything, but, of course, she had nothing with which to compare. And to be fair to Black, he probably gave these students a better rounded feel for *all* parts of archaeological research than is sometimes the case when digging is emphasized to maximize the accumulation of field data. Jim Kellar, who succeeded Black at Indiana University, says that in his experience, Black treated females just as he did males.

Few field schools are now ten weeks, and this experience set Bettye squarely on the path of concentrated archaeological fieldwork. Black was impressed enough with Bettye's interest in archaeology that at the end of the summer he wrote the chair of the sociology department at the University of Chattanooga, who had written Bettye a letter of recommendation, saying:

> Miss Broyles has a definite "flair" for archaeology and, as you stated in your letter of June 4th, is intensely interested in the subject. So far as her future interests are concerned her best opportunity for employment is in the field of museum work. She can do restorations, is quite adept at sketching and I am confident that, with a bit of training, she could make exhibits such as dioramas. She is quite persistent and once she starts something in which she is interested she will finish it—which in itself is an admirable trait. Her notebook—a requirement of all session participants—was the most complete of any.

Because of the switch in majors, Bettye had to take a senior seminar in the fall of 1954 and did not graduate until spring semester of 1955, just before her twenty-seventh birthday. She used those spring months to take further steps toward her goal. Armed with her newfound knowledge of excavation techniques, she found a site to dig. It was on land farmed by a friend of her father's, but she did not know at the time that it was TVA property and not hers to dig without permission. The site, a low mound, was on an island in the Tennessee River, and she and her mother took a boat to the site each day for two weeks, staying at a fishing camp nearby. She made a contour map of the site, excavated, inexpertly she now realizes, what turned out to be a late Woodland occupation, with at least two burials. An article about Bettye's work appeared in a local paper with a headline reading: "Finding Ancient Skeletons Like Hidden Treasures to Young Feminine Archaeologist" (fig. 6.2). This is the first of many newspaper articles on Bettye's work in which the journalist remarks on how unusual Bettye's situation was: "Betty [sic] is launching out on a career that is quite rare for a pretty 26 year old girl like herself. . . . She's going to be an archaeologist."

Bettye is apologetic now about her naivete. While doing the analysis, she learned of an FBI publication on measuring human bones. She wrote and received a letter back from J. Edgar Hoover himself with copy of *A Guide to the Identification of Human Skeletal Material*. Her report was published in the TAS's journal (Broyles 1955), with the encouragement of the editor, T. M. N. Lewis, the well-known archaeologist at the University of Tennessee in Knoxville (see chapter 4).

More important, in May she attended her first Society for American Archaeology (SAA) meeting, in Bloomington, Indiana. When she arrived, Black was the only person she knew. She asked him about summer work, and he introduced her to Melvin (Mike) Fowler, at the time with the Illinois State Museum, who was recruiting students for a ten-week field season at Modoc Rock Shelter. Bettye claims that Fowler later told her that because she was proficient in mapping, he mentally crossed another female off his list and put her on.

Bettye remembers that one afternoon at that meeting, Joffre Coe, director of the Archaeological Research Laboratories at the University of North Carolina, sat down beside her and struck up a conversation. He invited her to a gathering in George Quimby's hotel room—her introduction to this time-honored part of archaeological social life. She met several of the reigning men in southeastern archaeology who were to become good friends, employers, and colleagues.

First Jobs: Illinois, Georgia, North Carolina, and Elsewhere

On June 13, 1955, Bettye was at the field camp near Modoc with fourteen others for the first of four seasons of summer fieldwork in Illinois (figs. 6.3, 6.4). Alice Beck (Kehoe) was another crew member who went on to become a professional archaeologist. Bettye recalls that the big army surplus tents

A

B

Fig. 6.2. Photos from *Chatta-nooga Free Press* article, July 13, 1955, of Bettye Broyles excavating a Late Woodland (Hamilton) mound in the Watts Bar reservoir: (a) Bettye at a small dumpy level, with her mother holding the stadia rod; (b) Bettye shoveling dirt from her excavation area; (c) Bettye using fine tools to excavate around a burial. (Photos courtesy of Bettye Broyles.)

C

where the crew slept were really uncomfortable. "Everything was always damp, even clothes kept in a large steamer trunk. And there were a lot of daddy-long-legs that also occupied the tent."

That summer, Bettye made her first attempt at drawing artifacts. She remembers that Carl Chapman from the University of Missouri visited the field camp and Bettye's first drawings were shown to him. Nothing was said at the time of the professional drawing skills of Chapman's wife, Eleanor, as Bettye was somewhat embarrassed to learn later.

At the end of the 1955 field season, Bettye went back to Chattanooga. In September, Mike wrote, asking if she would come to the Illinois State Museum for three months to do the drawings for the Modoc report. Illness in her family delayed her arrival in Springfield until November. Mike could offer no salary, but Bettye went anyway. At the end of those three months, Thorne Deuel, director of the museum, decided he wanted her to illustrate a book, so she worked on a contract basis for several more months, until Deuel found money to put her on the regular staff. That began a stay of more than four years, working first with Mike Fowler (fig. 6.5), then with Joe Caldwell.

Fig. 6.3. The 1955 field crew at Modoc Rock Shelter. *Front row, left to right:* Paul Parmalee, Bettye Broyles, Anne Renouf, Mary Edmonston, Joan Bay, Doris Trojcak (botanist), Alice Beck (Kehoe). *Back row, left to right:* Michael Fowler, Melvin Fowler (director), Ron Wyatt, Judson Mygatt, Joe Vogel, Jack Tarr, Bill North, Clifford Von Arx, Dick Keslin (assistant director), Jim Schoenwetter, and Bill Edmonston (cook). (Photo courtesy of the Illinois State Museum.)

Fig. 6.4. The 1956 field crew at Modoc Rock Shelter. *Back row, left to right:* Pennington Wimbush, Joe Vogel, John S. Tarr, Melvin L. Fowler (director), Bennett Graham, James Gillahan, name unknown (from Prairie du Rocher, Illinois), name unknown (graduate student from Minnesota), Paul Parmalee. *Front row, left to right:* name unknown (project bookkeeper), Bettye Broyles, Phyllis Anderson (Morse), Dena Ferran (Dincauze). (Photo courtesy of the Illinois State Museum.)

Fig. 6.5. Bettye Broyles working at the Illinois State Museum with Melvin Fowler (holding pot) and another worker whose name is unknown. (Photo courtesy of the Illinois State Museum.)

Fig. 6.6. Bettye Broyles doing surveying work in Illinois in 1956. (Photo courtesy of the Illinois State Museum.)

The fieldwork at Modoc in 1956 lasted from June 13 to August 13. The crew included two other women who went on to become professional archaeologists: Phyllis Anderson (Morse) was then a graduate student at the University of Michigan, and Dena Ferran (Dincauze) a graduate student at Barnard College (see fig. 6.4). Bettye told Fowler about Bennett Graham (now senior archaeologist for the TVA and a lifelong friend), a young high school friend of hers, known from the TAS. Fowler hired Bennett for the 1956 season, and again in 1957 for work at the Twenhaufel site where Bennett was Bettye's rod man as she mapped that site (1 mile by 3/4 mile area in 6-inch intervals). A newspaper article about that summer's work lists her as "temporary assistant curator of anthropology [at the Museum] and field party cartographer."

Dena Dincauze (personal communication, 1996) remembers that Bettye "was a Presence. Her energy and competence were unquestioned; she had almost total control of the transit and stadia rods, insisted on accuracy, and was blindly obeyed" (fig. 6.6). Dena says Bettye had an "impressive wardrobe of city clothes," undoubtedly of her own making. Bettye was older than the other students—which, Dena says, took her "out of our youthful society and fooling around." Bettye had her own tent, which she said was "heaven" after enduring the army tents the year before. She built a wooden floor for it herself and was able to hang her clothes on a rack!

Bettye's job that first winter was helping Mike process the material from the summer's excavation, but she was also able to develop her artistic skills by making pen and ink illustrations of artifacts. In the museum's 1959 publication on four seasons at Modoc, Fowler acknowledged Bettye's contribution: "The laboratory analysis and preparation of this report has been long and tedious. Bettye Broyles participated in all phases of this work. Whether she was engaged in cataloging specimens, tabulating bone fragments, preparing charts and drawings, or proofreading the manuscript and checking references her interest has been unflagging and her aid invaluable."

Bettye's main job at the Illinois State Museum, during the non–field-season months, was organizing and updating the state site files. This work involved going through paper records and publications and picking up information on sites from amateurs and newspaper articles. She traveled all over the state recording collections and sites, and again newspaper articles often followed. In April 1959, the *Decatur Review* reported: "Miss Broyles was here as the result of a story in the March 25 *Review* which told of discovery of a large stone ax head found by William S. Berry at his home across from Spitler Woods State Park. . . . According to Miss Broyles, this is the first site discovered in the county. She said there are only two other counties, Ford and Marion, in the state that haven't been marked on their maps."

By 1957, Mike Fowler had gone to the University of Wisconsin, and Joe Caldwell was the curator of anthropology at the museum. A position description for Bettye, dated September 25, 1957, gives her title as "Preparator I," her salary as $350 a month, the "working title" of her position as "assistant in anthropology," and the duties and work performed as:

1. I carry on the usual duties of Assistant in Anthropology under direction of the Head Curator and the Curator of Archaeology
2. I assist in investigating sites by survey and excavation.
3. I clean, preserve, label, and catalogue archaeological and osteological material recovered in excavation or secured by loan or exchange, etc.
4. I aid in the preparation of anthropological publications, especially in preparing drawings, diagrams, and maps to illustrate them.
5. I compile, type, and file archaeological site survey records.

Once Joe Caldwell arrived, Bettye spent much time preparing the illustrations for a revised version of his Ph.D. dissertation, which was published in 1958 by the American Anthropological Association as Memoir Number 88, *Trend and Tradition in the Prehistory of Eastern United States.*

During her time in Illinois, she spent her vacations visiting her family in Chattanooga but often included finding an excavation or mapping project in which to become involved. In 1957, she spent several weekends helping with excavations at Russell Cave in northeastern Alabama, less than an hour's drive from Chattanooga. Four men, all friends of hers from the Chattanooga Archaeological Society, had leased the cave for a year of excavations. Their work was important enough that Bettye got their permission to borrow all the artifacts, analyzed the recorded information, and published the report in the TAS journal (Broyles 1958)—the first publication on what is now Russell Cave National Monument (she also submitted an article on this research to *American Antiquity,* but it was not accepted).

While vacationing with her mother in Florida, she found that Bill Sears was working on the Lighthouse Mound nearby. Bettye volunteered many days on that project. Bill taught her how to use a machete to clean off the mound but failed to tell her about the poison ivy. In 1957, at a TAS meeting in Chattanooga, Lewis Larson invited her to make a map of the Etowah site (in northwest Georgia), which she did. According to Larson (personal communication, 1996), it is still the only good working contour map of the site. After the Etowah work, Bettye attended her first meeting of the Southeastern Archaeological Conference in Macon, Georgia.

In the fall of 1958, Dick Keslin, who had been the field assistant during her first season at Modoc, invited her to map the Saline Springs site in eastern Missouri. All these experiences increased her contacts and friendships with archaeologists, mostly in the southeastern states, and led to her move from Illinois to Georgia in 1959.

In August 1959, she went to work for A. R. Kelly, then professor of anthropology at the University of Georgia. Kelly said he would let her supervise her own excavation, and that was enough incentive for her to make the move. She spent the rest of the summer at the Mandeville site in the Walter F. George Reservoir in southeastern Georgia, where she lists her position as "cartographer." She met Jim Kellar, who also had worked at Angel Mounds, and Ed McMichael, who later offered her a job in West Virginia. The first summer, these two men were the field supervisors (Kellar recalled that "Doc" Kelly visited the site only once or twice a week). Bettye tells some good stories of her arrival at the field camp and of her encounter with Ed McMichael before and after one of the evening parties. One of her jobs was to drive home the drunks. The second season, Kellar worked on another mound, Ed left for a job in West Virginia, and Bettye, Frank Schnell, and one other person (name not recalled) became a "committee" in charge of excavation in Mound A, a large pyramidal mound with an unusual small Swift Creek core mound.

That winter and the next she worked in Kelly's Laboratory of Anthropology on the University of Georgia campus. She lists her duties as "supervising laboratory work, planning exhibits for loan to schools in Georgia, and illustrating archaeological reports" (see Kellar, Kelly, and McMichael 1962). Kelly suggested she study the many Swift Creek Complicated-Stamped sherds and try to reconstruct complete designs (designs that were made by using carved wooden paddles to stamp damp clay). This research meant trips to the Kolomoki site to trace designs from the vessels in the museum there, and to the Ocmulgee National Monument to study the National Park Service collections, including those from the Fairchild's Landing site. Bettye perfected a technique of copying the complex designs; it involved cutting small pieces of tracing paper and following the grooves of the incised designs for a portion of the sherd or pot, then cutting another piece and doing the same in an overlapping section, until the complete design from the round pot was copied. The pieces of tracing paper were then overlapped and adhered to a flat piece of paper from which the final drawing was made. Not really a "tracing" she says, but a more accurate replication of the tooled design made by the potter. (Some of her designs accompany chapter titles in this book.)

Bettye continued her interest in these designs after she left Georgia, accumulating hundreds of drawings attached to four-by-six-inch cards. She eventually was able to recognize what she thought was an individual potter's art work from different sites; she could say, "I drew that design a couple weeks ago on another pot from. . . . " And most famously, she recognized a single paddle from a flaw in its design which she found repeated on pots from Georgia and northwest Florida, some hundred miles apart. In 1968 she published a report on this research in the *Bulletin of the Southeastern Archaeological Conference* (Broyles 1968a).

In the summer of 1960, after a few weeks at Mandeville again, she supervised fieldwork at a Lamar site nearby. Her report on this work appeared in the Laboratory of Anthropology's publication series (Broyles 1963). During this time, Joffre Coe was urging her to start graduate work at Chapel Hill. "He offered me my own reservoir, if I would come." She went to North Carolina in the spring of 1961 and spent the first six months in the field in the Wilkesboro Reservoir area, doing survey work and testing nine sites.

By this time, Bettye was thirty-two years old and had six years of archaeological field and laboratory experience. The spring survey work at

Wilkesboro Reservoir was the first in which she worked completely on her own (with two local men as crew), an experience that she came to love. Arrangements were made for her to live in the town of Wilkesboro, but that meant a nearly twenty-mile trip in and out of the reservoir area each day. She noticed a number of abandoned houses in the reservoir area, so she got permission to live in one of them, under what might be called "primitive" but adequate conditions—and entirely alone. Bettye says now that she thought nothing of this and was never afraid. She did not have a gun, but she knew how to use one; she had been taught by her father and had been on the rifle team in college. She would not stay alone in the field now nor would she advise anyone else to these days—"there are too many nuts out there now," she says.

Back in Chapel Hill, her father helped her buy a house so that she could establish residency and qualify for in-state tuition. During that summer she also worked in Coe's lab and did the illustrations for his well-known publication, *The Formative Cultures of the Carolina Piedmont,* published in 1964 by the American Philosophical Society. She was nominated for a Woodrow Wilson Fellowship, and although she received only an "honorable mention" and no money, Coe did share with her part of Glenn Black's letter of support: "This girl has great talent! She is a craftsman. Her drawings are works of art and she can turn out as pretty a dig as you can and that is saying a lot! I hope she obtains the Fellowship but in any event that she gets to work with you. It will be good for her to get away from Georgia, I would think."

In the fall of 1961 she began classes. This experience was not an unqualified success. By the end of the spring 1962 semester, a C in one course put her on probation for graduate work. She was considerably older than her fellow students and does not remember any particular friends. Her enthusiasm for academic work was not great, and she did not continue beyond this one year.

During that academic year and the following summer and fall, she worked for Coe in various capacities, which she describes again as "supervising lab and fieldwork, working on site records, and illustrating archaeological reports" (see Coe 1964). In the summer of 1962, she supervised fieldwork in a reservoir area on the Roanoke River on the Virginia-North Carolina border. Coe did not usually tolerate women in the field, but as with Black, the association with Coe honed her field techniques and provided her an excellent mentor in identification and analysis of material from southeastern sites.

She was looking, however, for more permanent full-time work. John Corbett, departmental consulting archaeologist with the National Park Service, encouraged her to take a job with the Amerind Foundation in southern Arizona. Despite the lure of working in the Southwest, the job required a three-year contract to work on analysis of pottery from Casa Grande—but no fieldwork. That did not appeal. By this time, Ed McMichael, whom she had known from the work at Mandeville, received his Ph.D. and was working for the West Virginia Geological and Economic Survey as their only archaeologist. He offered her a job to work with him in West Virginia— LOTS of fieldwork. In the early spring of 1963, she moved all her belongings to Morgantown, West Virginia, to begin what were to be the most significant years of her career.

West Virginia, Almost Heaven?

In the course of the next twelve-and-a-half years, Bettye did more archaeological work in West Virginia than anyone else, before or since. She traveled the state recording sites and collections, and she and Ed tested dozens of sites in an effort to get a handle on the cultural history and chronology of the state. The West Virginia Archaeological Society had been active since 1948, and its members provided much of the information on the location and condition of sites and opened doors to local people. In 1970, not long after Ed McMichael left to teach at what is now Indiana State University at Terre Haute, she became head of the Section of Archaeology.

Detailing all the field projects in which Bettye was involved is difficult because they multiplied as each year passed. The projects with which she is most identified are her four seasons of work at the St. Albans site, which, by her own admission, is probably her greatest contribution to southeastern archaeology; and near the end of her time in the state, a season on Blennerhassett Island, which was important largely because of the significance of the historic Blennerhassett Mansion site in American history. It was near here that Aaron Burr was arrested and charged with treason.

She spent her first field season, three months in the summer of 1963, in Randolph County, excavating in three mounds and a village site. While these Middle Woodland sites produced a good amount of information, that summer also changed Bettye's personal life. The Hyre Mound was owned by Mary Hyre (sometimes written Hyer), whose son, Herbert, was a "confirmed bachelor," at least he so confided to Bettye. Herbert was a rural mail carrier in Upshur County, and his visits to the site on his mother's property that summer turned into a courtship. Herbert and Bettye married in April 1964, a few months before she began her excavations at St. Albans.

By this time, Bettye had completed building a house in Morgantown. So long as Bettye was working, Herbert told her that he was not responsible for her upkeep, and although he made a small cash contribution to the cost of the house, he was only there on weekends. In fact, her memory of the three years of that marriage is largely one of arguments, culminating in Herbert's flat refusal to move to Morgantown, and presumably Bettye's refusal either to give up her work or move to Upshur County. There was no question in Bettye's mind about the conflict between marriage and career; she had a fulfilling and challenging job and she didn't want to give it up. This was not Herbert's idea of a wife's role. The result of this stalemate was divorce in 1967. By that time Bettye was deeply committed to the St. Albans site.

The St. Albans site is on the banks of the Kanawha River about fifteen miles west of Charleston. U.S. Highway 60 runs closely parallel to the river at this point, and the state highway department owns the site. It was first reported to the Geological Survey in the spring of 1963, before Bettye's arrival, by an amateur archaeologist, when "the waters of the Kanawha River were unusually high, causing large sections of the bank to break away" (Broyles 1966b:2). Ed McMichael visited and found several Kirk Corner-Notched projectile points (dating ca. 6000–5000 B.C. in North Carolina) in the eroded bank at a depth of nine feet. Later that year he brought Geological Survey core drilling equipment and took six cores. "Depth of the cores ranged from 28 to 36.5 feet below the present surface. Layers of burned earth and charcoal were found in zones of varying thickness from the top to the bottom of each core sample" (Broyles 1966b:3). Here was a potentially deeply stratified and quite old site.

Bettye began excavation at St. Albans in June 1964 and continued in the summers of 1965 and 1966, digging for a total of almost seventeen months during that period (fig. 6.7). Her preliminary report on these three seasons ended with the following summary: "The St. Albans Site is important for several reasons: First, it is one of the deepest stratified sites thus far discovered in North America [eighteen feet at that point], and second, it is one of the oldest [six radiocarbon dates from hearths, the youngest 6210 B.C. ± 100 years, the oldest at 7900 B.C. ± 500]. Third, each occupation zone is separated from the one above and below by a sterile zone of either clay or sand. Fourth, only one type of projectile point has been found in each occupation zone, showing that only one type of point was being used at any given time" (Broyles 1966b:41–42).

Fig. 6.7. Excavations at the St. Albans site. (Photo courtesy of Bettye Broyles.)

Bettye lived in a trailer next to the site, both for ease in transportation and to protect the site. She usually did have a gun with her in rural West Virginia but still had no qualms or fear of living alone. In the fall of 1964 a newspaper reporter found her at St. Albans and reported a familiar theme. "Lady Archaeologists almost as rare as stratified sites" is the heading for a sidebar on an article about the St. Albans excavations. Bettye was interviewed as a woman in a man's profession: "Women in the field are discriminated against to some extent, the assistant state archaeologist says, with some institutions hesitating to put a woman in charge of field expeditions."

Her fieldwork in West Virginia to that time was summarized quickly (dug three mounds, recorded 189 sites, spent the summer at St. Albans), but the article then went on to show that Bettye pursued more "normal" female activities as well: "During her 15 months in the state, Miss Broyles has found time to meet and marry Herbert Hyre, an Upshur county man and design their new home in Morgantown. She has constructed most of their furniture . . . and has reupholstered the overstuffed pieces. . . . This woman archaeologist also can prepare and serve a full-course dinner for 32, make her own clothes, and [she] plays the piano. On the other hand: Her professional activities require her to be able to handle a crew of men on an excavation, diagram mounds and village sites, photograph her finds, and give slide lectures before other professional archaeologists."

The Geological Survey gave her an assistant, but her crews the first two years at St. Albans consisted of local men on welfare. She got whomever she was assigned, which could change daily. One time she remembers having a one-armed man for a few days; she put him to screening dirt. Although the men generally were good workers, uncovering the complexity of the St. Albans site meant that she and her assistant had to do all the fine work, and the going was very slow. By the end of the second season she had a profile cut of eighteen feet, showing the stratigraphy of cultural deposits (hearths and scattered charcoal mostly), separated by "clean" layers of flood-lain sand, silt, and clay. She had radiocarbon assays from some hearths, dating early to middle Archaic occupations.

To handle the tremendous amount of dirt that needed inspection, she devised a sluicing system, inspired by a television show she saw about working gold deposits in Alaska! With an electric pump, jury-rigged screens, and corrugated tin to channel the water back into the river, the efficiency of sifting the dirt increased manyfold. She gave a paper on this technique at the annual SEAC meeting and published a report with illustrations in the SEAC Bulletin (Broyles 1969b). Don Dragoo at the Carnegie Museum in Pittsburgh and others soon copied this time-saving system.

The cores and the excavations proved the significance and potential of the site, but the water table and the need for elaborate precautions against slumping complicated possibilities of getting to deeper deposits. During the fall of 1966, the "Preliminary Report: The St. Albans Site (46 Ka 27), Kanawha County, West Virginia" was published in the *West Virginia Archaeologist* (which Bettye edited). This report was used as the basis for a National Science Foundation (NSF) proposal that Bettye wrote for the next season of work. The proposal was funded, but not in time for the 1967 season, so that summer was spent in survey and testing in other parts of the state.

With the NSF funds, the 1968 season at St. Albans, working slightly upstream from the previous excavations, brought the excavated depth to about twenty-four feet. A hearth was found at this depth, but there were no associated artifacts. More hearths and more projectile points and lithic debris were found, but no new point types, and the full depth of the deposits was not reached. She worked into the late fall (November), with only three people as crew. To reach the deepest charcoal layers would have required more complicated and more expensive techniques because of the high water table. No funds were available from the Geological Survey or the highway department for that work, and excavations at the St. Albans site came to a halt.

On January 1, 1969, Richard Jensen joined the Section of Archaeology, and was appointed its head on July 1. Jensen had a crew in the Cheat River Valley, and Bettye did fieldwork in the proposed Rowlesburg Reservoir with a National Park Service (NPS) grant of three thousand dollars. She hired five West Virginia University students for eight weeks, recording twenty-three sites and excavating seven of them. In those days, three thousand dollars went a long way. Bettye also did survey work, with NPS funds, in five other proposed reservoirs in the southern part of the state. This pattern of long and varied field seasons, often lasting into November, continued throughout her time in West Virginia.

In the winter, like every archaeologist, Bettye worked on reports of the fieldwork, including continued analysis of the St. Albans material. In the winter of 1969–70, she also wrote another grant request to the National Science Foundation, for $31,250, for three full months of fieldwork and nine months of analysis. Unfortunately, this request was not funded, and Bettye did no further excavations at St. Albans. In 1971, Bettye's "Second Preliminary Report: The St. Albans Site, Kanawha County, West Virginia" was published by the Survey as *Report of Archaeological Investigations No. 3*. It contains the same basic description of the fieldwork but includes five appendices of specialized analyses, including her descriptions and illustrations of eleven projectile point types, in which she names several new types.

The failure of the NSF grant request was not the end of Bettye's involvement in the site. The sloughing bankline of the Kanawha River continually exposed artifacts, and collectors were always pecking away. Although the site was in the highway right-of-way, this was before state highway departments had to pay attention to archaeological sites. Bettye and others brought the situation of the loss of bankline and site features to the attention of the West Virginia Antiquities Commission (of which she was a member), pointing out that the site was on state property and should be protected under the state Antiquities Act. But she could get no response.

Some collectors at the site were members of the Kanawha chapter of the West Virginia Archaeological Society, and although Bettye and other leaders of the society warned them of the danger of digging into the bank, and that removing artifacts was illegal on state property, on February 1, 1974, a sixteen-year-old boy, "digging for arrowheads" according to the newspaper account, was buried under mud and wet clay. He was rescued, but again, on February 17, three more youths so undermined the bank that all three were buried "for about 15 minutes" (although all were rescued). On that day, Sigfus Olafson, a well-known amateur archaeologist and also a member of the Antiquities Commission, wrote Bettye, sending copies of the newspaper articles about both incidents and saying "Something has to be done or you might as well forget about that site."

Within a month, Bettye compiled a summary about the site and its situation, importance, and legal status, and a history of efforts to protect it and to keep people from digging (Broyles 1974). She copied correspondence and newspaper accounts and distributed them widely. She wrote to prominent archaeologists, and to the National Park Service, asking that letters be written to the governor and to the Antiquities Commission, and many in the professional community did respond. But it was the cave-ins that caught the attention of local authorities, and signs were posted by the highway department, and patrols from the town of St. Albans were increased. Of course, Bettye remembers, "amateurs" just took down the signs and used them as shovels.

There was no question that this extremely important site had unique stratigraphy that might clarify the geomorphology of this particular stretch of the Kanawha River. The St. Albans site was placed on the National Register of Historic Places, but it continued to drop into the river. In the early 1990s, the West Virginia Highway Department contracted for more archaeological studies because the bankline was eroding to such an extent that Highway 60 was threatened. The bank was cut back and riprap applied. Extensive geomorphological studies were done, providing data on the sediments and profiles. The city of St. Albans obtained an Intermodal Surface Transportation Enhancement Act (ISTEA) grant from the Federal Highway Administration and contracted for development of a "Research Design and Management Plan" for the site (Michael Aslinger, personal communication, 1996). The western boundary of the site is now defined, and the archaeologists working on this research will be able to summarize all previous work. Perhaps the next time you drive through southwestern West Virginia, you can stop by the road and read an interpretive sign about the prehistoric occupation of the Kanawha River Valley, documented first by Bettye Broyles.

Although Bettye spent every season in the field on survey or testing, the St. Albans site was the most significant one in her career. She is associated with it and it with her; those four seasons of investigation were the high points of her career and put West Virginia archaeology on the map. Starting in 1965, Bettye gave talks about the site at professional meetings several times a year—to the Ohio Valley Archaeological Conference, SEAC, and

Fig. 6.8. Bettye Broyles and John Corbett at the Society for Historic Archaeology meeting in South Carolina, 1975. (Photo courtesy of W. J. Hranicky and *Popular Archaeology.*)

SAA. She was also a popular banquet speaker at state archaeological societies outside West Virginia—Tennessee, Virginia, Maryland, Delaware,
Pennsylvania, and the Eastern States Archaeological Federation. Attendance
at these meetings afforded her important input from her colleagues, and she
was a constant attendee at regional and national meetings (fig. 6.8).

Because there was always the hope that funds would be available to get
to the bottom of the site, and presumably because of the press of other
fieldwork, no "final" report interpreting her finds at St. Albans was ever
prepared, although the "Second Preliminary Report" described all the work
done in the four seasons.

Let me interrupt this chronological narrative of Bettye's archaeological
activities, to give an idea of what she did with her energy in her "spare time."
In 1968, she took over the editorship of the newsletter of the SEAC, and soon
thereafter of the *Bulletin* (she typed the stencils on her own typewriter at
home); she was voted "secretary-treasurer" at a time when there were no
official officers. In 1972 she did the local arrangements, planned the program, and hosted the SEAC annual meeting in Morgantown. She edited the
journal of the West Virginia Archaeological Society; she was secretary of the
ESAF in the late 1960s and early 1970s. She was West Virginia's representative on the SAA's Committee on Public Archaeology, and she taught an
evening class in archaeology each semester for six years at West Virginia
University. She attended an average of five national or regional archaeologi-

cal meetings a year, partly, of course, because she was an officer or editor, but also to recharge her batteries. The energy noted by friends and colleagues starting in the mid-1950s continues to this day.

One other thing that many archaeologists do in their "spare time" is to work on museum exhibits. James Price, the director of the Geological Survey, asked Ed McMichael to "do something about a museum" to tell of the Survey's archaeological research, but Ed had never gotten anything started. Finally, in the summer of 1966, Price asked Bettye to "do something" and she quickly prepared large-scale drawings of proposed exhibit cases and lists of where the artifacts would come from (some to be borrowed from amateurs). Price liked the plans.

"As soon as I got in from the field, I asked Daddy and Mother to come up for a visit. It wasn't possible to get unpainted paneling in Morgantown, so Daddy brought 10 sheets with him from Chattanooga. We spent about a week constructing and wiring the cases. Two of the Survey staff helped with painting and lettering. By the time of the October meeting of the West Virginia Archaeological Society, we were ready for the grand opening. It was all done in less than a month!" The exhibits were on display for many years but were removed shortly after Bettye left.

As in all states in the early 1970s, the National Park Service was providing funds in West Virginia for survey and testing of proposed reservoirs, and Bettye and the staff of the Section of Archaeology were kept busy with this work. She also was a participant in the National Youth Science Camp doing "public archaeology" before public archaeology was cool. This camp, begun in 1963, was a program unique to West Virginia, in which two high school students from each state came to West Virginia in June for an introduction to various kinds of science through lectures by a large number of guest speakers from all over the United States. First Ed McMichael and then Bettye gave these one hundred students a taste of archaeology for a week, sometimes two. This was Bettye's first efforts at "public education" in the field, although she had worked previously with amateurs and collectors.

Several years later she wrote some short popular articles on West Virginia's past and her excavation projects for *Wonderful West Virginia* and *Outdoor West Virginia,* published by the Department of Natural Resources (Broyles 1969d, e, 1970, 1971a). In one of the articles she describes the life of a shaman in the first person, and in another she portrays life in a Fort Ancient community of A.D. 1600–1700 by a first-person account of a woman of that village. Bettye says she was inspired to do this by Madeline Kneberg's writings (see chapter 4).

In 1970, she chose what she thought was a small prehistoric site with a stone cairn to test with these Science Camp students, and found, upon removal of the stones, that it was an early eighteenth-century cabin site. Herewith began Bettye's work as a historic archaeologist, her attendance at the annual meetings of the Society for Historical Archaeology, and even her nomination for president of the SHA in 1973 (although she was not elected). She continued excavations at this site for two years.

In the fall of 1972 and winter/spring of 1973, the pace of work and exciting activities grew. In addition, Daniel Fowler was hired on July 1, 1972, as a full-time archaeological assistant. Danny had been working for the Section of Archaeology for several years, starting as a student on Bettye's crew at St. Albans. He did many of the preliminary surveys of reservoirs and worked with Bettye over the years in many capacities. He was to have a significant role in her future as well.

Sometime in the fall of 1972, Bettye proposed that the Geological Survey and the State Highway Department sign an agreement for the Section of Archaeology to do all the Highway Department's required archaeological work (under NEPA and the new Federal Highway Administration regulations). Enacted in early 1973, this was one of the first such "blanket contracts" in the country. In the fall, she was invited to a three-day meeting in Baltimore sponsored by the National Park Service and the Federal Highway Administration to explain this new agreement and how such an arrangement would benefit any state highway department.

In the fall of 1972, the Blennerhassett Island Historical Commission contacted the Section of Archaeology, asking for a budget and proposal to survey the island and test the area where the Blennerhassett Mansion was thought to be. The commission hoped that, if there were significant remains, some sort of reconstruction might be possible as their contribution to the national bicentennial celebrations planned for 1976. As a result of the proposal that Bettye wrote, the commission awarded the section $7,000 for work in the summer of 1973. That summer's work also included $9,400 from the National Park Service for survey in three proposed reservoirs, and $1,500 from the Highway Department for testing at a bridge replacement project. There was also a test at the Grave Creek Mound site, the largest Adena Mound, scheduled for development by the State Parks and Recreation Department. As head of the section, Bettye was responsible for the logistics, staff, and success of all these projects. She hired two graduate students for the daily supervision at Blennerhassett Island, one for the historic site and one for survey and testing of prehistoric sites.

Blennerhassett Island is in the Ohio River, near Parkersburg, West Virginia. It was visited by George Washington in 1770 and was chosen by Harman Blennerhassett in 1799 as the site of a mansion for his new wife. The historical significance of the house is that Aaron Burr was visiting just before he was arrested for treason on December 10, 1806. (Blennerhassett was also arrested as a co-conspirator; both men were indicted but not convicted.) The mansion burned accidentally in 1811. It was huge for this part of the frontier, costing $40,000 to construct and having a two-story central section and curved porticos connected to square end rooms. During the summer of 1973, the foundation of the central section, east portico, and kitchen were located, to the accompaniment of a great deal of publicity in Parkersburg newspapers. In addition, a Fort Ancient village and cemetery were tested and had sufficient potential to warrant a full season of excavation. There was talk of plans for reconstruction of a portion of the site as illustrative of the island's long history. Bettye wrote a report on this first season's work in the winter and submitted it to all involved (some of the funds came from a matching Historic Preservation Fund grant to the Antiquities Commission).

The summer of 1974 was equally busy and exciting. E. Thomas Hemmings was hired to oversee the major excavations at the Fort Ancient village and cemetery, and Bettye was the supervisor for the five months of excavations at the Blennerhassett Mansion. She invited an archaeologist from Ohio State University (OSU) to bring students to work at Grave Creek Mound. But in May of that year, Robert Erwin, now director of the Geological Survey, criticized her administrative abilities (although she pointed out that she had generated $140,000 in funds for 1974 fieldwork) and continued to "insult" her publicly at meetings. His motives were puzzling to her then and the experience continues to be a thorn in her memory.

The project at Grave Creek Mound turned out to be one of the nails in Bettye's West Virginia coffin. The site is adjacent to the West Virginia Penitentiary and had been under the control of that agency for many years. Bettye explained to the OSU professor that Moundsville was a small rural West Virginia town, and that the penitentiary was within sight of the excavation area. Students should dress in jeans and shirts, and under no circumstances should the women on the project wear shorts and halters. Bettye told him "Do not bring any long-haired students with you—they are not acceptable in West Virginia. I would rather have sent a Black out to do a survey than somebody with long hair." A front page article in the Wheeling Sunday paper, June 23, 1974, prominently showed a photograph of a young female "anthropology student" in shorts and halter, with the state prison showing in the background. It happened that Governor Arch Moore was from

Moundsville, and "he was getting phone calls saying 'get this bunch of long-haired hippie degenerates out of Moundsville.' I had to take the blame for this," Bettye told us. She vividly recalls that the furor ended with her having to close the excavation, turn back $40,000, and find somewhere else for those students to work for the next two months! The head of the Geological Survey was not pleased, to say the least.

The work on Blennerhassett Island, however, went well that summer, with more publicity for both of the excavations. Gore Vidal, who had written a novel on Aaron Burr, came for a visit, and there were always local bigwigs from Parkersburg and the State Capitol dropping by. There was, however, continued dissension which Bettye could feel building; there was the stress of the problems at the Grave Creek site and the displeasure of her boss, and there were personality problems, perhaps even some jealousy on the part of some of her staff. One of the "rules" at the Geological Survey was that staff did not talk to reporters. If a newspaper wanted to do a story, staff were to contact the Survey first. Tom Hemmings did not clear his remarks to newspapers with the Survey, and Bettye felt that he had some feelings of professional superiority. In addition, Danny Fowler was making a concerted effort to gain favor with the Blennerhassett Commission, seemingly at Bettye's expense. There was also the pressure of many reports "in progress" and the need to produce results from this highly visible bicentennial project as well. A list Bettye generated in the spring of 1973 showed fifteen reports in various stages of completion.

Bettye went about her work as usual through the winter of 1974 and spring of 1975 but knew that what she thought was a good relationship with the director of the Survey was somehow broken. She worked hard on the analysis of all the material from the Blennerhassett Mansion in the winter of 1974, and the report on the first season was submitted on time. But progress was slow on the detailed analysis and that was a source of criticism. However, the call from Robert Erwin's office on September 2, 1975, and the formal letter of termination that followed, came as a shock.

Bettye still does not feel she knows the *real* reason for her dismissal. In a letter she wrote to Erwin on September 11, she mentioned various reasons given during the meeting on the second: "insubordination to authority" and "continued divisive actions within the Archaeology Section." She wrote to the governor objecting to the dismissal; several colleagues wrote both to the Geological Survey and to the governor. She requested a hearing, but relations had broken down so much that no repair was possible. Bettye found her office cleaned out within the week. The bitterness remains.

On Her Feet in Mississippi and Alabama

Bettye stayed in Morgantown for only a few months. Her many friends and colleagues in the Southeast were aware of her situation, and Bennett Graham asked Bob Thorne (at the University of Mississippi and another of Bettye's old friends) to contact her about doing a three-month survey of the proposed Yellow Creek Nuclear Power Plant in northeastern Mississippi on Pickwick Lake. Bob and Bettye discussed the project at the SEAC that fall, and by the first of February 1976, Bettye had settled into a cabin in J. P. Coleman State Park in Mississippi to begin the survey, with Charlie Hubbard as her assistant. At the end of the three months, enough information was collected to indicate that there were sites needing testing. A new contract between TVA and the University of Mississippi was concluded and Bettye was hired to supervise that research. She worked two-and-a-half years straight in the field on this project, living in one of five trailers that the TVA provided. In the summer when crews were hired, the other trailers were used for lab, dining room, and dorms for students. Bettye supervised all of the testing and impact mitigation for sites found in the initial survey, and in the winter, she did shoreline surveys on weekends (because she loved to get out in the woods and look for sites) and worked on the analysis of the artifacts, making drawings of stone tools and maps for the reports (Thorne, Broyles, and Johnson, 1981).

During that initial three-month survey, she also worked on the description and drawings of artifacts from the Blennerhassett Mansion. At the end of June (while the new TVA contract was being negotiated), she returned to West Virginia to again be a staff member for the National Youth Science Camp, excavating with the students on an old Civilian Conservation Corps camp garbage dump. She continued giving talks to local groups and working on the Blennerhassett analysis. She commuted to Chattanooga quite a bit because her mother was ill and died in 1977. Bettye then put her house in Morgantown up for sale.

After completion of the Yellow Creek project, Bettye spent a year doing a resurvey in three Corps of Engineers' reservoirs in northern Mississippi, again for Bob Thorne. The contract with the university called for relocating and assessing a percentage of the known sites during drawdowns in the lakes and interviewing local collectors. It was not a survey to locate "new" sites, and this was a requirement to which Bettye objected: "I can't walk over a site and see artifacts and not give that site a number and put it on the map." She solved the dilemma by ignoring this restriction, working extra hours doing surveys on her own to record all sites that she found (Thorne et al. 1982). You can get a feel for those days of surveying on her own as she describes working in northern Mississippi:

> I would walk a mile or more out over the mudflats [from the drawn down lake] and have nightmares because of the old house sites. I kept dreaming that I'd stepped into a well and no one would be able to find me. A lot of times in the mornings the little eroded gullies would be frozen and I would just walk across them, but in the afternoon when I walked back I would have to walk a mile or more out of my way to get around them. Sometimes I would build little bridges with logs or dead limbs to cross these gullies. I thoroughly enjoyed doing those surveys, but it's one of those things I really should not have done by myself.

Bettye's final field project was in 1983 in Colbert Ferry Park on the Natchez Trace, in Alabama, where she worked with Jay Johnson of the University of Mississippi. Bettye had moved back to Chattanooga by this time and was living with her father. She remembers driving to the field area in early December in a snow storm. Jay arranged for her to live in a log house ("I was blown away by the 18-inch logs, 12-foot ceilings, and open dog trot," says Jay), during what proved to be the coldest, most miserable winter she ever remembers. Bettye's advice is "don't ever let a man pick a place for you to live in the field." Big fires in the fireplace did not heat the one room she lived in, but she stuck it out—again because she loved the work and being by herself.

By the time that project was over, she had symptoms of Crohn's disease, making it difficult for her to do fieldwork. She was always on soft money, project by project, in the work in Alabama and Mississippi, and she decided it was time to "retire," at least from archaeological fieldwork.

Going Back to Tennessee

In the summer of 1985 she started building her new house in Chattanooga with her father's help. She put up all the walls, floors, siding, and windows but hired others to do the sheetrock and roof work. It took until 1987 to finish, and she and her father moved in. The *Chattanooga Times* did a feature story on Bettye and her house in September of that year, saying: "She wields a claw hammer with authority and runs a circular saw with ease. She talks of floor joists, T-squares, planes, and rafters. She knows building materials as well as any construction foreman." And, the article quoted Bettye as saying: "I know I'm doing something that most people—even a man—wouldn't tackle. But I've been doing a man's work for 30 years."

Each room in the house has a different theme. One bedroom has things from the Southwest; one is the Ancestors Room, with historic family photographs and coverlets; one bedroom is Mexican, and another is going to be Oriental. Her grand piano is on a balcony, where one wall has shelves filled floor to ceiling with her bottle collection. The den or study is lined with double sets of shelves for her archaeological library, and spread over everything are the records of Rhea County. Her computer is almost lost in a sea of papers, ashtrays, and Coke cans ready for recycling.

Once she decided to do no more archaeology, Bettye immersed herself in local history. By 1986 she was appointed Rhea County historian and president of the Rhea County Historical Society. One of the society's activities is maintenance of a small museum, in the basement of the county courthouse. The displays feature the famous Scopes trial because the Rhea County courthouse is where it took place. Bettye has been transcribing various county records as well as working on her own family history, and in 1993 she received the Ramsey Award from the East Tennessee Historical Society. She joined the United Daughters of the Confederacy and, of course, is already an officer in that organization. In 1997, the UDC awarded Bettye the Jefferson Davis Medal for "dedication to the preservation of Confederate history through her research and publications of Rhea County, Tennessee, and its people during the War Between the States." This is the first such medal awarded to a member of Bettye's UDC chapter in its seventy-five years of existence.

Bettye cared for her father until his death in 1989. Since then, the pace of her activity has not slackened, although the complications of living with Crohn's disease limit some of the traveling she would like to do. She now weighs what she did when she was in high school. Her hair, which was dark as a teenager, and which was gray in the 1970s, is now white (fig. 6.9). Anyone who talks with her on the phone would recognize the voice and laugh of this strong woman.

Fig. 6.9. Bettye Broyles at home in
Chattanooga in November 1994.
(Photo by Hester Davis.)

The Legacy

Bettye's contributions to southeastern archaeology are found in subtle places, but they permeate the lives of her colleagues. She kept SEAC alive and well for nearly eight years; she put West Virginia on the archaeological map through descriptive reports and articles in regional journals and papers presented at innumerable meetings. She has an unfinished manuscript of nearly two hundred pages summarizing Fort Ancient burial customs in West Virginia, and a detailed report on more than five hundred burials from the Buffalo site plus nine other sites excavated by Ed McMichael and herself up to 1973.

She wrote no books; she was not a theoretician. She was a meticulous "old-fashioned" dirt archaeologist who had no patience for slackers in the field. She could hold her own in any backroom archaeological social gathering but was always, and continues to be, something of a loner. Her legacy in West Virginia is contained in dozens of basic descriptive reports on sites and collections from all over the state and in their continued use by everyone working there today.

When pressed to think about who or what might have influenced her in her career, or her own influence for that matter, she was unable to pick out an individual. In the 1950s in the Southeast, the only woman she knew doing archaeology was Madeline Kneberg (Lewis). She saw and talked with Madeline at meetings of the TAS, but she remembers no particular heart-to-heart talks about becoming an archaeologist, or how a woman can fit into this man's profession. She always thought of her male counterparts as colleagues and friends, not as competitors, and she never felt she was treated any differently. The subtle situations are there, however: Glenn Black recommended that she go into museum work, not field archaeology; Thorne Deuel did not let her take charge of any field project; Bob Thorne did not think she should be driving a truck around the wilds of northern Mississippi by herself. But those colleagues whom she admires—Mike Fowler, Joffre Coe, A. R. Kelly, Bob Thorne—treated her as an equal. In the field and at meetings, as Dena Dincauze says, she was "a Presence." After being completely out of archaeology for more than ten years, it was to a room full of friends and a standing ovation that she was presented with the SEAC's Distinguished Service Award at its meeting in Knoxville in 1995, which included this statement:

WHEREAS Bettye Broyles is one of the small, very small, number of women who made her distinct contributions to southeastern archaeology at a time when there were few female mentors, but who had and has the support and friendship of most of the best known of her southeastern male cohorts, and
WHEREAS we wish to acknowledge the path which Bettye opened for many of us, and because we have not forgotten her, nor she us.

Bettye has great memories of good times in the field and at meetings. One of her legacies contains the details of a busy life and the growth of archaeology in the Southeast. Bettye kept three bulging scrapbooks (1955–57) and two large boxes of file folders with material from 1958 to the present, which contain notices of meetings, the newspaper accounts of her projects, significant correspondence—all of the things that made this story possible. If more archaeologists were so inclined, the archives and history of our profession would be much richer for historians.

In the September 1985 newspaper article, Bettye is again quoted as saying: "I was once asked, 'Is there anything you can't do?' There probably is, but there isn't much I haven't tried." What an exciting life to look back upon! Many of her friends have recalled her influence on them (although she claims some of the students she supervised in the field "probably never want to hear my name again"), and two are quoted here:

Bettye devoted the productive years of her life to the satisfaction of archaeological and anthropological goals, and probably gave more of herself than anyone should be reasonably expected to give. I am pleased to say that I had the opportunity to work with her and there is no question that she contributed to my understanding of archaeology in the Southeast.—Robert Thorne, Center for Archaeological Research, University of Mississippi, September 1996

I just finished my first summer in the field full time since 1976. I was apprehensive about whether I could do it and I'm several years younger than Bettye was when we worked together [in the early 1980s]. Another thing struck me as I struggled to repair screens, keep pumps running, put the truck back together and get it unstuck. Many of the skills needed to be successful in the field are traditionally male skills. Bettye was never bothered by that tradition. She is a better carpenter, a better shot, and has more time in a four-wheel-drive than most people. This, combined with the fact that she has a passion for archaeology and solid training in the finest tradition of fieldwork in the Southeast, makes Bettye one of the best field directors in the region. She was certainly the best I ever worked with.—Jay Johnson, Center for Archaeological Research, University of Mississippi, September 1996

Postscript

Reading about one's life spread out on pages for everyone to see has not been easy, especially when you have spent ten years trying to ignore an impulse to get out of the car and walk across a freshly plowed field or walk the shore line of Watt's Bar Lake when the water is down. When I decided to give up archaeology, it was not an easy choice, but it had become necessary.

There has been so much emphasis recently on women in archaeology and the fact that I was a "pioneer." I must say, in 1955, no one bothered to tell me that this was a man's field, or that there were few females doing fieldwork. I just knew that "come Hell or high water" this was something I wanted to do.

I thoroughly enjoyed my thirty years in archaeology and would not trade them for anything. My sincere thanks go to all individuals along the way who helped me and to the members of the Southeastern Archaeological Conference who will always occupy a special place in my memory. A special thanks to Hester Davis for her friendship and her "careful handling" of my life.
Bettye J. Broyles, 1996

Selected Bibliography of Bettye J. Broyles

1955   Preliminary Report on Excavation of the Whites Creek Woodland Mound. *Tennessee Archaeologist* 11 (2):63–68.

1958   *Russell Cave in Northern Alabama.* Tennessee Archaeological Society, Miscellaneous Paper 4.

1962   A Lamar Site in Southwest Georgia. *Proceedings of the Eighteenth Southeastern Archeological Conference* [1961], pp. 55–56.

1963   Excavation of 9 Cla 51, A Lamar Site in Southwest Georgia. *University of Georgia Laboratory of Archaeological Series Report* 5:29–47.

1964a   Mill Pond Site, 46 Me 2. *West Virginia Archeologist* 17:10–45.

1964b   Mounds in Randolph County, West Virginia. *Eastern States Archeological Federation Bulletin* 23:9.

1966a   Excavations at the St. Albans Archaic Site, 1964–1965. *Eastern States Archeological Federation Bulletin* 25:11.

1966b   Preliminary Report: The St. Albans Site (46 Ka 27), Kanawha County, West Virginia. *West Virginia Archaeologist* 19:1–43.

1968a   Reconstructed Designs from Swift Creek Complicated Stamped Sherds. Proceedings of the Southeastern Archaeological Conference. *Southeastern Archaeological Conference Bulletin* 8:49–55.

1968b   Prehistoric Man in the Kanawha and Ohio Valleys. *Proceedings of the West Virginia Academy of Science* 40:32a–41a.

1969a   Comments on Materials and Chipping Techniques Used at St. Albans. Proceedings of the Southeastern Archaeological Conference. *Southeastern Archaeological Conference Bulletin* 9:31–32.

1969b   The Sluicing System Used at the St. Albans Site. Proceedings of the Southeastern Archeological Conference. *Southeastern Archeological Conference Bulletin* 9:45–55.

1969c   Distribution of Southeastern Archaic Projectile Points in the Ohio Valley. Proceedings of the Southeastern Archaeological Conference. *Southeastern Archaeological Conference Bulletin* 11:31–36.

1969d   Prehistoric Man in the Kanawha and Ohio Valleys, Part I. *Outdoor West Virginia.* Department of Natural Resources, Charleston.

1969e   Prehistoric Man in the Kanawha and Ohio Valleys, Part II. *Outdoor West Virginia.* Department of Natural Resources, Charleston.

1970   A Fort Ancient Squaw's Life. *Wonderful West Virginia.* Department of Natural Resources, Charleston.

1971a   Mystery of the Buried Cabin. *Wonderful West Virginia.* Department of Natural Resources, Charleston.

1971b   Second Preliminary Report: The St. Albans Site, Kanawha County, West Virginia. *West Virginia Geological and Economic Survey Report of Archeological Investigations* 3.

1971c   Fluted Points in West Virginia. *West Virginia Archeologist* 20:46–56.

1972a   The Canfield Collection. *West Virginia Archeologist* 22:31–62.

1972b   The Canfield Collection. *West Virginia Archeologist* 23:31–45.

1973a   Fort Ancient Mortuary Customs in West Virginia. Unpublished manuscript in possession of the author.

1973b *Blennerhassett Island Archeological Project: Season I.* West Virginia Geological Survey.

1974   The St. Albans Archeological Site, Kanawha County, West Virginia: Preservation or Destruction? Report in possession of the author.

1975a A Late Archaic Component at the Buffalo Site, Putnam County, West Virginia. *West Virginia Geological Survey Report of Archeological Investigations 6.*

1975b Blennerhassett Island Project. *Popular Archaeology* 4(4):39, 41.

1975c Blennerhassett Mansion: An Early Nineteenth Century Eden on the River, Seasons I and II (1973–1974). Unpublished manuscript, in possession of the author.

Broyles, Bettye J., compiler and editor

1967   Bibliography of Pottery Type Descriptions from the Eastern United States. *Southeastern Archaeological Conference Bulletin 4.*

7

Best Supporting Actress?

The Contributions of Adelaide K. Bullen

ROCHELLE A. MARRINAN

Southeastern archaeology has been advanced by the contributions of several husband and wife collaborations. Phyllis and Dan Morse, Madeline Kneberg and Thomas M. N. Lewis, and Adelaide and Ripley Bullen come immediately to mind. While Phyllis Morse pursued graduate studies in archaeology but did not complete a Ph.D. because of family responsibilities, she continued to be a vitally involved contributor to the field. Kneberg's substantial and innovative collaborations with Lewis generally preceded their marriage (chapter 4). Adelaide Bullen's involvement in archaeology, particularly southeastern archaeology, was a life choice channeled by her husband's career change and by other economic, social, and geographic factors during the times in which she lived. She was not yet an adolescent when World War I raged. The Great Depression came as she entered her twenties. World War II presented career opportunities that influenced her throughout her life. While her education and early work were conducted in New England, the majority of her adult life was spent in Florida.

Early Years

Adelaide Kendall was born in Worcester, Massachusetts, on January 12, 1908, to Grace Marble Kendall and Oliver Sawyer Kendall. She had one sibling, a sister Harriet. She married Ripley Pierce Bullen on July 25, 1929, at the age of twenty-one. Their two sons were born while she was still in her early twenties. Dana Ripley Bullen II was born in 1931 and Pierce Kendall Bullen in 1934. Ripley, born in 1902, had received a degree in mechanical engineering from Cornell in 1925 and worked for General Electric in engineering research and sales. He maintained an avid interest in archaeology, however, conducting excavations and participating in scholarly organizations. In 1939, he was a founding member of the Massachusetts Archaeological Society.

By 1940, his interests in archaeology had developed to the point that he left General Electric to accept a position with the Robert S. Peabody Foundation for Archaeology at Phillips Academy, Andover, Massachusetts. He began graduate work in anthropology at Harvard, and Adelaide became an undergraduate at Radcliffe. Together they attended the University of New Mexico Summer Field School in the Chaco Canyon locality in 1941. Their activities in the Southwest led to three publications. Their first joint publication (1942) reported fieldwork on a cave site, Tres Piedras, near Taos, New Mexico. Their one-week excavation addressed the problem of purported Puebloan and Plains Indian interactions near andesite outcrops in this area. They concluded that Plains Indian influences were not demonstrably present and proposed that the site was better understood as a temporary campsite for hunting parties.

Adelaide's paper (1945a) on stuttering provides a cross-cultural examination of the problem of speech disorders. She had gathered data among the Navajo during the summer of 1941, but she also used unpublished data for Oceania and Australia provided by Margaret Mead, Reo Fortune, Lloyd Warner, and Joseph Birdsell. She reported the incidence of stuttering in American society at about 10 percent, against its rarity in Navajo and Oceanic societies. She considered anxiety and emotional maladjustment in American society to be the root causes of stuttering. Somatotyping (the attempt to achieve a standardized classification of human body types) was also applied in a minor way, but it would remain a research interest for the remainder of her career.

Adelaide's (1947) paper "Archaeological Theory and Anthropological Fact," revisited the problem of using ethnohistorical data in archaeological interpretation as urged by William Henry Holmes (1905). The materials in question were small ceramic vessels and effigy animals that had been variously interpreted by archaeologists as children's toys, shrine furnishings, or magico-religious ritual (cult) items. Her tone was strong in its advocacy of the use of ethnohistoric data ("to catch our archaeology alive") in the Southwest, adding meaning to excavated materials (Bullen 1947:133).

She received the A.B. degree *cum laude* from Radcliffe in 1943, at the age of thirty-five, certainly an unusual accomplishment for a woman of her age in those days. She continued graduate studies in cultural and physical anthropology at Harvard (1943–48), working with Earnest A. Hooten and Clyde K. M. Kluckhohn. During this period, Ripley and Adelaide took part in a number of excavations, but two are particularly important. One of their earliest papers, in what we now call African-American archaeology, was published in 1945. "Black Lucy's Garden" details the excavation and material remains of the home of Lucy Foster, a freed slave. This paper contains a discussion of the field techniques, the material culture, and an ethnohistorical account. Today, we would add artifact counts, calculate a Mean Ceramic Date, and add other treatments that have emerged since the late 1960s, but this paper is an excellent early treatment of a domestic site related to slavery and the circumstances of free persons of color.

While they were still living in Massachusetts, a second paper reports their excavation of two burials on Tiverton Island, New Hampshire (1946). Historic burials of two children, thought to be racially mixed (Native American and African), are reported. With this paper, Adelaide began her role as interpreter of human remains in their joint reports and occasionally as a service to other excavators.

Today, we would characterize much of her work as applied physical anthropology (for example, 1945b). Many of the early projects on which she worked had applications in support of the war effort and were classified (for example, 1948). She was particularly interested in stress and fatigue, considering these from the perspective of somatotyping, a major research interest of many physical and cultural anthropologists prior to World War II. Somatotyping began with the efforts of German psychiatrist E. Kretschmer in the early years of the twentieth century to link mental disorders with body type. In the United States, it was pioneered by W. H. Sheldon, who examined "normal" individuals (that is, non-psychiatric cases). Since this approach required standardization of methodology and large numbers of subjects, Sheldon and his colleagues devised methods using photographs taken against a gridded background. The anterior, posterior, and lateral full-body photographs were used to measure body build. Sheldon used college males as his subject population, and most available data at the time were derived from male subjects (Wells 1983:2–12).

Many of us remember the requirement for naked photographs, "posture pictures," routinely taken at many academic institutions into the 1960s. At the 1995 annual meeting of the American Association of Physical Anthropologists, the subject of these photographs was raised. It was reported that Sheldon's original photographs, deposited in the National Anthropological Archives at the Smithsonian Institution, had been de-accessioned and destroyed (Boaz 1995). Subsequent research showed that these materials had been returned to their respective universities when the Smithsonian determined that Sheldon's estate lacked clear title to the photographs. Yale University reportedly burned its photographs (including alumni former President George Bush, First Lady Hillary Rodham Clinton, and actress Meryl Streep).

In 1946, Adelaide Bullen and Harriet L. Hardy presented data for college women (175 Radcliffe College women) based on "posture pictures." Their paper also considered fatigue and discussed the degree of masculinity in women's body builds (androgyny, gynandromorphy, or masculinity). As the authors attest, there was then a lack of adequate data on women subjects that would support such characterizations as "weak masculine" or "feminine," terms that were commonly used by male researchers. Adelaide conducted this work as a Research Anthropologist in the Radcliffe College Health Center (1943–44).

While still a graduate student (from 1946 to 1948), she was a civilian consultant to the Department of the Army and a member of the Fatigue Laboratory staff at Harvard. One outcome of her research was a paper on the effects of the drug Pregnenolone. This drug had been given to aviators to combat fatigue, with marked positive results (Graham-Bryce, Bullen, and Forbes 1945). They reported little effect among the nonmilitary subjects they tested. Pregnenolone was tested in an effort to enhance performance under stress and was abandoned and forgotten as steroids were developed. Recently, it has re-emerged as one of the new "smart drugs" since it is a physiological precursor to all other steroid hormones without the harmful side effects associated with steroids (Vitamin Research Products, Inc. 1997).

The Florida Years (1948–87)

Ripley served as a Harvard teaching fellow from 1943 to 1945. In 1948, he accepted a position as assistant archaeologist with the Florida Board of

Parks and Memorials and was based in Gainesville. At this time, the Board of Parks also included Hale G. Smith and John W. Griffin, who were based in Tallahassee. In 1952, the Board of Parks and Memorials was disbanded and its data and collections were sent to the Florida State Museum in Gainesville. Ripley moved to the museum, which was reorganized, and a new department of social science established. Ripley became the first curator of social sciences and served as department chair for seventeen years.

Adelaide was involved with the museum by 1949, but on a voluntary basis. She was involved in archaeological inquiries from the outset. In 1950, the Bullens published their first Florida article in *American Antiquity* on the Johns Island site in Hernando County. It follows the usual style of the time, with heaviest concentration on those elements that could assist chronological placement. Subsistence and environmental data recovered from the site are not quantified but are treated in an impressionistic manner.

Over the years from 1950 to 1976, the Bullens jointly authored ten papers on Florida sites: Battery Point, Hernando County (1953, 1954); Cape Haze Peninsula, Charlotte County (1956); Summer Haven, St. Johns County (1961a); Wash Island, Citrus County (1961b, 1963b); Lemon Bay School Mound, Charlotte County (1963a); Ross Hammock, Volusia County (Bullen, Bullen, and Bryant 1967); Cato Site, Indian River County (Bullen, Bullen, and Clausen 1968); and the Palmer Site, Sarasota County (1976b). In addition to this work, Ripley published more than sixty papers on various sites in Florida. Adelaide was involved in many of these excavations, often living away from Gainesville for lengthy periods of time (fig. 7.1).

In 1950, the Florida State Museum (now the Florida Museum of Natural History) was the principal institution in Florida engaged in archaeological research. Florida State University had formed its department of anthropology and archaeology in that year under the chairmanship of Hale G. Smith, who was joined shortly thereafter by Charles H. Fairbanks. The University of Florida had a department of sociology and anthropology, in which John M. Goggin was the archaeologist. The role of these academic departments would grow rapidly, but when the Bullens came to the museum, they were the principal representatives of the archaeological community to the citizens of the state. While investigations had been conducted by Wyman in the 1870s and Clarence B. Moore and others in the late nineteenth and early twentieth centuries, the archaeology of Florida was not well known.

The Bullens were a cosmopolitan couple. Their New England roots and family wealth made them an attractive pair, and many of their initial projects were the result of contacts with wealthy landowners, but there were draw-

Fig. 7.1. Adelaide Bullen standing next to the limestone stele excavated by Ripley at the Crystal River site, ca. 1966. (Photo courtesy of the Florida Museum of Natural History.)

backs. Neither had been part of Works Progress Administration (WPA) projects in the Southeast. This work had forged strong bonds among the male field supervisors who became the postwar leaders in academic departments throughout the region. These men also returned to academic institutions on the GI Bill, received advanced degrees, and began teaching and conducting field research with their students. For example, in 1949, an anthropological conference was held at Rollins College in Winter Park. *The Florida Indian and His Neighbors* (Griffin 1949a), a publication synthesizing what was known about Florida archaeology, does not include Ripley Bullen. It does rejoin a number of archaeologists whom we identify with WPA archaeology: Gordon R. Willey, James B. Griffin, Charles H. Fairbanks, and John W. Griffin. Only John W. Griffin (1949b:45–54) acknowledges, in his overview of historical archaeology in Florida, any use of Ripley's work.

After Goggin's death, Fairbanks joined the department of anthropology at the University of Florida in 1960, and he immediately began to build a strong generalized department. He attracted a loyal, growing student following. In this environment, the lack of graduate degrees hurt both Adelaide and Ripley. Academic faculty and students viewed them as inadequately prepared for their positions given their lack of postgraduate degrees—particularly Ripley. While there seemed to be genuine respect for Adelaide's graduate work, neither was made part of the teaching faculty, even in a courtesy role. Although students worked with both Bullens at the museum, there was a rift between the department of anthropology and the museum. Other museum curators, William H. Sears, James A. Ford, and William R. Bullard, were given courtesy or joint faculty status, and students were encouraged to enroll for directed studies with them. This discrimination led students to view the Bullens's field methodology, for example, as being out of date. It also led to their exclusion from the kinds of intellectual stimulation that classroom teaching and research contribute to career development.

Ripley and Adelaide were founding members of the Florida Anthropological Society in 1948. Both served as officers and editors of the *Florida Anthropologist* and were lifelong supporters of this society. Adelaide served as interim editor and then editor from 1954 until 1956. One has only to examine preceding and succeeding issues to see the improvement in the quality of the publication during her editorship. The bulk of their Florida work is reported in this journal. In returning to the matter of their lack of southeastern roots, it is notable that Ripley published only twelve articles or contributions in the various publications (*Bulletin, Newsletter,* or *Proceedings*) of the Southeastern Archaeological Conference beginning in 1953, and Adelaide published nothing through the Southeastern Archaeological Conference. As chairman of social science at the museum, Ripley initiated the Contributions in Social Science series. The first issue was their jointly authored Cape Haze Peninsula report (1956). This series survived until 1973, several years after Ripley stepped down as chair.

In 1949, Adelaide is officially listed as associate in anthropology at the museum. In addition to accompanying Ripley on field trips, she continued to write on her earlier work, particularly on somatotyping (1952, 1953a) and a book-length treatment of fatigue (1956). Adelaide's paper entitled "Qualitative and Quantitative Theory as Applied to Body Build Research" won the Florida Academy of Sciences' Phipps-Bird Award for the best article published in 1953. These research interests were largely supplanted by the volume of work that Ripley's museum position produced and the need for analysis of skeletal remains. Adelaide provided osteological analysis and physical anthropological summaries for a number of projects, beginning with Caribbean remains (St. Thomas and St. John) in 1962 and the Goodman Mound (Florida) report in 1963. "Florida Indians of Past and Present: Why the Seminoles Survived," published in 1965, presents a comprehensive overview of Florida's native groups, with special emphasis on the Seminoles. This paper provided an archaeological and ethnohistorical contribution to a compendium of Florida history edited by Charlton W. Tebeau and Ruby L. Carson.

As Carol Mason (1992:97) has noted, Adelaide was one of a number of women researchers who labored on with little recognition. Sometimes, her contributions were unlisted in the Table of Contents. For example, in the Burtine Island report that Ripley published in 1966, he simply quoted her report within the narrative of his paper. Another Florida analysis appeared in 1973 as an appendix in *Excavations on Amelia Island in Northeast Florida* by E. Thomas Hemmings and Kathleen A. Deagan.

Perhaps Adelaide's most significant osteological analysis was her 1972 paper entitled "Paleoepidemiology and Distribution of Prehistoric Treponemiasis (Syphilis) in Florida." In this overview of the evidence of treponemal infection in prehistoric Florida, Adelaide concluded that treponemal disease was present as early as the Late Archaic (at the Tick Island Site, Volusia County) but was more pronounced in Weeden Island and continued into the European Contact. This paper is frequently cited (for example, in a recent overview of treponemal diseases in the New World by Rothschild and Rothschild [1996]).

In 1975, Adelaide officially declined to undertake further osteological analysis on indigenous skeletal remains. A cryptic note in her personnel file reads, "Yesterday afternoon Mrs. Bullen told me that, for reasons connected with Indian reaction to osteological studies, she has decided not to do any detailed analyses of the FSM collections. She will only do general observations connected with publication of wider scope than osteology. For that reason, she indicated her approval for me, students, or other qualified investigators to study any of our collections of human skeletal remains. Maples 1975."

This reaction seems very early to what, in the succeeding decade, became a full-blown problem for osteological studies. When I read this note, I considered it more a passing of the guard. William R. Maples, a physical anthropologist best known for his forensic work, had joined the museum staff. Ripley had retired as chair in 1969. After the death of his successor, William

R. Bullard, Jr., and the departure of E. Thomas Hemmings, Maples became department chair and the primary osteological researcher at the museum.

The Caribbean Area

As early as 1962, Ripley became actively engaged in archaeology in the Caribbean. Adelaide was also involved in this work, as she lists these localities as areas to which she traveled for "major projects" on her University of Florida Academic Staff Biographical Information Sheet in 1977. Beginning in 1962, the Bullens began to publish jointly authored papers related to the Caribbean: St. Thomas and St. John (Bullen, A. 1962b), Barbados (Bullen, A. and R. 1966a, 1968a), St. Martin (Bullen, A. and R. 1966b), Bahamas (Bullen, A. and R. 1966c), Grenada (Bullen, A. 1968; Bullen, A. and R. 1968; Bullen, R. and A. 1968), St. Lucia (Bullen, R. and A. 1968c; Bullen, A. and R. 1970; with Branford 1973), St. Vincent (Bullen, R. and A. 1972), Jamaica (Bullen, R. and A. 1974b), Trinidad (Bullen, R. and A. 1976c), Guadeloupe (Bullen, R. and A. 1973b), the Dominican Republic (Bullen, R. and A. 1973a), and Puerto Rico (Bullen, R. and A. 1974d). They also presented several general overviews drawn from their widespread experience in the region (1967, 1976a).

Their involvement in Caribbean archaeology was very extensive and supportive of local archaeologists (fig. 7.2). Ripley published numerous solo papers and a number of joint papers coauthored with individuals from the various islands where they worked (for example, Bullen, Bullen, and Branford 1973; and Bullen, Bullen, and Kirby 1973). As they had done in Massachusetts and Florida, the Bullens were founding members of the International Congress for the Study of Pre-Columbian Cultures of the Lesser Antilles founded in 1961. This congress meets every other year, usually on one of the island nations of the Caribbean. Adelaide and Ripley attended every meeting until his death in 1976. In 1977, the congress, dedicated to Ripley, met in Caracas, Venezuela. Adelaide worked devotedly to prepare Ripley's bibliography, which was published as a part of the *Proceedings of the Seventh International Congress for the Study of Pre-Columbian Cultures of the Lesser Antilles, 1977, Caracas.*

I have a copy of that bibliography. Attached to it is a card that reads, "With the compliments of Adelaide K. Bullen, Adjunct Curator of Anthropology." She graciously sent copies to colleagues, young and old. It is in this bibliography that I initially searched for an understanding of her contributions but found the going rough since she did not indicate those publications

Fig. 7.2. Adelaide and Ripley Bullen excavating at the Chancery Hill site, Barbados, 1966. (Photo courtesy of the Florida Museum of Natural History.)

for which she was senior author. The Adelaide Bullen that I remember was a striking, beautiful woman with a ready smile. She was unassuming and devoted to Ripley. She was always immaculately dressed. She had a very personal touch with students and colleagues. She was intensely private.

Within the pace of life, work, and publication of the many projects that the Bullens undertook, Adelaide continued her interests in physical anthropology. She served as editor for the physical anthropology sections of the *Handbook of Latin American Studies* published jointly by the Library of Congress and the University of Florida Press. These publications (1969, 1971) provided comprehensive overviews of current physical anthropology. Her last publications on fatigue and somatotyping occur as late as 1967 (1967a, 1967b), but it is clear that this work continued to be of more than passing interest to her. Her last public lecture, delivered in 1978 to a chapter of the Florida Anthropological Society, concerned her fatigue work.

Adelaide formed her own publication company, Kendall Books. She published Ripley's *A Guide to the Identification of Florida Projectile Points* in 1975. She also republished both "Black Lucy's Garden" and the "Bibliography of Ripley P. Bullen." Adelaide listed poetry and juvenile fiction as interests on her University of Florida biographical information form in 1977. In 1975, she published her own juvenile fiction in *Jim Tall and Count Small*. This book recounts the relationship of two circus performers, a tall man and a midget. It seems to be built on her interests in body types but addresses loyalty and friendship in the face of difficult circumstances. She was a member of the Authors League of America, the Authors Guild, National League of Pen Women, and the National Society of Literature and the Arts. She was a lifelong Episcopalian.

Adelaide Bullen was a Fellow of the American Anthropological Association and the Royal Anthropological Institute of Great Britain and Ireland. She was a member of the American Association of Physical Anthropologists and the Society for Applied Anthropology. She listed the Society for Research in Child Development and the World Federation for Mental Health as organizations in which she held memberships. She was also a member of the Florida Academy of Sciences and had been elected to Sigma Xi, the interdisciplinary scientific honorary.

After Ripley's death and after she completed his bibliography, Adelaide continued her curatorial responsibilities at the museum. In 1977, she was listed as adjunct curator of anthropology. Kenneth S. Bullen (no relation to Ripley), a volunteer in the museum, was assigned to assist her. Several years after Ripley's death, she married Kenneth Bullen. In failing health for several years, she died at her home in Gainesville on May 17, 1987.

As a young girl, I read the accounts of southwestern archaeology written by Ann Axtell Morris (1933). My impression of them now is that I was vaguely offended by her inclusion in the field parties as an extension of her husband's interests. I did not want to think that I, as a female, had to marry an archaeologist to gain access to the field. I had not thought about Morris for more than thirty-five years until I came to consider the life achievements of Adelaide Bullen.

Today, it would be easy to dismiss Adelaide Bullen as a woman who subordinated her career to that of her husband's, since it does seem reasonable to conclude that her involvement in archaeology was a direct result of her husband's pursuit of an archaeological career. Her position at the museum was totally voluntary for almost thirty years—she was never salaried. But a superficial dismissal would deny her the serious consideration she richly deserves and lessen the importance of the work she accomplished and the lives she touched. It would be far more fitting to see her as a full partner in a productive relationship that lasted a lifetime.

Bibliography of Adelaide Kendall Bullen

Bullen, Adelaide K.

1945a   A Cross-Cultural Approach to the Problem of Stuttering. *Child Development* 16(1–2):1–88.

1945b   Transcript of a course on *Music in Industry* at the Institute of Musical Art of the Juilliard School of Music, pp. 93–94, 96, 98–103. American Society of Composers, Authors, and Publishers, New York (mimeographed).

1947   Archaeological Theory and Anthropological Fact. *American Antiquity* 13:128–34.

1948   Vocational Incidence of Seven Body Types in 567 U.S. Army Women. Prepared for Military Planning Division, Office of the Quartermaster General, under contract W44–109-qm-1078, Project No. 64-02-01, work Phase 5, Department of Anthropology, Harvard University, Cambridge (mimeographed).

1952   Some Problems in the Practical Application of Somatotyping. *Florida Anthropologist* 5:17–20.

1953a   Qualitative and Quantitative Theory as Applied to Body Build Research. *Quarterly Journal of the Florida Academy of Sciences* 16(1):35–64.

1953b   Introduction to papers from "The Development of High Civilizations in Hot Climates Symposium." *Florida Anthropologist* 6(4):101–102.

1956   *New Answers to the Fatigue Problem.* University of Florida Press, Gainesville.

1962a   Comments on the Aging Population of Florida. In *Aging in a Changing Society,* pp. 158–60. Eleventh Annual Southern Conference on Gerontology. University of Florida Press, Gainesville.

1962b   Report of Skeletal Findings. In *Ceramic Periods of St. Thomas and St. John Islands, Virgin Islands.* The William L. Bryant Foundation, *American Studies* 4:25–27.

1963   Physical Anthropology of the Goodman Mound, McCormack Site, Duval County, Florida. *Contributions of the Florida State Museum, Social Sciences* 10:61–70.

1965   Florida Indians of Past and Present. In *Florida from Indian Trail to Space Age,* vol. 1, edited by Charlton W. Tebeau and Ruby L Carson, pp. 317–50. Southern Publishing Company, Holly Hill, Florida.

1966   Report on Skeletal Findings. In Burtine Island, Citrus County, Florida. *Contributions of the Florida State Museum, Social Sciences* 14:11–12.

1967a   Human Variation in Industry. *VII Congrès International des Sciences Anthropologiques et Ethnologiques Moscou* 2:66–74. Hayka, Moscow. 1964 Conference.

1967b   Individual Variation in Nervous and Mental Fatigue on the Job. *Cinquième Congrès Caraïbe pour la Santé Mentale,* 1965, pp. 104–11. Fort-de-France, Martinique.

1968   Field comments on the skull excavated in 1967 at Caliviny Island, Grenada, W.I. *Proceedings of the Second International Congress for the Study of Pre-Columbian Cultures of the Lesser Antilles,* pp. 44–45. Barbados.

1970   Case Study of an Amerindian Burial with Grave Goods from Grand Anse, St. Lucia. *Proceedings of the Third International Congress for the Study of Pre-Columbian Cultures of the Lesser Antilles, 1969,* pp. 45–60. Granada.

1972   Paleoepidemiology and Distribution of Prehistoric Treponemiasis (Syphillis) in Florida. *Florida Anthropologist* 25(4):133–74.

1973   Some Human Skeletal Remains from Amelia Island, Florida. In Excavations on Amelia Island in Northeast Florida, by E. Thomas Hemmings and Kathleen A. Deagan. *Contributions of the Florida State Museum: Anthropology and History* 18:72–87.

1975   *Jim Tall and Count Small.* Kendall Books, Gainesville.

1977   Biographical Information Sheet for Adelaide Kendall Bullen (dated May 16, 1977). Ms. on file, Personnel files, Ford Library, Florida Museum of Natural History.

1978   Bibliography of Ripley P. Bullen. *Proceedings of the Seventh International Congress for the Study of Pre-Columbian Cultures of the Lesser Antilles, 1977,* pp. 11–25. Caracas.

Bullen, Adelaide K., contributing editor

1969   Physical Anthropology. In *Handbook of Latin American Studies* 31:179–98. Library of Congress, University of Florida Press, Gainesville.

1971   Physical Anthropology. In *Handbook of Latin American Studies* 33:166–83. Library of Congress, University of Florida Press, Gainesville.

Bullen, Adelaide K., and Ripley P. Bullen

1942   A Pueblo Cave at Tres Piedras, New Mexico. *American Antiquity* 8:57–64.

1945   Black Lucy's Garden. *Bulletin of the Massachusetts Archaeological Society* 6(2):17–28.

1946   Two Burials at Tiverton, Rhode Island. *Bulletin of the Massachusetts Archaeological Society* 8:5–6.

1950   The Johns Island Site, Hernando County, Florida. *American Antiquity* 16:23–45.

1953   The Battery Point Site, Bayport, Hernando County, Florida. *Florida Anthropologist* 6:85–92.

1954   Further Notes on the Battery Point Site, Bayport, Hernando County, Florida. *Florida Anthropologist* 7:103–8.

1961a   The Summer Haven Site, St. Johns County, Florida. *Florida Anthropologist* 14(1–2):69–73.

1961b   Wash Island in Crystal River. *Florida Anthropologist* 14:69–73.

1963a   The Lemon Bay School Mound. *Florida Anthropologist* 16:51–56.

1963b   The Wash Island Site, Crystal River, Florida. *Florida Anthropologist* 16:81–92.

1966a   Barbados, a Carib Centre. *The Bajan and South Caribbean* 155:20–22. Bridgetown.

1966b   Three Indian Sites of St. Martin. *Nieuwe West-Indische Gids* 45(2–3):137–44.

1966c   The Early Peoples of the Bahamas. Report of the First Bahamas Conference on Archaeology, p. 19. San Salvador. Sponsored by the Center for Latin American Studies, University of Florida. New Haven (mimeographed).

1968   Salvage Archaeology at Caliviny Island, Grenada: A Problem in Typology. *Proceedings of the Second International Congress for the Study of Pre-Columbian Cultures of the Lesser Antilles, 1967,* pp. 31–43.

1970   The Lavoutte Site, St. Lucia: A Carib Ceremonial Center. *Proceedings of the Third International Congress for the Study of Pre-Columbian Cultures of the Lesser Antilles, Grenada, 1969*, pp. 61–86.

Bullen, Adelaide K., Ripley P. Bullen, and Eric M. Branford

1973   The Giraudy Site, Beane Field, St. Lucia. *Proceedings of the Fourth International Congress for the Study of Pre-Columbian Cultures of the Lesser Antilles*, pp. 197–98. St. Lucia.

Bullen, Adelaide K., and Harriet L. Hardy

1946   Analysis of Body Build Photographs of 175 College Women. *American Journal of Physical Anthropology* 4:37–68.

Bullen, Ripley P., and Adelaide K. Bullen

1956   Excavations on Cape Haze Peninsula, Florida. *Contributions of the Florida State Museum, Social Sciences* 1.

1967   Archaeology of the Lesser Antilles. *The Bajan and South Caribbean* 169:16–18. Bridgetown, Barbados.

1968a   Barbados Archaeology: 1966. *Proceedings of the Second International Congress for the Study of Pre-Columbian Cultures of the Lesser Antilles, 1967*, pp. 134–44.

1968b   Salvage Archaeology at Caliviny Island, Grenada: A Problem in Typology. *Proceedings of the Second International Congress for the Study of Pre-Columbian Cultures of the Lesser Antilles, 1967*, pp. 31–43.

1968c   Two Stratigraphic Tests at the Grand Anse Site, St. Lucia. In *The Amerindians in St. Lucia*, edited by C. Jesse, pp. 21–41. St. Lucia Archaeological and Historical Society.

1972   Archaeological Investigations on St. Vincent and the Grenadines, West Indies. The William L. Bryant Foundation, *American Studies* 8.

1973a   Settlement Pattern and Environment in Pre-Columbian Eastern Dominican Republic. *Boletin del Museo del Hombre Dominicano* 3:315–24.

1973b   Stratigraphic Tests at Two Sites on Guadeloupe. *Proceedings of the Fourth International Congress for the Study of Pre-Columbian Cultures of the Lesser Antilles, St. Lucia, 1971*, pp. 192–96.

1974a   Further Notes on the West Bay Site. *Florida Anthropologist* 27:119.

1974b   Inferences from Cultural Diffusion to Tower Hill, Jamaica, and Cupernoy, St. Martin. *Proceedings of the Fifth International Congress for the Study of Pre-Columbian Cultures of the Lesser Antilles, Antigua, 1973*, pp. 48–60.

1974c   Stone Mortars in Florida. *Florida Anthropologist* 27:169–70.

1974d   Tests at Hacienda Grande, Puerto Rico. *Fundacion Arqueologica, Antropologicae Historia de Puerto Rico, Boletin Informativo (Edicion Especial)* 1:1–6.

1976a   Culture Areas and Climaxes in Antillean Prehistory. *Proceedings of the Sixth International Congress for the Study of Pre-Columbian Cultures of the Lesser Antilles, Guadeloupe, 1975*, pp. 1–10.

1976b   The Palmer Site. *Florida Anthropological Society Publication* 8.

1976c   Three Stratigraphic Tests along the Eastern Shore of Trinidad. *Proceedings of the Sixth International Congress for the Study of Pre-Columbian Cultures of the Lesser Antilles, Guadeloupe, 1975*, pp. 28–34.

Bullen, Ripley P., Adelaide K. Bullen, and William J. Bryant
1967   Archaeological Investigations at the Ross Hammock Site, Florida. The William L. Bryant Foundation, *American Studies* 7.
Bullen, Ripley P. Adelaide K. Bullen, and Carl J. Clausen
1968   The Cato Site Near Sebastian Inlet, Florida. *Florida Anthropologist* 21:14–16.
Bullen, Ripley P., Adelaide K. Bullen, and I. A. Earle Kirby
1973   Dating the Troumassee Decorated Cylinder: A Horizon Style. *Proceedings of the Fourth International Congress for the Study of Pre-Columbian Cultures of the Lesser Antilles, St. Lucia, 1971*, pp. 197–98.

8

Yulee W. Lazarus

From Avocational to Professional in Northwest Florida

NANCY MARIE WHITE

When asked if she thinks women contribute something special to archaeology, Yulee Lazarus says yes, women have a different sense of appreciation for the artifacts and their origin and use, and a more personal application to the work. She also thinks women recognize better the need for a sense of humor. She says, "Only a woman (not I!) would glue an eggshell back together for a better view; call herself 'Hale Smith's dishwasher' as she washed and marked sherds; refuse to reach into a bag of sherds for fear of bugs (!); recognize a g-string on a clay figurine; and appreciate that the potter must have been left-handed judging by the direction of the scroll design."

Another of the women noted yearly in the Southeastern Archaeological Conference bulletins, Yulee was an avocational who became a professional museum director; her name is synonymous with archaeology in the Florida panhandle. She does not have a professional degree in archaeology but earned an A.B. in history in 1936 from Florida State College for Women (later Florida State University [FSU]). Her career track is notable today for

the modern goals of research combined with public archaeology. Yulee retired in 1985 but continued research and writing. Her story is a fascinating
one, set in a region of the South with a rich archaeological record.

Entrance into Archaeology

Yulee Way was born in Orlando in 1914, and she remembers early interests
in Florida history, especially regarding family connections to David Yulee,
Florida's first senator (in 1845; Tebeau 1971:172–73). She was encouraged by
family friend Fred Hanna, a historian at Rollins College in nearby Winter
Park. At FSU she took a course in Florida history and research techniques
taught by Katheryn Abbey, who later married Fred Hanna. The course was
useful later for archaeology. (Fred Hanna was still teaching in 1948–52 when
Hester Davis attended Rollins College; see chapter 10.) In 1935 Yulee met
William Lazarus on a blind date. He was an aeronautical engineer from Pennsylvania and, at that time, assistant manager of the Orlando municipal airport.
Right out of college in 1936 she married Bill and her career became "that of
a wife!" (fig. 8.1). They moved around in association with the military, and
they had two children (son Martin is deceased and daughter Suzan Cameron
now lives near Tampa). Yulee's entrance into the world of archaeology came

Fig. 8.1. Yulee and Bill
Lazarus, 1946, at home
in Orlando, Florida.
(Photo courtesy of Yulee
Lazarus.)

Fig. 8.2. William C. Lazarus, aeronautical engineer and notable avocational archaeologist, early 1960s. (Photo courtesy of the Temple Mound Museum, Fort Walton Beach, Florida.)

when she was planting grass in the yard of a new house. She and Bill had moved in 1953 from Ohio to Fort Walton Beach's Eglin Air Force Base, where he had switched from the military to civil service. They bought a home on Choctawhatchee Bay, close to the Gulf of Mexico, on a prehistoric site. Their inquiry at FSU about the sherds they had dug up was answered by Charles Fairbanks and Hale Smith, who were, she says, delighted that someone in the panhandle was interested.

No professional archaeologist had worked in northwest Florida since Gordon Willey (1949). Fairbanks and Smith became good friends, Yulee says, and "opened the door for us to have a new life. They had despaired of help in the prehistory of this area of Florida until we turned up!" They grabbed her husband immediately and she "went along for the ride." Since she had been a history major, Bill said, "you like old things; well, this is very old!" Bill, as a civilian consultant and later chief scientist at the Air Force Base, worked on advances in aviation, Yulee says, but on weekends they went back in time (fig. 8.2). The local community thought they must be looking for gold, since nothing else could be of much value, but they persisted, recovering artifact materials and data and building up local interest as they worked with the professionals.

Fairbanks came 150 miles from Tallahassee to teach a night anthropology class in this small city, brought in by a local arts group, and also to observe the Lazaruses' fieldwork. By 1958, they were excavating at the famous Middle Woodland Buck Mound (8Ok11; Moore 1901:435; Lazarus 1979a). It was important that professionals verify that a particularly noteworthy prehistoric ceramic vessel originated at this site and was not brought in by Bill and Yulee from Central America, as they had been accused. This unusual Weeden Island polychrome vessel was broken at the time of deposit, and all the body pieces of the human effigy were recovered. The face was not found until a later excavation season (1966, a year after Bill's death), farther down the slope of the mound, the whole vessel possibly having been dashed to the ground in some ceremony and the pieces having flown in many directions. The Lazaruses' salvage operations revealed Buck Mound to have a shell walkway around it, a small plastered truncated cone feature, evidence of a structure, and a ceremonial dog burial, as well as human burials, mostly cremations, and elaborate mortuary pots and figurines. The famous pot, which Fairbanks called a funerary urn, is now restored and well known throughout the Southeast. It is painted red, black, buff, and white and shaped like a hunchbacked, topknotted, possibly sneering person who appears to be sitting on a two-legged stool. It has been widely published (for example, Dickens 1982:28, 58) and has traveled to many exhibitions; its latest representation graces the cover of the most recent synthesis of Florida archaeology (Milanich 1994).

Yulee helped Bill publish their findings (for example, Lazarus, W. 1961, 1962, 1964, 1965), and they set up a temporary museum in a little local real estate office converted to new use. Exhibits and operation were by an all-volunteer group, including the local Arts and Design Society. During the summer of 1960, Fairbanks was in Fort Walton Beach conducting excavations with the Lazaruses at the famous Fort Walton Temple Mound, 8Ok6. At this time the Chamber of Commerce was having their usual pirate show for tourists, and he suggested that they make a model from a bona fide pirate ship. He helped Yulee with the research, referred her to the state of Mississippi archives, and translated the Spanish reports she found of true pirate activities. The Chamber still uses the model of the *William Augustus Bowles*.

The Lazaruses gave presentations at both popular and professional meetings. Bill called them "dog and pony shows"; for example, at the 1963 Florida Anthropological Society meeting, he spoke while she operated both the slide and movie projectors. They encouraged Hale Smith to meet with city officials on the idea of a public museum. Smith also reviewed artifacts and exhibit design, and, as Yulee says, "he even read my history booklet in his office to advise me (more likely the only way to get me out of the way!)." Local people helped with the museum, but Yulee thinks nothing would have been accomplished without Fairbanks, Smith, and other professionals, who even "scrounged parts and pieces toward exhibits," repairing or redesigning them when necessary.

The Fort Walton Temple Mound Museum

Yulee regards her greatest accomplishments as carrying on with Buck Mound after her husband's death and publishing the report on it (Lazarus 1979a), as well as a volume on pottery of the Fort Walton period (Lazarus and Hawkins 1976) and other works, and of course the completion of the Fort Walton Temple Mound Museum, which opened in June 1972. It stands on U.S. Highway 98, not far from bars and airbrush T-shirt shops, adjacent to the temple mound itself, a short distance from the sea. Yulee credits Bill with the original idea and enthusiasm, though it is hard to picture her ever lacking in enthusiasm herself. The presence of the military base provided a well-educated local population perhaps atypical of the rural deep South. People were therefore receptive to the idea of a larger, formal museum. In addition it would be good for the tourist-centered economy of this part of the Gulf Coast. The Fort Walton Temple Mound is the closest to the water of any in northwest Florida; the seafood economy of prehistoric Florida peoples was easy for modern residents or tourists to appreciate.

The city of Fort Walton Beach had evolved from a small Confederate camp and fishing village to a bootleg liquor and gambling area during the prohibition era (Al Capone was said to have laundered money there often). It was an important region during World War II, when it boasted the largest U.S. Air Force Base in the world (Eglin) and other military installations. Such a population continued to enjoy the various and notorious recreational activities, though gambling was shut down in the 1950s. In the postwar (and pre–Disney World) decades, the city became the center of the "Playground Area" of northwest Florida. A building boom in housing and hotels increased both tourist business and the resident population, including the continued huge military presence and many retired military personnel unwilling to give up the mild climate and outdoor recreation (Jahoda 1967). However, it was recognized by 1960 that the greatest threat to the local economy was world peace and disarmament (!), and so other development avenues such as recreation and tourism had to be targeted (Hutchinson

1961). Thus the museum fit nicely into the general view of regional planners. It remains one of only a few owned and operated by a city, as well as one of the best small museums in the country.

The museum project instigated greater interaction among professionals and community members, who put in many hours of labor on the building. Even the architect was awarded a plaque from the American Institute of Architects in 1970 for design. The *New York Times* noted that the "Temple Mound Museum, although small in size, makes up for this in the importance of its archaeological findings" (Wright 1967).

Bill Lazarus died of cancer in November 1965; Yulee was no longer just along for the ride; she had to start driving. She says, "This whole way of life for me has of course come by accident and has filled the void after [that] loss and given [me] drive [over the] years to accomplish something started and unfulfilled by Bill. To have so many people interested and helpful has proven worth the effort." Though some advised her to return to school for a Ph.D. in archaeology, she was more interested in finishing what had been begun, as a memorial to her husband but also as an accomplishment for herself. (Now she notes that she has been a widow longer than she was a wife or a single woman.) Thus she became a professional.

The city of Fort Walton Beach hired Yulee in 1968 as director of the museum (fig. 8.3). She had to learn quickly what a museum did. The intent to have a tourist attraction with class, tied to the prehistoric mound site, quickly made it the most highly rated institution in the city. From a population of 96 people in 1940, the city was growing immensely (reaching more than 21,000 by 1990, with a projection of over 170,000 for all of Okaloosa County by 2000). Especially because of the military and scientific presence, the county ranked near the top in Florida for most college graduates. The city stationery Yulee used describes Fort Walton Beach as "the home of the Sonic Boom" and "Northwest Florida's playground on the Gulf of Mexico and the Heart of the Miracle Strip." The Miracle Strip is a portion of U.S. Highway 98 that runs along the Gulf Coast from Apalachicola through Panama City and west to Pensacola. The especially touristy portion has earned the designation as a "redneck riviera," complete with tacky miniature golf courses featuring thirty-foot-high plastic pirates and dinosaurs, a mini shopping mall inside a fabricated stone mountain, a giant pirate ship-type building on the water enclosing restaurants and stores, and, away from all this, the white-sugar sand beaches that are among the most beautiful in the world. While much of this was being built, Yulee made sure that the triangle of land surrounding the temple mound at the east end of town was

Fig. 8.3. Yulee W. Lazarus and Fort Walton period (Mississippian) pottery vessels, early 1970s. (Photo courtesy of the Temple Mound Museum, Fort Walton Beach, Florida.)

developed with a bit more sophistication for archaeological (or what we would call today heritage) tourism.

Northwest Florida has a rich prehistoric record (Willey 1949). The Fort Walton Temple Mound (Fairbanks 1965; Lazarus and Fornaro 1975; Lazarus and Hawkins 1976) became the type site for the local variant of Mississippian culture (late prehistoric chiefdoms) here. (Ironically, as with other archaeological constructs, later research has proven the inaccuracy of this choice; the site is at the western edge of Fort Walton site distribution and is apparently characterized by more typical Mississippian shell-tempered pottery labeled under the heading "Pensacola culture," while the pottery of the Fort Walton archaeological "culture" is mostly grit-tempered [White 1982].) The Fort Walton Temple Mound was recognized as an Indian site but rather neglected, except for one curious attention: it had a little cottage on top of it and some entrepreneurs had put up a sheet and shown the first movies in town on this makeshift screen. The documents show that a lengthy correspondence with politicians and government bureaucrats was required to convert the slum neighborhood around the mound into an attractive city facility under the U.S. Housing and Urban Development's Neighborhood Development Program. Community support was always there for Yulee; two local real estate agents even cared enough to buy the east side of the mound base and preserve it until the federal and state grants aided the city to complete the purchase of the total area.

The mound now has concrete steps over its ramp, descending southward toward the highway (fig. 8.4). There is a reconstructed "temple" on its summit with large, painted wooden birds on the roof and freestanding displays inside (fig. 8.5). The temple building was one of Yulee's last projects there and she describes it as pure joy. So many people had said, well, if there was a building on top of the mound, what was it like? It had to be built. The mound summit was prepared first with heavy equipment. Some archaeologists feared damage to important deposits, but mostly horse and cow bones were unearthed. Later cuts into the mound slope uncovered a screen door but also evidence of Early Woodland Deptford occupation (possibly even a mound) beneath the late prehistoric temple mound (Lazarus and Fornaro 1975).

Fig. 8.4. Fort Walton Temple Mound in the 1970s, on U.S. Highway 98, with concrete steps and ramp, shell and concrete pillars along the sidewalk, before reconstruction of temple on top. Museum is adjacent on the right (out of the picture). (Photo by Nancy White.)

Fig. 8.5. Reconstructed temple building on top of Fort Walton Temple Mound. (Photo courtesy of the Temple Mound Museum, Fort Walton Beach, Florida.)

Much of the fun of this project was in seeing how much other professionals will do for archaeology after they get involved and fascinated with it. For example, over the open log walls the temple roof is of cement but treated carefully with muted black, yellow, and brown, and striations to look like thatch. The architect was proud of his design. Visiting archaeologists thought it was great; Yulee quotes Stu Neitzel (of Mississippi) as saying it was the best idea he ever saw, and with a permanent roof such as this, who would want true thatch?! The carved wooden birds were done by a local man who worked from ceramic rim effigies and historical references. Yaupon holly bushes (used to make the famous southeastern Indian "black drink") complement the oak, cedar, and pecan trees on top and around the mound and museum.

On the east side of the mound, at the base of another staircase leading down from the summit, is the elegant museum building. Its external walls have modeled motifs from various prehistoric ceramics. Yulee worked to make it highly scientific yet accessible. Exhibits proceed in chronological order by archaeological culture. The Weeden Island segment includes a separate case for the famous polychrome mortuary urn (fig. 8.6), and there are many other noteworthy ceramics. The remarkable Early Woodland (Alexander or Deptford) bowl from a site on the beach (Lazarus, W. 1965:95, figure 6) has unusually large tetrapods and a net-marked band around the top that stretches in one place and contracts in another; this can be seen because time was spent piecing it back together, even though, as Yulee mentions, William Sears said it would never occur to him to glue it back together since it was just a pot. Other artifacts include stone tools, shell beads, and unusual items such as a small ceramic paddle for treating the surfaces of Middle Woodland pottery, displayed on a rotating stand to show its complicated-stamped design on one side and check-stamped pattern on the other.

There are replica and modern equivalents of ancient foods, pigments, and other natural products; a real prehistoric canoe; a diorama of a stickball game. The Buck Mound dog burial is displayed as it was removed in situ (and identified and analyzed at Harvard by zooarchaeologist Barbara Lawrence). A wall is adorned with brightly colored paintings replicating Swift Creek Complicated-Stamped paddle designs from Middle Woodland pots. Hands-on displays at a touch "table" give kids and others the opportunity to grind corn or push a pump drill up and down, and replicas of such artifacts can be purchased at the gift shop. Yulee and her helpers recognized the benefits of close contact with museum materials and appealing to youngsters long before such ideas became important in museum philosophy and design. One exhibit even showed colorful plastic diggers and shovels on top a tiny temple mound (fig. 8.7).

Fig. 8.6. Yulee Lazarus, retired director, in the Temple Mound Museum, Fort Walton Beach, Florida, 1997, with display of the famous mortuary "urn" from Buck Mound. (Photo by Nancy White.)

Fig. 8.7. Exhibit showing representation of temple mound excavations in the Temple Mound Museum, Fort Walton Beach, Florida, in the 1970s. Tiny plastic figures shovel soil into a screen, and a miniature notebook lies open on the ground. (Photo by Nancy White.)

The extensive collections at the Temple Mound Museum are utilized by many thesis writers, contract archaeologists, and other researchers. Even twenty years ago (when the gift shop at Moundville, Alabama, sold real projectile points), the wonderful gift shop offered everything: academic books and monographs, miniature reproductions of prehistoric Florida pots by local artisans, and Mexican and Central American Indian crafts. Yulee took "busman's holidays" in Central and South America to gather modern native craft items for sale and to interact with other archaeologists and museum people. She also went on American Museum Association summer tours in Europe.

Research and Public Archaeology

While running the museum Yulee continued to conduct research, publishing in the *Florida Anthropologist* and elsewhere, writing historic works for local and museum audiences. She estimates she has worked at some one hundred archaeological sites herself. She built up the museum's research collections and continued to catalog donated materials, examine and monitor newly uncovered sites, and seek professional collaboration to interpret new finds. A correspondence file archived at the Florida Museum of Natural History (at that time the Florida State Museum) shows her ongoing interaction with the state's archaeologists (I am grateful to Jerald Milanich for locating this file). Letters to and from Ripley Bullen, the department of social science chair and editor of the *Florida Anthropologist* for a time, show she supplied specimens for documentation in his Florida projectile point guide (Bullen 1975). Many times she sent artifacts to Gainesville for better identification, and Bullen returned them with comments. There is an interesting sequence of correspondence as she requested advice in trying to document some monetary value for the exhibits and especially the polychrome urn, unique and priceless but requiring evaluation for insurance purposes. The quandaries evolved further as she tried to deal with the problems of donors wanting tax write-offs for their artifacts, and wanting to know if artifacts appreciate over time.

She was involved constantly with the public, in many ways. One was a booklet she wrote called *Indians of the Florida Panhandle* (1968). With this project Yulee remembers well the important experience of balancing the intended audience, the archaeological scholarship, and the support sources. A citizen member of her own museum board told her to make the booklet sexier and give the woman on the cover holding the pot more figure and less clothing!

Dealing with the public has its down sides, but a constant positive emphasis for Yulee and her staff was the value of getting children involved. The superintendent of schools agreed to place a teacher for three years to develop an education department, which first hired a graduate in museum training from Cooperstown, New York, and then two local teachers who had been trained in archaeology and museum tours. The latter, Anne Dilworth (Weihe) and Joyce Nunnery, have been faithful museum workers ever since (Lazarus 1990). These teachers went to the elementary and secondary schools with portable cases of artifacts.

Yulee also got lawbreakers involved when selected inmates from a nearby prison helped with museum projects. One was the most avid excavator she ever saw, learning quickly to shave straight walls and perfect corners. Yulee and Joyce allowed him the privilege of driving Joyce's classic Thunderbird upon occasion (which was probably strictly forbidden; transporting stolen vehicles across state lines had been his undoing!). When the project was finished he kept calling to see when he could be allowed out to dig again, but there were not more opportunities. Yulee does not know what direction his life took when he left prison but wonders if he went on to be a professional (archaeologist, that is).

Doing urban archaeology in a small but busy, growing city involved Yulee in other projects impossible to divorce from public participation. When highway officials wanted to widen U.S. 98 in front of the mound, in the late 1960s, heavy equipment cut into undisturbed shell midden, and the outcry from the museum was rapid. Since this occurred just before Labor Day weekend, the archaeologists were given four days to salvage whatever was possible, and the construction crew even lifted off the sidewalk for better accessibility. On both sides of the road was the original shell heap from the first prehistoric camps on this shore, dating to long before the building of the mound (not to mention the beachwear/souvenir shops). Santa Rosa/Swift Creek pottery and other prehistoric cultural evidence was recovered. This being the last prime tourist weekend of summer, the traffic was heavy. Yulee remembers the eerie feeling of being in a big hole with cars whizzing by just beyond the edge, wondering if the excavation walls would hold and hearing tourists stop every so often to see what was going on. One can just visualize the scene (with haircuts and tacky bermuda shorts of typical 1960s tourists).

When the Florida Anthropological Society instituted an award in 1986 for accomplishments in archaeology by an avocational researcher and excellence in working with the public, they named it after Bill Lazarus; the first recipient of the Lazarus Award was Yulee (even though by then she was a professional). Her local fame continues to expand; in May 1995 she was featured on national television news on C-span. When originally contacted about being interviewed, she had just finished a project documenting the first thirty years of the history of the city's Chamber of Commerce (begun in 1946) through research on the accumulated minutes of their board meetings. She was eager to get to the next project, so immediately began writing her answers to the interview questions. (She says, "I never have wanted just to sit home and knit!") Later, she met with my field crews and me (fig. 8.8) during succeeding summers (1993 and 1995) for live/videotaped interviews and came up with directions to a new microbrewery in town for a group lunch. This establishment, just east of the former location of the Buck Mound, distributed to customers a "Brews and News" newspaper with stories of local history and prehistory, including a photo of the Buck Mound mortuary urn. When we visited Yulee in 1997 for another chat on top the temple mound, a local television news crew mysteriously showed up.

Friendly competition and surprise at an amateur's expertise usually characterized the attitude of male professionals toward her, Yulee thinks. She

Fig. 8.8. Yulee Lazarus, March 1996, standing in front of the shell-encrusted west facade of the Temple Mound Museum, Fort Walton Beach, Florida, wearing a University of South Florida public archaeology T-shirt, designed by Scott Mitchell. (Photo by Nancy White.)

does admit to an occasional negative reaction from a less educated man and sees some difference in the kinds of contributions women can make. She thinks women can better provide the early training and appreciation for archaeology that children need but notes that women are generally more accepted in a public role than as learned, scientific practitioners. She finds that artifacts have perhaps more appeal to women as craft and art, and that women in her audiences could appreciate prehistoric women having to make their own dishes! She wonders if a man would have the patience to glue together that eggshell, pieced together by an FSU coed on one of Fairbanks's historic digs in south Alabama. But she asserts that famous southeastern archaeologists were always cooperative and glad to have her interest. Of any disadvantages to being a woman, she says, "I'm sure there are some but I didn't really run into any." She advises students today not to be narrow in outlook but to get a broad background, especially in general anthropology, and as much experience as possible in all angles of archaeology.

Yulee Lazarus was a pioneer in an area that is now recognized as a requirement for all professionals: public archaeology. As noted elsewhere in this volume, we are just coming to the realization that all archaeology is public archaeology in one form or another (for example, McGimsey 1972; Smith and Ehrenhard 1991; the forthcoming proceedings of the 1995 Chacmool conference entitled "Public or Perish"; the recent Distinguished Lecture by Sabloff [1996] to the Archaeology Division of the American Anthropological Association; Jameson 1997; the Society for American Archaeology's

1998 workshop on enhancing training in public archaeology [Bender and Smith 1998]). Yulee needed to get everyone from local working-class fisherfolk and military types to business people and local politicians interested in the value and attraction of the human past, and she did it with extraordinary success.

Selected Bibliography of Yulee W. Lazarus

Lazarus, Yulee W.
1968   *Indians of the Florida Panhandle.* Temple Mound Museum, Fort Walton Beach, Florida.
1970   Salvage Archaeology at Fort Walton Beach. *Florida Anthropologist* 23:29–42.
1971   Clay Balls from Northwest Florida. *University of South Carolina Institute of Archaeology and Anthropology Notebook* 3:47–49.
1975   Another Ceramic Chungke from the Florida Panhandle. *Florida Anthropologist* 28:123–24.
1979a   *The Buck Burial Mound: A Mound of the Weeden Island Culture.* Temple Mound Museum, Fort Walton Beach, Florida.
1982   *The Fort Walton Temple Mound and Museum: History in Headlines.* Temple Mound Museum, Fort Walton Beach, Florida.
1985   A Temple Style Shelter on the Fort Walton Beach Temple Mound. In *Indians, Colonists and Slaves: Essays in Memory of Charles H. Fairbanks,* edited by K. W. Johnson, J. M. Leader, and R. C. Wilson, pp. 145–53. *Florida Journal of Anthropology,* Special Publication No. 4, Gainesville.
1986   The Indianola Inn Shell Midden Mound (8Ok6sm). *Florida Anthropologist* 39:253–56.
1987   The Case of the Face-Down Burial from Site 8By39, Bay County. *Florida Anthropologist* 430:321–27.
1989   Fort Walton Wonders: Four Odd Artifacts Found in the Florida Panhandle. *Florida Anthropologist* 42:158–62.
1990   The Temple Mound Museum, Remembering the First Twenty Years. *Florida Anthropologist* 43:116–25.
Lazarus, Yulee W., editor
1979b   Design Motifs and Comparison. Temple Mound Museum, Fort Walton Beach, Florida.
Lazarus, Yulee W., and Robert J. Fornaro
1975   Fort Walton Temple Mound: Further Test Excavations, DePaux 1973. *Florida Anthropologist* 28:159–77.
Lazarus, Yulee W., and Carolyn B. Hawkins
1976   *Pottery of the Fort Walton Period.* Temple Mound Museum, Fort Walton Beach, Florida.
Lazarus, Yulee, William C. Lazarus, and Donald W. Sharon
1967   The Navy Liveoak Reservation Cemetery Site, 8SR 36. *Florida Anthropologist* 20:103–17.

9

"This Ain't the English Department"

A Memoir of Becoming an Archaeologist in the 1950s at Florida State University

Carol I. Mason

The first problem I had when I arrived on campus that fall was finding the anthropology department. I had already told my friends and relations that the department at FSU was one of the most important on campus. After all, hadn't the chairman actually written to me two years before as I sailed out of high school declaring anthropology as a major? "Come to FSU" he had said on stationery that was wonderfully heavy, official, and full of attractive symbols. Even his signature, Hale G. Smith, sounded solid and dignified. Surely there was an Anthropology Hall to match: something centrally located, covered with ivy, nobly designed, and full of skeletons and potsherds. It certainly was not an obvious feature of the collegiate landscape as I wandered back and forth trying to arrive on time for my first appointment. After much asking and staring at useless campus maps, I was directed first towards geology—after all, I was told, doesn't anthropology have something to do with dinosaurs? And finally, patient and bored upperclassmen suggested that I check out the dining hall. The dining hall?

The Florida State University Anthropology Department

The large dining facility stood at right angles to Landis Green, that broad empty field in front of the dorm of the same name, and all the nearby women's dorms were connected in mysterious ways by stairways and corridors to that self-same dining hall. Very convenient for dinner, but where anthropology fitted in was anybody's guess. I went up the broad steps and into the darkish foyer—big dining halls opened to the left and to the right where subdued clatter made dreadful note of preparation for the next meal. Over all lingered that dim smell, anywhere recognizable as an olfactory patina from years of bad cooking and the death of many appetites. Straight ahead of me was another broad set of steps going upwards, stone steps leading eventually to an even broader, open landing facing windows directly over the entranceway below. This surely was the place: to the left was a set of doors leading to what seemed to be a small art gallery and an even smaller museum that was wrapped partially around it. And to the right ought to have been the anthropology department in a warren of offices and classrooms immediately above the dining halls. The right hand was in fact not anthropology at all but the immense and impressive school of hotel and restaurant management, a monument to the importance of the tourist industry to the state of Florida and a constant painful reminder of what really counted in university life. Ahead of me across the broad landing and contrasting with the opulence of the hotel and restaurant management entranceway, a narrow white door, a little weather-beaten or more precisely, student-worn, displayed "anthropology" in small letters. Yes, at last, the promised land, but it could not have been much of a promised land since it was flush against the front wall of the dining hall, and I could see Landis Green through the windows directly in front of me. No matter, I went through the door where a warning bell jangled above my head and narrow steps led up to the right. The steps themselves were reassuring with pieces of chunky statuary and odd tools and weapons displayed against the wall. Up and up I went, into what was the large loft over the dining hall, an attic that topped everything else and served as home to the anthropology department.

"One of the things you need to know about anthropology departments," intoned Hale G. Smith peering at me over his glasses, "is that they are always in the basement or the attic, one or the other." "It has to do with the expansion of the scope of science," he explained apologetically and hunched back over his desk.

Looking back on it, I cannot conceive an odder or more appropriate place for that distinctly odd and wonderful department. Perched high over the campus, it was disembodied, in a world of its own physically, and only tangentially tied to the common concerns of university life. In a real sense, it created its own environment, and its very shape and organization gave it an openness of communication within itself that allowed everyone to pool knowledge and experience. The attic did not even have offices. The large open space had been loosely subdivided: a secretary sat at her desk just inside the door; Hale Smith was behind her to the right in a chaos of papers, books, and artifacts with his desk facing inward, towards his attic. To the left and across from the secretary's desk was Charles H. Fairbanks, surrounded by bookcases, typewriter, files, and miscellany. Beyond in an untidy attempt at separating a small classroom space from work space with tall dividers were a large workroom with sinks, paint, lumber, and tools; the high drafting desk belonging to the artist-in-residence; storage facilities; and long tables. Open storage of box after box of artifacts lined the walls in shelves that reached all the way to the attic ceiling. It was not quite the cool lap of science that I had fallen into, but the atmosphere breathed of the life of anthropology, and that was heady stuff. I can remember seeing for what seemed like months the carcass of some bird spread out on one table waiting for someone to skin it. "Someone" never came, but the invitation was out to students and faculty alike to "do" what needed to be done in the common pursuit of knowledge.

The—to me—untidy department was the result of several administrative pulls: first, of course, it was home to the academic faculty and to the students who trailed up the stairs to the attic for small class instruction. Additionally, it was space for research, where artifacts could be laid on tables, collections analyzed, and the labor of anthropology carried out. Cleaning, cataloguing, map making, artifact reconstruction and stabilization—all of these things took place within the department, the left hand always knowing what the right hand was doing. Second, the department was also home to the museum staff, at that time an artist and a museum curator. They were somehow involved in the planning and execution of exhibits in the museums below, both the anthropology museum and the art gallery. Exhibits were often actually built in the department, and students became the pool of volunteer labor in much of the actual work. Deadline times when exhibits were to open often created a frantic feel to life in the anthropology department as everyone scurried about to make sure the university at large, should it ever appear at one of our rather intimate opening teas, would find everything ready. The crosscurrents of academic anthropology with both an anthropology museum and an art museum gave an enriched experience to undergraduates, whose feet were literally in both worlds.

How this particular department took shape, I do not know. It was still comparatively young when I was a student there, and much of its exuberance, personality, and character came full blown from the personality and character of Hale Smith. He was not quite what I expected from his letter of two years before: there was nothing remotely solid or imposing about him. A tall man, thin and even spidery, he was an original even within a profession that produced or attracted more than its fair share of originals. Highly unconventional, he faced life with a wry and self-deprecating humor, a developed sense of the ridiculous, and a low tolerance for the pompous, the self-righteous, or the fake. His approach was always low-key—unless, of course, someone did not do what was promised or needed to be done; in an open department, imaginative cursing at full voice could not be hidden. We undergraduates always wanted to know when and how he had one ear pierced and why he collected strange hats and why he had that odd predilection for horse jokes.

The other half of the department was Charles Fairbanks, with a fresh degree from Michigan and ready to make up for time lost in the ranks of the National Park Service. He immediately became the intellectual center of the department, attracting archaeology students and eventually even those anthropology majors who had given their allegiance to Robert Anderson, Fairbanks's predecessor and—from what I could tell—a most charismatic and inspiring teacher. Fairbanks himself was always an inspired teacher. Perhaps because he was new to the teaching profession, he was an enthusiastic professional from day one. If good teachers are created by themselves having been taught by good teachers, then Chicago and Michigan and perhaps even Swarthmore gave him the models for what he became. For us as undergraduates, he was always ready for discussion, ever ready with apt references, and a delight to talk to. He was quintessentially the scholar-model we wanted to become. And maybe because there were so few people around to talk anthropology with, he talked to us, neophytes as we were.

Undergraduate education is not often a favorite pastime at institutions with graduate departments: undergraduates are seldom on a footing with the graduate school elite and sit low on departmental horizons. In the 1950s, undergraduates were all there were except for a few master's candidates, a very few, seldom more than one at a time. Undergraduate majors were taken very seriously, and their education was the departmental business. I suppose deans were impressed by numbers of majors, and the department in self-interest had to cherish us. I like to think we were all in it together, students and faculty, participating in a calling, a profession that was an intellectual delight, endlessly stimulating through the questions it posed and the answers it proposed. It was a marketplace of ideas, and I cannot recall that period of intense intellectual excitement without great pleasure and special joy. It was like being Miranda in a world without Caliban.

The True Word of Anthropology

How students were educated was multilayered and quite complex. First, of course, were formal courses. Anthropology at FSU began with a two-semester sequence of cultural and physical anthropology; as an upperclassman transfer student, I took them both together. The physical anthropology, taught by Smith, was handicapped by a lack of really appropriate texts and an absence of any kind of teaching aids such as fossil casts or slides. We used Howell's *Mankind So Far,* witty and erudite, and were sent to Hooton's *Up from the Ape* and whatever else we could find in the anthropologically inadequate university library. Hale Smith was not the world's most exciting classroom teacher; I thought at the time that such a larger-than-life personality was uncomfortable, even shy, in front of a classroom of undergraduates. Fairbanks, the first edition of Beals and Hoijer in hand, was wonderful, capable of hopping on desks to demonstrate whirling a churinga and always ready to set a class at an intriguing problem and let it swing in the wind as it grappled with possible answers. Introductory anthropology was amazingly good fun. I hope the undergraduates of today have an equally lively time in those first anthropology classes, something I doubt, given the almost universally uninspiring texts and the currently dull state of anthropology.

We, of course, were all primed and ready to carry the true word of anthropology's comparative approach wherever it might do some good. Like Margaret Mead in her "It-isn't-so-in Bongo-Bongo" period, we tried to see how cross-cultural comparison might invalidate or support what universal generalizations other disciplines had to offer. Our most common victim was the poor sociology faculty, condemned to face intolerably self-righteous anthropology majors, convinced that we knew the path to truth. Smith sent us regularly to sociology courses: "you need to know the enemy," he declared in that flat, nasal midwestern accent that years in the Florida panhandle never even slightly modified. But in justice he pointed out to us that the sociologists now on campus, ancient relics though they seemed to us, had in fact made our way easier by being the first to feel the brunt of community anti-evolutionary criticism in the days before anthropology was more than a twinkle in the eye of the university. By facing the heat first, sociology made anthropology's discussion of human origins more matter-of-fact, reasonable, and less controversial.

With the exception of introductory courses, formal anthropology courses never drew vast numbers of students. Even area courses in North American ethnography were cozy sessions that met around one of the tables in the department. Students generally knew one another and arrived early and left late; occasionally an older special student was admitted, in my time a retired dentist, who took every course and whose broad experience and tart comments enlivened the discussions.

How courses entered the curriculum was mysterious. The catalog courses covered the standard anthropological four fields except for linguistics, which no one at all was qualified to teach. But beyond those standard courses was a gray area with "magic" numbers that allowed faculty to offer whatever courses seemed needed. We were all required to take introductory courses, area courses, history of anthropology, archaeology, and a more advanced physical anthropology. Some areas were well covered—North America and the Circum-Caribbean, which was of special interest to Smith and where he had actually done some ethnographic fieldwork. Fairbanks, however, was always concerned that our primary New World emphasis was limiting, and he was open to suggestions about other areas. He taught both African Ethnography and Peoples of Oceania, courses that certainly required him to work harder; we did not appreciate his labors then, convinced that he knew everything anyway, but in view of modern specialization, it was a remarkable tour de force. Undergraduate students—if they were paying attention—came out of FSU well prepared academically and singularly unsuited for graduate school, where a common misapprehension assumed that no southern institution, no matter how well-stocked with Michigan Ph.D.s, could possibly produce students who knew anything at all.

We were from the beginning educated to be anthropologists, apprenticed and encouraged to think of ourselves as potential professionals. Anthropology courses beyond the introductory level were aimed at broadening our backgrounds, giving us a grasp of the literature, and making sure we knew how to find out what we needed to know. We were being prepared for the likes of Michigan or Berkeley or Pennsylvania. We were familiar with the faculties at graduate institutions, knew who was where and who was who.

For example, when I first went to national meetings as an undergraduate, I did not need to be told who George Peter Murdock was or what he had accomplished when I found myself sharing an elevator filled with illustrious name tags. I had even read in *Social Structure* and worried over the boundaries of African culture areas and hoped some Murdockian mana might fall on me just for having been in that elevator. I can remember being introduced to Cora du Bois and Margaret Mead, long before the latter took to pink pantsuits and a staff of prophet-like dimensions. Once I even had dinner with A. L. Kroeber—well, we were actually *in* the same dining room at the same time, and that almost qualifies as an intimate brush with greatness. I found it curious when I went to graduate school that few of my fellow students "knew" the profession, and I did not think it odd at all that at least some faculty there did yeoman work in pushing the graduate student cadre into learning who the professionals were, at least in the areas of their immediate concern. I had already been through that phase of the game: FSU undergraduates were treated as professionals *en esse*, fledglings aiming at becoming part of the flock, and no one seemed to doubt that we would go to graduate school, earn degrees, and take our places as members of the guild.

Since I was hoping to become an archaeologist, I spent time learning who was who in archaeology. Fairbanks and Smith took pains to push me in the right direction. My first presentation at a professional meeting was a brief report on a small site whose pottery was peculiar and worth drawing to the attention of people outside Florida. I gave my report at the Southeastern Archaeological Conference at Ocmulgee, where the whole membership met in a single room in the basement; and I faced Griffin, Ford, Alex Krieger, and Tono Waring in the front row with dozens of archaeologists whose work I had read or had heard of lined up behind them. Even then I understood that anthropology was a social institution, and the more one understood how the networks ran and who peopled them, the sooner one might figure out how to operate within the system as a whole. In pursuit of this goal, I met people and matched accomplishments with faces and personalities. I suppose I was the only undergraduate who knew everyone's name, even including middle ones: it was James Bennett Griffin and Gordon Randolph Willey and John Mann Goggin.

No archaeologist, no matter how short his intended visit to the department, ever escaped without being offered hospitality at dinners or parties or given the opportunity to speak to classes. Neither Smith nor Fairbanks ever let a big fish get away. When Carl Guthe arrived unexpectedly on campus, probably on his way to a Florida vacation, word of his coming was passed to Smith as he was explaining manioc leaching to a class in Circum-Caribbean ethnography. His response was to leap up from the table and glare at his little circle. "Next to God Almighty," he muttered and rushed out. Before we could gather wits scattered by his departure, Carl Guthe was in the professorial chair, and we were miles away from manioc.

Local archaeologists were more frequent visitors. John Goggin from the University of Florida came through fairly regularly, and we sometimes combined our forces and did fieldwork together. There was always a bit of good-natured competition with the people from Gainesville, and we enjoyed our outings and the chance to mutually show off. Goggin himself was a charming man, glass eye and all, and he treated FSU undergraduates as serious participants in whatever intellectual pursuit was his current passion. When I was there, it was olive jars, Seminole pottery, and majolica. Underwater archaeology was to come later although he once involved the FSU department in surface collecting the bed of the Ichetucknee River for artifacts. As I recall, the exciting objects recovered from that expedition were fossilized alligator coprolites, conversation pieces of unlimited interest.

Fairbanks and Smith also felt that we needed to be exposed to points of view that were peculiar, to say the least. At that time in southern states, it was not unusual to meet people with extraordinary ideas about the biology of race, ideas that had become quaint or worse in biology but existed as living, breathing concepts in the minds of large numbers of people. One speaker, only a little to the left of Nott and Gliddon, talked to anthropology classes and provided astonishing insights into the thinking of parts of the community outside the university. Confronting such ideas and trying to mount counter-arguments against them was a valuable experience, particularly since we somehow thought that progress in biology had swept them away long ago. The living reality did in fact leave us shaken but taught us how to meet these ideas without becoming shrill with indignation and thus losing the advantage in argument.

Confronting ideas did not mean mounting battle against those who held them. Fairbanks and Smith taught us by example to meet the lunatic fringes clustered around the skirts of anthropology with courtesy and separate ideas from persons. It did not always work that way, but it was a standard that did not allow the easy path of dismissing unsavory opinions out of hand without being able to understand why these ideas were untenable. In the years to follow I had ample opportunity to practice what was preached, and I am grateful for having learned a little of how to educate and not alienate.

A considerable amount of learning at FSU occurred informally, either in the department itself or below in the dining halls. Being upstairs from the dining halls gave the anthropology staff and students a decided advantage in extracurricular communication. There was an almost perennially open snack area where soft drinks and empty calories were grudgingly supplied to all comers. We gathered around long tables in the shadow of a giant Coke machine, watching in disbelief as Fairbanks, building his formidable reputation as a consumer of Cokes, downed bottle after bottle. For reasons I cannot recall, the theater department seemed always to have representatives in the dining hall snack area, and we all crammed in around the same table and solved the mysteries of the universe from the perspectives of the humanities as well as the social sciences.

Informal learning was also a byproduct of the active departmental social life. Unlike my experience in graduate school, as an undergraduate I knew faculty on a social basis. Faculty wives and children were part of departmental life, and none of us shared the common belief among undergraduates that off-campus professors spent their time in earth-filled boxes in cellars. The department had a string of dinners and parties in faculty homes, outdoors, in the department itself, and in student homes. Excuses for socializing were endless, including even Leslie White's birthday, the day de Soto left the Tallahassee area, and, of course, in honor of visiting firemen. Armadillo roasting was not yet on the list. Once we had a surprise birthday party for Fairbanks, featuring a chocolate cake gorgeously decorated with weeping eyes, bilobed arrows, and eye-in-hand designs. Most often parties were simple affairs, more a time for socializing than a culinary or gustatory occasion. Among the most complex of these involved parching and preparing the leaves of the *Ilex* plant so that we might emulate our betters by drinking the black drink. Brewed mild with sugar and ice, it was a very acceptable tea. I was, of course, disappointed.

The department had a strong esprit de corps. I expect physical separation from the rest of the university helped nurture it as did the small size of the faculty, few majors, and a relatively small population of students who took anthropology courses. At the time, anthropology was under-funded, fostering a feeling that it was treated as less equal than other social sciences and creating a strong feeling of "us" versus "them." We majors were certainly different from other students in that we spent more time with each other than with friends, roommates, or other members of our graduating class. The majors were themselves a diverse group, ranging from married men and women with off-campus apartments to singles living in dorms on campus. No matter where we came from, our loyalty to the department was strong;

and we regarded ourselves as professionals, perhaps only on the first rung but certainly on our way up.

Fieldwork

Fieldwork was important. When Robert Anderson was on campus, students did ethnographic work in the Plains. One of our number had spent a summer with the Crow, learning something of the language and discovering to his astonishment how dependent modern Crow were on Robert Lowie's famous Crow ethnographies. In my time, with a department consisting of two archaeologists, both very active in their discipline, opportunities for archaeological fieldwork were many. Fairbanks, coming from a strong background in southeastern archaeology and a dissertation centered on the Mississippian occupation of the Macon Plateau, was feeling his way into the archaeology of Florida. He wanted to learn as much as he could; and his students became his henchmen, day laborers, and fellow tillers of the intellectual soil. Fairbanks and Smith spent weekend after weekend surveying sites, retracing Willey's footsteps in places like Wakulla County, and testing sites that had yet to be excavated. And we anthropology majors went along. I can remember that the worst possible tragedy was a Saturday morning of solid, steady rainfall when no work could be done at all, and Fairbanks's "Maxim No. 1" was invoked: "You can't do archaeology in the rain."

The department had its own truck, a strange paneled truck that memory recalls as being a hideous and impossible shade of maroon. At one time we lashed a cow skull to the radiator just to give it some distinction, but nothing could make it anything other than a rattletrap with a serious cough. It was spacious, though, capable of holding piles of equipment plus numbers of students sitting on the floor amid the field packs, shovels, and screening tables. It probably was World War II surplus and it probably was unsafe, but no one really cared. It was a magical vehicle that carried us into strange places to dig holes in the ground or survey sites from one end of the panhandle to the other.

The first fieldwork I was involved in at FSU was a weekend testing operation in a farm field near Lake Jackson, only a short distance from the actual Lake Jackson site. Why we were there or what we expected to find I do not recall, but I remember the bright fall day and the smell of earth as we went down in those pre-metric six-inch levels looking for "something." The only thing I remember finding in that hole was oyster shells, a peculiar thing in the middle of a farm field but unimportant to us since no artifacts or signs of human occupation accompanied them. However, it was a thrill to be actually "doing" archaeology under professional direction at last, even if the only comments I heard at the end of the afternoon were Smith's "okay, fill it up." This kind of testing, survey, and simply visiting sites had the effect of opening up for students a view of the landscape that was multilayered. Here was a farm field, but yesterday it had been something else; there was a subdivision, but once it had been a village of people whose voices were silent and whose presence was forgotten. Slowly, students acquired a feel for the past that made them responsible recoverers of what had happened in prehistory and spokesmen for ways of life now gone forever.

Sometimes fieldwork involved rescue and recovery. One afternoon Smith was notified that a dugout canoe had been found in a nearby lake. Dugout canoes were not all that unusual in bodies of water in Florida; the dugout had been the common mode of transportation for Indian and non-Indian alike for centuries. How many dugouts had been located in lakes was probably a respectable figure, but Smith and Fairbanks somehow managed to become excited at the prospect of a big, waterlogged piece of wood whose makers were unknown, whose cultural affiliation was probably unknowable, and whose date in terms of years was speculation at best. It was their duty to the past: the canoe *had* to be rescued. It needed to be taken out of the water, loaded on a trailer, hauled to the dining hall and up the steps to the landing, where we were all going to learn how to stabilize and preserve waterlogged artifacts.

Wearing swimsuits, we arrived at the lake and rowed out in flat-bottomed boats to dead center. I for one stared disconcerted at the green and slimy water, goodness knows how deep, lying spread out before us. Fairbanks and Smith were already in the lake, and I was trying to think up an excuse—any excuse—not to have to get into that nasty-looking water. Hale Smith, his arms full of rope and the dark shape of the canoe under his chin, knew exactly what I was thinking. "This ain't the English department," he bellowed, "get in here and grab that rope!" I slid into that horrid water, sure I would never rise again, and helped secure the canoe. From that point on it was sheer dog work, hauling and pushing, dragging and lifting. And somehow we moved that immense, heavy dugout up the dining hall steps and up the stairs beyond into the broad landing. There it stayed, the object of solicitous attention as day after day, week after week, we impregnated it with acetone and hoped for the best. Out of context, undatable, unbelievably big and clunky, that canoe was a departmental albatross, capable of telling nothing to earnest students of the past beyond the solid fact of its existence, a monument to the dedication and muscle-power of anthropology in action.

Besides dugout canoes, there were few occasions when we did not check on what people called in to report or what they brought in to be identified. In the latter category I remember a strange pot covered with crawling alligators that some enthusiast had purchased—probably in a dark alley—with the assurance that it was ancient Maya or authentic ancient something-or-other. It was so obviously wrong that even I, only beginning to understand the breadth of Meso-American ceramics, could see that this particular object was a crude fake. The embarrassed purchaser donated his expensive mistake to the department where it sat on a shelf behind Fairbanks and became part of the teaching collection as well as a source of amusement. It wasn't an alligator coprolite, but it was almost as funny.

More seriously, we were once called out to look at a piece of Spanish chain mail recovered near Panama City or, at least, that was what we were told. Where it really came from, no one ever knew. The chain mail was patently authentic, the biggest piece any of us had ever seen outside a museum, and we were shown where it purportedly had been found. The place was so odd that neither Fairbanks nor Smith felt any need even to put in a test pit. The person who found the chain mail—somewhere—and reported it for whatever obscure reason to the department kept it more or less incommunicado from that point on. He was a former FSU student who had incidentally failed introductory anthropology. "Never fail students," Smith growled *sotto voce* all the way back to Tallahassee: "never fail students . . . probably an authentic de Soto relic . . . we will never see it again" along with strings of unprintable comments on the ancestry or lack thereof of that particular ex-student. It may have been a real de Soto artifact, and Smith was right—we never saw it again.

One of the ongoing projects of the department was locating Spanish missions and their associated Indian communities. We relocated with Fairbanks all the missions known to Smith and re-established datums in sites previously tested, preparatory to some excavations of our own. We came to know what to expect surface collecting probable mission sites and how to deal with what were to me initially very unfamiliar artifacts. The most poignant objects that came from the missions were the tiny peach pits, testimony to the march of domesticated plants from one continent to another. I always wondered what Indians thought of peaches and what Spanish missionaries thought in their turn of beans and squash or even pecans. Sometimes we arrived too late to learn anything: once we hunted for the tiny remnants of a mission not a hundred feet away from bulldozers and within sight of Tallahassee as vast highway systems carried away what we wanted to know. In the days before highway salvage or cultural resources management, an acknowledgment of the presence of the past was all too often a luxury; we were in the way, and nothing waited for us.

The department ran a summer field school, the place for detailed instruction in archaeological field techniques. The summer I participated, the site was a mound on Ocklochonee Bay, at that time a beautiful and uninhabited piney woods where wild turkeys were common and interesting snakes abounded. The mound was one of C. B. Moore's relics, trenched by his crew "in all directions," and we were curious to learn exactly what that meant and why that particular approach to mound excavation was less useful than any other. Fairbanks and his family lived on the coast for the summer while we commuted from the campus in Tallahassee in the maroon truck. We left before dawn, giving campus security something to think about as we insisted, scruffy-looking and lingering about in the dark, that we were only "going to class." All of us converged at the site as the sun rose, still early enough to avoid the summer heat and just late enough to see what we were doing.

Fairbanks was a careful and patient teacher. He showed us how to see an archaeological site as an unrepeatable experiment and how to extract as much as possible in the process of carrying it out. We all surveyed; we all drew extensive field maps; we all kept field diaries and drew features. It was an important summer, and the small crew worked hard. We learned to care for field equipment and to feel concern for the merest speck of dirt left on shovels and trowels at the end of the day. The Florida piney woods, beautiful though they are, took their toll in heat, humidity, mosquitos, and sheer exhaustion. That we came away from many weeks of hard labor and intense learning with as much enthusiasm as we began was testimony to the fact that learning by doing generates its own momentum if it is done right.

Besides archaeology, a major activity was watching the wild pigs along the highway to and from the site. Were they really descendants of de Soto's pigs as Fairbanks insisted or did they come from somewhere else? Sometimes crunched by cars, they were prey of vultures walking stiff-legged in and out of their remains. Nothing, even feral pigs, escaped the relevance test of the anthropological net nor Fairbanks's dry caution to "keep moving or the vultures will get you."

One of the extensive field trips we took was a tour of sites in Georgia. We covered Ocmulgee, Etowah, Kolomoki, and the Eagle Mound with time out to pay our respects to the department in Athens. Ocmulgee and Kolomoki were sites where fieldwork was no longer being done; Etowah was in the process of excavation and for that reason held particular charm for those wanting to learn how big projects were handled. Museums associated with these sites were examined in minute detail and judged for their effectiveness from the vantage point of our backgrounds in museum work. We were, of course, experts by then or so we thought ourselves to be. Fairbanks, genial as always, never seemed to find shepherding us around any great hardship, and we profited immensely from what he had to say about the sites, the museums, the archaeologists, and the restaurants. Being an archaeological tourist broadens experience in a way no amount of reading will do; accompanied by a knowledgeable guide, those same archaeological tourists take more steps towards professionalism. The habit of looking at sites, examining their settings, and acquiring a feel for the landscape was one of Fairbanks's many intellectual gifts to his students. Even today I cannot travel by car without planning to see what is out there to be seen, relevant to my trip or not.

The most peculiar field trip we participated in was to the Garden of Eden; yes, *that* Garden of Eden. A gentleman to the west of Tallahassee, a southern lawyer in a marvelously theatrical white suit and hat, was convinced he had the Garden of Eden in panhandle Florida. That he wanted to build some sort of religious resort on the premises was perhaps behind his conviction that he had in fact the appropriate biblical spot, but his enthusiasm was real. He had contacted Smithsonian scholars, who had identified native gopherwood on his property, the material out of which Noah had built his ark, and that was the most important proof he had of the presence of the Garden. What he wanted of Smith and Fairbanks was a further imprimatur on his speculations, and perhaps he did not really care what they thought. That they came, students in tow, was enough. We all followed him around the beautiful woodland to a series of miraculous locations: the place of Adam's creation, where Eve was created from Adam's rib, the location of the building of the Ark, and great giants' graves fulfilling the comment "that there were giants in the earth in those days." As a student, I was simply flabbergasted at the cool recitation of all these wonders and the polite silence of my mentors. Their only real comment was to suggest that the giants' graves just might be tree falls, but it fell on deaf ears. After the tour, our host took us to a local cafe for a lovely catfish dinner, and everything was pleasant and hospitable. And what we learned was how to behave in the face of delusion, how to recognize a situation where discussion was fruitless, and when to save our intellectual weapons. Tilting at windmills is pointless. It was an excellent catfish dinner, however, and perhaps it does no harm for the Garden of Eden to be in panhandle Florida. I hope, though, that the FSU anthropologists did not wind up in brochures right beside the Smithsonian Institution as one of the authenticators of the Garden of Eden Resort.

The Museum

The museum below the department was first and foremost a teaching museum although it attracted a public beyond the university community. It was quite small, described once by Smith as a "telephone booth" museum, and consisted of a broad corridor that made a right angle turn around the art gallery and ended in a large room behind the gallery. Such a small museum required imagination and a certain willingness to risk in order first to entice visitors in and then sustain their interest. Smith always operated on the principle that something "red and wiggly" needed to be near the entranceway to pull people up short and move them down that corridor and into the museum. The well-lit art gallery straight ahead was an important competitor for a visitor's interest and only a strong pull would move them left into the anthropology museum corridor.

When I was a student there, the prevailing museum philosophy was erected on coats of flat black paint with very creative lighting and startling color contrasts in the exhibits themselves. My first essay into museum volunteering was to stand ready to paint panels with flat black paint. No need to tell anyone there that I had never painted anything before in my life; there really should not have been any trick to it, but my first panels needed four coats. Brush strokes were *not* appreciated, runny edges were criticized, and I learned fast that using tools and handling brushes were skills I needed to have. I even learned what a Phillips-head screwdriver was, something I had been sublimely ignorant of all my life. Eventually I graduated from lower-level grunt work into lettering, moving from the status of untutored laborer into being a museum person. At one point I became organizer of the museum office, presumably because I ended up knowing where everything was. And finally, of course, I learned to plan and help design exhibits themselves. We worked at night mostly, entertained by music over the museum sound system; our repertoire included *Guys and Dolls* and *South Pacific,* and that was it. By the end of the first semester, we could all sing along with Ezio Pinza and never make a mistake.

The first exhibit I helped mount was the Gundrum collection of Antillean artifacts. How to deal with these heavy ground stone objects was a major problem; they were beautiful and spoke volumes about the complexity of Antillean life, but they were plain and gray and did not lend themselves to easily reaching the public in any way calculated to inform. The solution was to put the zemis, stools, waist-weights, and other stone artifacts on geometric forms painted bright orange. The museum itself was the flat black backdrop to brilliantly lighted orange spots. The museum visitor moved through the dim hall from one lighted nook to the next, each time shocked by the expanse of orange and spotlights with the artifacts apparently floating in the air or standing on orange supports. Color and light substituted for the absence of exhibit cases and anything else that smacked of traditional forms of display.

The museum was deeply influenced by the close proximity of the art gallery. The work of artists was a constant stimulus for the planning and execution of artistically satisfying anthropology exhibits, and the anthropology museum was hand in glove with the world of art. The influence was two-way, of course. In the generation before my time, an artist, Taizo Miake, had been curator of the art gallery and at the same time wrote a master's thesis on the nature of art that clearly owed a substantial debt to the ideas of Leslie White and to discussions with anthropological colleagues. Smith himself was artistically inclined and did his own "arting." His drawings and sculpture were more often amusing than otherwise, but his closeness to the world of art was a resource that underpinned the excellence of that little telephone booth museum. Fairbanks had just participated in planning the major exhibit installation at Ocmulgee National Monument, and his knowledge and skills were a perfect counterpoise to the art emphasis of the museum. He always reminded us that museum exhibits were not only works of art but important means of public education. I am convinced of the usefulness of art to museum display, but an art emphasis had the effect of preventing my appreciation of boring, old-fashioned museum exhibits whose enormous virtue in illustrating the range of artifacts is such a help to an informed visitor who needs more than one beautifully displayed object.

The department offered a course in museums and museum techniques that culminated in the preparation and mounting of a large exhibit. The year I took the course, the subject was religion, and we worked at building something that covered the diversity of religious practice as well as the commonalities of behavior in all religions. I was assigned an exhibit on the Southeastern Ceremonial Complex, which involved borrowing one of the Etowah figures and building an exhibit that did justice to that amazing statue. What we did not have in the way of pertinent artifacts to display, we made ourselves. I produced, under Fairbanks's direction, a very reasonable facsimile of a shell gorget from Tennessee, which for all I know is still in the department, along with replicas of corn husk masks made by students and Chilkat blankets painted on oil cloth. We even mounted a display on the Native American Church using peyote cactuses selected from local variety store displays of ornamental cactuses, possible in an innocent time when only we knew what they were. Smith operated on the principle that every student coming out of that course should be capable at the end of mounting a perfect exhibit whose central object should be a single buffalo chip. The buffalo chip challenge haunted many a student's imagination, but we all felt we could do it given enough black paint and spotlights.

Creating exhibits was sometimes difficult, given grandiose plans and limited funds. We learned to use the most unlikely objects for most unlikely purposes: metal bases for paper ice cream cups painted flat black were perfect stands for pottery and were carried off one by one from the dining hall. Smith was an inveterate scrounger, always on the lookout for building materials or whatever else he could beg, borrow, or trade for use in the department or in the museum. Nothing was ever discarded or thrown away that had the least possible future use—pack rat behavior was a way of life. Some of this was responsible for the general disheveled air the department often wore; it is hard to store lumber, sheets of plywood, or cans of paint in an inconspicuous manner.

Almost no cases were available in the museum, and those that were served in the back room where more or less permanent exhibits were installed. The lack of cases meant that exhibits were often literally within touching distance of visitors. We had to plan the flow of people, creatively design exhibits so as to discourage close encounters, and tie down everything in more or less invisible ways. Amazingly enough, few things actually disappeared from museum exhibits in spite of what was almost no security at all. Some of our "security" was clever—labeling easily reached peyote cactuses with cards announcing that they had been sprayed with deadly poison and hoping visitors might actually believe it, at least enough *not* to touch. A pair of children's moccasins was once purloined but returned by shamefaced children after a public appeal, but such incidents were very rare.

Given the strong museum involvement and the powerful archaeology orientation of the department, material culture was always high on the list of things students needed to be concerned with. Fortunately the John V. and Mary Carter collection of Peruvian ceramics and textiles had been given to the university even before the department was created and became a treasured resource for teaching as well as museum display. The pottery had at one time been shoe-polished, a sacrilege not easily forgiven by Smith, who never failed to use it as a lesson in how-not-to-do-it. He taught a course in material culture that he wanted to call "Pots and Pans, Sticks and Stones," but even a curriculum committee used to the eccentricities of the anthropologists could not stomach that, and it flew under a more prosaic title. In the course, students learned to identify objects, determine probable place of origin, understand function, and become familiar with use. We all practiced with blowguns on the landing in front of the museum, hoping to impale our hotel and restaurant management neighbors. We never reached the point of sophisticated analysis in that course, mental templates or theories about the nature of objects, but we made a valuable beginning in appreciating the range of possibilities "out there" and feeling cultural differences through the things made and used by different peoples. Part of the final exam in that course was a table full of objects to be identified, the total impact of which was only slightly diminished by Smith's having neglected to remove some of the tags.

Objects surrounded students, and the significance of material culture was never undervalued. From Robert Anderson's soul pot looking benignly over classroom space to Smith's walrus penis bone and Fairbanks's prized booger mask, there was always some "thing" to think about. Tylor's definition of culture, which Fairbanks had made us memorize, plainly included objects even though not in the famous list as did Leslie White's definition, derived in part from Tylor's. We were untroubled as yet by culture concepts that declared that culture had nothing to do with the detritus of human life, the material remains so dear to archaeological hearts. We were archaeologists—or were to become archaeologists—and it was an archaeology never divorced from anthropology as a whole. How else could we function except in contexts supplied by anthropological theory? When the 1960s ringing cry that archaeology must be anthropology or it is nothing became such an oriflame, those of us who had begun our work in Florida at the tiny FSU department only shrugged our shoulders and asked "what's new about that?" After all, the major archaeological journal in Florida is the *Florida Anthropologist,* published by the Florida Anthropological Society and going strong since the 1940s.

The study of material culture has had its ups and downs, its ins and outs of fashion, but in the training of undergraduates at FSU, it was a constant. The consciousness of things and the connectedness conferred by their contemplation has never left me. I am still enchanted by the world of objects, the skills of those who have put something of their humanity into creation, and the liveliness of imagination that characterizes our species. And as for those anthropologists who cannot tell a fluted point from an ulu—or even worse, do not care—I have nothing but sympathy. They are missing a lot.

Postscript

All of the above was written many years after the event, and I have moved my area of anthropological interest from the Southeast to the Great Lakes region. Those undergraduate years are far behind, but their peculiar vividness even at such a temporal and spatial distance convinces me that I received an excellent grounding in anthropology and a sound basis from which to grow as a scholar.

Being a woman in a department without women faculty members did not seem to be worth being concerned about. My mentors and role models were anthropologists, and not having women as mentors and role models did not adversely affect me. I realize that I am supposed to feel deprived without having had women to model myself after, but I never felt in the least disadvantaged. Faculty were people, human beings, and as one of the species, I felt equally at home among them.

What was hard to endure was the general treatment of women on the campus as a whole. It was the very opposite of allowing women a full voice in their own affairs: we were not supposed to wear slacks or shorts on campus, unless discreetly covered with a raincoat; women could not leave campus without signing out; and the rules pertaining to dorm hours and visitors seemed to me even at the time hopelessly archaic. I was always in trouble for inappropriate dress and signing out with destinations as unspecific and suspicious as "to the woods" or "along the coast." I came to care little for the university as a whole, something the alumni office has never learned, and its—then—lack of commitment to scholarship and its general absence of intellectual tone. The anthropology department, by contrast, was a place where scholarship was valued and students treated as more or less rational beings.

The department did include women, from the ranks of undergraduates to that scarce and peculiar creature, the anthropology master's candidate. One year our graduate student cadre of two included a young Cuban woman, Mercedes Cros y Arrue, who had come out of Batista-controlled Cuba and who had tales to tell of university life there under that regime. Mercy was new to anthropology, but she was bright and eager; and—for once—we undergraduates became her mentors and guides. For a short time, she lived with the Smiths in their back bedroom, and I can remember her trying to teach a group of us, Hale included, the cha-cha-cha in his living room.

Paid student assistants in the department included women undergraduates; as I remember, there was but one at a time so the post was a conspicuous one. Unofficial assistants included anyone who made even the slightest move towards volunteering. I helped grade exams, monitored exams in some of the introductory courses, and hunted up references in the library. Besides being an always-there volunteer in the museum, I "sat" with the museum on Sunday afternoons when someone needed to open it up, turn on the lights, and make things look as if it were a bustling place. I cannot recall any discrimination in favor of one sex or another—we were all warm bodies, and in that department, being clearly breathing was enough to earn a student a place on the team.

There was one older woman who spent time in the department, and I cannot recall ever being surprised that she was there. This was Ina VanStan, a graduate student in some part of the university—home economics, I think—who was studying the Peruvian fabric collection. She was an authority on fabrics, and her work was meticulous and intense. Some part of what she did was published in the Notes in Anthropology series put out, mimeographed and stapled to begin with, by the department.

I don't know, but looking back on it, I might suspect that Chuck Fairbanks went out of his way to make sure I met prominent and not so prominent women in anthropology. Perhaps they were simply people he knew, and he never thought about gender at all, just the usefulness of introducing an eager undergraduate to professionals. I met Frederica de Laguna, Ruth Underhill, and Marian White, but I met many equally prominent men as well.

When it was time to apply to graduate school, women students were seriously encouraged and promoted. I know that the letters of recommendation I needed, and there were a lot of them, were supplied expeditiously and cheerfully. I was given advice on where to go, what kinds of courses to take, and what to avoid. When I was awarded my first fellowship, the department celebrated with one of its famous parties. Such support from the department served as an immediate encouragement to students, whether male or female, and perhaps the successful launching of a graduate into the world of post-baccalaureate training was the ultimate mark of success for the department's whole regime.

Graduate school was the first major hurdle to be faced on the way to a professional career; in some respects, it was neither as intense nor as interesting as undergraduate anthropology at FSU. It is not diplomatic to point that out, of course, and I had one very bad moment as a graduate student when in a group of archaeologists at an SAA meeting, John Goggin asked me in a very loud voice whether I considered myself Fairbanks's student or had transferred my allegiance to the graduate faculty. I cannot remember how I evaded his embarrassing question within earshot of all concerned, but I can say here that I will always consider myself one of Fairbanks's students, his first from the FSU group to finish with a Ph.D. and always I hope emulating his enthusiasm, intellectual honesty, good humor, and unending kindness to earnest beginners.

Going from FSU to a much larger institution was in one way a piece of cake: I had been armed with a critical bit of information that not all fellow graduate students had received in THEIR undergraduate educations. When I first stood on the steps of Angell Hall wondering where the department might be, one look at the building convinced me that there was no attic, and I straightaway headed to the basement.

Carol Ann Irwin Mason: A Biographical Sketch

Rochelle A. Marrinan

Her eyes are arresting. It may be the glasses, which make them seem over-large, or her intense look as she discusses her career, archaeology, and the teaching of anthropological archaeology. Her own education was directed by the young men of the WPA archaeology cadre who dominated the departments of anthropology at many universities across the nation, particularly those of the South. Hers is the outlook of one who has seen cycles of change within the discipline. Her take on those changes voices concern for the anthropological groundedness of the discipline in the face of paradigm shifts, various technical innovations, and trendiness. She says, "Too many archaeologists today remind me of field technicians who haven't a clue that what comes out of the ground represents the lifeways of extinct societies and real people."

Carol Ann Irwin Mason, as a young coed from Jacksonville, Florida, spent her junior and senior undergraduate years at Florida State University in Tallahassee. As a girl, she had been interested in history and things past. During the innumerable mummy movies she watched, she knew that she could be the archaeologist; that she would be able to deal more effectively with the mummies than the movie star archaeologists appeared to be.

She enrolled at Florida State only a few years after it had transformed from a women's college (Florida State College for Women) to a co-educa-

Fig. 9.1. Carol Irwin and unknown student with Charles H. Fairbanks (*center*) in Florida, ca. 1956. (Photo courtesy of Carol Mason.)

tional institution (1948). She joined the department of anthropology in the first years of its existence (founded in 1950). Her memoir chronicles both the early years of this department and the careers of its principal members: Hale G. Smith and Charles H. Fairbanks (fig. 9.1). As Carol Ann Irwin, she graduated *cum laude* from Florida State in 1956. In retrospect, she says, "The people who encouraged me were mainly men. The most important influence on my life as a scholar was Charles H. Fairbanks, who never seemed to think that I would not finish my degrees and go on to be a professional."

Graduate work was undertaken at the University of Michigan, the *alma mater* of both Smith and Fairbanks. She attended as an NSF Fellow from 1956 to 1958. She says:

I had three heady years of NSF fellowships. I got mine through the usual application to NSF; I was surprised to discover that I was a recipient since part of the NSF protocol at that time was a comprehensive exam in the closest allied field. It turned out that NSF had never heard of anthropology—there was NO appropriate exam, and I was told to take the comprehensive exam in the closest allied field. The nearest thing was psychology, about which I was as ignorant as two undergraduate courses could make me; however, the exam was mul-

tiple guess so I must have managed. What was fun was getting the telegram at my dorm on the FSU campus—a real telegram, just like the movies! And the anthro department threw a party in honor of its first NSF fellow. I also got fellowships at Illinois and California and was on a list somewhere else, but the very generous NSF fellowship I had laid out for Michigan so that's where I went. Wherever Jimmy Griffin was.
. . .

Fairbanks had arranged for her to conduct research on WPA-excavated materials from Ocmulgee National Monument in Macon, Georgia (fig. 9.2). Through Fairbanks's contacts, she was employed as a "combination tour leader and researcher" for two summers. She was a full-time researcher for a period of six months in the Ocmulgee collections. She took the master's examinations at Michigan, which she says, "even at this distance I feel cold chills just remembering." She received the master's degree from the University of Michigan in 1957, not from Florida State as has been recorded elsewhere (Walker 1994:31). It is clear, from her own words, that James B. Griffin had a direct impact on the development of her work and thinking in archaeology. In a recent tribute to Griffin, she wrote, "James B. Griffin has been one of the eternal verities in my archaeological landscape for as long as I can remember. My first teachers were his students, and many of the archae-

Fig. 9.2. Carol Irwin Mason at her desk, Ocmulgee National Monument, Macon, Georgia, 1958. (Photo courtesy of Carol Mason.)

Fig. 9.3. Carol and Ronald J. Mason excavating a burial mound near the Little Eau Pleine River, Wisconsin, ca. 1960s. "The ROMANCE of archaeology, sure enough." (Photo courtesy of Carol Mason.)

ologists I met in those early years at meetings or in the field were also part of the Michigan 'crowd.' I had probably heard more Jimmy stories than most people by the time I went to Michigan to collect them in my own right" (Mason 1998).

As an ABD, she became director of archaeological field research for the Neville Public Museum in Green Bay, Wisconsin. She also taught at St. Norbert College in West De Pere and for the University of Wisconsin system in Green Bay and Menasha. Her dissertation, "The Archaeology of Ocmulgee Old Fields, Macon, Georgia," was completed in 1963 (Ph.D., Michigan). She continued to teach in the University of Wisconsin system and collaborate with her husband, Ronald J. Mason, whom she married in 1958 (fig. 9.3). Of her husband, she says, "I met my husband romantically in Leslie White's history of anthropology course, where I impressed him by knowing Tylor's definition of culture right off the bat (naturally!!! Fairbanks made us all learn it)."

Fig. 9.4. Carol Mason and her husband preparing samples in the field on Rock Island, Wisconsin, ca. 1970s. The hat, she says, is from Florida days. Hale Smith collected strange hats and encouraged students to wear them in the field, a custom she still observes. (Photo courtesy of Carol Mason.)

Throughout the 1970s and 1980s, she conducted fieldwork for Lawrence University, Appleton, Wisconsin. The Masons have been married for forty years and have two grown children who have become "competent, responsible, and delightful adults." Their children always accompanied them to the field (fig. 9.4). She says, "It isn't easy having a family AND being a practicing scholar at the same time. I did a lot of teaching at night and in a part-time capacity for many years. I am not sorry for missing a lot of meetings because of family life and having to say 'no' to opportunities I might otherwise have accepted. But there IS more to life than archaeology."

In addition to her professional contributions, she is an award-winning cook, having won second prize in the Wisconsin section of the National Chicken Cooking Contest and first prize in the Applefest Cooking Contest. She loves opera and is a non-professional Dickens scholar. She trains border collies—her current two hold obedience titles and are Canine Good Citizens and Registered Therapy Dogs. A piece of dog fiction, "Holmes, Watson, and Me," was published in the American Kennel Club *Gazette* in 1991 as the Second Place Winner in its Annual Fiction Contest. She also makes chocolates in her spare time.

I first heard of Mason from the late Theron A. Nunez, Jr., a professor of Mexican ethnology at the University of Florida in 1971. Nunez, a master's student of Fairbanks, had been a graduate student in the department at Florida State when Mason was there. He was a member of the crew when Mason enrolled in her first field school. One anecdote he related about her was that she never "used the bushes" when they were in the field, but Mason laughs and rejects this story as a faulty remembrance. He also told me that she was an avid reader of science fiction and mentioned her book, *Anthropology through Science Fiction* (1974), which she edited with Martin Harry Greenberg and Patricia Warrick. My copy was a gift from Charles Fairbanks. She says, "I wrote it on a portable typewriter in a cabin on an island in Lake Michigan—we were excavating a site by day, and I was writing at night. It was fun but hectic as I sent chapters off by boat. I did not have much of a chance to see what I had written as a whole until the book came out. A lot of people have told me over the years what fun it was to come to anthropology through s-f; students enjoyed the stories and understood the anthropological lessons."

As a member of the faculty at Florida State University and one of the last doctoral students of Charles Fairbanks, I first read "This Ain't the English Department" with great interest. For the past three years, I have read this paper, a few pages each week, to students in my archaeological method and theory seminar. I began with the intention of informing them about the evolution of their own department, but I have realized that Carol's words accomplish much more. She speaks in this memoir about the ways in which an anthropology student, particularly an archaeology student, is enculturated in a small department. She explores the passing of archaeological lore and norms of professional conduct. Her words say to students, "I have sat in your seat and I have succeeded in this field" (fig. 9.5). She also reminds me of the importance of formal and informal student-faculty interaction and support. She speaks to the joys and trials of fieldwork and projects demanding more effort than initially anticipated. She reminds us, with her example, how we have become who and what we are.

On the trip to the 1997 Southeastern Archaeological Conference Meeting in Baton Rouge, two van loads of Florida State students stopped briefly in Fort Walton Beach, Florida, to visit the Temple Mound Museum. Several of the students from the archaeological method and theory class made the trip. Yulee Lazarus came out of retirement for a few hours to give the students the tour of the mound and museum and have yet another lunch at the microbrewery near the Buck Mound. One display in the museum featured

Fig. 9.5. Carol Mason and statuary friend at Brennan's restaurant for breakfast and interview, New Orleans (during SAA meeting), April 1996. (Photo by Nancy White.)

a dugout canoe. The students, many of them now interested in underwater archaeology, asked Yulee about its origin. She said, "Oh, that's something Hale and Chuck sent over for the museum. They had it around the department at FSU." Carol's dugout canoe, from the slimy depths of a Tallahassee lake, was there on display for all to see.

A Southeastern Bibliography of Carol Irwin Mason

Mason, Carol I.

1959   Dating English Pipestems. *Florida Anthropologist* 12(3):71–72.

1963a   The Archaeology of Ocmulgee Old Fields, Macon, Georgia. Ph.D. dissertation, Department of Anthropology, University of Michigan, Ann Arbor.

1963b   Eighteenth Century Culture Change among the Lower Creeks. *Florida Anthropologist* 16(3):65–80.

1963c   Comments on Mouse Creek and Yuchi Identification. *American Antiquity* 28(4):550–51.

1963d A Reconsideration of Westo-Yuchi Identification. *American Anthropologist* 65(6):1342–46.

1964 Natchez Class Structure. *Ethnohistory* 11(2):120–33.

1971 Gunflints and Chronology at Ocmulgee National Monument. *Historical Archaeology* 5:106–9.

1973 Historical Archaeology at Ocmulgee National Monument. Ms. on file, National Park Service, Southeast Archeological Center, Tallahassee, Florida.

1985 Archaeological Analogy and Ethnographic Example. In *Indians, Colonists, and Slaves: Essays in Memory of Charles H. Fairbanks, Florida Journal of Anthropology, Special Publication* 4:95–104.

1992 From the Other Side of the Looking Glass: Women in Archaeology in the 1950s. In *Essays in the History of American Archaeology*, edited by Jonathan Reyman, pp. 91–102. Avebury/Ashgate Publishing Co., Brookfield, Vermont.

1998 James B. Griffin: A Memoir. *Midcontinental Journal of Archaeology* 22(2):144.

10

Hester A. Davis

A Legend in Public Archaeology

NANCY MARIE WHITE

One of the most familiar names in American archaeology is that of Hester Davis of the Arkansas Archeological Survey, who has done arguably more than anyone else to promote public archaeology, starting long before it was the cause célèbre it is now (for example, McGimsey 1972; Smith and Ehrenhard 1991; the forthcoming proceedings of the 1995 Chacmool conference entitled "Public or Perish"; the Distinguished Lecture by Sabloff [1996] to the Archaeology Division of the American Anthropological Association; Jameson 1997; the Society for American Archaeology's 1998 workshop on enhancing training in public archaeology [Bender and Smith 1998]). Hester has been called the "messiah" and "patron saint of conservation archaeology" (Mayer-Oakes in Lipe and Lindsay 1974:142), someone who has taken "the initiative to speak out on ethical and public issues and assume responsibility for the new administrative and educational tasks in archaeology, achiev[ing] considerable power, influence, and renown" (Dincauze

1992:136). She has combined research with advocacy and the broader message of archaeology in public education to achieve a fascinating career.

Early Influences and Field Experience

Hester Ashmead Davis is a direct descendant of Lucretia Coffin Mott, the famous Quaker abolitionist. Her paternal grandfather was a Harvard geology professor, and both parents were from old New England families. Her father had a degree in natural sciences from Harvard. The family ran a Massachusetts apple farm during the summer and went to Florida in the winter, where he taught natural history at Rollins College in Winter Park. There he also directed the tiny Thomas R. Baker Museum and later organized the founding of the unique Beal-Maltbie Shell Museum, which Hester's mother directed after his death in 1943. Hester was the youngest of five children who all went on to have professional careers in art, theater, archaeology, and natural resources. She grew up working outdoors and describes experiences, starting at about age seven, such as camping on Florida field trips, collecting shells, and banding birds.

Hester's first archaeological experiences were also in the family context. During the summer of 1939, her brother Mott was a Harvard graduate student doing his first fieldwork at Awatovi in northern Arizona on the Hopi reservation. Her sister Penny, a graphic artist for Harvard's Peabody Museum, had also been hired, to make scale drawings of the kiva murals. Penny related the summer's adventures and Hester could not help but become interested. Later, ten-year-old Hester was in Florida when Mott, Penny, and a group of Harvard archaeology grad students calling themselves the Excavators' Club came to visit over Christmas break. This group went on field trips, published their own journal, and included individuals such as Chester Chard (now retired; formerly at the University of Wisconsin) and John Rowe (UC Berkeley). They had come to excavate at the Palmer-Taylor Mound in Seminole County (E. M. Davis 1996). Hester visited the site and thought it was all pretty neat.

Her father died when she was twelve, and it affected Hester such that she became unhappy in school and even flunked algebra her first year of high school in Winter Park. Her older siblings were all gone by then, she says, "so there was my poor mother with this perfectly awful teenager who wouldn't talk to her about why she wouldn't talk to her." She was sent to boarding school at Northfield School for Girls in Massachusetts, a college prep and co-op school where all the girls worked to help pay for room and board.

Summers she was with her brothers running the apple farm, cooking, canning, cleaning, scrubbing, and gardening.

At boarding school her favorite subject was history, and for a graduation present her mother and sister took her on a car trip to California, visiting places of historical and natural interest along the way. They met people whom Penny knew from Harvard. At Canyon de Chelly, David de Harport took them to distant ruins that tourists usually did not see. Even more memorable was the visit to Bat Cave in New Mexico, being excavated at that time by Herb Dick, a graduate student at Harvard (later of Trinidad College, Colorado). This site had produced the earliest domesticated maize known at the time in the New World (Dick 1965:95; cf. Wills 1988). The crew camp was out in the middle of the San Augustin Plains, and they gave Hester and her family a tent to throw their bedrolls in because there were too many rattlesnakes to make sleeping outside safe. They stayed two or three nights, watching excavations during the day and playing pinochle at night with the crew, great fun.

Returning to Florida, Hester attended Rollins College, where it cost her only fifty dollars per semester as a county resident and daughter of a staff member. Her brother Mott had taken a job as an archaeologist at the University of Nebraska by then. At Rollins she majored in history but took the one anthropology course offered, from Frederick Sleight, who was the organizer of the "Florida Indian and His Neighbors" conference there (Griffin 1949). She attended the whole conference and remembers many people she got to know later, such as John Griffin, Jimmy Griffin, and Hale Smith. After her sophomore year, Penny suggested she apply for work at the Peabody Museum, which had been the highlight of her own life. When Hester wrote, "probably embellishing what little contact I ever had with archaeologists," she was accepted on the Upper Gila Expedition in New Mexico. As her sister drove her to Denver in June 1950, she remembers, the North Koreans were crossing the 38th parallel, inciting the conflict that was so paramount in that phase of American history. After a bus ride from Denver she was met in Albuquerque by Mary McGimsey, wife of field director Bob McGimsey, who was then a Ph.D. candidate at Harvard. The crew camp was north of Quemado in west central New Mexico. A typical Peabody facility, it had a kitchen and an attached ramada for dining. The field assistant was Bob Baker, who was later exhibits designer at the Arizona State Museum. The crew included archaeologists Charles Rosaire and Hal Eberhardt of California and Art Rohn, later of Wichita State. There were only two other women, Mary McGimsey, the project photographer, and Hester's tent-mate Agnes

Bierman. The cook, Lindsey Thompson, Hester knew about from her siblings' tales of Awatovi. He produced pies and other specialties on a big wood stove and was so famous in the Southwest that anyone working in the region would visit the camp. Hester worked in field and lab, drawing artifacts and loving the minutiae of record keeping.

The principal site, Trechado Spring Site 616, was a multi-room pueblo; she worked in a two-meter square on two 10 cm levels (Harvard always used metrics) that yielded nothing. The pueblo had probably been hastily abandoned and partially burned, for many artifacts remained on the room floors. An exciting find was a subadult female skeleton sprawled out on top of the roof rubble. A hole in her skull that could have been made by a stone axe led to the interpretation that she must have been killed while running across the roof, which then burned and fell during the final attack on the pueblo. The floors had broken pots and jewelry, and the skeleton had a necklace with thousands of black stone beads interspersed with shell and turquoise beads (McGimsey 1980:36–170). It was all an exciting start to one's archaeological career. The two-month project was not for pay, but the museum agreed to cover crew expenses. Bob and especially Mary McGimsey, who did the food buying (a good expedition wife's job), must have budgeted well because, after returning home, Hester was sent a check for one hundred dollars for her two months' expenses, an added bonus to the great experience. The other rewarding aspect of the project was the informality of the relationships with people, particularly men. She says she wasn't into the dating game, coming from a girls' school and not good at small talk; but working together on a project was an appealing, comfortable way to relate to the opposite sex.

That fall she continued at Rollins, where she was elected secretary of the 500-person student body, and was even then an activist. The college president, Paul Wagner, hired to straighten up the finances, was slashing budgets. Cutting a losing football team and men's dorm housemothers raised little opposition, but this changed when he began removing favorite and tenured faculty members and possibly collaborating with a finance officer to falsify budget records. Hester helped lead a three-day strike of the student body, which included a sit-down in front of the administration building and catching the finance officer sneaking out the back door with some files. This was in 1951, long before college strikes became commonplace. The trustees eventually agreed with the students and fired the president. Another memorable extracurricular activity in college was working on the staff of the nondenominational chapel, which she enjoyed immensely, though she mentions hardly having been in a church since then. The combination of political activism and rewarding quiet work have characterized her life for a long time.

The next summer Hester returned to the Upper Gila project, this time directed by J. O. Brew and Wat Smith. Her job was to keep records and organize the lab. She remembers Brew's wife and rowdy sons, Alan and Lindsey, ten and eight, who once set fire to the sagebrush, and who sneaked into Thompson's kitchen to steal chocolate doughnuts. (Alan is now an anthropology professor in Minnesota and Lin is a lawyer in Tucson). There were also perhaps five Harvard students, all men, including Dwight Heath, who went on to do archaeology in Central America. Discussing her future during this field project, Hester was advised by Brew not to go into archaeology unless she developed a particular talent such as her sister had in art. Smith advised her to go to graduate school at some place like the University of Oregon, where archaeologist Luther Cressman was known to take women on his crews. (Margaret Mead [1972:131], whose first husband was Cressman in the 1920s, many years before he became an archaeologist, said she thought "he liked women better than men, as people.") She applied to Oregon and was accepted and given an assistantship. Graduating from Rollins on her twenty-second birthday, Hester was awarded the Algernon Sydney Sullivan Medallion for academic and leadership abilities.

During the summer of 1952, before beginning graduate school, she got a job with the Smithsonian's River Basin Surveys project, with which her brother Mott had put her in contact. She traveled by bus to North Dakota and worked two months for Dick Wheeler as crew member, photographer, and cook. Bob Stephenson, director of the River Basin Surveys at the time, didn't want women in the field, but there had been a lot of pressure upon him. Wheeler did not care and had two small daughters of his own who were with him some of the time. Two women were accepted for that crew, but one never came, so Hester was the first experiment with women on River Basin Surveys. She says she did not cause any trouble, so apparently they figured they could continue this practice. She was not even supposed to be the cook. The family with whom she lived was to do the cooking for the whole crew; the men lived in an abandoned schoolhouse a mile away. But Wheeler discovered that the woman who was cooking was also feeding her family of six on the project food budget, so that agreement ended and Hester cooked for the whole crew at the schoolhouse on two Coleman stoves.

Graduate School and Applied Anthropology

At the end of the summer she hopped on another bus for Eugene, Oregon, and grad school, where she had to start taking anthropology courses. Her most memorable professor was Homer Barnett, just back from two years in the South Pacific advising the U.S. government on the administration of the islands that were made Trust Territories after World War II. He lectured about those experiences ("Gosh, putting anthropology to work for others," says Hester), and she decided, "by golly, I was going to save the world through anthropology." So she never did do fieldwork with Cressman (though she remembers getting sloshed on his sherry at his party for grad students). Her assistantship was with Bill Laughlin, a physical anthropologist/archaeologist who worked in Alaska but who did not take women to the field. For her one hundred dollars per month over nine months for two years, she remembers accomplishing useful things for him: transcribing the diary of a Russian priest named Venuminov, who was a missionary to the Aleutians, and helping him measure physical attributes of Indian children on the Umatilla reservation. Because of Barnett's influence, she was then figuring on a career in cultural anthropology. The summer of 1954 was spent working at the Population Reference Bureau, a small research agency in Washington, D.C. She investigated population changes resulting from European contact on various South Pacific islands.

It was the era of Eisenhower, who had started the "Point Four Program" similar to the Marshall Plan, to help what were then called "underdeveloped countries." Hester found out about a special graduate program at Haverford College, funded for five years by the American Friends Service Committee, to train people in cross-cultural skills needed in countries that had been devastated by the war. She was accepted in the fall of 1954 into this program, which provided an M.A. degree in social and technical assistance with a year's concentrated work. One of a group of nine grad students, she first spent a week in Philadelphia slums painting houses, then went to Haverford, main-line Philadelphia at the opposite extreme from the slums, to hear government and academic experts. Then anthropologist Gordon Macgregor led the group on an ethnographic project with the Cherokee Indians in North Carolina, where they learned how to relate to other cultures and build houses and agricultural and sanitary facilities. Her student group included a woman who had been a U.N. translator, an older man from Denmark who had been a government administrator, a Japanese architect, a German engineer, and a man trained in sanitation, altogether four women and five men. For six weeks over Christmas and in January, they lived in Big Cove on the reservation, in an abandoned church and schoolhouse. Hester recalls visiting families, contributing to pie socials, and helping in the school and the fields.

Then during spring semester one memorable class was a reading course on the South Pacific with Margaret Mead, who came down once a week from New York to Bryn Mawr, which had a cooperative agreement with Haverford. Hester read all of Mead's and Malinowski's writings and had to write the longest paper she'd ever done, perhaps fifty pages, which earned a B-, the lowest passing grade. Mead wrote that it had "the theoretical orientation of a 3rd-grader." Hester was incensed but, reading it years later, she realized Mead was correct. She also wrote a paper on a portion of the Cherokee study and soon got her M.A. But she realized she had no talent to give other countries except anthropology. She had come to the program already possessing what the other students had been looking for, but now there was no place for her in the needs of other countries. So she applied to the University of North Carolina's master's program. Luckily, anthropologist John Gulick was just beginning a study of contemporary Cherokee through the Institute for Social Science at Chapel Hill. She went there with an assistantship in the fall of 1955.

The summer just before beginning at North Carolina, however, she returned to archaeology. Brother Mott hired Hester out of his field school budget, needing a photographer but also a cook. She said, "what the hell, I can do both," and went to western Nebraska near Scottsbluff. The project was testing of Forager sites, which Hester calls just about the least interesting archaeology imaginable. By the next year, as a graduate student in cultural anthropology, she was commuting between Chapel Hill and the Cherokee reservation with other students involved in Gulick's work, living in the same abandoned schoolhouse. She gathered data for a thesis entitled "Social Interaction in the Big Cove Community," on family locations and interactions within this tiny settlement that was the most conservative among the Cherokee communities. In a year and a half, by spring 1957, she had another master's degree, though without ever having worked in archaeologist Joffre Coe's lab (which he has never let her forget). She also likes to recall that Lewis Binford was beginning study at UNC as she was finishing, and she paid him the princely sum of twenty-five dollars to draw the map for her thesis.

Answering a job ad in the American Anthropological Association *Newsletter* took Hester next to the Midwest. The University of Iowa College of Medicine was beginning a research program called the Institute for Agricultural Medicine, funded by the Kellogg Foundation. For a project on the Iowa farmer they sought someone in anthropology with a farm background and knowledge of German, for research in an Amish community. The only qualified applicant, Hester knew no German, so the project was redesigned to allow her to find placement with any farm family. She drove to Iowa City in spring 1957 in her first car, a Chevy sedan. Anthropologist Tom McCorkle, from California, was in charge of the project. After a couple months orientation she moved down to Washington County, southeast Iowa, where she found a family who needed household and farm help in return for her room and board. Thus she could do participant observation.

She also hung around with archaeologists in Iowa City, only fifty miles away; one was Rey Ruppé, whom she had met in New Mexico. She volunteered in the archaeology lab and helped publish the Iowa Archaeological Society Newsletter. Somehow she persuaded her bosses at the Institute to give her six weeks off in the summer so she could participate in Ruppé's University of Iowa archaeological field school as cook (fig. 10.1). She also

Fig. 10.1. Hester Davis serving coffee to Jim Scholtz, University of Iowa field school, 1958. (Photo courtesy of Hester Davis.)

went on weekend digs and made many good friends, including Adrian Anderson, later Iowa State Historic Preservation Officer, Dale Henning, Charlie Keller, now retired from the University of Illinois, and Jim Scholtz, who was later hired at the University of Arkansas Museum.

After thirteen months with the farm family, Hester returned to Iowa City to write up research results. At the fall AAA meeting she gave her first professional paper: "Open Country Culture," about the Iowa farmer. By this time, however, she realized she did not want to be a cultural anthropologist. She thought she had not been good at getting information from people she was living with, much less anyone else, and wondered what business it was of hers trying to find out these personal things about people. In the fall of 1958 she started writing to individuals in her network of contacts in archaeology, and she encountered good luck again. Bob McGimsey had begun a job at the University of Arkansas. He and Rey Ruppé had been together at Harvard, and she remembers Rey getting a card from Bob from Fayetteville and saying, "good god, Arkansas! We'll never hear from him again!" But McGimsey had gotten the legislature to create a laboratory of archaeology at the university and, when it remained unfunded, he talked the dean into creating a full-time museum position. Hester was hired in July 1959 as a "preparator." This is a genuine museum job title, referring to exhibits preparation, but she had to do everything since there was no other full-time person.

Archaeology in Arkansas

In 1960 she started teaching in the anthropology department, the museum methods course, which continued yearly for six years. McGimsey was the archaeologist in a sociology/anthropology department, and Fred Voget was the cultural anthropologist. When Voget took a leave of absence and then announced, during the middle of fall registration in 1961 that he was not coming back, Hester and Bob split his courses. She agreed to teach Indians of North America but it led her to dislike teaching, since she was thrown into it with so little time to prepare—one weekend's notice before the first class. She stayed a day ahead in the reading and talked fast enough so nobody had a chance to ask questions.

For the first four months of 1961, McGimsey was off on a research project in Panama, leaving Hester in charge. It was a legislative session and the man who had been responsible for creating the laboratory of archaeology legislation was angry at the university for not doing anything about his project, so he dropped in some legislation that moved the lab to the department of parks. It was a political crisis. With McGimsey in Panama, Hester learned quickly about ham radio in order to communicate with him. With his advice, relayed by Hester, the university negotiated with the legislator and the crisis was resolved. Soon after, Hester and Bob began the long political process of establishing a formal archaeological program for the state.

Hester was appointed assistant director of the museum in 1963. Other professional endeavors included her first SAA paper in about 1960, on the potential of salvage work at Beaver Reservoir in northwest Arkansas. From that area's dry bluff shelters the museum already had a large collection of perishable materials, which had never been written up. Hers was a descriptive presentation, including information on other work in the region. She also did various field studies (fig. 10.2), especially survey and salvage at sites

Fig. 10.2. Hester Davis in the field, possibly at Denham Mound, Arkansas, about 1961. (Photo courtesy of Hester Davis and the University of Arkansas Museum.)

damaged or about to be destroyed by construction. This research could not help but influence her archaeological approach. Reporting on emergency work on the lower Arkansas River in 1965, for example, she noted three conclusions: major Woodland occupation existed, surveys should be conducted before construction, and some information is better than none at all (Davis and Baker 1974:56).

Hester's work with avocational archaeologists became intense in Arkansas. When she arrived in 1959 there was a Northwest Arkansas Archaeological Society started by an active amateur. He was recruiting all over the state, mostly artifact collectors and sometimes dealers. Whole pots looted from mounds had long been items to collect, trade, or sell in Arkansas. A Mississippian head pot from Mississippi County, painted and modeled in the deceased's portrait, even forty years ago commanded a price of thousands of dollars. Hester and Bob McGimsey decided there should be a statewide society supported by the museum; they joined the NWAAS and got the mailing list. There was also at that time a Western Arkansas chapter of the Oklahoma Anthropological Society, and Hester got their mailing list too. In 1960 the Arkansas Archaeological Society was formed from that nucleus. With a monthly newsletter and ever-increasing membership, this group became involved in much of the survey and salvage fieldwork and also was to become very politically active.

From 1959 through 1965, with the Arkansas legislature meeting every two years, there was continual activity to get a statewide archaeological program. In 1966 the Legislative Council created a committee to decide what the state should do to get such a program that would keep its own heritage within Arkansas and not let valuable artifacts be grabbed for big east coast museums. One powerful legislator tried to get this archaeological program because he wanted someplace to have his collection. By this time there were about five hundred members in the Society. Many were politically powerful and lobbied their legislators at the personal level. In a rural state such as Arkansas it is common to have coffee with your representative at a local cafe. All the lobbying combined with another fortuitous political event. In the years between 1959 and 1966, the university had no funds for "new programs." In addition, Governor Orval Faubus had vetoed an antiquities bill that would have protected sites on state land, saying that hunting arrowheads was a perfectly good activity for the citizens of Arkansas and he didn't want to deprive them of it. But then Winthrop Rockefeller was elected governor in November 1966. He knew about historic preservation and archaeology, his family having been involved in development at Colonial Williamsburg. He supported the whole program, and the Arkansas Archeological Survey was created on July 1, 1967. The legislation also created the position of State Archaeologist, to which Hester was named, and which she has held ever since. (Amazingly enough, she was not the first woman state archaeologist; Joan Freeman, now retired, had the position in Wisconsin with that state's Historical Society a few years earlier.) Another notable feature of the program was its creation as an agency associated with higher education, rather than as a commission with politically appointed overseers.

From state-level politics it was only a short hop for Hester to the national scene. The legislature appropriated budgets for two years, but any surplus could not be carried over. After the first two years, McGimsey did not want to give back any funds. He and Hester came up with an idea of how to spend the surplus: a project bringing Phillips, Ford, and Griffin (1951) back to the Lower Mississippi Valley to evaluate how things looked in 1968 as compared with 1939. By then Jim Ford had died, and Phil Phillips had a prior commitment, but Griffin thought it was a great idea. A series of meetings, held in Greenville, Mississippi, Poplar Bluff, Missouri, and Edwardsville, Illinois, involved some fifty archaeologists from Louisiana, Mississippi, Tennessee, Missouri, and Illinois.

At this time everyone was discovering the extensive land-leveling that was going on in the valley, due to federal projects, particularly those of the Soil Conservation Service (SCS). The push in the late 1960s was to flatten the land with a big leveler, a tractor with an angled blade, to make room for the wider machinery that could till more rows at a time of cotton and especially soybeans. Any bumps such as natural levees got in the way. Important sites from Archaic to Mississippian were being deep plowed, cut down, completely removed. The SCS confidently estimated that "in less than 25 years, all levelable land in Arkansas will have been cleared and leveled" (Davis 1996a). The conferences focused on what should be priorities for investigations in the face of such widespread destruction, and whether there was even any choice. The participants agreed that the destruction was increasingly due to federal involvement, such as farming practices spread through the SCS. They invited John Corbett, chief archaeologist with the National Park Service, to discuss what might be done. After all, it was just as devastating as flooding sites in a reservoir, yet there was no money, no protection.

Thus originated the national campaign to get all federal agencies to identify sites appropriate for the National Register of Historic Places. The Historic Preservation Act had passed in 1966 with that requirement, but agencies such as the SCS and especially the Army Corps of Engineers were saying that they had no authority to fund archaeology, that it was the Park Service's responsibility. The argument needed to be made to Congress that sites were

Fig. 10.3. Arkansas Archeological Survey Members, August 1968. *Left to right:* Frank Schambach, Hester Davis, Burney McClurkan, Jim Scholtz, Martha Rolingson, Bob McGimsey, Ken Cole, Dan Morse, John Huner. (Photo courtesy of the Arkansas Archeological Survey.)

disappearing and that all federal agencies should be authorized to spend their own money to identify and preserve them. McGimsey went to Senator William Fulbright with the whole campaign, including a draft of federal legislation he and Carl Chapman of Missouri had put together. Fulbright said he'd be glad to support the effort but he thought it would take five years minimum. He was right. The Moss-Bennett Bill, which became the Archeological and Historic Preservation Act, was not passed until 1974.

Meanwhile, Hester helped write the famous booklet *Stewards of the Past* (McGimsey, Chapman, and Davis 1970), to make professional archaeologists, landowners, and the public aware of site destruction and preservation goals. Chapman produced some sixty thousand copies through the University of Missouri (and it was reprinted elsewhere). McGimsey also published *Public Archaeology* (1972). It is interesting that the national effort, which quickly gathered data from all other parts of the country on federal action threatening sites, originated in Arkansas and southeast Missouri. It is also interesting that involvement with avocational archaeologists was important from the start in the creation of the Survey (figs. 10.3, 10.4) and the legislative campaign. Besides advocacy writings, the whole endeavor produced much-needed lab/field manuals and other publications for avocational archaeologists and students (for example, McGimsey and Davis, n.d.).

Remarkably consistent was the clear message of all this effort, as expressed so well in *Stewards of the Past*, for the average local resident, business person, or archaeology student: that we cannot postpone our responsibility to save everyone's basic heritage of the past, and that destruction is forever. This clarity of expression and widespread promulgation of the message, so important in public archaeology, was crucial. The SAA, under president Joe Ben Wheat, created the Committee on Public Archaeology (COPA, which originated as the Committee on Public Understanding of Archaeology). Hester became the second chair (after Carl Chapman), and COPA expanded to include one archaeologist in each state, to spread information on pending legislation. A bill was introduced each session of Congress, which means three times over those six years, by Senator Moss and Representative Bennett. Hester sent out notices of the bill numbers, dates of hearings, names of members of the committees hearing the bill, sample letters for archaeologists to write their own congressional representatives,

Fig. 10.4. Hester Davis on Arkansas Archeological Society excavation, July 1969, Marked Tree, Arkansas. (Photo courtesy of Hester Davis.)

and exhortations to all professionals to take action. This was the activity that raised the consciousness of archaeologists about the need for political savvy, as well as eventually turning COPA into the political network of the SAA, rather than being the public education committee (which came later). Enhancing the visibility of the campaign were Hester's seminal writings in strategic national venues. The lead article in an *Archaeology* magazine was entitled "Is There a Future for the Past?" (Davis 1971), a phrase which was picked up and repeated to the point of sounding trite today, Hester thinks. With the help of Dick Ford, the SAA representative to the American Association for the Advancement of Science (AAAS), an article entitled "The Crisis in American Archaeology" (Davis 1972a) came out in *Science* as well.

Hester admits that those were heady times, and things reached the next order of magnitude when the forum became international. She contributed what she labels a very enjoyable task in organizing a symposium for the SAA in 1975 that was to have important repercussions upon archaeology in England. She invited four British archaeologists and got funding to bring them to speak about their rescue archaeology efforts: Henry Cleere, then executive director of the Council on British Archaeology; Peter Fowler, honorary secretary of the Council of British Archaeology; Andrew Saunders, chief inspector of ancient monuments and historic buildings; and Tom Hassall, director of the Oxfordshire Archaeological Unit.

This was also the SAA meeting featuring the discussion about certifying archaeologists (that later led to formation of the Society of Professional Archaeologists [SOPA], now the Registry of Professional Archaeologists [RPA]). The 1974 bill had passed and agencies needed lots of archaeologists; anyone with field school experience could set up in business to do the work. A mechanism was needed for agencies to know who was a professional. The SAA and the National Park Service had sponsored the Airlie House Seminars in 1974 (fig. 10.5) to address the nature of cultural resources and state-of-the-art management of them (McGimsey and Davis 1977). The debate on accreditation at the 1975 SAA business meeting was spirited and acrimonious—a shouting match. The British thought this was great. They learned the term "cultural resources management" and got ideas for new approaches to rescue and heritage issues (cf. Cleere 1984, 1989) that led directly to their forming their own professional organization, the Institute for Field Archaeology. Hester is justly proud of these kinds of international results.

While Hester credits McGimsey with the accomplishment of the Arkansas Archeological Survey, with herself in an auxiliary role, obviously she was

Fig. 10.5. Hester Davis,
fall 1974, at SAA's Airlie
House Seminars. (Photo
courtesy of Hester Davis.)

a major player as events expanded beyond the state. The Airlie House Report cartoon detailing steps in Milking the Archaeological Cow (fig. 10.6) lists her among the milkers, the people at the SAA seminar discussing the issues in McGimsey's stall (not the milkmaids, the recorders). Little can be written about public archaeology and CRM without reference to her major works (for example, Davis 1982, 1991, contributions to federal publications such as Davis 1990, 1996a). The evolution of her thinking has led the profession from the early days of alarm over site loss to exploring legislative action and heritage tourism, from concern about the concept of archaeological significance to worry over the mounting problems of collections curation. After passage of the Moss-Bennett Bill, Hester created and taught a graduate seminar in public archaeology from 1974 to 1991. This teaching was pleasant, because there was a message for the students about real world archaeology. She is now a full professor in the department of anthropology, and she has even helped change professional recognition of the composition of the field to include practitioners with M.A. degrees, as she is herself (Davis 1996b:44).

Fig. 10.6. Milking the Archaeological Cow, with Hester Davis listed as a milker. (Reprinted from McGimsey and Davis 1977:67, with permission of the Society for American Archaeology and Stanley South. Drawing by Jim Frierson.)

The Legend Continues

Hester was apparently the first non-Ph.D. elected to the SAA Executive Committee (in 1975). She ran for SAA president as well (but lost, thank goodness, she says) and is currently chair of the SAA Ethics Committee, having had a trial by fire as SOPA grievance coordinator several years ago. She has been president of SOPA (1979–80), ASCA (American Society for Conservation Archaeology, 1979–80), the Southern Anthropological Society (1977–78), the Southeastern Museums Conference (1969–71), and recently the Southeastern Archaeological Conference (SEAC), and she is an academic trustee of the Archaeological Institute of America. One of eleven founders of SOPA, she was also a founder of ASCA and of the National Association of State Archaeologists. She has also served in editorial positions: for the SAA (assistant editor, 1960–67), SEAC (1965–74), the Council of Affiliated Societies (1993–present), the Arkansas Archeological Survey (1980–present), the Arkansas Archeological Society (1965–present), the Southeastern Museums Conference (1964–71), and the *Journal of Field Archaeology*'s "Public Archaeology Forum" for many years. Other official and non-official positions are far too numerous to list.

On the international scene, she was a member of the Board of Trustees for US/ICOMOS, the United States' committee for UNESCO's International Council on Monuments and Sites (all members of the United Nations have such a committee), and has been appointed chair of the US/ICOMOS Archaeological Heritage Management Committee. She was appointed by President Clinton to the Cultural Property Advisory Committee, which advises the USIA (United States Information Agency) when a foreign country requests import restrictions on its antiquities illegally taken out for import into the United States. Having a presidential appointment means that she can now be addressed as "the Honorable Hester A. Davis."

Hester's alma mater Rollins College gave her a Distinguished Alumna Award in 1996; in 1987 Rollins had awarded her an honorary "Doctor of Humane Letters." She muses, however, that many people in government agencies know she does not write humane letters. In 1994, SOPA noted her equivalent of something like two hundred years of service on every major archaeological organization, sometimes up to six at a time, and gave her the Seiberling Award for public service (fig. 10.7). The SAA presented her their first Award for Excellence in Cultural Resource Management and the Dis-

Fig. 10.7. Hester Davis at the creation of the Seiberling Award by the Society of Professional Archaeologists, 1986. *Left to right:* Bob McGimsey, Congressman John Seiberling (being the first recipient of the award), George Gumerman, Davis; she received the award in 1994. (Photo courtesy of Hester Davis.)

Fig. 10.8. Hester Davis plugging in her electric shovel. (Photo courtesy of the Arkansas Archeological Survey.)

tinguished Service Award. She is also recognized as the owner of the famous electric shovel (fig. 10.8), created for her by her brother Hugh (see Rathje and Schiffer 1982:358).

A keen interest in history has always characterized Hester's work, including the history of archaeology, well before it became a fashionable topic. A paper she presented at the 1989 SAA symposium on women in the profession (a landmark topic for that time) concerned women's involvement in the network of archaeologists writing/receiving the newsletter *Teocentli*, started by Carl Guthe in 1926 and currently edited by McGimsey and herself. She found there had always been participation by women, and that it increased over the years to as much as 25 percent, surprising for this informal, personal newsletter shared among an arbitrarily assembled group. Her last statement in the paper is "women have been and will always be a part of archaeology."

In sum, Hester professes to be not only proud of her contributions, working so intensively with amateurs, native Americans, and public interpretation (fig. 10.9) on the local to international level, but also satisfied at finding such a good niche in which to make organizational and leadership contributions. She says she is probably one of the few people who truly enjoys serving on boards and committees and going to business meetings. Her tradeoff, of course, is having so little opportunity for fieldwork, the attraction of the discipline in the first place. Even on an Arkansas Archeological Society dig, she is a teacher and also usually the photographer, not down in the unit troweling.

Asked what advice she would give to people beginning to study archaeology today, Hester emphasizes finding and developing a specific talent, if only for a fallback job. It is important to have a contribution one can make that is indispensable, whether it is theoretical archaeology, graphic artwork, or some other specialty. She remembers that, even when at Oregon, starting in cultural anthropology, she learned to use the Leroy lettering set, difficult for a left-hander, thinking it would be useful for mapmaking. As for the debate on the necessity of doing fieldwork to be a professional archaeologist, Hester agrees with the SOPA criteria, saying it is important to have dug a 10 cm level, drawn a profile, known what the problems of fieldwork are, and gotten the basic training and supervisory experience. Then, as with her own prime example, one can find other niches to fill later.

With a scholarly yet down-to-earth presence, Hester also has an ever-present twinkle in her eye and a nose for where there might be fun. Now so solidly associated with Arkansas, she still speaks with a mild New England

Fig. 10.9. Hester Davis with Quapaw Robert Whitebird and Arkansas Humanities Council Executive Director Jane Browning at dedication of the Crossroads of the Past exhibit, Toltec Mounds Archeological State Park, 1988. (Photo courtesy of the Arkansas Archeological Survey.)

Fig. 10.10. Hester Davis relaxing with laboratory work, fall 1993. Photo was taken for Women in Science exhibit of the University of Arkansas Museum. (Photo courtesy of Hester Davis.)

accent. She admits that her own personal response to archaeology, what she enjoys most about it, is the picky work in the lab (fig. 10.10). It is similar in motion and mindset to what she enjoys doing for relaxation—fine embroidery, quilting, and needlework. She thinks lab work is a great stress-reliever. Attention to detail may have set the stage for the picky work of administration, as well. Hester's life is a constant stream of details of meetings and programs, writing and editing and speaking. A friend once asked if she regretted never marrying and never getting a Ph.D. and the recognition it might have brought; Hester replied that she had a "perfectly good life." Assuming she would eventually get married, she decided in her early forties that maybe that was not going to happen. She also recounted the story of a man who once asked her to marry him, with the comment that he could picture her working happily in a little vegetable garden behind the house the two of them would inhabit; she said no thanks. But she has always enjoyed being a woman in a field where there are more men than women. McGimsey has been a good mentor, and her work environment has been egalitarian. She says that except for one occasion at an SAA meeting, she has never had any bad experiences with men.

Research for this chapter included speaking with *Arkansas Times* journalist Leslie Peacock, who has often covered Arkansas archaeology in detail. Peacock pointed out in a long letter (September 1996) how folks in Arkansas see nothing unusual about Hester or any women in archaeology. As the coordinator of the Society digs for several decades, the field school for amateurs and the certification program, Hester is the first person anyone interested in archaeology meets. Peacock says, "it's not some guy in khakis who's halfway expecting you to show up in heels, or suggests you head over to the lab. Then, after you get over to the site, you are just as likely to run into a woman director as a man . . . Martha Rolingson or Ann Early . . . Hester has become the heart of amateur archaeology in Arkansas, made them, as the support group for the professionals, her life's work."

Hester's high-visibility career illuminates the point that one does not have to be a high-powered theoretician or chance upon some crucial discovery to make a major contribution. It is inappropriate to say that Hester Davis consciously chose this route for herself rather than a (perhaps more male?) role of achieving recognition through research. She did not set out to do what she did for recognition but saw a job that needed doing and (in more womanly fashion?) jumped in and did it. And, of course, did it very well. Her work to save sites and educate the public has had far more lasting value than any faddish theoretical orientation of the moment, and an impact upon the discipline that few strictly research-oriented archaeologists could ever hope to achieve. As one of the very first to recognize public archaeology and its value, she has "become a legend the most!" But she also has made it her gift to the profession and, to paraphrase her own statement (about the National Historic Preservation Act; Davis 1996a:44), she has changed forever the future of the past.

Selected Bibliography of Hester A. Davis

Davis, Hester A.
1966   An Introduction to Parkin Prehistory. *Arkansas Archeologist* 7(1–2):1–40.
1971   Is There a Future for the Past? *Archaeology* 24(4):300–306.
1972a   The Crisis in American Archaeology. *Science* 175:267–72.
1972b   Inventory of the Archeological and Historical Resources of the Lower Mississippi Alluvial Valley. Report to the National Park Service, Southwest Region.
1974   Comment on Paper by D. S. Miller: Certification for Archaeologists and Amateurs. *Proceedings of the 1974 Cultural Resource Management Conference, Museum of Northern Arizona, Technical Series* 14:157–60.
1976   Applied Archaeology. *Proceedings of the Southern Anthropological Society* 10:72–80.

1979   Approaches to Archeology in the Historic Preservation Program. *American Society for Conservation Archaeology Newsletter* 5(6):10–15.

1980   A Case of Limited Vision? Archeology and Historic Preservation. *American Society for Conservation Archaeology Newsletter* 7:26–28.

1981   A State Plan for Archeology in Arkansas. *American Society for Conservation Archaeology Proceedings* 7:11–15.

1982   Professionalism in Archaeology. *American Antiquity* 47:158–63.

1983   Prehistoric Inhabitants of the Jackson County Area. *The Stream of History, Journal of the Jackson County Historical Society* 20(1):3–10. Newport, Arkansas.

1984a   Approaches to Ethical Problems by Archeological Organizations. In *Ethics and Values in Archaeology*, edited by E. Green, pp. 13–21. The Free Press, New York.

1984b   Introduction. In *Motifs of Ancient Man: A Catalogue of the Pictographs and Petroglyphs in a Portion of the Arkansas River Valley*, by P. C. Sherrod, pp. xi–xix. University of Arkansas at Little Rock, College of Sciences.

1986   The Arkansas Cherokee: An Invisible Archeological Resource. In *Visions and Revisions: Ethnohistoric Perspectives on Southern Cultures*, edited by G. Sabo III and W. Schneider, pp. 48–58. *Proceedings of the Southern Anthropological Society* 20. University of Georgia Press, Athens.

1987   Doing It the Hard Way: Arkansas' Two State Plans. In *Proceedings 1986*, edited by F. Ruffini and J. Montgomery, pp. 2–7. American Society for Conservation Archaeology.

1988   Learning by Doing: This Is No Way to Treat Cultural Resources. In *Archaeological Heritage Management in the Modern World*, edited by H. Cleere, pp. 275–79. Unwin Hyman, London.

1989a   Women in *Teocentli:* Inroads in the Old Boys Network. Paper presented at the annual meeting of the Society for American Archeology, Atlanta.

1989b   Is an Archaeological Site Important to Science or to the Public, and Is There a Difference? In *Heritage Interpretation*, vol. 1, *The Natural and Built Environment*, edited by D. Uzzell, pp. 96–99. Belhaven Press, London.

1989c   The Future of Archaeology: Dreamtime, Crystal Balls, and Reality. *American Journal of Archaeology* 93:451–58.

1990   *Training and Using Volunteers in Archaeology: A Case Study from Arkansas*. Archaeological Assistance Program Technical Brief 9. U.S. Department of the Interior, National Park Service, Washington, D.C.

1991   Avocational Archaeology Groups: A Secret Weapon for Site Protection. In *Protecting the Past*, edited by G. S. Smith and J. E. Ehrenhard, pp. 175–80. CRC Press, Boca Raton.

1992   Archaeology in the Next 25 Years. In *Past Meets Future: Saving America's Historic Environments*, edited by A. J. Lee, pp. 181–89. Preservation Press, Washington, D.C.

1996a   Peril or Potential. The Future of the Past in the Alluvial Valley. *Common Ground* 1:46. National Park Service Archeology and Ethnology Program, Washington, D.C.

1996b   NHPA and the Practice of Archaeology. *CRM* 19(6):42.

Davis, Hester A., contributing editor
1982   *A State Plan for the Conservation of Archeological Resources in Arkansas.*
        Arkansas Archaeological Survey Research Series 21, Fayetteville.
Davis, Hester A., editor
1970   *Archeological and Historical Resources of the Red River Basin.* Arkansas
        Archeological Survey Research Series 1, Fayetteville.
Davis, Hester A., and Charles M. Baker
1974   *Emergency Survey and Testing in the Lower White River and Arkansas Post
        Canal Area, Arkansas.* Arkansas Archeological Survey Research Report 3.
        Fayetteville.
Davis, Hester A., Carol Spears, and Nancy Myer
1975   *White River Basin.* Arkansas Archeological Survey Research Report 5. Fay-
        etteville.

11

Martha Ann Rolingson

From Paleo Points to Platform Mounds

NANCY MARIE WHITE

A major figure in Arkansas archaeology for three decades, Martha Rolingson continues extensive research and public archaeology with the Arkansas Archeological Survey at Toltec Mounds Archeological State Park, not far from Little Rock. At this famous multimound site she has explored questions concerning the development of domesticated plants and the extent of food production in relation to social complexity, as well as the mound builders' different site planning strategies. She has developed research designs different from those used at simple habitation sites to investigate mound construction and function through time. She came to this point via Kentucky archaeology, the University of Michigan, and an early fascination with southwestern U.S. anthropology.

The Lure of the Southwest

Martha was born in Wichita, Kansas, of parents whose own fathers were both Methodist preachers. Her mother and father had both been raised in parsonages, moving around every two years from one church to another. Both parents did graduate work in history at the University of Kansas. Her father switched to journalism after his M.A., working for various newspapers, moving to the *Denver Post* when Martha was ten. Her older brother is a chemist (now retired). Though her mother did not work professionally outside the home, she was active in the church. An uncle was also a Methodist minister who taught at the University of Denver.

Her father was also an avocational photographer, and the family did a lot of weekend hiking in the Colorado mountains. Annual vacation trips were oriented toward both nature and history. When Martha was thirteen, they visited Mesa Verde, and the following summer, the Rio Grande valley and pueblos and archaeological sites in New Mexico. At age seventeen, she and her family made a memorable trip through New Mexico again and on to Juarez, Mexico, visiting museums, native peoples, and ruins (fig. 11.1). Martha developed an early familiarity with cameras that has served her well in the field, and she has had a major interest in travel as a pastime, continuing

Fig. 11.1. Martha Rolingson, December 1954, in front of a cliff dwelling at Walnut Canyon, Arizona, on a family vacation. (Photo courtesy of Martha Rolingson.)

to join her family in vacations through the years. She has a bowl they bought at Santa Clara pueblo, back when native women were just starting to make pottery for sale. She remembers it cost about five dollars, which was all that could be allotted for souvenirs at a time when both she and her brother were in school. There was also the Denver Museum of Natural History, which the family visited often. A Christmas present of C. W. Ceram's *Gods, Graves, and Scholars* and Ann Axtel Morris's books about archaeology enhanced her fascination with the subject.

Martha attributes her early interest in archaeology partially to the romantic point of view of a teenager but also to her family's strong emphasis on real history and archaeology rather than the popular ideas. She read *Natural History* magazine and saw role models such as marine biologist Eugenie Clark but noticed that most women in archaeology were married to archaeologists. In high school English class she asked to do a term paper on archaeology, and the resulting study of cenotes at Chichen Itza considerably impressed the teacher. Other early interests included playing piano and organ, and she was the assistant organist at her church. She got burned out on music, however, and did not know what kind of future she wanted, but she thought archaeology was fun. She declared an anthropology major her freshman year at the University of Denver. She lived at home, had scholarships, and worked part time to help pay for college. When she told the only full-time anthropology professor, Arnold Withers, that she wanted to be an archaeologist, he was very supportive; she remembers his saying, "What kind?" (classical or American), as opposed to "what for?"

At this time Frederick Douglass was at the Denver Art Museum as curator of ethnographic materials. These were housed in a separate late-nineteenth-century building, the Chappell House, where he used them in his evening classes. There was a session on pottery, one on silver jewelry, and so on. When he became ill and later died of leukemia, those courses were taken over by Kate Peck Kent, who had published a major report on fabrics but was afterwards less active professionally as she was raising a family. Martha remembers the building being packed with Plains Indian clothing on racks, pots, baskets, Northwest Coast house parts, South Pacific stuff, an "abysmal curation situation but just absolutely fascinating." The students spent one evening a week drawing and studying these materials. The class included some other women; one now runs an Indian craft shop in Denver. The anthropology-geography majors numbered only about ten in that period from 1953 to 1957. Two others went on in archaeology, Frank Swancara and James Maxon, the latter working in the Great Basin. The archaeology students went on field trips: a geographical survey of the town of Farmington, a visit to Aztec Ruin and Chaco Canyon. Martha also remembers James B. Griffin of the University of Michigan, a reigning figure in eastern U.S. archaeology whose student she would later become, visiting Denver to give an impressive Archaeological Institute of America lecture on Hopewell. He had brought a Hopewellian platform pipe, and after the talk he lit it up and began to smoke it.

No field archaeology was offered at Denver, so in 1956 Martha went on the University of Colorado's field school directed by Robert Lister. They dug at a mesa-top pueblo, MV875. There were many women in that field school though most were not career-oriented; some were teachers. They stayed at Mesa Verde National Park, where the superintendent was Jean Pinkley, the only woman in the National Park Service at that time. Because there were so many women, they used the old CCC dormitory and gave the men a house used for seasonal rangers. There was an adjacent building for a dining hall, kitchen, lab, and group area. Every student took a turn staying in camp for lab work, where one of the chores was to start a fire in the wood-burning stove for the girls' shower. There was only cold water, very cold at about seven thousand feet elevation, in that dorm. Florence Lister cooked for the group and supervised lab work, a typical role for an archaeologist's wife (Lister 1997). They were often visited by University of Colorado archaeologist Joe Ben Wheat, who was working at a site near the park. He was accompanied by his wife, another individual in the more typical role, who had training in archaeology but was attached to a man running things. Side trips were made to modern pueblos and other sites in New Mexico, always keeping holistic anthropology in mind.

During her college studies Martha knew of other women in the field, since many were visible in southwestern anthropology (Babcock and Parezo 1988; Parezo 1993c). For example, though Ruth Underhill was then retired from the University of Denver, her books were used in class. Marie Wormington was at the Denver Museum of Natural History. Seeing no problem being an anthropologist, but unsure about job possibilities, Martha had also taken the education requirements. She graduated Phi Beta Kappa with a B.A. in anthropology and education in 1957. Now she was on her own, and it was time to get away from home. She did not know whether she should go to Arizona, where so many others were headed. Withers recommended going to grad school in a different geographical area to get a different viewpoint, and the notion of going East appealed to her. However, having been turned down for a NSF fellowship and a University of Kentucky Museum assistantship, she could not afford to attend graduate school. So she applied for teaching positions.

That summer Martha was an interviewer for a federal Great Plains Health Study in Kit Carson County, eastern Colorado, in the town of Burlington. The project was directed by Gordon Macgregor with the Division of General Health Services. It studied attitudes toward regional health conditions, so there was good experience asking questions of strangers. In the fall she accepted a position teaching with the Minneapolis public schools, a big venture for a self-described shy woman. She enjoyed the colder climate and had a car and a nice roommate. But she remembers five sessions a day of seventh-grade geography, where the students ruled the classroom, and she realized that she did not really want to be a teacher. Midway through that year, Douglas W. Schwartz of Kentucky wrote and asked her to reapply. Thus she began a museum assistantship at Kentucky in the fall of 1958 and welcomed the chance to get a perspective on the East.

Eastward to Kentucky and Michigan

At the University of Kentucky, Martha worked with Schwartz in museum collections, education, and lab work. She gave talks and designed one temporary exhibit a month, a huge chore of planning, painting, and hammering. Other department faculty at the time were cultural anthropologist Frank J. Essene and physical anthropologist Charles E. Snow. Fellow students included John W. Walker (later of the National Park Service Southeast Region), R. Berle Clay (later state archaeologist of Kentucky), Brenda Johnson Clay (in cultural anthropology), Charles Hudson (later at the University of Georgia), Robert C. Dunnell (later at the University of Washington), Donald L. Hardesty (later at the University of Nevada), Jon N. Young and his wife Karen (from the Southwest), and Lee H. Hanson (who later went to Canada). Martha was the only woman in archaeology there, unlike in Colorado. But she remembers a fairly supportive intellectual environment (fig. 11.2). There was good access to museum collections. Her first publication (1961), in the *Transactions of the Kentucky Academy of Science*, came from doing an independent study on a small Mississippian site in west central Kentucky, the Kirtley site, that had been excavated by the WPA in the 1930s. She does recall the summer of 1959, processing materials coming in from the field, alone in the lab, while the men were excavating the Tinsley Hill site in the Barkley Reservoir on the Cumberland River.

At some point Martha became interested in Paleo-Indian archaeology for her thesis research. Little was known about it in the state, and the strategy

Fig. 11.2. Physical an-
thropology class at the
University of Kentucky,
taught by Charles E.
Snow, 1958–59. Martha
is being measured by
Francis E. Johnston.
(Photo courtesy of
Martha Rolingson.)

she developed included writing to amateurs and setting up interviews. She
drove all over the state visiting collectors and photographing their materials.
She says her standoffish attitude prevented any problems, even though she
worked alone. One exception to this was when mathematics graduate student Martha Watson accompanied her on a trip to western Kentucky to see
several collections. She had an address for someone way down in the Green
River bottomlands, outside of Paradise. This tiny town, in the middle of
nowhere, was the closest town to Indian Knoll and thus important in the
archaeological literature. They drove into a solid fogbank, down a narrow
dirt road, looking for this farmhouse near Paradise. It was spooky, but they
found the collector and he was very nice. Martha was grateful for a compan-
ion on that trip.

The Paleo-Indian survey was very basic. The only diagnostic artifacts
then were points, few of which had been found in excavated contexts. Much
later, feminist archaeologists would point out the gender-based division of
labor in artifact studies. Gero (1994), for example, noted how large projectile points (macho weaponry, for thrusting, penetrating, killing) have become more often the subjects of study by male investigators, while the re-
touch flakes, or any tiny tedious-to-count-in-the-lab items have been more
within the realm of what women commonly study. But these associations
were not in effect in 1959–60 (if indeed they are any more now), and Martha
had the precedent of Marie Wormington (for example, 1957), who was *the*
authority on Paleo-Indian in the 1950s and 1960s (in fact, she was asked if
she was following in Wormington's footsteps). Martha thinks that the image

of women as tedious-job housekeepers in the lab is a recent one and that it has an alternate side, as well: if it is a special and valuable talent, what is the difference between ghettoization and specialization?

The work on Paleo-Indian culture in Kentucky was published as a monograph in 1964. It began the documentation of one of the least-known portions of Kentucky prehistory, recording classic projectile points and demonstrating the denser distribution of these early sites in northern and western Kentucky. This work established the base for later, more specific research. With thesis and coursework completed, Martha encountered trouble with the language exam. Without any foreign language study in college, she took the Spanish exam hoping high school Spanish was enough, but she flunked it, then sat in a college class, took the exam again, and flunked it again. To make sure the last chance was not blown, she went home to Denver and studied for the month of June, went back and passed the exam, and was awarded her M.A. in the summer of 1960. Without any excavation experience beyond that as an undergraduate in Colorado, she then went with Doug Schwartz and his wife, two children, and a doctor friend to Grand Canyon National Park in July. They flew in by helicopter and surveyed Nankoweap Canyon, an easterly tributary stream on the north side of the Canyon (Schwartz 1963).

Returning to Kentucky in 1960–61 as museum curator, Martha managed collections, gave talks, and prepared exhibits, including one of birds and mammals for the zoology department and a traveling exhibit on Kentucky prehistory, which she took to four university extension centers (fig. 11.3). During that year she developed with Schwartz a successful NSF proposal entitled "Analysis and Synthesis of Kentucky Paleo-Indian" and began investigations on four sites: Morris and Parrish, excavated by the WPA in the late 1930s and early 1940s; the Roach site, on a portion of land between the Tennessee and the Cumberland Rivers that was inundated by Kentucky Lake; and the Henderson site on the Cumberland River. Some WPA site materials had never been washed or taken out of the bags, or the field notes examined. The Henderson site (now also inundated) had been recorded during surveys for the Barkley Reservoir but not well investigated. The decision was made to test there, providing Martha's first field experience in Kentucky, six years after her field school.

She was thought at that time not to have had enough experience to run a field project. Fellow graduate student Berle Clay was her assistant but had more field experience, so they ran it cooperatively, for a month in the summer of 1961, with a crew of six. It was OK for the crew to have women

Fig. 11.3. Martha and Charles E. Snow in the archaeology lab, University of Kentucky, with a traveling exhibit she designed and took to various schools throughout the year. (Photo courtesy of Martha Rolingson.)

because the supervisors were mixed, but Martha thinks perhaps there were no other mixed crews in Kentucky before that. They stayed at a Corps of Engineers' abandoned house in Eddyville, did their own cooking, and had to have the fellows crawl under the house and duct-tape the pipes in order to get enough running water. They tried to find the Roach site, though it was underwater. Getting maps and permission at the Corps office to go to the land between the two rivers, she was warned about the abundance of snakes there but went anyway. The project resulted in a 1966 publication in the university's anthropology series titled *Late Paleo-Indian and Early Archaic Manifestations in Western Kentucky*, coauthored with Schwartz. This monograph extensively documented the four sites, which had shell middens and later components as well, but which provided good data for exploring relationships between Paleo and Archaic. The research expanded the growing but still small database for Paleo-Indian, including smaller regional and temporal distinctions.

In the spring of 1963 Martha did research for the River Basin Salvage program. For one project, the proposed Grayson Reservoir on the Little Sandy River in eastern Kentucky, she worked alone, contacting landowners and doing a surface survey. She remembers being in the mountains and thinking that if anything happened to her, such as falling and breaking a leg, nobody would ever find her. Another project was the Laurel River Reservoir, for which Schwartz did the survey and she was the senior author of the report with him. A third project was for the Soil Conservation Service watershed protection program in south-central Kentucky; she did the survey for this one as well, and was senior author of the report. As a boss and teacher, Schwartz was supportive, and he obtained funding to continue her work and called on her for several projects.

During this time many students were talking about going on elsewhere to graduate school. Clay went to Southern Illinois. Martha applied several places, including Chicago and Michigan. She accepted a teaching assistantship at the University of Michigan in the fall of 1963 and was put in with the cultural anthropology students, across campus in Angell Hall, instead of with the other archaeology students whose work was in the museum building. At that time there was a traditional (and unfortunately too typical) rivalry between the Museum of Anthropology and the Department of Anthropology (Quimby and Cleland 1976:xxxi). Martha had little interaction with other archaeology students, and because she already had an M.A., she thinks the department had a harder time figuring out what to do with her. She was a teaching assistant alternately for Robert Burns's ethnology class, then for archaeologists Richard Keslin and Jim Fitting. Ethnology was big enough to have several teaching fellows, another of whom was Phyllis Morse. The ethnologist Burns was the father of Ken Burns, who did the Civil War television series and others. Martha's only archaeology course at Michigan was Griffin's North American archaeology. She took a bypass exam as a substitute for the archaeology core course taught by Arthur Jelinek, the other major archaeologist in the graduate program and the museum.

During the summer of 1964, Martha was hired by Griffin as field assistant for Jim Fitting at the Green Point site near Saginaw, Michigan. This was an interesting eleven-week project with a large, mixed crew, though Martha was the only supervisory woman. They dug twenty-foot-square units, Martha's being the one over the riverbank that extended six to eight feet deeper than all the others, full of artifacts and ash beds. It was dug in four ten-by-ten-foot units and followed apparent strata. It was a surprise because the ground surface was completely flat there; nobody had suspected the river had shifted over that far and that all the trash that had been dumped over the riverbank would be so neatly layered.

Martha was not involved in the write-up of that site, however, and halfway through her second year at Michigan, a call came from Schwartz in Kentucky saying he was taking a leave and asking her to teach his classes for a year. This would mean interrupting grad school, and he needed a quick decision. There was not even time to discuss it with Griffin, her advisor, who was out of town. She thinks Griffin might have been startled that she not only was leaving but also made the decision without him. Jelinek said she should not leave without at least giving preliminary exams a try. That meant studying for and taking prelims on top of taking classes and teaching assistant sections. It was a rough semester, but she passed the exams on the first try.

Michigan had an NSF summer fellowship program for students who were teaching assistants during the academic year. Martha then was awarded one of these and so could spend the summer of 1965 working hard toward the second language exam, in French (Michigan accepted the Spanish from Kentucky). They allowed a passing grade in a two-semester French course to substitute for the exam but agreed to let Martha take one semester of the class and try the exam if she passed the class. She spent the summer studying French and reading for her dissertation work. She passed everything and left after two years in Ann Arbor to return to Kentucky.

Back on the UK campus from 1965 to 1968, she taught Schwartz's graduate courses, was acting director of the Museum of Anthropology, and conducted dissertation work. This research involved writing up a dozen of the Green River Archaic sites in western Kentucky using museum materials. There was no excavation involved in this either, and Martha notes that, because she did so much work on museum collections, she probably had less excavation experience than anyone else when she later came to Arkansas. During the summer of 1967 there was a short field season on Eagle Creek north of Lexington, a River Basin Salvage project with a mixed crew of four. The rest of that summer and the remainder of those years were spent by herself in an off-campus maintenance building with no air-conditioning, "sorting and measuring and describing 50 bazillion Archaic projectile points," going through notes and Webb's site descriptions, looking for temporal variation and continuity in all those large shell mound sites.

It was really a continuation of her earlier work on Paleo and Archaic. And again, it was projectile points, though other stone tools too. She also reanalyzed burial contexts of sites and realized that the earlier Kentucky archaeologists had not saved broken tools, point tips, or flakes at all (a common practice in earlier decades in the Southeast). She had only points and stems, but it was plenty; she ended up with a five-hundred-page dissertation on the collections from twelve Archaic sites investigated by the WPA. It is interesting that Martha was not the first woman whose archaeology Ph.D. committee was chaired by Griffin; the first had been Marian White in 1956 (Bender 1994).

By May 1967 Martha had produced a finished dissertation draft and was ready to give her first SAA paper, made more challenging because somehow her slides were switched for someone else's. The dissertation story itself is a good one. The draft she had handed in had not yet been returned when Griffin, her chair, called to say he was leaving for a sabbatical and if she wanted to get done before he left she needed a finished dissertation that summer. She finally got the draft back from the rest of the committee, Fitting, Volney Jones, and Michigan geologist Bill Ferrin, and finished some eighty figures. There was considerable support from people in the museum at Kentucky, especially Louise Robbins, who was also working on a dissertation. In those days, final dissertation copy was typed onto a stencil then printed on 100 percent rag paper, an expensive process. Martha's dissertation defense was scheduled for early September, to meet Griffin's deadline and also the deadline for graduate school paperwork. Martha was running continuously from typist to print shop in a flurry of activity, with maybe two hours of sleep a night for several days, to get it done on time. When she finally finished, the print shop man asked how she was going to get it up there to Michigan. When she said she would drive, he said, no you're not! And Louise said, no you're not! There was talk of renting an airplane to fly up to Ann Arbor, but that was too expensive. So Louise Robbins drove her to Ann Arbor. They jumped into Louise's station wagon, zipped by the print shop for the last pages, and headed up the road with Martha sitting cross-legged in the back collating the pages. About an hour into the trip Martha realized it was not all there. They called the man at the print shop, who found the missing pages, and they turned around to go back for them. As they zoomed up to the print shop the man stuck his hand out with the pages. They grabbed them and flew north again, driving all night, arriving in Ann Arbor at 5:00 A.M. They stopped outside town and sacked out in the back of the wagon for some sleep, then made it to turn the manuscript in and get it stamped and off to the binder's by 8:00 A.M. The binder required twenty-four hours, during which Martha had to register for summer school in order to graduate, not an easy task as this was the week for fall registration. In a fog by then, she remembers the defense as anticlimactic. She repaid Louise by proofreading and checking all the figures and statistical tables for all the skeletons from the Fort Ancient site for her dissertation (probably an even trade). At the museum/department party in December celebrating the degree, Martha was presented with a treasured gift: her own trowel mounted on a walnut base with a plaque.

At Kentucky Martha continued museum duties and fieldwork; she also had taught graduate courses for two years, as a graduate student herself. Schwartz decided at the end of his leave (at the School of American Research in Santa Fe, where he remains today) that he was not coming back, so they continued Martha in the temporary position while they did a search for a permanent museum director. Having completed graduate work by fall 1967, she moved from the position of instructor at the university to assistant professor and was then assigned to teach undergraduate classes. But she realized that she was not going to be considered for the director position. The department was growing in the direction of medical and social anthropology, with work in the Appalachians, and figures such as Marion Pearsall and Margaret Lantis. Archaeology was being de-emphasized. By late 1967, she realized she had better check out the job market. Attending the AAA meeting in Washington, she applied for the position just opened with the Arkansas Archeological Survey, interviewed there in March, got the job and moved there in July 1968, where her career has expanded ever since.

Arkansas Accomplishments

Hester Davis notes that when they interviewed potential station archaeologists in Arkansas, they would take candidates from Fayetteville to Conway, through Little Rock and, in this case, down to Monticello, because they required approval by the host college authorities too. When the Arkansas Archaeological Survey was created in 1967, funding was provided for only three research stations around the state. To spread them around geographically from Fayetteville in the northwest, where the coordinating office was, they had chosen Arkansas State University in Jonesboro in the northeast, Henderson State University in the southwest, and Arkansas AM&N in Pine Bluff. In 1968, four more stations were added, including Arkansas A&M (now the University of Arkansas at Monticello) in the southeast. The Survey (see fig. 10.3) had previously hired Burney McClurkan for the Monticello station but had encountered a difficulty. By coincidence at that time, the board of trustees of the college in Monticello had been involved in a bad lawsuit brought by a former English professor who had been fired, probably for politically incorrect ideas, and had raised a terrible stink. This man had a beard, and his appearance had made a lasting impression. When McClurkan, having accepted the job, turned up bearded in a routine interview, he was deemed unacceptable and the embarrassed Survey had to renegotiate a different post for him at Arkansas AM&N at Pine Bluff (a historically black institution). When they brought Martha to Monticello, one of the interviewers said to Hester, "well, at least this one doesn't have a beard!"

After accepting the job, Martha completed one last field session in Kentucky in June 1968, on a River Basin Salvage contract for the National Park Service to test some sites at Cave Run Reservoir in the eastern mountains, not far from Morehead. She had a mixed crew of eight, including grad student assistant Mike Rodeffer and his future wife, Stephanie Holschlag. They ended up with an abysmal old house that had already been bought up to be removed for the reservoir, so the locals had helped themselves to the electrical wiring. There was no running water either, just cold well water for bathing, and an outhouse. Some of the girls refused to shovel because it would give them unsightly muscles. Then it turned cold and started raining, for eighteen out of twenty-one field days. They were never dry or warm; the shallow Mississippian site filled with water. They bailed the units but it immediately bubbled back in. Finally, the Park Service said they could go to the other sites and try again later. Many crew members then had to leave after the scheduled three weeks, so only Martha and Mike stayed to finish, profiling walls and backfilling. By then it had quit raining and gone from 50 degrees to something like 100. After that they rushed back to Lexington to get it all written up in time for her to arrive in Arkansas by July.

At Monticello for four years, Martha taught courses, did research and survey archaeology, and adapted to small-town life. She became a popular dinner and party guest and remembers never getting to eat much because people were so curious and interested in her they never stopped asking questions. "How did you get to be an archaeologist?" "I can't imagine a woman archaeologist!" "What church do you go to?" And in field situations, two persistent questions: "Where are you from?" (because of her accent) and "Why aren't you married?" She answered that she was having too much fun doing archaeology to get married. But she did not get any grief for being unusual and knows that she was more effective working alone since, if she drove up to a farm to ask permission, the farmer would automatically talk to any man along, even a student assistant, and not to her (a situation still routinely encountered in the field by many women, unfortunately). When she was alone they had to talk to her. She realized she had been accepted when people started asking where she was farming; she thought she must look as though she fit in instead of being a weird stranger.

As the first station archaeologist in southeastern Arkansas, Martha had responsibility for seven counties. At that time the archaeology of the area was practically unknown. The first tasks were to record sites, obtain surface collections, rough out a culture history, and develop a research program. She worked mostly with amateurs and collectors, doing intensive survey and excavation of five sites. Research objectives included investigating the interaction of prehistoric peoples of the Boeuf Basin with neighboring groups, and two projects were developed. The first was a response to massive site destruction due to agricultural practices. Janet Ford, then a Tulane University graduate student, was hired as Martha's assistant, and they tested six sites in 1969 and collected data and materials on many others in the eastern (delta) portion of southeast Arkansas. They inventoried impacts from land leveling and other human activities, urgently noting the race to record all this threatened evidence ahead of the machines and management policies of destruction (Ford and Rolingson 1972).

The second project was a survey adjacent to Bayou Bartholomew, on the western edge of the Boeuf Basin. The wife of a prominent farmer in Ashley County took an interest in archaeology, shared her collections, and introduced Martha to many sites and people. Not confined to a limited field season, the project could include revisits to sites under different conditions for thorough characterization. This work resulted in records on one hundred sites and test excavations at four of them in 1970 and 1971 (Rolingson 1970, 1971b), finally published more extensively later (Rolingson 1993). Later, she defined the Bartholomew Phase in southeast Arkansas as a short-lived, possibly intrusive, Plaquemine adaptation extending beyond the lower Mississippi Valley, the previously defined range of this regional Mississippian variant. Up to that time Bartholomew Phase sites had been assumed to be of the Caddoan tradition. The settlement pattern included everything from small temple mound ceremonial centers to individual houses and camps, all well correlated with physiographic zones. Her appraisal also included a discussion of meander belt channel shifts in the Arkansas and Mississippi alluvial valleys and their effects on prehistoric human adaptations in the last millennium (Rolingson 1976, 1983).

In 1971–72, Martha was also conducting survey in the swampy jungle of the proposed Felsenthal National Wildlife Refuge on the Ouachita River. She found survey conditions extremely difficult, with "the few existing roads . . . nearly impassable much of the year due to flooding" and considerable effort needed to reach and evaluate sites (Rolingson and Schambach 1981:3). This work resulted in a report to the National Park Service and a later work on the Shallow Lake site (Rolingson and Schambach 1981). Some of the reporting had to be delayed because Bob McGimsey, director of the Survey, called her to work in Fayetteville. So in the fall of 1972, having had, Martha says, her fill of small-town south Arkansas, she went to the "big city" (Fayetteville's population was then under thirty thousand), where she stayed until 1979. The position was primarily administrative. It included working with the director, the state archaeologist, various governmental agencies, and the University of Arkansas Museum. She organized the publishing of reports on research projects and was responsible for Survey/Society training and certification programs for amateurs, and for the contract archaeology program. There was no station archaeologist for the northwest region, so she worked with local amateurs and served as state archaeologist for six months when Davis was on leave in 1975. In addition, she taught classes in the anthropology department.

The seventies also saw Martha elected secretary of the Southeastern Archaeological Conference, serving from 1973 to 1978 and helping to draft the initial constitution, as well as serving the Society of Professional Archaeologists on boards and committees. Meanwhile she continued analysis of earlier years' work in southeast Arkansas. The Shallow Lake site was a multi-mound and midden site in the Ouachita River bottomland of the Felsenthal National Wildlife Refuge. Excavations by station archaeologists at Mound C showed it to be a clay cap on top of the remains of a circular structure dating to the thirteenth century. Martha worked on the monograph, which included descriptions of components from preceramic through the sub-mound Coles Creek through Mississippian, and discussion of environment, ceramics, subsistence, and intra-site variability (Rolingson and Schambach 1981). In addition to all this work, by 1976 Martha had started research at Toltec.

Toltec Mounds

Now preserved in Toltec Mounds Archeological State Park in Scott, on an abandoned meander channel in the Arkansas River Lowland, this eighteen-mound and earthwork complex is famous in the southeastern United States. It is known for an archaeological record that does not fit smoothly into accepted notions of Woodland and Mississippian archetypal culture, or stereotypes of prehistoric maize agriculturalists' complex society (for more on Toltec mounds and imaginative interpretations of prehistory there, see chapter 15). The first field season at Toltec was in 1976. Controlled surface collections were combined with the 1894 plat map to establish locations of various now-leveled mounds. In 1977 Martha took the University of Fayetteville's field school there for five weeks for the first excavation season, involving work on Mound D. In 1978 she hired Michael J. Kaczor and a crew of sixteen for twelve weeks, and she also worked with Judith Stewart, field director for the University of Arkansas field school, and her student crew for five weeks. The Arkansas Archeological Society training program also took place for two and one-half of these weeks. During this frustrating season there developed strange conflicts among the groups, with the field school students wanting the classes given to the training program people and the latter saying they ought to be covering what the field school was getting, and both groups working (and complaining) on Mound D, and the paid crew elsewhere. Martha spent much time trying to calm everyone down in this summer of the "three-ring circus." She remembers storming into camp hot, tired, hungry, and fed up with the whole scene, grabbing a cold drink and walking up to Hester Davis saying she would never do this again. Hester said nothing in reply.

Of course Martha did do it again, often, finally moving in 1979 to the Toltec Mounds Research Station in Scott and establishing her own home in North Little Rock. In 1979 there was a hired crew for the summer and also the Society dig again (fig. 11.4), and in 1980 another hired crew. Kaczor continued as field director until 1983 when the money ran out. The work has carried on for more than two decades (fig. 11.5). Martha considers this the most satisfying portion of her career, developing her ideas on the site and prehistoric cultural evolution in the region, working with hypotheses, and having them grow and change.

The 40 ha Toltec Mounds site is surrounded by an earthen embankment and ditch 1.6 km long, and the major occupation dates to the period from A.D. 500–1000. It had long been considered a Mississippian center, especially because of its impressive size, number and size of mounds, plaza, and flat-topped platform mound. Martha's work demonstrated that it was much earlier, with only small amounts of evidence for later and earlier occupations. The cultural adaptations of its inhabitants were explored in a 1979 symposium entitled "Toltec Mounds Research Project: Northern Coles Creek Culture in the Arkansas River Valley" at the Southeastern Archaeological Conference in Atlanta. Those and subsequent discussions led Martha to develop the concept of the Late Woodland Plum Bayou culture, spanning

Fig. 11.4. Toltec Mounds State Park, July 1979, consultation about soils and mound fill. *Left to right:* John Belmont, Michael Kaczor, Martha Rolingson, and John House. (Photo courtesy of the Arkansas Archeological Survey.)

Fig. 11.5. Toltec Mounds State Park, November 1982, with University of Arkansas at Little Rock field school. Martha demonstrates shoveling technique that will make soil flip over into the screen. (Photo courtesy of Martha Rolingson.)

the late Baytown and early Coles Creek periods in the chronology of the Lower Mississippi Valley. Typical characteristics include a predominance of plain grog-tempered pottery and abundant lithic materials of predominantly pebble cherts, comprising assemblages of flake tools including bifaces and arrow points. There are similarities with Coles Creek culture, but that is 100–200 km to the south in the Lower Mississippi Valley, and platform mounds are slightly later in Coles Creek. Plum Bayou pottery is plainer and quite distinctive beyond the general similarities with Coles Creek, and in most Lower Mississippi Valley sites, stone is scarce. Clearly Plum Bayou is a distinctive regional manifestation (Rolingson 1982a).

As for the Toltec site itself, all investigations have been hampered by the fact that it is severely damaged by human and natural processes. However, an enormous body of data has been recovered and much reconstruction is possible. The embankment has no postmolds or indication of defensive use; its design was carefully laid out before construction. Major mound building seems to have taken place from A.D. 700–1000. Some mounds were platforms for dwellings, and Mound C was an accretional burial mound (Miller 1982:42). Martha's current view on the embankment is that it is the predominant feature of the site in terms of size and work effort. It was probably constructed rapidly and involved corporate activity and a leader. It may have defined the site as a sacred space; it is certainly closer in concept to Woodland enclosures than to Mississippian spatial design.

Ceramics and other evidence demonstrate continuity from submound to later occupations within Plum Bayou. Some mounds are earlier, some later, and Mound B, the large platform, was apparently continuously in use. Later investigations have explored the low mounds damaged by farming activities. Excavations on Mound D at the south end of the plaza took place in the late 1970s; a decade later, three seasons of work went into excavations at Mound S, and there were other field projects in the park as well. Now Martha has turned her attention back to Mound D and a comprehensive report. One thing that has changed is the dating of the site. There had not been good features from which to obtain more precise dating of artifact assemblages, and Martha recognizes that getting radiocarbon dates out of midden materials is more chancy. Four recent dates were later than expected but internally consistent. They extend the occupation of the site for one hundred or more years. Furthermore, now that there are other dates from other parts of the site, it is clear that the prehistoric inhabitants never viewed this as a complex with eighteen mounds, because they were using the mounds serially or sequentially, abandoning some and building others. Building and using

Mound S back in A.D. 750, they had a completely different concept of the site than did the folks who built Mound D at A.D. 1000. As a result, there are changing perceptions of what the site might have been like to the people who were using it. The recent major synthesis demonstrates that Mound D was a low platform built between A.D. 950–1050; the submound floor produced archeomagnetic dates of A.D. 800–860 (Rolingson 1998).

This and other recent work has produced a wealth of biotic materials as well, confirming a diffuse subsistence pattern, utilizing a wide variety of species. From the beginning, they were growing maize, but it is unclear how dependent the people were upon it, because they were also growing little barley, maygrass, chenopod, and amaranth. The maize may have started out small, as just another garden crop. Maybe it was a sacred or otherwise special food, but there is no evidence of dependence upon it as a principal crop. To complicate the picture even more, the most maize from the site is from the earliest mound that has been dated, not the latest one. Much new work has also documented status-related artifacts and raw materials, and the efforts and distance of travel that would have been necessary to obtain them. However, no evidence for elaborate mortuary patterns has yet been recovered. Plum Bayou settlement patterns are not well known beyond the vicinity of Toltec, which had been assumed to be a center for higher-ranking people in a hierarchical Late Woodland system. Clearly it was a central locale within local and interregional exchange networks, but a study by Nassaney (1992) showed more evidence for communal society, not rule by a few elites using force to obtain surplus or mobilize production and exchange.

As research continues, archaeological knowledge has been expanded using the Toltec data. One notable study Martha carried out with P. Clay Sherrod presents detailed comparative measurements of Toltec, Cahokia, and other mound centers in the Mississippi Valley to establish some insights into prehistoric astronomical and engineering knowledge. Principles for planning construction of ceremonial mound centers were seen to include celestial orientation, especially mound alignment conforming to the solstices and equinoxes, and a standard unit of measure equaling 47.5 m for mound spacing distances. Both began use at least by Coles Creek times, and the distance module, at least, continued in use through Mississippian times. Moving beyond the material evidence, some glimmer of the complexity of thought and society of late prehistoric times can be inferred (Sherrod and Rolingson 1987). Lately, Martha has thought that mounds may not have been constructed to use as calendrical markers per se; their positioning and that of houses and other features may reflect a symbolic plan, building on earth in the same arrangement as the celestial world to integrate the physical and the cosmological.

Reflections on a Continuing Career

Martha has moved around in the Arkansas system, accomplished all this admirable research, and continued contributions in the training of new archaeologists and certifying avocationals in the Society program (fig. 11.6). Though she has not taught university courses lately, and though she misses having had graduate students, she is still teaching every year as she runs various projects. Lately she has appeared on television (A&E network) in an "Ancient Mysteries" program on mound builders. She has always enjoyed the job and appreciated its advantages. For example, at many of the Arkansas research stations there is relative isolation; people are stuck out there by themselves with no colleagues to talk to, with less access to a good anthropological library. Even when the stations are associated with small colleges, there is still nobody around doing the kind of work the Survey archaeologist is doing, and the emphasis is upon teaching; research is not encouraged. On the other hand, the close contact that might breed discord within departments of anthropology is also absent. But still, professionals only get together rarely, at annual meetings and a few other occasions when there are research problems in common. As far as other aspects of the work environ-

Fig. 11.6. Ann Early and Martha Rolingson in the archaeology lab during the Survey/Society training program at the Holman Springs site, July 1986. (Photo courtesy of the Arkansas Archeological Survey.)

ment are concerned, Martha thinks a major advantage has been pretty equal treatment and absence of bickering between genders. Whether this is due to McGimsey's management style or the presence of Davis or the large number of other women in the Survey is hard to determine (fig. 11.7). She notes the Survey hiring practice that identifies applicants only by initials so that the names and genders of the candidates are unknown.

Of all her professional responsibilities, Martha has enjoyed the research the most. She is now a full professor. She says it has never been dull over the past forty years, including thirty years of commitment to Arkansas archaeology. There has been much satisfaction also in moving around and exploring such different geographical and research areas. She remains active, attending meetings and interacting constantly with fellow professionals (fig. 11.8). She has noted (1997) that women in her age group in the profession are few and says in retrospect that she has "the sense of being caught at the front of a wave. When I started graduate work in 1958 there were few women in archaeology but, by the time I finished in 1968 they were all over the place."

Concerning her career style in archaeology, in Dincauze's (1992:132) terms, Martha remains single, as have many other women in archaeology. She says, somewhere along the way she realized she was not going to get married, and the career is more fun; there are no regrets. She has had a colleague tell her that she needed a wife (reminiscent of the classic statement in Syfers 1972, 1973: who *wouldn't* want a wife?), and she recently remarked that what she needed was a clone or two. She has strong ties to her

Fig. 11.7. Martha Rolingson and Hester Davis in a moment of serious decision making during the Survey/Society Training Program at Toltec Mounds State Park, June 1988. (Photo courtesy of Martha Rolingson.)

Fig. 11.8. Martha Rolingson, Patty Jo Watson, and Hester Davis appreciating Martha's basket collection in the library of her home in North Little Rock, October 1995. (Photo by Nancy White.)

parents and finds time for other active pursuits, from travel to needlepoint. The latter is restful and creative fun, as seen on her office wall in the beautiful needlepoint Mississippian bird dancer of her own design, after the original from Etowah (fig. 11.9).

Martha does recognize a general difference in the approaches of men and women in archaeology: men being used to others doing for them, delegating little tasks that they would not usually do unless absolutely forced to, and women used to going ahead and doing it all themselves. She finds boring some of the minutiae of lab work, preferring to hand the artifacts to someone and say, here, number these. But beyond just processing, Martha needs to handle the materials herself, see what connections there are, use her decades of training for understanding more than would someone who is just there to number specimens or has only a few weeks of training. She thinks perhaps this is not the case on most projects, especially contract work, where the processing, cataloguing, and classification are done by lab workers and the tables and figures come back to the male PI, who then writes the report from these documents, without the closer connections to the raw data.

Is there a different point of view that women may have in archaeological interpretation? Martha reminds us that the expansion in all of archaeology has enormously widened the range of interests. When southeastern archaeology was small, research interests were more narrowly defined. There were

Fig. 11.9. Martha Rolingson's original needlepoint of Mississippian bird dancer figure, based on the representations from Etowah. (Photo courtesy of Martha Rolingson.)

fads, and anyone doing research on an unpopular topic was mostly ignored. Her Paleo-Indian work was accepted because "early man" studies were popular. She says, "If I had tried to talk about the tasks of women and the division of labor in the late Paleo-Indian period, I would have been ignored. Today that would be an interesting and acceptable topic."

As for advice to those studying to be archaeologists, she encourages strong determination to get the work done, whether you are criticized or not. There might be rough times, but there is great satisfaction in giving a good paper or turning out a report, giving people an original piece of research. Furthermore, she cautions that it is important to remember you are an anthropologist in the field; this means adapting to the cultural-social environment. She says, if letting a man do things for you in a gallant southern manner makes a woman's position more acceptable, then go ahead and let him do it. Politeness goes a long way toward helping people feel comfortable while working together, a concept she thinks has become downgraded recently.

Martha has had good relationships with colleagues and workers, both male and female. She thinks she has faced variable situations and encountered some discrimination, but it has not been overwhelming. There has been help along the way, she states, as well as stumbling blocks. Today we ask why women in the past did not protest the limits on acceptable tasks. But in the late 1950s and 1960s there simply was no choice. At Kentucky in 1959, she says, it would have done no good to protest being left in the lab while the guys went out into the field. She did learn a lot in the lab, and, had she protested, there would have been no job for her at all, not to mention future difficulty in relationships with faculty. She has herself (1997) described a large sample of women's archaeological contributions in the mid-South region and pointed out the gaps in our knowledge between those who have published and those in support activities who are difficult to document. But she is proud to say that today women *can* demand more of a choice. One of the reasons we can is that pioneers such as Martha Rolingson set the precedent.

Selected Bibliography of Martha Ann Rolingson

Boyd, L., and Martha A. Rolingson
1978   *Toltec Indian Mounds Site: Search for the Past.* Arkansas Archeological Survey, booklet no. 1.
Early, Ann M., and Martha A. Rolingson
1977   A Field Training for Amateur Archaeologists: The Arkansas Example. In *Teaching and Training in American Archaeology, a Survey of Programs and Philosophies,* edited by William P. McHugh. *Southern Illinois University Museum Studies* 10, pp. 176–91.
Rolingson, Martha A.
1961   The Kirtley Site, a Mississippian Village in McLean County, Kentucky. *Transactions of the Kentucky Academy of Science* 22 (3–4):41–59.
1963   An Archeological Survey of the Grayson Reservoir. Manuscript on file with University of Kentucky Museum of Anthropology and National Park Service Southeast Region, Tallahassee.
1964   *Paleo-Indian Culture in Kentucky.* Studies in Anthropology No. 2. University of Kentucky Press, Lexington.
1968   Preliminary Excavations in the Eagle Creek Reservoir, Grant and Owen Counties, Kentucky. Manuscript on file with University of Kentucky Museum of Anthropology and National Park Service Southeast Region, Tallahassee.
1970   Archeological Investigation of Bayou Bartholomew, 1969. *Proceedings of the Arkansas Academy of Science,* vol. 24. Fayetteville.
1971a   Lakeport: Initial Exploration of a Late Prehistoric Ceremonial Center in Southeastern Arkansas. *Arkansas Archeologist* 12 (4):61–80.
1971b   The Ashley Point. *Arkansas Archeologist* 12 (3):50–52.

1971c   Settlement Pattern of the Plaquemine Culture along Bayou Bartholomew. *Southeastern Archaeological Conference Bulletin* 13. Morgantown.

1972a   Report on the Preliminary Site Survey of the Felsenthal National Wildlife Refuge. Manuscript on file with the Arkansas Archeological Survey, Fayetteville, and National Park Service Southwest Region, Santa Fe.

1972b   Preliminary Report on the Test Excavation at Coon Island Site. *Field Notes. Newsletter of the Arkansas Archeological Society*, no. 88.

1974   Archeological Reconnaissance of the Upper Petit Jean Watershed Site #9 Project, Sebastian County, Arkansas. Manuscript on file with Arkansas Archeological Survey, Fayetteville and Soil Conservation Service, Little Rock.

1976   The Bartholomew Phase: Plaquemine Adaptation in the Mississippi Valley. In *Cultural Change and Continuity*, edited by Charles E. Cleland, pp. 99–119. Academic Press, New York.

1982a   *Emerging Patterns of Plum Bayou Culture: Preliminary Investigations of the Toltec Mounds Research Project*. Toltec Papers II. Arkansas Archeological Survey Research Series 18. (Author of four articles; editor of six articles.)

1982b   Public Archaeology: Research and Development of the Toltec Site. In *Arkansas Archaeology in Review*, edited by Neal L. Trubowitz and Marvin D. Jeter, pp. 48–75. Arkansas Archeological Survey Research Series 15.

1983   Floods and Forests: Clues to the Mississippi Valley Floodplain Environment in Southeastern Arkansas and Significance for Prehistoric Settlement. *Southeastern Archaeological Conference Bulletin* 20:162–67.

1984a   Archaeology and Prehistory in Public Parks, Southeastern North America. *Mid-Continental Journal of Archaeology* 9(2):155–71.

1984b   Discovery of Use of Engineering at Prehistoric Indian Communities. Field Notes. *Newsletter of the Arkansas Archeological Society* 200:9–11.

1986   Public Archaeology at Toltec Mounds State Park. In *Archaeological Parks: Integrating Preservation, Interpretation, and Recreation*, edited by Mary L. Kwas, pp. 17–22. Tennessee Department of Conservation, Division of Parks and Recreation, Nashville.

1988a   An Assessment of the Significance of Clay-tempered Ceramics and Platform Mounds at the Toltec Mounds Site. In *The Emergent Mississippian: Proceedings of the Sixth Mid-South Archaeological Conference*, edited by Richard A. Marshall, pp. 107–16. Mississippi State University, Occasional Papers 87-01. Starkville, Mississippi.

1988b   Archeological Investigation of the Greer Site, 3JE50. Arkansas Archeological Survey Project No. 657. Report submitted to Little Rock District, U.S. Army Corps of Engineers, Little Rock, Arkansas.

1989   The 1988 Society Dig at Toltec Mounds State Park. *Field Notes. Newsletter of the Arkansas Archeological Society* 227:7–11. Fayetteville, Arkansas.

1990   The Toltec Mounds Site: A Ceremonial Center in the Arkansas River Lowland. In *The Mississippian Emergence*, edited by Bruce D. Smith, pp. 27–49. Smithsonian Institution Press.

1992   Excavations of Mound S at the Toltec Mounds Site: Preliminary Report. *Arkansas Archeologist* 31:1–29.

1993   Archeology along Bayou Bartholomew, Southeast Arkansas. *Arkansas Archeologist* 32:1–138.
1996   Elements of Community Design at Cahokia. In Symposium Papers, "The Ancient Skies and Sky Watchers of Cahokia: Woodhenges, Eclipses, and Cahokia Cosmology" edited by Melvin Fowler, *Wisconsin Archaeologist* 77 (3/4):84–96.
1997   Contributions of Women to Mid-South Archaeology. Paper presented to the Mid-South Archaeological Conference, Jonesboro, Arkansas.
1998   *Toltec Mounds and Plum Bayou Culture: Mound D Excavations.* Arkansas Archeological Survey Research Series 54, Fayetteville.

Rolingson, Martha A., and J. Michael Howard
1997   Igneous Lithics of Central Arkansas: Identification, Sources, and Artifact Distribution. *Southeastern Archaeology* 16:33–50.

Rolingson, Martha A., and Marvin D. Jeter
1986   An Assessment of Archaeological Data for the Tchula Period in Southeastern Arkansas. In *The Tchula Period in the Mid-South and Lower Mississippi Valley,* edited by David H. Dye, and Ronald C. Brister, pp. 93–101. Mississippi Department of Archives and History, Archaeological Report No. 17.

Rolingson, Martha A., and Michael J. Kaczor
1987   *Toltec-DELOS Artifact Inventory System and Dictionary* (Version 1.0). Arkansas Archeological Survey Technical Paper No. 7a. Fayetteville.

Rolingson, Martha A., and Michael J. Rodeffer
1968a   Archeological Excavation in Cave Run Reservoir, Kentucky: Progress Report, 1968. Manuscript on file with University of Kentucky Museum of Anthropology and National Park Service Southeast Region, Tallahassee.
1968b   The Zilpo Site, BH37, Preliminary Excavations in the Cave Run Reservoir, Kentucky: 1968. Manuscript on file with University of Kentucky Museum of Anthropology and National Park Service Southwest Region, Tallahassee.

Rolingson, Martha A., and Frank Schambach
1981   *The Shallow Lake Site. 3UN9/52 and Its Place in Regional Prehistory.* Arkansas Archeological Survey Research Series 12.

Rolingson, Martha A., and Douglas W. Schwartz
1963a   Archeology in Watershed Protection Projects: A Sample with Recommendations. Manuscript on file with University of Kentucky Museum of Anthropology and National Park Service Southeast Region, Tallahassee.
1963b   Archeological Survey of the Laurel River Reservoir. Manuscript on file with University of Kentucky Museum of Anthropology and National Park Service Southeast Region, Tallahassee.
1966   *Late Paleo-Indian and Early Archaic Manifestations in Western Kentucky.* Studies in Anthropology No. 3, University of Kentucky Press, Lexington.

Sherrod, P. Clay, and Martha A. Rolingson
1987   *Surveyors of the Ancient Mississippi Valley.* Arkansas Archeological Survey Research Series 28, Fayetteville.

12

Elizabeth S. Wing

A Patient but Persistent Vision

ROCHELLE A. MARRINAN

Elizabeth S. Wing received the Fryxell Award, for excellence in archaeological science, from the Society for American Archaeology at the 1996 annual meeting in New Orleans. In the audience that gave her a standing ovation, I thought about what her patience and hard work had achieved. That year also marked thirty-five years of involvement in building both the institutional base and the scientific knowledge that is now taken for granted by students and professional collaborators. Donald Grayson (1997:577) has recently characterized Liz Wing as "one of North America's most quietly influential zooarchaeologists." She is a member of the cadre of scholars and researchers (including Volney Jones, Kent V. Flannery, Richard A. Yarnell, Paul W. Parmalee, and Stanley J. Olsen, in the United States) who have pioneered the emergence of subdisciplinary specialties now broadly termed environmental archaeology. These individuals labored to establish their roles and data as legitimate for answering anthropological and archaeological questions.

First impressions often leave vivid memories. Mine was formed during a brief meeting at the Florida State Museum (now the Florida Museum of Natural History—FMNH) in 1971. She stood about 5 ft 2 in, had brilliant blue eyes, and graying blonde hair. She was reading Margaret Ashley Towle's *Ethnobotany of Pre-Columbian Peru* (1961; see chapter 2, this volume). I had come with her graduate student, Stephen L. Cumbaa, to ask permission to work on a faunal sample for a field school paper. In the weeks and months to come, I would use her range (the area within the museum where the site collections were stored) and the comparative collection to analyze material from 8Al169 (Melton Village site). It was the first encounter of a long relationship that is both professional and personal. At the time of our meeting, Liz was well along the path to being recognized as one of the American founders of the specialty we today recognize as zooarchaeology but not yet on the path that would broaden into environmental archaeology.

Anna Elizabeth Schwarz (Wing) was born in Cambridge, Massachusetts, on March 5, 1932. Her father, Henry F. Schwarz, was born in Connecticut, a New Englander descended from German grandparents. His grandfather, F. A. O. Schwarz, founded the toy store that bears his name today. Maria Lisa Schwarz, her mother, was from Austria. Her parents had married in Europe and were expecting Liz, the first of their three children, when they arrived in this country. Caroline and Henry were born six and nine years later, respectively. Her father taught Eastern European history at Wellesley College. German was spoken at home. She attended the Winsor School in Boston and was graduated in 1951. Bouts with scarlet and glandular fevers delayed her graduation one year.

She was interested in animals early in life. One of her earliest memories is of collecting a whole bucket of earthworms from a newly spaded garden and proudly presenting them to her parents. While the "wonderful writhing mass" was not greeted with enthusiasm, she acknowledges that it probably signaled her preadaptation to skeletal preparation (Wing 1990b), a necessary skill for the career she would develop.

Barbara Lawrence, a mammalogist at the Museum of Comparative Zoology (MCZ) at Harvard, was one of the first friends her mother made in this country. Lawrence, who died in 1997, made arrangements for Liz to be a summer volunteer at the museum, beginning in high school. Lawrence spoke with other curators on the staff whom she felt could tolerate a young volunteer. The work was menial but interesting. Liz particularly remembers dusting glass on the bug cases and changing the alcohol in the hermit crab collection. She worked for the zoogeographer Phillip Darlington, arranging his map and beetle collections; the diversity of the latter collection remains a vivid memory.

She also worked for Liska Deichmann, curator of crustaceans. Deichmann was single, a woman of great personal force who was not swayed by public opinion or fashion. Fondly called "the Great Dane," Deichmann once took a great fancy to the borrowed jeep that Liz drove to the museum. She asked to test drive it and got stuck, much to Liz's teenage embarrassment. Ruth D. Turner, a research associate in malacology, was another woman on the staff. Some of the women, like Lawrence, had begun as volunteers at the MCZ and stayed on to become curators. While Lawrence held no advanced degree, she was initially employed as an assistant to the curator of mammals, Glover M. Allen, in field collection maintenance. Liz remembers Allen's leading an expedition to the Far East from which Lawrence, as a single female, was excluded. Instead, Lawrence went alone to the Far East collecting in Borneo, China, and the Philippines. When Allen died, Lawrence became curator of mammals. In those days, Liz recalls, "there was more of an apprenticeship approach in museum curatorship." She credits the interaction among the curators and departments with forming an early interdisciplinary awareness.

Barbara Lawrence had begun to identify faunal remains from archaeological sites just before Liz left for graduate studies. Lawrence had been asked to identify "bags of bones" by archaeologists, but Liz recalls Lawrence's excitement about Robert Braidwood's Near Eastern projects. Braidwood had a very broad view of archaeology, and the team approach of the interdisciplinary group he assembled was much appreciated by Lawrence.

After completing high school, Liz entered Mount Holyoke College. Given her father's employment, attending Wellesley seemed inappropriate. She says she chose Mount Holyoke because it was enthusiastically recommended by one of her high school teachers. She "waited tables and fed salamanders for $.75 per hour" during her undergraduate years. She completed a B.A. in biology at Mount Holyoke in 1955 and embarked upon a career in biology at a time when medical research dominated the discipline. She was directed to microbiology and medical research, but her interests continued to be in whole animal biology. She spent one summer at the Jackson Memorial Laboratory, Bar Harbor, Maine, among a group of college students. In this program, she served as a laboratory assistant to Phillip White, a tissue culturist, who had developed the artificial fluids that were used to grow cell cultures. In White's lab, she explored cellular biology but was not swayed.

As she considered where to enroll for graduate studies, she asked the advice of Ann Haven Morgan, an ecologist who had retired from Mount Holyoke before Liz came to school there. Morgan, author of *Fieldbook of Ponds and Streams* (1930) on marsh and wetland ecology, and a biology textbook (*Kinship of Animals and Man*) in 1955, continued her field interests in the Mount Holyoke area after retirement. Morgan's advice, and the advice of others Liz consulted, narrowed her choices to the University of Chicago or the University of Florida (UF). At a time when most graduate programs in biology were investing heavily in microbiology and cellular level studies, both schools offered a variety of courses oriented to natural history.

When she visited the University of Chicago, she was warned that her car might be stolen if she parked on the street. While her car was not stolen, she "did not tempt fate by enrolling at Chicago." In choosing UF, Liz left the environment of private New England women's schools and colleges for life at a southern public university that had only become coeducational in 1947. She also transplanted to the South at a time when forces for profound social change were building. The University of Florida would not be racially integrated until 1962.

Once the decision to attend UF was made, Liz arrived by train with hardly more than a suitcase. She was more worried about finding a place to live than anything else. She found cheap but substandard housing near campus. A roommate kept an opossum in the apartment and there was a hole in a closet wall that allowed the neighbor's cat to show up unexpectedly. Once she got settled, her mother sent her belongings, addressed to the biology department, in an ancient, battered trunk (a humorous but embarrassing event). Liz says that when her mother first saw her accommodations in Gainesville, she wept. Her mother, she says, never liked her living arrangements, ever.

She studied with James Layne, a young assistant professor of biology and mammalogist, who had arrived in the same semester. She recalls receiving only encouragement in the department even though she was one of the few women in graduate studies at the time. Her master's thesis (1957) investigated pocket gopher (*Geomys pinetis*) reproduction, and the resulting publication in the *Journal of Mammalogy* (1960) was her first in the field of whole animal biology as well as her last. For her thesis, Liz trapped and dissected 325 pocket gophers. She investigated various aspects of breeding behavior including age of sexual maturity, number of pregnancies, litter size, and population dynamics. This work was conducted within a fifteen-mile radius of Gainesville using a Lambretta scooter to get to collecting sites.

At UF, Liz also entered the South and southern culture. The natural environments of the South had fascinated her since her first trip to Florida in 1953. Then she had traveled alone by train (as far as Jacksonville) and bus (to Miami) to visit family friends in Coconut Grove. She began graduate studies at a time when race relationships were heating up for the struggles to come.

She was a single female student at UF when many biology classes were entirely male. Being the lone female member in class often brought different assignments or expectations from professors. The botanist John Henry Davis conducted his plant identification field trips from his vehicle at a speed of around thirty-five mph, screeching to a stop for brief plant identifications, and then rushing on. He was known to leave laggard students. He expected Liz not only to keep up with the class but also to make sandwiches for all participants. As a single female, she was often excluded from nighttime collecting trips. These differences, that today would be considered discriminatory, were, she says, "of a different time."

While James Layne guided her work in mammalogy, John Mann Goggin was her guide in anthropology. Liz's first contact with Goggin came as the result of the divorce of two graduate students who were analyzing vertebrate materials excavated by Goggin and Irving Rouse on Trinidad. When the couple broke up, the work was turned over to Liz because the sample was largely mammalian. Since Liz was working on Goggin's material, she audited his survey course and then took several graduate courses from him.

If Liz's education as a female biology student differed from that of her male counterparts, so did her experience in anthropology. Her exposure to archaeological field methods came not as a member of a field crew, but as a chaperone. During her masters work, Liz married Jim Wing, and her altered status made her the perfect chaperone for Goggin's coed field groups. Goggin is to be credited with bringing Liz's research interests to zooarchaeological problems, introducing her to field methods, and providing early contracts and professional contacts.

It is also important to note that Liz was one of the students who participated in Goggin's early underwater archaeological investigations (figs. 12.1 and 12.2). Goggin had two male assistants, one of whom was a former Navy diver, to administer the "formal" training. Liz made her initial dive, under Goggin's training scheme, as a cave dive at Ginnie Springs (north of Gainesville). She dove to seventy-five feet, in a winding cave descent, with

Fig. 12.1. John M. Goggin assists Elizabeth Wing in donning her scuba gear for a dive, ca. mid-1950s. (Photo courtesy of Elizabeth Wing.)

Fig. 12.2. Liz Wing prepares to dive in one of Florida's numerous clear springs, ca. mid-1950s. (Photo courtesy of Elizabeth Wing.)

a flashlight that required "frequent tapping to relight the bulb." Subsequent dives in the Suwanee River at the Oven Hill site and Ichetucknee River near the Spanish mission site at Fig Springs were much less traumatic. Liz does not remember all of the sites they investigated since her task was "to manage people and she just went where they told her."

Her dissertation, "Succession of Mammalian Faunas on Trinidad, West Indies" (1962), grew out of her work with the faunal material from Trinidad and launched her career in zooarchaeological studies. Her doctoral committee was again chaired by James Layne with Archie F. Carr (herpetologist), James R. Redmond (physiologist), Clayton E. Ray (paleontologist), and John M. Goggin as members. She used Goggin's and Rouse's archaeological collections to investigate a biological problem associated with faunal succession: the question of when Trinidad became separated from the South American mainland. This study of this collection, which contained both paleontological and archaeological remains, launched her career in zooarchaeological studies.

The skeletal collections available to her at Gainesville were insufficient for the task of identifying Caribbean paleontological and archaeological faunas. Barbara Lawrence lent specimens on behalf of the MCZ as did other museum curators in New York (American Museum of Natural History), Basel, Switzerland (Natural History Museum), and London (Royal Victoria Institute). The early need for interinstitutional and international communication promoted ties to European colleagues that remain strong today.

During her graduate studies, Liz held an assistantship in the mammal collection at the FMNH. In 1961, she began to create the position she now holds, curator of zooarchaeology. J. C. Dickinson, director of the museum, had met Liz's parents during his graduate studies at the MCZ. He also served on her master's committee. Through his active encouragement, she was allotted space for a comparative collection and laboratory research. Her official title was interim assistant curator of zooarchaeology, and she began to accept contracts for faunal analysis from archaeologists working in Florida and the Caribbean. In 1969, a curatorship in zooarchaeology was established and Liz became assistant curator. Five years later, she was promoted to associate curator; in 1978, to curator. At the outset, she worked part-time. Her two children were both infants and this arrangement made the most sense for her. She credits the flexibility of this arrangement with her early success.

Through her affiliation with the museum, she produced a series of public service articles for such publications as *Florida Deer* (1965c), *Florida Wild-*

life (1966c), and the FMNH *Plaster Jacket* (1966a, 1975d, and Swift and Wing 1968). She also published a brief notice on pathologies in white tail deer dentition in the *Journal of Mammalogy* (1965a) based on her work with faunal collections from Florida sites. Increasingly, however, her work appeared in reports of archaeological investigations.

Goggin continued to be a major influence, providing both collections and recommendations to his colleagues. Another early collection with which Liz worked was from the site of Nueva Cadiz, on Cubagua Island, off the coast of Venezuela. This site, a pearl fishing community, was the first Spanish settlement in South America (Goggin identified the Nueva Cadiz type bead, an important early historic diagnostic artifact, from this site). Indigenous divers were brought from many different Caribbean and South American localities. Beyond developing an understanding of the use of local animals, she faced the problem of learning which animals were brought to the islands by Spaniards and people coming from the Caribbean and South America (Wing 1961:162). She found that local marine products were most heavily exploited at Nueva Cadiz and that the domestic animals present (swine and fowl) were brought to the site by the Spaniards. This question, however, about the movement of animals in the Western Hemisphere was to be one to which Liz returned repeatedly during her career.

Many early zooarchaeological reports seem superficial today since most of the samples were inadequate for the types of analyses currently expected. Very few samples were obtained with screens and even fewer with fine mesh screens. Flotation methods were being pioneered in Europe but rarely applied in New World sites until the 1970s. Often the faunal assemblage from an excavation represented only what the excavator had "observed" during the course of excavation; sometimes, the faunal materials were separated by the excavator and sent to a variety of specialists. Most samples were biased toward large bone fragments and, consequently, large mammals. While frequently discussed and cited as staple parts of prehistoric subsistence, molluscan fauna, for example, was rarely quantified. Liz recognized these problems yet managed to consistently address theoretical issues despite the serious limitations of most samples.

She worked quietly to change these conditions. She was systematically involved in the improvement of field techniques in order to improve the samples with which she worked. As a consultant, her field visits to projects provided the opportunity to observe field techniques and advise about collection of samples, in addition to obtaining local comparative material. From very modest collection and laboratory resources, Liz's scholarly work generally reflects the growth of zooarchaeology and its major preoccupations: subsistence reconstruction, human-environmental interactions, technology, domestication, and seasonality.

Liz's own work has had several major directions resulting from a variety of research opportunities. The most important contribution of her curatorship is the amassing of a comparative collection. This accomplishment supports a broad range of research interests. She has consulted with archaeologists primarily working in the southeastern United States, Caribbean, Central and South America. Her work has involved both prehistoric and historic collections. Domestication, particularly of New World animals such as the guinea pig, dog, and camelids (llama, and its relatives), has been a persistent concern. She has taught zooarchaeology to technicians and, formally, to students since 1970. Within all this activity, she found time to have a rather nontraditional family life.

Comparative Collections and Collecting

Faunal studies are limited by the quality of the comparative skeletal collection available. Faunal identification is accomplished by constant reference to a comparative collection of vertebrates and invertebrates from the study area. Such collections include mammals, birds, reptiles, amphibians, fishes, and invertebrate animals such as shellfish and crustaceans. When Liz began her work at the FMNH, such a resource was not available. She has, through years of effort, amassed one of the best institutional collections available today. Acquisition and curation of osteological materials from the variety of taxa likely to be required in the analysis of any archaeological faunal assemblage is no small task.

Liz began this effort for the FMNH in 1961 and continues the process today. A 1961 NSF grant to Clayton Ray and John Goggin supported her efforts at the outset. Because she did not yet have her doctorate, Ray and Goggin submitted the proposal. Her plan was to secure one specimen of each type of animal, beginning with mammals, then building for size and variability. John H. Rick assisted in the initial phase of collecting. In subsequent years and under other NSF grants, Liz would hire ichthyologists John Randall (Caribbean fishes) and Robert Rush Miller (Mesoamerican fishes) to assist her in collecting and identifying fishes for the comparative collection. The process of obtaining, preparing (measuring and defleshing), and accessing (numbering bony elements to prevent inadvertent mixing) of thousands of animals is tedious and often unpleasant. Identification of archaeological materials and the strength and adequacy of interpretations based on these identifications depend entirely on the reliability of the comparative collection.

Among the students who have passed through the lab, there is a long-standing joke about Cheez Whiz and baby food jars. Many of the comparative collection specimens are curated in these containers, particularly the early ones. Liz used many frugal approaches to obtaining the resources needed to build the zooarchaeology laboratory. Because the lab was in the natural sciences department of the museum until 1990, anthropology students were able to mix freely with students specializing in many other disciplines. Formal (classroom and lecture) and informal (brown bag lunches and parties) exchanges enriched the experiences of the anthropology students who studied in Liz's lab.

Many of the students who used the collections became involved in the process of collecting specimens, skinning and defleshing them, taking standard measurements and weights, and assisting with the process of maceration. The maceration task was difficult to accomplish within the museum, particularly after it moved from the Seagle Building in downtown Gainesville to its new facility on campus. The research collections are still located in this structure, now designated Dickinson Hall. In 1979, a special maceration house was built atop neighboring Bartram Hall, but even there, it was too odoriferous. Maceration still continues, as the task of adding to the collection never ends, but it is conducted at a distance from the museum.

My own introduction to collecting comparative specimens occurred during the summer of 1972, when I accompanied Liz and her children, Molly (aged ten) and Steve (aged seven), to West Mexico. Liz was a consultant for Stuart D. Scott of the State University of New York at Buffalo. Scott conducted a multi-year archaeological program in the coastal margins of the states of Sinaloa and Nayarit, south of Mazatlán. The group lived in a small shark-fishing village, Teacapan. Sharks caught by the village fishermen were sold to a local business and salted for meat, the residual carcass used for fertilizer. Each evening at dusk, when the fishermen returned from their day at sea, Liz would meet them and buy their collateral catch. Fish, because of their diversity, formed the majority of specimens collected that summer. Liz took standard measurements, gutted them, and filleted one side. Then the fish were salted and sun dried for transport to the FMNH.

Before we packed for our return trip through Guadalajara and Mexico City, where Liz would also consult with archaeologists, we had several days of rain. The most recently caught fish did not dry well. Even though the fish were heavily wrapped in plastic and bagged, our packages had a distinctive odor. In Mexico City, Liz's hotel reservation was not honored. As Steve said, "They said our luggage smelled bad." In another hotel, several blocks away, the packages were stored in a closet that was not opened until we left. This experience became even more humorous when our Florida-bound plane blew a compressor on takeoff and was forced to return to the terminal. Our luggage stood on the tarmac for several hours, becoming ever more fragrant. We finally arrived at Tampa Customs and Immigration around one o'clock in the morning. After a brief inspection of Liz's scientific permits, our luggage was passed through without comment, but not without notice.

As a consequence of her collecting activities, and those of her students, the zooarchaeology comparative collection of the FMNH numbers seventy-five hundred specimens, representing the southeastern United States, Central America, northern South America, and the Caribbean. This geographical coverage is a direct reflection of the areas within which Liz has worked. It is a resource used by colleagues and students from many institutions. Its strengths lie in the southeastern United States and the Caribbean. In addition to animals, both vertebrate and invertebrate, the lab now includes plants and soils.

Pioneering an Emerging Specialty

Until the late 1960s, archaeologists turned to biologists with expertise in nonhuman osteology for the identification of bone fragments recovered during excavation. In the main, these specialists contributed to archaeological reports by compiling species lists, often commenting on the size of the creatures relative to modern fauna and suggesting how the environments represented by the assemblage might have appeared in the past. This practice contributed to the dispersal of archaeological assemblages as specialists were sought, often for each class of remains. The absence of a specialist who could combine the various reports into something approaching archaeological interpretation resulted in most of this information appearing as addenda in reports, but rarely fully integrated.

The evolution of zooarchaeological studies represents the creation of an anthropological specialty from recognized scientific disciplines such as biology, zoology, malacology, and vertebrate paleontology. The students drawn to the founding cadre of scientists in this emerging field, however, came primarily from anthropology. The first hurdle for zooarchaeology (and similarly for archaeobotany) was achieving academic validity and acceptability.

In the United States, archaeological interpretation featured items made by humans, and recovery of faunal or floral remains was of less priority. Faunal remains fashioned into tools or ornaments received attention, but as components of the technological or ceremonial sphere, not as informative parts of subsistence or environment. Field techniques were not geared to recovery of such material and there was open sentiment against the considerable time and labor required to obtain controlled floral and faunal samples. Faunal and floral materials from archaeological contexts were termed "ecofacts," further undermining their significance and their integration in interpretations of human behavior. Certainly the momentum toward more rigorous field methods, encouraged by the "New Archaeology" of the late 1960s and 1970s, assisted the process of changing those attitudes.

Liz's persistence and dedication parallel the early problems of researchers whose areas of expertise bridged established scientific disciplines. While professors of anthropology saw expertise in zooarchaeology and archaeobotany as excellent skills for their students, they did not fully believe that such pursuits had validity beyond contributions to archaeological knowledge. In fact, they worried about their students getting too far away from anthropological questions. Demonstrations of appropriateness required years of patient contribution on Liz's part and the part of the cadre of scholars mentioned previously. Their work reflects the growth of zooarchaeology, archaeobotany, and the coalescence of the broader area of study termed environmental archaeology.

Subsistence Reconstruction in Florida

Liz's scholarly work was never mere species listing. Even in her earliest papers, there are modest efforts toward anthropological interpretation and the use of new concepts. Two early papers provide insight: the Wash Island site (1963a) and the Goodman and Jungerman sites (1963b). Her report on the Wash Island site, excavated by Ripley P. and Adelaide K. Bullen, presents some of the first systematic data on the prehistoric use of animals by Florida's indigenous peoples. The site is located near the mouth of the Crystal River on the Florida Gulf Coast; *Chelonia mydas* (the green turtle) was identified in the abundance of sea turtle remains recovered. Based on the presence of immature sea turtle elements, Liz interpreted season of occupation. She also discussed butchering techniques and food preparation practices, and she assessed local habitats present throughout the period of the site's occupation.

Liz's (1963b) report detailing the assemblages from the Jungerman and Goodman sites on the Atlantic coast applied species diversity measures (MacArthur and MacArthur 1961) to the problem of change through time in the stratified Jungerman site. She also compared and contrasted procurement techniques and relative ecological stability between the two sites. A brief chronological discussion was also included, given the occurrence of *Rattus* sp. (European rats) with a burial in the Goodman collection.

The cumulative effect of Liz's work for our understanding of Florida archaeology is not easily assessed. In the recent *Archaeology of Precolumbian Florida* (Milanich 1994), Liz is cited three times in the bibliography and once in the index. But there are more than a dozen published entries on Florida in her professional bibliography (1963a, 1963b, 1965b, 1966a, 1966c, 1975d, 1977b, 1978b, 1987, 1992, Wing and Loucks 1984, Wing and McKean 1987, Wing and Quitmyer 1992, and Marrinan and Wing 1980) and there are many other uses of data provided by her that are unattributed. It was not unusual for Liz's reports to be reduced to species lists for inclusion in reports and/or for the principal investigator to simply "integrate" all of the subsistence data himself. For example, Hemmings (Hemmings and Deagan 1973:iv–v) acknowledged that the subsistence data had been provided by Liz and then proceeded to synthesize them. Such treatment is not an uncommon occurrence for that period since many archaeologists believed that they should be able to represent the findings of paid consultants. It is of interest, however, that the analysis of human skeletal remains in this report, by Adelaide Bullen (1973), is included separately.

Another aspect of her importance to the development of subsistence knowledge in Florida lies with her students. She has directly influenced many archaeologists currently active in Florida: for example, Bonnie G. McEwan, Guy Prentice, Elizabeth J. Reitz, Michael Russo, Karen Jo Walker, Brent R. Weisman, and me. Others have used her services to contribute to their dissertations, research, or contract reports: for example, Judith A. Bense, Kathleen A. Deagan, William Marquardt, Jerald T. Milanich, James J. Miller, and Nancy Marie White. Information produced by Liz, her students, and technicians is so pervasive to the understanding of Florida archaeology today that it is impossible to quantify or qualify.

Although she labored alone in Florida, her contacts with zooarchaeologists outside of the United States remained firm. In Europe, the analysis of faunal remains was more developed and integrated into archaeological analysis. Liz was one of the few American members of the International Council on Archaeozoology (ICAZ), a group of practitioners who provided inspiration and support. The importance of this organization to her career growth is obvious. As she observed in 1990, "During the early years, I felt as though I worked in isolation and was particularly grateful for the support of members of ICAZ. It was most exhilarating to be in a whole room full of archaeozoologists as we were at Groningen [Netherlands] in 1974 rather than the lone person giving a paper on faunal studies in a sea of archaeologists."

These remarks were made at a plenary session of ICAZ, held in 1990, which featured personal comments on the field by the "founding mothers and fathers" of international archaeozoology (as zooarchaeology is known outside the United States). Remarks were also made by Sandor Bokonyi (Hungary), Anneke Classon (Netherlands), Angela von den Driesh (Germany), Sebastian Payne (Great Britain), and Nanna Noe-Nygaard (Denmark). Liz was among three Americans (Donald K. Grayson and John D. Speth) invited to participate in this session. At the 1990 ICAZ meeting, papers were presented in other sessions by five current or former students (Nina T. Borremans, Irvy R. Quitmyer, Elizabeth J. Reitz, Karen Jo Walker, and myself).

At the Southeastern Archaeological Conference in 1976, Liz outlined the potentials of the field of zooarchaeology in a paper entitled "The Role of Zoology in Archaeological Research." She made comments about what was required for training and addressed bias in the archaeological record. As her work increased, the greater was her awareness of the limitations, for interpretive use, of many of the collections submitted for analysis. By bringing bias problems to the attention of archaeologists, she worked very hard to eliminate the shortcomings of many samples submitted for analysis.

In 1977, "Subsistence Systems in the Southeast" was published in the *Florida Anthropologist*. It is a synthesis of data from forty-three prehistoric sites, thirty-six of which are in Florida. Liz used two approaches to reveal the kinds of procurement strategies in these sites spanning the time from Late Archaic to Historic (2500 B.C. to A.D. 1700). The first level of analysis produced constellations of animal resources for sites located in large geographical zones of the Southeast: inland, coastal ridge, and coast. A second approach involved the use of diversity (MacArthur and MacArthur 1961) and equitability indices (Sheldon 1969) to determine whether subsistence practices were generalized or specialized (based on minimum number of individuals—MNI). Two distinct clusters were generated: a small coastal cluster with three specialized fishing sites and a large, overlapping cluster of the other forty sites. While these outcomes do not seem particularly surprising today, the ability to demonstrate, from faunal remains, the relative specificity of resource selection was notable at the time.

From the early 1960s, Liz consulted with a number of southeastern archaeologists. As a member of the FMNH staff, she conducted analysis of materials for Ripley P. Bullen and William H. Sears. She later was involved in the Fort Center excavations conducted by Sears and his Florida Atlantic University students. Until his death, she continued to analyze materials for Goggin. The work of her museum and UF department of anthropology colleagues often produced faunal samples, but early on there was little funding to support analysis. These collections frequently became student projects. As archaeologists became aware of the potential of zooarchaeological analysis, interest in her services increased. Beginning with the late Roy S. Dickens, Jr. (Wing 1970a) in the late 1960s, she has consulted with archaeologists in the lower Southeast (principally in Alabama, Florida, Georgia, and South Carolina).

Increasingly, however, her consulting work took her to the Caribbean and Central America. In the Caribbean, she worked with collections excavated by William G. Haag (St. Lucia), Ripley P. Bullen (Grenada), Charles A. Hoffman, Jr. and Clayton E. Ray (Antigua), Hoffman (Bahamas, St. Kitts), and Irving B. Rouse (Puerto Rico). National Science Foundation grants supported travel to collect specimens for the comparative collection and for analysis of materials from Florida and the Caribbean.

Consultant to the Stars

From modest beginnings, her reputation grew. Although her first consultancies outside Florida came from archaeologists working in the Caribbean, she was asked by E. Wyllys Andrews IV, of Tulane University, to analyze materials from Cancun (Wing 1974c) and from Dzbilchaltun (Wing and Scudder 1980). She began research in Mesoamerican sites for Barbara Voorhies (in 1975), Olga Linares (in 1978), and Norman Hammond (in 1976) and in South America for Donald Lathrap (in 1975) and Anna Roosevelt (in 1978). She also began to attract long-term projects. In 1968, Liz joined the Japanese Andean research effort at Kotosh. Again, Barbara Lawrence proved to be an integral, although indirect factor. The Japanese archaeologists Seiichi Izumi and Kazuo Terada had initially asked Lawrence, but she had been too busy. She had recommended Kent V. Flannery because of his previous work in South America. He also was unable to participate and recommended Liz. Liz initially met with Flannery and the Japanese archaeological group in Washington, D.C., in 1965. One of the provisions of the project that she requested was the inclusion of a Japanese student (Takeshi Ueno) who learned zooarchaeological analysis.

Her report of this work was published in 1972 and includes a discussion of the roles of two domesticates, camelids (llamas and their relatives) and guinea pigs. She demonstrated a change in large mammal resource procurement and usage in the earlier and later periods at Kotosh from hunting to purposeful herd management. Because llamas were used as beasts of burden, fewer adult animals were represented in the faunal assemblages; more subadult animals were consumed. Guinea pigs were abundantly used as a food source, and historic records suggested that they were also used for medicine, divination, and sacrifice (Wing 1972).

She also worked with Stuart D. Scott in coastal West Mexico and Michael D. Coe in Vera Cruz beginning in 1968. Scott's project in the Marismas Nacionales of Sinaloa and Nayarit states included excavation of burial mounds which produced numerous dog burials (42), most from the site of Chalpa. She used the work of G. M. Allen (1920) and William G. Haag (1948) in her analysis of these ritual deposits. The dog burials were of particular interest to Liz, and their association with human and raccoon burials is explored in an unpublished paper (1970b). Regional mythology holds that a dog may act as a guide in the world of the dead. Raccoons, she suggests, were also used for this need, ostensibly if a dog were not available. Scott's data, and those of his consultants, have never been published and are, unfortunately, available only in mimeographed form.

Coe's project at San Lorenzo investigated Olmec lifeways. Her analysis of the subsistence base showed that, when raw counts of minimum numbers of individuals (MNI) were used as a basis for interpretation, aquatic vertebrate resources dominated the sample. However, when standard methods (for example, White's [1953] methods to estimate meat weight) were used, a reversal of this relationship (terrestrial animals assumed greater importance in the food base) was produced. This finding illustrated the kinds of problems inherent in faunal analysis, that is, the difficulty of determining how to move from bone fragments to a measure of nutritional contribution. Again, dogs were a major consideration. Given their provenience and associations in the Olmec samples, she concluded that dogs represented the major terrestrial food source.

One of the added benefits of archaeology is the opportunity to live in interesting, out-of-the-way places. Liz credits her two visits to San Lorenzo as being very important in providing insights about subsistence farming and life lived at a "barter level." There were no wheeled vehicles, and Liz rode to her work on a horse named "Rock and Roll." At San Lorenzo and in its environs, she collected specimens for the comparative collection. She found the local people pleasant and helpful to her efforts to learn where animals could be found and in collecting them. She said her informants "instantly recognized the limits of my vocabulary and explained things in those words."

As a part of this collaboration, she also provided the analysis for Coe's student, Barbara Stark, who was excavating at the Patarata site (Wing 1974a and 1977a). In these samples, she was again struck by the overwhelming importance of dogs to the prehistoric subsistence base. The use of dogs for human consumption, Liz proposed (1978c), was a particular adaptation to life in the coastal mangrove environment of Vera Cruz. In this study, she used the Santa Luisa site (excavated by her FMNH colleague S. Jeffrey K. Wilkerson), Chalahuites (excavated by the late James A. Ford, also of the FMNH at the time of his death), Patarata (excavated by Stark), and San Lorenzo (excavated by Coe). At each site, dog remains were clearly midden constituents, not from burials as they had been on the Pacific coast (Wing 1970b). To support her findings, she used the sixteenth-century observations of Fray Diego Duran attesting to the abundance of dogs for sale in the market and the high price of dog meat.

She also worked with Richard S. MacNeish as a member of the Ayacucho Valley Project. Her responsibility was the valley sites, locales under 2,000 m elevation, while Kent V. Flannery analyzed the puna sites (greater than 2,000 m). She compliments MacNeish on his ability to gather people for projects, to discuss ideas. She says that he often proposed "way out ideas" but was not rigid about those thoughts; he was open to suggestion and changed his opinions when warranted. It was an intellectually stimulating collaboration. Flannery she found "witty and incisive, a fund of knowledge." Although the archaeological data have not yet been published, the ethnological work on puna llama herders is available (Flannery et al. 1989).

Teaching Zooarchaeology

Students came into Liz's lab in a variety of ways. Some were hired as technicians and performed a number of different tasks including specimen preparation and sample analysis. In the early days, most of us arrived because we were introduced by our fellow students. She taught the first zooarchaeology class in 1970 and would continue in alternating years. The class was listed as an anthropology course and, through the years, the majority of students enrolling have been from that department. In addition to her position in the museum, she was granted joint appointments in Latin American studies (1969) and anthropology (1970). Currently, she holds joint appointments as professor of anthropology (since 1979) and professor of zoology (since 1988).

The format for Liz's course was a combination of readings from other researchers on methodological issues, ethnological case studies, and student analysis and reporting of a collection of previously unanalyzed faunal material. Many of the practical projects involved collections that had arrived at the museum lacking sufficient funds for analysis. Considerable work on Florida sites was done by members of these classes. Students acquired beginning skills in faunal analysis that allowed them to continue working as paid assistants in her lab. Others acquired skills that allowed them to develop ecologically oriented thesis or dissertation topics. Most important, Liz had the opportunity to influence the field approaches of many of the archaeology students enrolled at UF. Often, the problems students encountered with a faunal assemblage, in the practical part of the course, affected their field approaches. The practical experiences of this class taught students how to interact with a zooarchaeological consultant: what services a consultant should provide, when to involve a consultant, and how best to use the consultant's expertise.

In 1979, Liz collaborated with department of anthropology colleague and physical anthropologist Antoinette B. Brown to produce *Paleonutrition: Method and Theory in Prehistoric Foodways*. This book summarized the basic course content (Wing) and added the dimensions of osteological, chemical, and physical analysis of human remains (Brown) in discussions of human diet. Now out of print, it is an excellent introductory text for beginning students. It also includes an introduction to more advanced considerations such as allometric scaling, diversity and equitability measures, and nutritional analysis in a very accessible manner.

Liz began to serve on committees for master's theses (Cumbaa in 1972) and doctoral dissertations (Cumbaa and Marrinan in 1975) in anthropology. The first doctoral student for whom she served as chair was Kathleen M. Byrd (now of Northeast Louisiana State University) in 1976, followed by Elizabeth J. Reitz (now of the University of Georgia) in 1979. Her most recent doctoral student is Laura Kozuch (in 1998). In the late 1970s and early 1980s, there were often several masters and doctoral students in the lab simultaneously fostering a stimulating environment. It is in this context that the evolution of the laboratory from a zooarchaeology lab to an environmental lab began. The students and the lab technician, Sylvia J. Scudder, formed a working committee on minimum standards for collections. Their recommendations to archaeologists were edited by Liz (1983), published, and provided to potential principal investigators. The insistence on better field methods for the recovery of plant and animal remains resulted in more complex samples that required expansion of the work traditionally undertaken in the lab.

One of the most important samples for expanding the horizons of the lab was the Hontoon Island material excavated in 1982, and in subsequent years, by UF archaeologist Barbara A. Purdy. Preliminary samples from this inundated shell midden in the St. Johns drainage indicated that plant (wood, seeds, and plant parts) and animal remains were present and well preserved. Although Purdy opened only a 3x3-m unit in 1982, the resulting samples were so massive that the material could not be processed in the field. Consequently, material was bagged and processed in Liz's lab (Wing and McKean 1987, Wing 1987). The variety of plant remains interested Lee A. Newsom, whose master's thesis work (in 1986) was the motivation for her preparation in archaeobotany. The complexity of other samples provided the need for soils expertise, now provided by Sylvia Scudder.

During the mid-1980s, the UF department of anthropology undertook one of its largest contract projects at Kings Bay, a submarine base near St. Marys, Georgia. The department hired William H. Adams as the principal investigator. Irvy R. Quitmyer, who had worked as a technician in Liz's lab since 1979, was chosen to supervise the zooarchaeological work. A systematic sampling policy was negotiated for the archaeological impact mitigation from the outset, and an innovative study of hard clam (*Mercenaria campechiensis*) growth was initiated. The sampling program resulted in a study (Wing and Quitmyer 1985) documenting the effects of screen size on assemblage composition and its impact on interpretation. It showed that different screen sizes produced assemblages that, in turn, produced widely divergent interpretations.

The hard clam project, conducted in collaboration with Douglas S. Jones (of the FMNH natural sciences department), produced data on seasonal growth in captive hard clams and led to the development of indicators of seasonal occupation of coastal sites (Quitmyer et al. 1985). This technique was applied to the Kings Bay sites and resident collections in the zooarchaeology laboratory with available clam samples. The use of hard clams to assess seasonality has led to an understanding of both prehistoric sedentism and the effects of human exploitation on coastal molluscan resources.

Because Liz traveled widely for her consulting projects, she often included students or arranged for a doctoral student to take on a project for a dissertation. Cumbaa and I both participated in the West Mexican project. Byrd (1976) worked with Donald Lathrap in Ecuador. Reitz worked on Peruvian materials for Craig Morris. Susan deFrance worked on material from Puerto Rico for her master's thesis (in 1988) and on Don and Prudence Rice's Peruvian materials for her dissertation (in 1993). Both Reitz and deFrance worked on-site.

Occasionally, professionals and students from other institutions worked in her lab. Jane Wheeler came to Gainesville to work on Peruvian material. Her collaboration with Liz resulted in *Economic Prehistory of the Central Andes* (1988), a jointly edited work in which they both contributed papers. H. Sorraya Carr from Tulane University worked on collections for Hammond's Cuello project for her dissertation. The lab serves as a resource for national and international scholars.

Methodological Considerations

In addition to concerns about the quality of samples submitted for analysis, there were other problems that Liz considered. One significant difficulty for zooarchaeologists was translating bone fragments from archaeological contexts into meaningful quantities of meat from which dietary data could be extracted. In early papers, Liz had used White's (1953) approach to this problem by calculating the MNI and using White's values to produce pounds of usable meat. While it was helpful in conceptualizing the relative magnitude of contribution of various species, this approach permitted consideration of a very limited group of species (specifically mammals). Liz and her students would develop a very different type of bone-to-meat estimate, an estimate of biomass, using allometric scaling and data gleaned from the comparative collection. As the comparative collection was gathered, standard weights and measurements were taken. In addition, weights were taken as the hide, muscle, and intestinal contents were removed. This process allowed for calculation of bone weight to edible body portions. The method proposed (Reitz et al. 1987) provides a biological basis for estimating amount of meat represented by the bone fragments in a collection using the relationships of skeletal mass to body mass.

Liz was also concerned about the problem of data loss through various post-depositional processes such as predation and scavenging. As a part of William Marquardt's Southwest Florida Archaeological Project, she conducted an experiment designed to address such problems by creating two controlled midden deposits (Wing and Quitmyer 1992). The findings suggested a number of occurrences, both anticipated and unanticipated, that changed the assemblages in the test middens. Natural events such as flooding and red tide (a type of fish kill common to the Gulf Coast) affected a test midden site located very close to the water's edge. Overall, the recovery of material from this midden was very low since there was substantial loss of deposited material. The addition of remains that were not originally included as a part of the designed midden was also reported. The second midden site was located farther ashore, at a higher elevation. This midden also reflected significant loss of skeletal elements. Raw fish elements and MNI counts evidenced heavier predation than cooked. The results of this work suggested that what was recovered in midden deposits was considerably diminished, further complicating the task of reconstructing human diet—even when both plants and animals are recovered.

And on the Home Front

Liz's personal life was not routine either. On April 18, 1957, Liz married James E. Wing, Jr., a ceramic artist. Jim had been a neighbor, the roommate of a biology student who went out with Liz's roommate. Their first child, Mary Elizabeth (Molly), was born in 1961 and Stephen Richard followed in 1965. The Wing family lived in a rustic home on Bivens Arm, an alligator-infested lake on the wooded south edge of campus. Molly and Steve attended P. K. Yonge, the UF developmental school. While Molly graduated from P. K. Yonge, Stephen left the lab school for Gainesville High School where Liz and Jim believed he would receive a strong conventional background in biological science.

Liz was one of the first women many of us experienced who was the primary breadwinner for a family. In addition to his ceramic work, however, Jim farmed, planted the trees, dressed the lumber, built the new house, and cared for the animals (fig. 12.3). Their home was an oasis for students, and being invited to dinner was always a welcome treat. As well as being relaxing, it was educational. Jim and Liz had goats, pug dogs, a variety of chickens, guinea pigs, and a small flock of peafowl. There was always something to be seen or heard. Dinner was often something raised on the farm.

We got to know the Wing children. Molly was quiet and artistic. Liz and Jim encouraged her interests in music and illustration. Molly is married and

Fig. 12.3. Jim Wing
with Molly and
Stephen, ca. 1966.
(Photo courtesy of
Elizabeth Wing.)

now lives in Philadelphia with her husband and two daughters. Steve was
much more able to tolerate the students who annually grew more numerous.
As a boy, he had his own museum collections. I recall one Christmas when
his gift to Liz was three dead birds: a woodcock, an anhinga, and a bittern.
Each "gift" has made its contribution to the comparative collection. In his
teenage years, he was a member of the student group. Steve completed his
Ph.D. in ecology at the University of California at Davis in 1992. Currently,
he lives in New Zealand with his wife and daughter and teaches at the
University of Otago. Recently, Liz and Steve published their first collaborative work (Wing and Wing 1995) on prehistoric island biodiversity in the
West Indies (deciding the senior authorship by the flip of a coin).

Building a museum career is a task that requires considerable time in the
lab and in the field. Liz met that challenge in a variety of ways. Child care
was a need that was met by Liz, Jim, and several students over the years. Liz
recalls taking Molly to San Salvador when she was two or three. She says
there was no alternative at that time and she "assumed someone would be
available there to care for her." On one trip to Mexico, when the children
were five and nine, Jim accompanied her. By the time I met Stephen and
Molly, they were veteran travelers. In Mexico that year, Liz hired a local
woman to care for the children each day when her work took her to the field.
Looking back, Liz says that this sort of thing just worked out; "exceedingly
lucky" she says. Occasionally, the children spent the summer with their
grandparents in New England. Liz and Jim always sent a student with them

to make the trip and visit easier. Liz stresses the importance of part-time work in the beginning. She was pregnant with her first child when she completed her Ph.D. An NSF grant provided support and allowed her to work part-time as needed. This flexibility was critical in the earliest years of her career.

For more than twenty years, Liz and Jim lived close to campus. During this time, they purchased property in northern Alachua County about a half hour drive from the university. They planted pine trees and numerous fruit trees. Jim built their new home from their own lumber, set amid the fruit trees. They had gardens, a small herd of sheep, diverse types of fowl, and the occasional unusual pet (the most unusual was a water buffalo named "Baby Doc"). The new house was spacious and had a swimming pool.

In 1984, Liz was diagnosed with breast cancer. A family friend, Oliver Cope, had written the current definitive treatment of breast cancer. Liz read his work (Cope 1977) in the medical center library and decided on a conservative approach. She, with Cope's assistance, convinced her local surgeon to perform a lumpectomy rather than a radical mastectomy. Radiation therapy followed. Of this difficult time, she says, "it was important to face up to such a diagnosis and deal with it. The outcome need not be terrible." Jim, too, has had a recent bout with cancer.

A Few Summary Comments

In retrospect, the most important aspect of our education with Liz was the truly interdisciplinary activity of the research. Given the nature of the assemblages with which we worked, we consulted curators and students in vertebrate and invertebrate paleontology, malacology, mammalogy, ornithology, ichthyology, herpetology, and paleoecology departments within natural sciences. We attended classes given by many of the curators and competed with many of these students.

As anthropologists, we understood that we had to work to maintain these cross-disciplinary ties. One avenue was through intermittent rites of intensification (parties). The lab Christmas party was an annual affair, when all of the articulated skeletons were decorated for the occasion. A perennial favorite, Rocky Raccoon (a male skeleton prepared by Steve Hale), was dressed for the event with a Santa Claus hat, beard, and two red spherical, anatomically correct, ornaments. Lab parties were often rumored to have strange foods and roadkill offerings, but these were relatively rare and our reputation overblown. Another unusual party was the Mad Hatter Revue, held during the spring of 1981. Liz won the "most extensive use of unnatural substances" category with her Spanish bayonet and Styrofoam egg crate flower creation.

When one looks back over a lifetime of scholarly activity, it is easier to see the influences, opportunities, and paths that were taken. The time that Liz spent at the Museum of Comparative Zoology at Harvard as a young girl predisposed her to understand what could be achieved and to find ways to accomplish those ends. She had observed women, like Barbara Lawrence, overcome exclusion and succeed through personal tenacity. In acknowledgment of her debt to Lawrence, she was instrumental in creating the Barbara Lawrence Prize to honor the best graduate student paper at the annual meeting of the Society of Ethnobiology.

A current project of Liz and Elizabeth J. (Betsy) Reitz is a new book, an overview of zooarchaeology. A former student of Liz's, and frequent collaborator, Betsy directs the zooarchaeology laboratory at the University of Georgia's Museum of Natural History (fig. 12.4). This book (Reitz and Wing 1999) provides an introductory text that updates the advances in the field since the earlier *Paleonutrition* (1979).

The growth of zooarchaeological knowledge is incremental and requires the addition of data from site after site after site. Some of us have examined

Fig. 12.4. Bonnie McEwan, Rochelle Marrinan, Liz Wing, and Betsy Reitz on the University of Florida campus, 1994. (Photo by Martha McEwan.)

our collections and gone on to other pursuits. Liz, however, continues to provide the continuity and synthesis. In her lab, collections are re-examined frequently, as methods change. In a brief note, sent last fall, she told me that she was again teaching zooarchaeology. Further, she said that the students were analyzing some of the large collection from 8 Al169 (Melton Village site); she had noticed that I worked on that faunal collection. The Melton Village faunal assemblage had been the focus of Steve Cumbaa's master's thesis, and my field school paper had reported the material from a single pit feature. The opportunities that came from this experience, however, have truly been the most important in my professional career.

Elizabeth Wing has been quietly influential as a field researcher, as a consultant, and as a mentor. From circumstances of isolation, she has been joined by a succession of colleagues and students in studying an impressive array of sites, in providing overviews of various regions, and in tackling the study of domesticated animals in several areas of the Western Hemisphere. Recently, colleagues and students dedicated an overview of environmental archaeology to her (Reitz, Newsom, and Scudder 1996). Her years of work, island by island in the Caribbean, clearly show the introduction of the guinea pig from the South American mainland sometime after A.D. 900, but before European intrusion, demonstrating direct contact between the two areas (a fact known from stylistic similarities, but not demonstrated directly).

In a 1982 interview for the *Florida Anthropologist*, Liz estimated that the zooarchaeology laboratory included collections from more than four hundred sites from the southeastern United States, Caribbean, and northern South America (McGuire and Allerton 1982). Fifteen years later, the number is much greater. Perhaps her greatest measures of success are her influences on field methods, her fostering of a variety of specialties that have expanded the purview of the laboratory, and the impact of her ideas and skills on several generations of archaeologists. In Florida, and to an extent, in the southeastern United States, our understanding of prehistoric and historic subsistence, environment, technology, resource procurement strategies, and the role of domestic animals and plants has been impressively furthered by her life work. She has accomplished these things through persistence, force of character, exceptionally good humor, and open-minded interaction with colleagues, students, and consulting researchers.

Selected Bibliography of Elizabeth S. Wing

Wing, Elizabeth S.

1960   Reproduction in the Pocket Gopher of North-Central Florida. *Journal of Mammalogy* 41(1):35–43.

1961   Animal Remains Excavated at the Spanish Site of Nueva Cadiz on Cubagua Island, Venezuela. *Nieuwe West-Indische Gids* 2:162–65.

1963a   Vertebrate Remains from the Wash Island Site. *Florida Anthropologist* 16(3):93–96.

1963b   Vertebrates from the Jungerman and Goodman Sites Near the East Coast of Florida. *Contributions of the Florida State Museum to Social Science* 10:51–60.

1965a   Abnormal Dentition in Several White-Tailed Deer Jaws. *Journal of Mammalogy* 46(2):348–50.

1965b   Animal Bones Associated with Two Indian Sites on Marco Island, Florida. *Florida Anthropologist* 18(1):21–28.

1965c   Early History of Florida White-Tailed Deer. In *Florida Deer*, by the Florida Game and Freshwater Fish Commission, pp. 5–12.

1966a   Fossil Skates and Rays of Florida. *Plaster Jacket* 2. Florida State Museum, Gainesville.

1966b   Animal Remains from a Midden at Fort Walton Beach. *Quarterly Journal of the Florida Academy of Sciences* 30(1):57–58.

1966c   The White-Tailed Deer Early History in Florida. *Florida Wildlife* 20(5):10–13.

1967a   Aboriginal Fishing in the Windward Islands. *Proceedings of the Second International Congress for the Study of Pre-Columbian Cultures of the Lesser Antilles*, pp. 103–7.

1967b   One Man's Food Is Another Man's Poison. *Mill Reef Digger's Digest*, pp. 18–20. Antigua Archaeological Society, September,

1968a   Preliminary Note on the Faunal Remains Excavated from Several Sites in Sinaloa, Mexico. *West Mexican Prehistory, Part 2*, pp. 150–52. State University of New York at Buffalo.

1968b   Vertebrate Remains Excavated from San Salvador Island, Bahamas. *Caribbean Journal of Science* 9(1–2):25–29.

1969   Preliminary Analysis of the Subsistence Economy of Two Small Communities in the Marismas Nacionales of Sinaloa and Nyarit, Mexico. *West Mexico Prehistory, Part 3*, pp. 96–109. State University of New York at Buffalo.

1970a   Appendix 2: Faunal Remains from the Warren Wilson Site. In The Pisgah Culture and Its Place in the Prehistory of the Southern Appalachians, by Roy S. Dickens, Jr., pp. 294–99. Ph.D. dissertation. University of North Carolina, Chapel Hill.

1970b   Dog Remains from the Marismas Nacionales. Manuscript on file, Environmental Archaeology Laboratory, Florida Museum of Natural History, Gainesville.

1972   *Utilization of Animal Resources in the Peruvian Andes. Andes 4: Excavations at Kotosh, Peru*, edited by Seiichi Izumi and Kazuo Terada, pp. 32–352. University of Tokyo Press.

1973a   Notes on the Faunal Remains Excavated from St. Kitts, West Indies. *Caribbean Journal of Science* 13(3–4):253–55.

1973b   The Origins of Agriculture: Animal Domestication in the Andes. *Ninth International Congress of Anthropological and Ethnological Sciences.* Chicago.

1974a   Appendix 1: Subsistence at the Patarata Site, Vera Cruz, Mexico. In Patarata Island, Vera Cruz, Mexico, and the Role of Estuarine Mangrove Swamps in Ancient Mesoamerica, by Barbara L. Stark, pp. 435–48. Ph.D. dissertation. Yale University.

1974b   Factors Influencing Exploitation of Marine Resources. In *The Sea in the Pre-Columbian World,* edited by Elizabeth P. Benson, pp. 47–64. Dumbarton Oaks, Washington, D.C.

1974c   Vertebrate Faunal Remains. In *Excavation of an Early Shell Midden on Isla Cancun, Quintana Roo, Mexico,* by E. Wyllys Andrews IV, M. P. Simmons, E. S. Wing, and E. Wyllys Andrews V, pp. 186–88. *Middle American Research Institute,* Publication 31, Tulane University, New Orleans.

1975a   Hunting and Herding in the Peruvian Andes. In *Archaeozoological Studies,* edited by A. T. Clason, pp. 302–8. North-Holland Publishing Company, Amsterdam.

1975b   Informe Preliminar Acercera de los Restos de Fauna de la Cueva de Pachamacay, en Junin, Peru. *Revista del Museo Nacional T.* 41:70–80. Lima, Peru.

1975c   La Domesticacion de Animales en Los Andes. *Allpanchis Revista del Instituto de Pastoral Andina* 8:25–44.

1975d   Prehistoric Use of Animal Resources in Florida. *Plaster Jacket* 24. Florida State Museum, Gainesville.

1976a   Appendix 6: Faunal Remains from the Lubaantun Site. *Publications of the Peabody Museum of American Archeology and Ethnology,* pp. 379–83. Monograph 2. Harvard.

1976b   The Role of Zoology in Archaeological Research. Paper presented at the annual meeting of the Southeastern Archaeological Conference.

1977a   Animal Domestication in the Andes. In *Origins of Agriculture,* edited by Charles A. Reed, pp. 837–59. Mouton Press, The Hague.

1977b   Subsistence Systems in the Southeast. *Florida Anthropologist* 30(2):81–87.

1977c   Vertebrates. In *Prehistoric Ecology at Patarata 52, Veracruz, Mexico: Adaptation to the Mangrove Swamp,* edited by Barbara L. Stark, pp. 204–12. Vanderbilt University Publications in Anthropology No. 18. Nashville.

1978a   Animal Domestication in the Andes. In *Advances in Andean Archaeology,* edited by David Browman, pp. 167–96. Mouton Press, The Hague.

1978b   Subsistence at the McLarty Site. *Florida Anthropologist* 31(1):3–7.

1978c   Use of Dogs for Food: An Adaptation to the Coastal Environment. In *Prehistoric Coastal Adaptations,* edited by Barbara L. Stark and Barbara Voorhies. Academic Press, New York.

1979   Dog. In *McGraw-Hill Yearbook of Science and Technology,* pp. 161–64. New York.

1980a   Aquatic Fauna and Reptiles from the Atlantic and Pacific Sites. In *Adaptive Radiations in Prehistoric Panama,* edited by Olga F. Linares and Anthony J. Ranere, pp. 194–215. Peabody Museum Monographs, No. 5. Harvard University, Cambridge.

1980b   Human-Animal Relationships. In *In the Land of the Olmec,* by Michael D.

Coe and Richard A. Diehl, vol. 1, pp. 97–123, and vol. 2, pp. 375–86. University of Texas Press, Austin.

1980c Faunal Remains. In *Guitarrero Cave: Early Man in the Andes,* edited by Thomas Lynch, pp. 149–72. Academic Press, New York.

1981 A Comparison of Olmec and Maya Foodways. In *The Olmec and Their Neighbors: Essays in Memory of Matthew W. Stirling,* edited by Elizabeth P. Benson, pp. 20–28. Dumbarton Oaks Research Library and Collections, Washington, D.C.

1983a Domestication and Use of Domestic Animals in the Americas. In *World Animal Science,* vol. 1, edited by L. Peel and D. E. Tribe, pp. 21–39. Elsevier Publishing Company, Amsterdam.

1983b Spread in the Use of South American Camelids. In *Archaeozoology,* edited by Marian Kubasiewicz, pp. 201–15. Agricultural Academy, Szczecin, Poland.

1984a Faunal Remains from Seven Sites in the Big Cypress National Preserve. In *Deuxièmes Recontres d'Archéo-Ichthyologie,* edited by Nathalie Desse-Berset, pp. 169–81. Notes et Monographies Techniques, No. 16. Editions du C.N.R.S., Paris.

1984b Guinea Pigs: Early Man's First Pets? *Florida State Museum Notes* 13(3):4–5. Gainesville.

1984c Use and Abuse of Dogs. In *Contributions in Quaternary Vertebrate Paleontology: A Volume in Memorial to John Guilday,* edited by High Genoways and Mary R. Dawson, pp. 228–32.

1985 Foreword. In *Aboriginal Subsistence and Settlement Archaeology of the King's Bay Locality,* vol. 2, *Zooarchaeology,* edited by William H. Adams, p. ii. University of Florida, Department of Anthropology, *Reports of Investigations* 2.

1986 Domestication of Andean Mammals. In *High Altitude Tropical Biogeography,* edited by F. Vuillemier and M. Monasterio. Oxford University Press, Oxford.

1987 Integration of Floral and Faunal Data from Hontoon Island, Florida. *Archaeozoologia* 1(1):127–36. Actes du 5 Congrès International d'Archéozoologie de Bordeaux.

1988 Use of Animals by the Inca as Seen at Huanaco Pampa. In *Economic Prehistory of the Central Andes,* edited by Elizabeth S. Wing and Jane C. Wheeler, pp. 167–79. British Archaeological Reports, International Series No. 427. Oxford.

1989a Evidences for the Impact of Traditional Spanish Animal Uses in Parts of the New World. In *The Walking Larder: Patterns of Domestication, Pastoralism, and Predation,* edited by Juliet Clutton-Brock, pp. 72–79. Unwin Hyman, London.

1989b Human Exploitation of Animal Resources in the Caribbean. In *Biogeography of the West Indies,* edited by Charles A. Woods, pp. 137–52. Sandhill Crane Press, Gainesville.

1989c Human Use of Canids in the Central Andes. In *Advances in Neotropical Mammalogy,* edited by J. Eisenberg and K. Redford, pp. 265–78. Sandhill Crane Press, Gainesville.

1990a Animal Remains from the Hacienda Grande Site. In *Excavations at Maria de la Cruz Cave and Hacienda Grande Site, Loiza, Puerto Rico,* edited by I. Rouse and R. E. Alegria, pp. 87–101. Yale University Publications in Anthropology, No. 80. New Haven.

1990b   Comments before the Plenary Session of the International Congress on Archaeozoology, Smithsonian Institution, Washington, D.C.

1991a   Animal Exploitation in Prehistoric Barbados. *Proceedings of the Fourteenth Congress of the International Association for Caribbean Archaeology*, pp. 360–65. Barbados.

1991b   Dog Remains from the Sorce Site on Vieques Island, Puerto Rico. In *Beamers, Bobwhites, and Blue-Points: Tributes to the Career of Paul W. Parmalee*, edited by J. R. Purdue, W. E. Klippel, and B. W. Styles, pp. 379–86. Illinois State Museum Scientific Papers, vol. 23. Springfield.

1991c   Economy and Subsistence I: Faunal Remains. In *Prehistoric Barbados*, edited by P. L. Drewett, pp. 134–52. Archetype Publications, Denbigh, Wales.

1992   West Indian Monk Seal. In *Rare and Endangered Biota of Florida*. Vol. 1, *Mammals*, edited by Stephen R. Humphrey. University Press of Florida, Gainesville.

1993   The Realm between Wild and Domestic. In *Skeletons in Her Cupboard: Festschrift for Juliet Clutton-Brock*, edited by A. Clason, S. Payne, and H.-P. Uerpmann, pp. 243-50.

1994a   Patterns of Prehistoric Fishing in the West Indies. *Archaeofauna* 3:99–107.

1994b   The Past, Present, and Future of Paleonutritional Research. In *Paleonutrition: The Diet and Health of Prehistoric Americans*, edited by Kristin D. Sobolik, pp. 309–17. Center for Archaeological Investigations, Occasional Paper No. 22. Southern Illinois University, Carbondale.

1995   Rice Rats and Saladoid People as Seen at Hope Estate. *Proceedings of the Fifteenth International Congress for Caribbean Archaeology*, pp. 219–31. Puerto Rico.

Wing, Elizabeth S., editor
1983   *A Guide for Archeologists in the Recovery of Zooarcheological Remains*, pp. 1–16. *Florida Journal of Anthropology*, Special Publication No. 3

Wing, Elizabeth S., and Antoinette B. Brown
1979   *Paleonutrition: Method and Theory in Prehistoric Foodways*. Academic Press, New York.

Wing, Elizabeth S., and Norman Hammond
1974   Fish Remains in Archaeology: A Comment on Casteel. *American Antiquity* 39(1):133–35.

Wing, Elizabeth S., Charles A. Hoffman, Jr., and Clayton E. Ray
1968   Vertebrate Remains from Indian Sites on Antigua, West Indies. *Caribbean Journal of Science* 8(3–4):123–39.

Wing, Elizabeth S., and Lana Jill Loucks
1984   Granada Site Faunal Analysis. In *Excavations at the Granada Site*, edited by John W. Griffin, pp. 259–345. Florida Division of Archives, History, and Records Management, Tallahassee.

Wing, Elizabeth S., and Laurie McKean
1987   Preliminary Study of the Animal Remains Excavated from the Hontoon Island Site. *Florida Anthropologist* 41(1):40–46.

Wing, Elizabeth S., and Lee Ann Newsom
1993   Biological Remains. In Excavations at Heywoods, Barbados, and the Economic Basis of the Suazoid Period in the Lesser Antilles. *Proceedings of the Prehistoric Society* 59:128–34.
Wing, Elizabeth S., and Mary D. Pohl
1990   Appendix 8.2: Vertebrate Fauna from San Antonio, Rio Hondo, Belize, Operation 2, North. In *Ancient Maya Wet Land Agriculture*, Mary D. Pohl, editor, pp. 262–68. Westview Special Studies in Archaeological Research, Westview Press, Boulder.
Wing, Elizabeth S., and Irvy R. Quitmyer
1985   Screen Size for Optimal Data Recovery: A Case Study. In *Aboriginal Subsistence and Settlement Archaeology of the King's Bay Locality*. Vol. 2, *Zooarchaeology*, edited by William H. Adams, p. ii. University of Florida, Department of Anthropology, Reports of Investigations 2.
1992   A Modern Midden Experiment. In *Culture and Environment in the Domain of the Calusa*. Institute of Archaeology and Paleoenvironmental Studies, Monograph No. 1. University of Florida, Gainesville.
Wing, Elizabeth S., and Elizabeth J. Reitz
1980   Prehistoric Fishing Economies of the Caribbean. *Journal of New World Archaeology* 5(2):13–32.
1982   9.2.2. Pices, Reptilia, Aves, Mammalia. In *Duccio Bonavia, Los Gavilanes*, pp. 191–200. Editorial Ausonia-Talleres Graficos SA, Lima, Peru.
Wing, Elizabeth S., and Sylvia J. Scudder
1980   Use of Animals by the Prehistoric Inhabitants on St. Kitts, West Indies. *Proceedings of the 8th International Congress for the Study of the Pre-Columbian Cultures of the Lesser Antilles*. Arizona State University, Anthropological Papers No. 22: 237–45.
1983   Animal Exploitation by Prehistoric People Living on a Tropical Marine Edge. In *Animals and Archaeology*. Vol. 2, *Shell Middens, Fishes, and Birds*, edited by Caroline Grigson and Juliet Clutton-Brock, pp. 197–210. British Archaeological Reports, International Series, No. 183.
1991   The Exploitation of Animals. In *Cuello: An Early Maya Community in Belize*, edited by Norman Hammond, pp. 84–97. University of Cambridge Press, Cambridge.
Wing, Elizabeth S., and David Steadman
1980   Vertebrate Faunal Remains from Dzibilchaltun. In *Excavations at Dzibilchaltun, Yucatan, Mexico*, edited by E. Wyllys Andrews IV and E. Wyllys Andrews V, pp. 326–31. Middle American Research Institute, Publication 48. Tulane University, New Orleans.
Wing, Elizabeth S., and Stephen R. Wing
1995   Prehistoric Ceramic Age Adaptation to Varying Diversity of Animal Resources along the West Indian Archipelago. *Ethnobiology* 15(1):119–48.
Wing, Elizabeth S., and Jane C. Wheeler, editors
1988   *Economic Prehistory of the Central Andes*. British Archaeological Reports, International Series, No. 427. Oxford.

13

From the Hilly Flanks of
the Fertile Crescent to the Eastern
Woodlands of North America

PATTY JO WATSON

When the editors of this volume invited me to join them and two of the subjects (Hester Davis and Martha Rolingson) on a working weekend in Fayetteville, Arkansas, during October 1995, I was pleased to take on the role of catalyst or agent provocateur and thoroughly enjoyed the occasion. In fact, it was so much fun that I readily agreed to the suggestion that I make a modest contribution to the published volume myself by providing some account of how I was drawn out of Near Eastern prehistory and into southeastern archaeology during the 1960s, when long-term field projects directed by women were still rather rare in that part of the United States.

Getting into Caves

Some of the relevant background for my entry into eastern North American archaeology is detailed in a book called *The Longest Cave* (Brucker and Watson 1976). The gist of the story is that just before I went to Iraqi Kurdistan with Robert J. Braidwood's Iraq-Jarmo Project in the summer of 1954, I became engaged to one of my high school boyfriends, Richard A. (Red) Watson. While I was in Iraq, he was completing two years' active duty with the Air Force ROTC in Columbus, Ohio. There he met and joined a small group of other young men who were making frequent weekend trips to explore and map a private commercial cave within Mammoth Cave National Park: Floyd Collins' Crystal Cave. When the U.S. Congress appropriated sufficient funds a few years later to buy out the private owners of Crystal Cave, the ringleaders among the cave explorers and mappers (several of whom had recently acquired Ph.D.s in various scientific fields) incorporated themselves as a private, nonprofit group they called the Cave Research Foundation and negotiated an agreement with the National Park Service to continue their underground work, expanded to include geological and biological investigations. A period of intensive subterranean research, and equally intensive legitimation for the fledging organization, ensued. In the interests of the latter process, and as the wife of one of CRF's founders, I was under some pressure to initiate archaeological research in Salts Cave within Mammoth Cave National Park. Although I liked caving, having been introduced to it by Red shortly after my return from Iraq and immediately after our marriage in 1955, I could not have been less interested in starting my own research there because I was still a graduate student at the University of Chicago (in anthropology, with a minor at the Oriental Institute where Braidwood, my dissertation director, was based). I was deeply involved in Near Eastern prehistory, especially the origins of food production in what Braidwood called "the hilly flanks of the Fertile Crescent": upland zones in the Levant, southern Turkey, northern Syria, and Iraq, and western Iran. These foothills had been, and still were, home to wild ancestors of the first domesticated plants and animals.

So I tried to help by contacting New World archaeologists who might be interested in bringing a social science type research project into CRF. The most obvious person to do cave archaeology in Mammoth Cave National Park was Douglas Schwartz, then at the University of Kentucky. In 1958, Schwartz had completed some contracted work for the Mammoth Cave interpretive staff, which resulted in seven manuscripts describing and discussing various aspects of Mammoth Cave prehistory. He had also published an article and an interpretive booklet on the prehistory of the cave. However, I was unable to interest him in continuing any of the work he had begun in the cave and in the park. In the late 1960s, he left Lexington to take a new position at the School of American Research in Santa Fe.

My next attempt was to persuade the only other Eastern Woodlands archaeologist I knew, my graduate school colleague Joe Caldwell, to direct some attention to Salts Cave archaeology. Joe had come back to Chicago in the mid-1950s to complete a Ph.D., and we became good friends before he finished his degree and took a job as head curator of anthropology at the Illinois State Museum in Springfield.

Joe agreed to tour Salts Cave with me and a group of CRF scientists and cave-support personnel. We took him into the Salts entrance, through Upper Salts to a place called Grand Forks, then down the Corkscrew into Lower Salts, through the Quarter-Mile Crawl and the Quarter-Mile Crouch, to the most important place we knew: a passage called Indian Avenue. What made Indian Avenue so special was that it had been undisturbed by post-Columbian traffic before CRF cavers discovered it in the early 1950s. It is a beautiful canyon—nearly 1,500 m long—with in situ archaeological material strewn sparsely over the floor and side ledges.

When we climbed out of Salts entrance after being underground some eight hours or so, talking all the time about the archaeological potential of what we were seeing, Joe removed his hard hat, looked me straight in the eye, and said firmly, "Patty: I *never* want to go in there again! But I will get you some money from the Illinois State Museum Society and will ask Bob Hall to help you with the work." I inferred that Joe did not like the cave but was favorably impressed by the archaeology to the point of wanting to support work there in a very substantial way, if I would undertake it with his Illinois State Museum colleague, Bob Hall.

So that's how my career in southeastern archaeology began. I also followed Joe's suggestion some time later that I join the Southeastern Archaeological Conference and have been a member for more than three decades. It was not until years later, however, that I noticed that Kentucky is not really in the Southeast, as southeasternist archaeologists think of it: Kentucky (and Tennessee where I have also done a fair amount of cave archaeological research) are in the Midsouth; in fact, I eventually noticed, Kentucky is sometimes included in the Midwest. Hence, I found myself, a woman archaeologist—in contrast to the position of women in Near Eastern archaeology at that time—somewhat marginal to the discipline during the 1960s and pursuing a marginal kind of prehistory in a highly marginal locale: the dark zones of several big caves.

But I did not notice any of this marginality for quite a long time because it was so much fun following the ancient cavers through miles of big and small passageways, documenting what they left there, and trying to figure out what it all meant. Moreover, the dean of eastern U.S. archaeology, the ferocious Jimmy Griffin, gave me thirteen free radiocarbon dates on a variety of materials from Salts Cave and seemed to take our work reasonably seriously. Meanwhile, Joe Caldwell had alerted me to the potential of the human paleofecal material that is scattered generously throughout Salts (and Mammoth) Caves, so some of that was included in the Michigan date series. When it turned out to be as old as the rest of the remains Griffin had accepted for dating (that is, between 2,000 and 3,000 years before present), Joe and I knew the plant story encapsulated within the paleofeces was of great general importance. Accordingly, we submitted a proposal to the National Science Foundation for a project Joe nicknamed "Twenty Dated Dinners." The proposal was not funded, but I did manage to attract Dick Yarnell's paleo-ethnobotanical attention, and he became an integral member of the CRF Archeological Project. Dick and I gave a paper on Salts Cave archaeology and archeobotany at a Midwest Conference meeting at Ann Arbor in the mid-1960s, which now seems to me to have been a watershed event for the work itself (we subsequently published that paper in *American Antiquity:* Watson and Yarnell 1966). Dick and his wife, Jean Black Yarnell (who already had a specialist interest in *Iva annua,* one of the early cultigens represented in the cave paleofeces), joined many of our trips into Salts Cave during the late 1960s.

We recruited two other valuable team members, Louise Robbins and Lathel Duffield, both on the anthropology faculty at the University of Kentucky. Duffy and I had met as students at the 1953 University of Arizona Point of Pines Field School, but I first encountered Louise when I ventured to Lexington in the late 1960s in search of the Salts Cave mummy, supposedly curated there. The mummy was indeed there, and Louise, a physical anthropologist, agreed to extract tissue from it for radiocarbon determination and to examine the body, as her professor Georg Neumann had done for the Mammoth Cave mummy some thirty years previously. Louise went on to become a willing and very able collaborator in those early years of cave archaeology in and around Mammoth Cave National Park.

Before I actually showed up on the University of Kentucky campus in search of the Salts Cave mummy, and after Schwartz had declined to join us, I had also corresponded with Martha Rolingson, who was in Lexington when the Salts Cave work was getting started. She kindly agreed to come to Mammoth Cave to see what we were doing. We took her on the same itinerary Joe Caldwell had experienced, and although she was very pleasant and seemed to enjoy it, she never came back, perhaps because that was about the time she was relocating in Arkansas.

Shifting to Eastern North America

During the late 1960s, almost without my noticing it, preoccupied as I was with our little daughter, Anna (born in 1962), and with establishing myself as a professional archaeologist, my research center of gravity was shifting significantly toward eastern North America and away from western Asia. The process reached a point of no return sometime during the mid-1970s after two more field seasons in Turkey with Braidwood's Oriental Institute group, and two summers in New Mexico with the Cibola Project (directed by Steven LeBlanc, Charles Redman, and me). I had been definitively ensnared by Americanist archaeology, especially by the Kentucky research, which took off in a new direction when we began looking for sites that might contain archeobotanical data relevant to the early crop complex Dick Yarnell had documented at Salts Cave. We had moved to Washington University, St. Louis, when Red accepted a tenure-track position there in 1964. In 1968, I was offered a part-time job in the new anthropology department, which became a full-time assistant professorship in 1969. About the time my first Ph.D. student at Washington University, Steve LeBlanc, finished his degree, Bill Marquardt entered the anthropology doctoral program at Washington University, having just completed his M.A. at Kentucky. He and I embarked on a new, jointly directed effort in Butler County, western Kentucky: the Shell Mound Archaeological Project (SMAP), which—like the CRF Project in the Mammoth Cave System—is still continuing.

Because I came into eastern North American archaeology in a rather indirect manner, it took some time to feel as though I belonged there, especially as I did not know the basic data at all. For many years, I was only vaguely familiar with the projectile point types, pottery types, regional phase sequences, and other critical elements of time-space systematics in the Midwest, Midsouth, and Southeast. This was often a source of considerable amusement for some of my first-echelon graduate students, such as Bill Marquardt, Ken Carstens, and David Dye, who grew up in eastern North American archaeology beginning with undergraduate (or even high school) field experience and coursework. Having had the advantage of several years' familiarity and practice, however, I could always outrun and outmacho them underground, and I developed productive and mutually beneficial working relationships with each of them.

Early Cultigens

But I was still somewhat of an interloper in foreign territory in the mid-1970s when examination of flotation samples from SMAP test excavations at 15Bt5, the Carlston Annis mound (fig. 13.1), revealed several charred fragments of *Cucurbita pepo* rind. The identifications were made tentatively by two undergraduate anthropology majors at Washington University, Charles Miksicek and Clark Erickson, in 1976. Hugh Cutler, Missouri Botanical Garden, and Dick Yarnell, then at Emory University, confirmed this diagnosis, which meant we had found evidence for a third millennium B.C. cultigen in eastern North America. This was the oldest archeobotanical record for a domesticated plant in the East at that time and meant to Dick Yarnell, Bill Marquardt, and me that at least one tropical cultigen had arrived in the region prior to development of the agricultural complex so well documented in Salts Cave and Mammoth Cave. We now know that cultivated *pepo* gourd in the Midwest and Midsouth is much older than the Bt5 remains (Fritz 1990; Hart and Sidell 1997; Petersen and Sidell 1996; Smith 1992), and that it was independently domesticated there, probably by 6,000 years ago. But twenty years ago, our discovery of a domesticated plant in a Late Archaic

Fig. 13.1. Patty Jo Watson *(left)* and Louise M. Robbins, Shell Mound Archaeological Project, Logansport, Kentucky, with SMAP machine "Mark I" model; summer 1974 at 15Bt5, the Carlston Annis site. (Photo by Roger Brucker.)

context seemed to us to be "Big News." Nobody else paid much attention, however, and that was when I began to feel occasional twinges of marginality, which became more acute when Yarnell's carefully documented evidence for Early Woodland agriculture at and around Salts Cave (Yarnell 1969, 1974) was more or less written off as an aberration because it came from a cave: it was just "cave food," "prehistoric trail mix."

This situation never caused me to brood unduly, however, because the research was so rewarding in itself, and at least a few students and colleagues found it of interest. By now, after twenty plus years of work, we have made our case that the dark zones of big caves in the midcontinental karst are valuable repositories of significant archaeological information; and it is common knowledge that Archaic hunter-gatherers in eastern North America created an indigenous pre-maize agricultural complex including *Cucurbita pepo ovifera*. I do have one deep regret, however, and that is that Joe Caldwell—who died in 1973—did not live to see all the results of his $300-plus-Bob Hall grant to the CRF Archeological Project.

Reflections

To return to some of the feminist issues mentioned in the Foreword to this volume: it never crossed my mind during the period of my graduate work at Chicago and the subsequent years of pursuing Near Eastern prehistory that gender was an issue when it came to doing archaeology. My sister, Sharon, and I had been brought up in small-town Iowa and rural Nebraska by permissive, wholly supportive parents, grandparents, aunts, and uncles who seldom objected to anything we wanted to do, so long as there was not extreme danger to life and limb. Our childhood activities ranged from running loose for weeks each summer on various farms in southeastern Nebraska with our two first cousins (both also girls) and our second cousin, Marvie (a red-headed, freckle-faced boy a few years my senior), climbing the windmills, wading in the cow ponds, swimming in the horse tank, jumping out of the haymow onto hay piles, trying to ride yearling cattle, stalking the barn cats, driving the tractor, etc., to joining all the extracurricular groups our hometown school afforded: glee club and chorus, concert band, pep band, marching band, basketball. We also signed up for corn detasseling crews every summer while we were in high school, which was quite demanding work physically but also lots of fun because all our friends were there, too. We took for granted the sexually segregated crews and double-standard pay scale (sixty-five cents per hour for girls, seventy-five cents per hour for boys), even though everybody knew the girls worked harder and were more conscientious than the boys.

When I entered the graduate program at the University of Chicago in 1952 and found out about Robert J. Braidwood's work on the origins of agriculture and pastoralism, I soon gravitated into that part of the curriculum and became one of Braidwood's students, then one of his field assistants. Robert McCormick Adams was Bob's first Ph.D. student, I was his second, and there were several other women grads around the Oriental Institute. Sally Schanfield (later Sally Binford) was there during the late 1950s, eventually writing a dissertation on Saharan Pleistocene prehistory under the supervision of Clark Howell; Maxine Kleindienst, also an Africanist student of Clark Howell's, was another; and Hattula Moholy-Nagy was working on her M.A. and formed a member of our Institute gang. Braidwood's wife, Linda, was a professional archaeologist, a lithics expert, and a respected, life-long collaborator with her husband (Braidwood 1959). Finally, the senior field assistant during my first season (late summer 1954 to early summer 1955) in the Near East with the Braidwoods was Vivian Browman, who had just finished a Radcliffe M.A. based on her study of the Jarmo figurines. (Her advisor was Hallam Movius.) Vivian had been at Jarmo in 1950–51, knew the ropes very well, and was a great help to me from the time of embarkation in New York to the end of the season ten months later when the staff went their separate ways from Baghdad.

When Red and I got married in 1955, after my first Near Eastern fieldwork year, we of course intended to combine our lives, but we also wanted to combine our careers as much as possible. So, he took a year's leave from his graduate work in philosophy at the University of Iowa to earn a Master of Science in geology at the University of Minnesota with Braidwood's geological collaborator, Herbert E. Wright, Jr., whom I'd met during the 1954–55 season in Iraq. Herb and Red worked together many times in the following years, beginning with a season in Iran (1959–60), once more with the Braidwood Oriental Institute group (I was archaeological assistant but spent most of my time doing an ethnoarchaeological project in three living villages near the expedition headquarters in Kermanshah). Herb and Red's collaboration continued through two seasons in southeastern Turkey (1968 and 1970) when I was digging at a prehistoric site near Diyarbakir, and the Braidwoods were working at Çayönü. With our daughter, Anna, who was then six and eight years old, respectively, we lived with the rest of the Oriental Institute dig staff at a teachers' training college just outside Ergani in southeastern Turkey.

In the early 1970s, when I began turning myself into an eastern North American archaeologist, gender issues finally came inescapably to my attention. I was fairly well established as a professional at that point and rarely noticed Americanist male colleagues interacting with me differently from what I was used to among Old World scholars. If I did perceive some stand-offishness on the part of traditional, male Americanist archaeologists, I charged it up to the fact that I had entered their arena from an unusual direction and did not have experience and expertise comparable to theirs. But, I did eventually begin hearing from women graduate students at various schools about the problems they faced in getting appropriate attention from their male professors, in acquiring supervisory experience, and even in coping with greater or lesser amounts of sexual harassment. And I certainly noticed the influx of women graduate students into our own curriculum at Washington University.

When David Browman and I—the only archaeologists in the anthropology department from ca. 1970 to 1986—achieved tenured positions and were able to hire a third archaeologist who turned out to be another woman (Fiona Marshall), we experienced a gender shift toward women in our cadre of graduate student archaeologists, a trend that accelerated when Gayle Fritz became the fourth archaeologist to join the faculty. For several years now, nearly all of our top applicants have been women, a fact I attribute partly to the rather unusual gender balance (three women, one man) on the faculty, although there is also a national trend in the same direction (that is, more women entering graduate programs in archaeology, and more men entering private sector archaeology; see Zeder 1997).

In the early 1980s, when I was elected to the executive board of the Society for American Archaeology, I met and worked with a number of energetic and highly visible women. Leslie Wildesen was secretary, and Ruthann Knudson was tracking (and advocating) archaeologically relevant legislation in Washington D.C. Hester Davis had become known to everyone ten years previously during the push for the Archeological and Historic Preservation Act (the Moss-Bennett Bill) and was the coordinator of SAA's archaeological advocacy network. Dena Dincauze came in as president a few years later (1987–89) when I was appointed editor of *American Antiquity*. In fact, it seemed to us in the mid to late 1980s that the SAA's Committee on the Status of Women in Archaeology had become obsolete, so it was dropped. But that action was reversed very shortly thereafter when a new generation of women formed a different kind of constituency within the SAA. They faced different obstacles from those that had confronted their predecessors. Some of these problems arose because now that there were sufficient numbers of professional women, they were, for the first time in the history of Americanist archaeology in the United States, in direct and serious competition with men for fewer and fewer academic jobs. It was no longer a relatively clear-cut matter of women making their way into an androcentric—often even sexist—discipline. Rather it was more an overt competition for limited resources. The situation is different now (details are available in Zeder 1997) and will surely continue to shift and change, but the SAA Committee on the Status of Women in Archaeology is very active and likely to remain that way.

In conclusion, I wish to emphasize how much I enjoyed reading about the *real* southeasternist women archaeologists whose lives are described in this book. Although I came much later in my career than did they to archaeology of the Southeast (and the Midsouth and Midwest), I now feel more at home there knowing what they have accomplished and how deeply dedicated they have been to the region and its history. It is an honor to be a member of their archaeological community.

A Selected Southeastern Bibliography of Patty Jo Watson

Benington, Frederic, Carl Melton, and Patty Jo Watson
1962   Carbon Dating Prehistoric Soot from Salts Cave, Kentucky. *American Antiquity* 18:238–41.
Carstens, Kenneth C., and Patty Jo Watson, editors
1996   *Of Caves and Shell Mounds*. University of Alabama Press, Tuscaloosa.
Chapman, Jefferson, and Patty Jo Watson
1993   The Archaic Period and the Flotation Revolution. In *Foraging and Farming in the Eastern Woodlands of North America,* edited by Margaret Scarry, pp. 27–38. University Press of Florida, Gainesville.
Crothers, George M., and Patty Jo Watson
1993   Archaeological Contexts in Deep Cave Sites: Examples from the Eastern Woodlands of North America. In *Formation Processes in Archaeological Context,* edited by Paul Goldberg, David Nash, and Michael Petraglia, pp. 53–60. Monographs in World Archaeology 17. Prehistory Press, Madison, Wisconsin.
Freeman, J. P., G. L. Smith, T. L. Poulson, P. J. Watson, and W. B. White
1973   Lee Cave, Mammoth Cave National Park, Kentucky. *National Speleological Society Bulletin* 35:109–26.
Kennedy, Mary C., and Patty Jo Watson
1997   The Chronology of Early Agriculture and Intensive Mineral Mining in the Salts Cave and Mammoth Cave Region, Mammoth Cave National Park, Kentucky. *Journal of Cave and Karst Studies, National Speleological Society Bulletin* 59(1):5–9.

Marquardt, William H., and Patty Jo Watson
1983   The Shell Mound Archaic of Western Kentucky. In *Archaic Hunters and Gatherers in the American Midwest*, edited by James Brown and James Phillips, pp. 323–39. Academic Press, New York.
Marquardt, William, and Patty Jo Watson, with Mary C. Kennedy
In Preparation   *Archaeology of the Middle Green River, Kentucky.*
Munson, Patrick J., Kenneth B. Tankersley, Cheryl Ann Munson, and Patty Jo Watson
1989   Prehistoric Selenite and Satinspar Mining in the Mammoth Cave System, Kentucky. *Mid-Continental Journal of Archaeology* 14:119–45.
Robbins, Louise M., Ronald C. Wilson, and Patty Jo Watson
1981   Paleontology and Archeology of Jaguar Cave, Tennessee. In *Proceedings of the 8th International Congress of Speleology*, USA, edited by Barry Beck, pp. 377–88. Bowling Green, Kentucky.
Sobolik, Kristin D., Kristen J. Gremillion, Patricia L. Whitten, and Patty Jo Watson
1996   Technical Note: Sex Determination of Prehistoric Human Paleofeces. *American Journal of Physical Anthropology* 101:283–90.
Stein, Julie, Patty Jo Watson, and William B. White
1981   Geoarchaeology of the Flint Mammoth Cave System and the Green River, Western Kentucky. In *Geomorphology, Hydrogeology, Geoarchaeology, Engineering Geology*, edited by Thomas G. Roberts. Geological Society of America Fieldtrip Guidebooks 3:507–42.
Tankersley, Kenneth B., Cheryl Ann Munson, Patrick J. Munson, Nelson R. Schaffer, Samuel S. Frushour, and Patty Jo Watson
1997   Archaeology and Speleothems. In *Cave Minerals of the World*, edited by Carol Hill and Paolo Forti, pp. 266–70. National Speleological Society, Huntsville.
Watson, Patty Jo
1966   Prehistoric Miners of Salts Cave, Kentucky. *Archaeology* 19:237–43.
1969   Archeological Investigations in Salts Cave, Mammoth Cave National Park, Kentucky. *Proceedings of the 4th International Congress of Speleology*. Ljubljana, Yugoslavia, 1969, 4–5:403–7.
1976   In Pursuit of Prehistoric Subsistence: A Comparative Analysis of Some Contemporary Flotation Techniques. *Mid-Continental Journal of Archaeology* 1(1):77–100.
1977   Prehistoric Miners of the Flint Mammoth Cave System. *Proceedings of the 6th International Congress of Speleology* 6,Eb:147–49. Olomouc, Czechoslovakia, 1973.
1984   Ancient Indians of Mammoth Cave. In *1985 Science Year: The World Book Science Annual*, pp. 140–53. World Book, Chicago.
1985a   The Impact of Early Horticulture in the Upland Drainages of the Midwest and Midsouth. In *Prehistoric Food Production in North America: The Archaeological Background and Botanical Evidence*, edited by Richard Ford, pp. 99–147. Museum of Anthropology Publications, Anthropological Papers Series No. 75. University of Michigan, Ann Arbor.
1985b   Archaeology. In *Caves and Karst of Kentucky*, edited by Percy Dougherty, pp. 176–86. Special Publication No. 12, Series XI. Kentucky Geological Survey, Frankfort.

1986a Cave Archaeology in the Eastern Woodlands. *Masterkey* 59:19–25.

1986b Cave Archaeology in the Eastern Woodlands of North America. *Comunicacions: 9th Congresso Internacional de Espeleologia.* Barcelona, 2:199–201.

1986c Prehistoric Cavers of the Eastern Woodlands. In *The Prehistoric Native American Art of Mud Glyph Cave*, edited by Charles Faulkner, pp. 109–16. University of Tennessee Press, Knoxville.

1988 Prehistoric Gardening and Agriculture in the Midwest and Midsouth. In *Interpretations of Culture Change in the Eastern Woodlands during the Late Woodland Period*, edited by R. Yerkes, pp. 39–67. Occasional Publications in Anthropology No. 3. Ohio State University, Columbus.

1989 Early Plant Cultivation in the Eastern Woodlands of North America. In *Foraging and Farming: The Evolution of Plant Exploitation*, edited by D. Harris and G. Hillman, pp. 555–70. Unwin & Hyman, London.

1990 Trend and Tradition in Southeastern Archaeology. *Southeastern Archaeology* 9:43–54 (special issue edited by David Dye).

1991a The Origins of Food-Production in Western Asia and Eastern North America: A Consideration of Interdisciplinary Research in Anthropology and Archaeology. In *Quaternary Landscapes*, edited by Linda Shane and Edward Cushing, pp. 1–37. University of Minnesota Press, Minneapolis.

1991b Early Plant Cultivation in the Southwest and in the Eastern Woodlands: Pattern and Process. In *Puebloan Past and Present*, edited by M. Duran and D. Kirkpatrick. Papers of the Archaeological Society of New Mexico 17:183–200.

1996 Of Caves and Shell Mounds in West-Central Kentucky. In *Of Caves and Shell Mounds*, edited by Kenneth Carstens and Patty Jo Watson, pp. 159–64. University of Alabama Press, Tuscaloosa.

1997a The Prehistory of Salts Cave and Mammoth Cave, Mammoth Cave National Park, Kentucky, U.S.A. In *Proceedings of the 12th International Congress of Speleology* 3:29–30. La Chaux-de-Fonds, Switzerland.

1997b The Shaping of Modern Paleoethnobotany. In *People, Plants, and Landscapes: Case Studies in Paleoethnobotany*, edited by Kristen Gremillion, pp. 13–22. University of Alabama Press, Tuscaloosa.

Watson, Patty Jo, contributing editor

1969 *The Prehistory of Salts Cave, Kentucky.* Reports of Investigations No. 16, Illinois State Museum, Springfield.

1974 *Archaeology of the Mammoth Cave Area.* Academic Press, New York.

Watson, Patty Jo, and Mary C. Kennedy

1991 The Development of Horticulture in the Eastern Woodlands of North America: Women's Role. In *Engendering Archaeology: Women and Prehistory*, edited by J. Gero and M. Conkey, pp. 255–75. Basil Blackwell, Oxford.

Watson, Patty Jo, and Ronald C. Wilson

1984 Paleontological Remains from Pit of the Skulls, Barren County, Kentucky. *Cave Research Foundation Annual Report,* 1981, p. 23.

Watson, Patty Jo, and Richard A. Yarnell

1966 Archaeological and Paleoethnobotanical Investigations in Salts Cave, Mammoth Cave National Park, Kentucky. *American Antiquity* 31:842–49.

1985 Lost John's Last Meal. *Missouri Archaeologist* 47:241–55.

14

Grit-Tempered Women

The Editors

The South is much more than a geographical region. Apart from the beauty of its varied landscapes, its cultural terrain is a social web rife with contradiction, where the phrase "separate and unequal" is appropriate for both gender and racial interactions. It has been archly conservative, a place where ideal overshadows real, where manners have more importance than morals. Yet the women in this volume have adjusted to the rules and attempted to live their lives in fulfillment of their dreams and intellectual curiosity. They are a diverse group and most are not native-born. We have tried to understand them in the context of the history of their times and also the history of archaeology and anthropology (table 2).

The Paths Less Followed

The traditional path to a successful career in archaeology takes one through undergraduate and graduate programs in anthropology, fieldwork with increasing responsibility, and demonstration of competence in analysis, reporting, and critical thinking. With the male counterparts of our women, these steps are usually accomplished before the individual is thirty years of

Table 2. Timeline for women, history, and southeastern archaeology

Date	Margaret E. Ashley Towle	Isabel Garrard Patterson	Madeline Kneberg Lewis	American archaeology/international scene
1890–99		1894 born		1894–1918 C. B. Moore's investigations in Southeast; 1894 *Report of the Mound Explorations of the Bureau of Ethnology* (Thomas)
1900–1909	1902 born		1903 born	1903 *Aboriginal Pottery of the Eastern United States* (Holmes)
1910–19				1914–18 World War I
1920–29	1924 A.B., Oglethorpe 1926 Boas's student, Columbia U. 1926 Shinholser Mound 1927 Arch. Survey of Georgia 1929 with Moorehead, Etowah 1928 Columbus area survey			1929 stock market crash 1929–41 Great Depression
1930–39	1930 married Gerald Towle; 1932 *Etowah Papers*	1934 began public support of archaeological programs with newspaper articles 1937 chair of archaeology established U. Ga 1939 deSoto celebration	1931 U. Chicago student work on human hair 1936 M.A., U. Chicago 1936 Beloit College 1937 Shireland Mound excavation 1938 to U. Tenn. Lab	1933 SEAC founded; WPA archeology 1934 SAA founded 1933–38 New Deal 1939–45 World War II

(continued)

Table 2—*continued*

Date	Margaret E. Ashley Towle	Isabel Garrard Patterson	Madeline Kneberg Lewis	American archaeology/international scene
1940–49	1941 member SAA 1944 Gerald Towle died 1944 Botanical Mus. volunteer 1948 Peruvian ethnobotany		1940 U. Tenn faculty (teaching) 1941 Chickamauga project 1946 *Hiwassee Island*	1945–49 radiocarbon dating (Libby) 1948 *A Study of Archaeology* (Taylor) 1945–89 Cold War
1950–59	Publications on Peruvian area 1958 Ph.D., Columbia U.	1950 Bull Creek Notes in first issue of *Early Georgia* 1955 died	1951 early projectile point forms, Tenn. area publications 1955 *First Tennesseans* 1958 *Tribes That Slumber*	
1960–69			1961 *Eva*; married T. Lewis; retired to Florida	
1970–79				
1980–89	1985 died			
1990–99			1996 died	

Date	Bettye J. Broyles	Adelaide K. Bullen	Yulee Lazarus	Carol Irwin Mason
1900–1909		1908 born		
1910–19			1914 born	
1920–29	1928 born			
1930–39			1936 A.B., history, FSU	1934 born
1940–49		1941 U. New Mexico field school, Chaco 1942 first dual publication 1943 A.B., Radcliffe 1943–48 grad studies, physical anthropology; Harvard fatigue research		

1950–59	1950 student U. Chattanooga 1953 family trip to Southwest 1954 Angel Mound field school 1955 B.A., U. Chattanooga Modoc, Ill., State Museum	1945 *Black Lucy's Garden* 1948 moved to Florida 1949 FSM volunteer; Fla. Anthro. Society founded 1950 Johns Island 1953 Battery Point 1954–56 ed. *Florida Anthropologist* 1956 Cape Haze	1953 bought house in Ft. Walton Beach; contact with FSU dept. 1958 Buck Mound	1955 FSU undergraduate 1955–56 Florida fieldwork 1956 NSU fellowship; U. Mich. grad studies 1956–58 Ocmulgee research 1957 M.A., Michigan 1959–60 St. Norbert teaching
1960–69	1963 W. Va. Geological Survey 1964–67 St. Albans site 1967 Rowlesburg Research Project	1961 Summer Haven, Wash Island 1964–77 Caribbean excavations reports 1966 Ross Hammock	1960 Ft. Walton Temple Mound excavations 1965 Bill Lazarus died 1967 Naval Live Oaks 1968 hired as museum director 1967 Cato site	1960–61 U. Wis., Green Bay 1961–present U. Wis., Fox Valley 1963 *Culture Change among Lower Creek*; Ph.D., U. Mich. 1964 Natchez class structure 1960–present Wisconsin
1970–79	1970 head archaeology section 1976 U. Mississippi	1972 Treponemal Synthesis 1975 juvenile fiction 1976 Palmer site; Ripley Bullen died 1978 last public lecture	1972 Temple Mound Museum opened	
1980–89	1984 retired	1987 died	1986 Fla. Anthro. Society established Lazarus award; Yulee first recipient	

(continued)

Table 2—*continued*

Date	Hester Davis	Martha Ann Rolingson	Elizabeth S. Wing	Patty Jo Watson	American archaeology/ international scene
1930–39	1930 born 1939 Explorer Club at Palmer-Taylor Mound	1935 born	1932 born	1932 born	1930s Great Depression; federal relief archaeology
1940–49	1948 trip to SW visiting archaeologist friends of siblings; enrolled Rollins College; 1949 attended Florida Indian and His Neighbors conference		1949 museum comparative zoology summer volunteer		1945–89 Cold War
1950–59	1950–51 Upper Gila Expedition member 1952 B.A., Rollins Coll.; U. Oregon grad studies 1955 M.A., Haverford Coll.; Nebraska forager sites 1957 Iowa College of Medicine program 1959 Arkansas Archeology Lab	1952 trip with family to Southwest 1955 U. Colorado field school, Mesa Verde 1956 B.A., U. Denver	1950–51 comp. zoology summer volunteer 1955 B.A., biology, Mt. Holyoke; U. Florida grad studies; 1957 M.A., U. Florida, biology 1959 NSF summer grant, Trinidad	1952 U. Chicago grad school 1953 U. Arizona field school 1954–55 Near East fieldwork 1959 Ph.D., U. Chicago 1959–60 Near East fieldwork	1952 *Measurement of Stone Prehistoric Design Developments in the Southeastern United States* (Ford) 1956 *Method and Theory in American Archaeology* (Willey and Phillips); culture history, syntheses; first stirrings of "New Archaeology" (late 50s); science and computers
1960–69	1960 teaching museum methods; Arkansas Archeological Society formed	1960 M.A., U. Kentucky; Nankoweap Survey 1960–61 museum curator 1961 Kirtley site report	1961 interim asst. curator zooarchaeology, FSM 1962 Ph.D., U. Florida, biology	1960s research, Salts Cave, Ky. 1968 Near East fieldwork; teaching Washington U. 1969 *Prehistory of Salts Cave*	1961–75 Vietnam War 1962 *Archaeology as Anthropology* (Binford) 1967 *Computer*

Period					
	1963 named museum director 1967 Arkansas Arch. Survey founded; named Ark. State Archeologist	1964 *Paleoindian in Kentucky*; Green Point site 1965–68 U. Kentucky Museum; 1966 *Late Paleoindian and Archaic in Western Kentucky* 1967 Ph.D., U. Michigan 1968 joined Ark. Archeological Survey (Monticello)	1964–67 NSF summer research, Jamaica, Bahamas, San Salvador Is., Yucatan 1968 Japanese Kotosh project; M. Coe–Vera Cruz Project 1969 asst. curator zooarch., FSM 1969–72 Scott–West Mexico		*Applications in Archaeology* (Cowgill) 1968 *New Perspectives in Archaeology* (Binford and Binford) "New Archaeology" and reactions
1970–79	1970 *Stewards of the Past*; COPA chair 1971 *Is There a Future for the Past?* 1972 *Crisis in American Archaeology* 1976 founding member SOPA	1970 Boeuf Basin, Bayou Bartholomew surveys 1971–72 Felsenthal NWR 1972 Fayetteville Station 1973 secretary SEAC 1976 Toltec research begun	1970 asst. prof. anthro., U. Florida 1971 MacNeish–Ayacucho 1974 assoc. curator zooarch., FSM 1975 Lathrap–Ecuador; 1978 curator zooarch., FSM 1979 Granada project	1970s Mammoth Cave and Shell Mound, Ky., projects mid-1970s Near East and New Mexico fieldwork 1974 *Archaeology of the Mammoth Cave Area*	Era of Watergate 1970 *Explanation in Archaeology* (Watson, LeBlanc, and Redman) 1974 Moss-Bennett bill passed 1976 SOPA founded
1980–89	1982 *Ark. State Archeology Plan*	1980s long-range research program at Toltec	1980 Huanaco, Peru 1981 U.S. rep. ICAZ; St. Eustasius–U. Leiden 1989 *Paleonutrition*	1980s Mammoth Cave and Shell Mound, Ky., projects	1980s expansion of CRM and contract archaeology 1984 *Archaeology and the Study of Gender* (Conkey and Gero) 1985 *Postprocessual Archaeology* (Hodder) 1989 end of Cold War; Reaganomics
1990–99	1994 SOPA Sieberling Award; SAA Excellence in CRM; SAA Distinguished Service Award	1998 *Toltec Mounds and Plum Bayou Culture: Mound D Excavations*	1996 SAA Fryxell Award	1990 "Trend and Tradition in Southeastern Archaeology"; SAA Fryxell Award 1990s cave research Ken., Tenn. 1996 *Of Caves and Shell Mounds*	1990s Postmodernism; cognitive-processual archaeology; explosion of gender studies

age. Additionally, this formal and informal education is usually experienced in an environment of networks of friendship, competition, admiration, and support. This was not, for any woman featured in this volume, the normal course.

The women whose careers we have described have had to be grit-tempered. In the same way that the potter needs to mix the aplastic with the clay to obtain desired results such as strength, resilience, resistance to fracture and wear, our women have had to mix into their personalities a persistence, a gritty strength to keep going in the face of enormous challenges. They often have appeared mild-tempered or even-tempered, but we think that is just the effects of smoothing the outside surface; the interior composition is basic to characterizing the type, as any archaeologist knows.

Perhaps the most isolated and least known of our women was Margaret Ashley Towle. In her life story, we are again reminded that we are anthropologists who learn about our target populations through the method of archaeology. We recognize the quest for empirical data with which Franz Boas sent his students from Columbia University into the "otherness" of non-western cultures or remote places. Margaret Ashley conducted archaeological research in rural Georgia a decade after the work of C. B. Moore ended (e.g., Moore 1918). She was sent to test-excavate sites with the goal of establishing an archaeological chronology. For Margaret Mead (1972) to undertake the unknown in Samoa and New Guinea, or Zora Neal Hurston (1942) to collect data in Harlem and in Florida jook joints under the active mentoring hand of Boas in the 1920s was not much different than for Margaret Ashley to venture into the wilderness forests of south Georgia with the same guidance, set up with a local Boy Scout in much the same way Mead obtained help from local missionaries.

We cannot be sure that Margaret Ashley gave up her career for marriage, but whatever problems her husband faced, she returned to active involvement in archaeology after his death. She worked, without pay, until her own death, providing analysis of data on plant materials, principally from Peru. The tragedy for southeastern archaeology is that she felt her southeastern work and data were worthless. If she was ashamed of the methods of the 1920s, she must have been unaware that they were typical for the times and nonetheless useful for future researchers. It is also common Western female psychology to view her own work as inadequate (a trait we wonder why more men do not consider). Given the isolation in which she worked, her lack of confidence, and the passage of time and disciplinary changes, it is not surprising, and that is all the more horrifying, that she would destroy her data.

While Columbia University produced many anthropological pioneers, as archaeology became more systematic in the South, after the time of Margaret Ashley, leadership of the WPA projects devolved on archaeologists from several major institutions: Chicago, Michigan, and Harvard. In the WPA groups, there were no supervisory female field archaeologists in the Southeast, though we have noted the work of Harriet Smith in 1941 at Cahokia (chapters 4 and 5). There were women in graduate programs, but none were included in the supervision of fieldwork and field projects. When we remember the leaders of this period, we think of Kelly, Ford, Phillips, Griffin, Willey, Fairbanks, Jennings—all men.

Madeline Kneberg, trained at Chicago with many of these historic figures in anthropology, was active during this time, but she was in charge of the University of Tennessee laboratory in which materials from numerous field projects were analyzed. She did not come to this work along a traditional educational path. She had already considered several careers—opera, nursing, medical school—and made the life changes that seemed more in keeping with her own interests (and her own heart and her own circumstance). While her training was in physical anthropology, she helped to write many major reports on Tennessee sites. Her lengthy success in Tennessee was made possible by her organizational skills, methodological rigor, and supportive management of people. She was not a self-promoter. She enjoyed long working relationships, with Tom Lewis and others, and was the most well-known woman in southeastern archaeology for decades. Her meticulous work in archaeological and skeletal analysis, synthesis and reporting, even helping living Native Americans recover their own heritage, is a monumental legacy. But even with her obvious prominence and substantive academic contributions, her career still slips "under the shadow of the laboratory tent" (Woodbury 1991).

Another role that was possible for women in the WPA days was that of patron. Isabel Patterson may be the least important to primary archaeological research of the women profiled in this volume, but her patronage of A. R. Kelly and others assisted with landowners, funds, and public recognition. We could see her as an archaeological "groupie" but that would cheapen the importance of her role. Her advocacy and assistance of John R. Swanton and the de Soto Commission reverberate into today's professional deliberations. Her work for this commission reminds us of the emotional content of this event, the attachment of people to their past, the other kinds of value beyond science that derive from archaeology. In a time of great international uncertainty, Isabel Patterson's promotion of the de Soto anniversary provided a cause, pageantry, and large-scale effort in public archaeology.

By any measure, the most invisible women were the African Americans who worked in various WPA projects. The "separate but equal" doctrine and Jim Crow laws created an effective ceiling for their life hopes. The total number of women who worked in WPA projects will probably be forever unknown, as are most of their names. Women who have been interviewed, or their families, point out the importance of this experience in their lives, yet there is no legacy of this, even in the African-American community. We believe that, because this employment was not a path out of their situations, but a temporary condition within oppression, it remains unknown. For these women, and doubtless also the black men similarly working in archaeology from the very beginning, this unusual employment represented an opportunity to support their families rather than any hope of social mobility. The situation for the many white women working on these projects may have been different, but most of them are equally unknown (see fig. 1.4). The lab workers, administrative assistants, and typists all made contributions whose nature and scale remains for the most part unrecognized.

Bettye Broyles represents the greater opportunities in the postwar years for college education. Her post-baccalaureate training was field-based and experiential. She never earned a master's degree. Her personality, drive, and native intelligence helped her succeed, with a steely core that allowed her to take charge without the backing of senior male mentors. She was an active member of professional societies, and her work on behalf of the Southeastern Archaeological Conference has been underappreciated, though she came to be the major female presence at SEAC after Madeline Kneberg's time. Unusual for her time among our subjects, she combined the working-class ethic and love of fine detail—drawing, mapping—to excel in the physical labor of the field as well as in the laboratory. We wonder, too, if Bettye's ousting from West Virginia would have gone differently had she been a man. Perhaps having a tough female supervisor without the "proper academic pedigree" was too much of a challenge for male egos; we all know many cases where the rise to power of a man in similar circumstances was not only tolerated but supported through "old boy" networks.

Adelaide Bullen is the most distant and difficult to profile of the women presented here. The completion of an undergraduate degree at the age of thirty-five and after having two children is surprising for a woman of her social class. Her preparation was in physical anthropology, but her devotion to a husband who was consumed by archaeology brought her squarely into osteological analysis, report preparation, and fieldwork. She is one of three New Englanders (with Davis and Wing) who, transplanted to the South, remained to have productive careers in the region. We will never know the character of her intellectual contribution to her husband's work, but her own "basic archaeological dog work" (Mason 1992:97) has enduring value.

Yulee Lazarus also worked in isolation off the traditional archaeological career path. She took up the responsibility for her husband's interests, both public and scientific, doing these things for love and for the public good. Yulee's work stressed research and education. Her efforts contribute a sense of place to residents of a beach-side region of the South that annually swells with tourists. She found academic archaeologists who advocated for her and provided educational direction and advice on museum development. From mentors such as Smith and Fairbanks, she received that formal archaeological training indirectly, outside the academy.

From Carol Mason's memoir, we gain insights relative to the educational environment of the 1950s and one woman's experience within it. We see also the formal continuing influence of the Chicago field schools and Chicago-Michigan academics. Mason's path to establishing herself as a professional archaeologist was perhaps the most traditionally "womanly" of the individuals we have considered. Because of her marriage and family involvement, however, she has not taught in a "major" department of anthropology, she is less well-known than her abilities warrant, and she has not been able to support her research interests with large competitive grants.

Hester Davis created her own niche. Her path into archaeology was rooted in the interests and networks of her older siblings. When her own educational undertakings failed to satisfy her, she fell back on archaeological employment and applied many of the techniques of her anthropological training in the archaeological sphere. Her training of the hundreds of avocational volunteers in Arkansas is testimony to her management skills and personal energy. In Arkansas, nationally, and internationally, politics created the opportunities, but Hester Davis was a pioneer in creating the system that currently exists for site protection and preservation, professional ethics and standards, and all other facets of public archaeology.

Martha Rolingson has "walked the walk and talked the talk." Hers was more the traditional male archaeologist's path, but perhaps with somewhat different results. She received her Ph.D. from a premier program and came out of the dusty WPA collections and into the field. Her work, however, has been largely underappreciated and has garnered less limelight and prestige than it would have if she were a man with the same educational pedigree (especially a pushy man). Her early investigations into Paleo-Indian and Archaic cultures are primarily reported in University of Kentucky report series and her later research in Arkansas publications. These outlets are very respectable but perhaps do not command the same attention in the discipline that national and international publications do. The supportive and female-friendly environment of an organization such as the Arkansas Archeological Survey has the downside that it is not associated with a Ph.D.-granting institution. Much the same way that older women gain status in many cultures through ties of obligation from their progeny, the status of academics is enhanced through their students, especially highly placed ones. Nonetheless, Rolingson's career shows a quiet persistence and solid determination, and the beauty of work done so thoroughly and imaginatively, with much more to come.

Elizabeth Wing came to southeastern archaeology sideways through biology. Her involvement with John Goggin provided the opportunity for employment that gave the flexibility to work part-time. She was able to have a family and career, accomplishments supported by her husband, Jim. She has perhaps received less recognition than other premier zooarchaeologists. But, she is famous for her training of cadres of graduate students and her major contributions to environmental archaeology, including on the international scene. As specialist studies become less a topic for appendices and more crucial for fundamental understanding of human behavior in the past, her contributions may be more appreciated.

As she points out herself, Patty Jo Watson also came to the Southeast from the "margins," not only via the Old World, but also beginning in a natural environment—caves—that most certainly was not the mainstream place for fieldwork. Even the paleoethnobotanical focus of her work was then a specialty subject. For Watson, as with several other women profiled here, her husband's interests (in this case, caves) were an influential factor in her career. Unlike most of the other women, however, she did not subvert her own interests or become "support staff" but maintained her identity as she gradually became more interested in the research herself. Watson became an equal partner, making her own separate but complementary contribution and becoming recognized as a premier scholar. She is also the only woman featured in this book to have a traditional tenured position in a Ph.D.-granting program (nonetheless she originally took a part-time job at the institution where her spouse received a tenure-track position).

Each of these women was isolated from mainstream archaeological practice in the Southeast in some fashion, if only by being female. They were isolated from each other as well, some by time, others by distance. Had they not been, would we be more aware not only of their work but also of the contributions of a handful of other women whose names we have seen? Further, would we continue not to notice the absence of both women's labor (as archaeologists, as wives, as technicians) and women's ideas in theory, practice, methodology, and interpretation? Would there have been a need for this book? Or might they already have been legendary, like so many of the male figures they worked with? Certainly their stories are just as colorful and amazing, even more so considering the barriers they faced, and the grace, humor, and style they maintained in the face of them as they did the work they so thoroughly enjoyed.

Women and the South

Just as women anthropologists in the Southwest may have been attracted to the power of that desert landscape, we like to think that especially the fieldworkers among women archaeologists in the Southeast were drawn to the immense beauty of this lush landscape, the close green branches, trumpet and muscadine vines in pillars and arches, passion flowers "with their white and purple rays . . . the streaming hot shade of the wilderness . . . the snakes in the sudden cool . . . like thousands of silver bells, the frogs [ringing] through the swamp . . . ," as Eudora Welty puts it in "At the Landing" (1980:257). Another attraction of course may have been the extraordinarily rich and diverse material record and evidence of complexity in cultural evolution. Then there is the dilemma of the contemporary cultural environment.

The South has a long history as a rural, conservative region, and much has been debated about the archetypal dominant male figure, the power of the behind-the-scenes woman, the Good Good Ole Boys and Bad Good Ole Boys of Florence King's (1976) hilarious *Southern Ladies and Gentlemen* and other profound characters behind the stereotypes. King's chapter entitled "'I'd Be More than Happy to Carry You Upstairs Ma'am' or: the Cult of Southern Manhood" describes the South as a gynecocracy emphasizing respect for women, if sometimes in quirky, unwanted, or ridiculous ways. Journalist Molly Ivins (1991:124), equally hilarious, notes that one of the nicest things about southerners is their large tolerance for eccentricity. The various meanings of being a southerner, despite class and racial difference, can be deconstructed, in contemporary "redneck discourse," to demonstrate a common anti-bourgeois lifestyle and love of the outdoors, but a decidedly male attitude (Kirby 1995).

Many of the women in our study were not from the South, but all had to work in the South, with men, doing archaeology. Perhaps these alternately endearing/aggravating Southern cultural characteristics are what made their work possible. The fact that there were so many more women than expected when we began this study is perhaps traceable to the same social and intellectual atmosphere that allows the women to do the work and do a good job but not make too big a deal of it because other things are more important. Perhaps it is because the South was considered lagging in intellectual endeavor and men trained in anthropology preferred jobs anywhere but there (Hudson 1996). There is also the possibility that many of the women were content not to be totally in charge, famous, or responsible for the whole deal because of the way they were socialized. The role of helpmate to one's husband in archaeology is a revered one, with a long tradition of lively, fascinating, and exceedingly competent women very happy in it (for example, Morris 1933, Braidwood 1959 and so many others; recently, Hudson 1993, Lister 1997, Gradwohl 1997). But warm acceptance of that role tends to minimize the value of the solid work and contributions to regional data, method, and theory that many women have made. The role of helpmate is always destined to be undervalued; we have no evidence, for instance, that Adelaide Bullen was ever paid for her work. Riley's (1998) review of Florence Lister's (1997) autobiography has only one sentence about Florence herself, without reference to her archaeologist husband. A new biographical treatment of Lewis Binford shows a 1956 photo of him and Stanley South in the field in North Carolina with an attractive woman who is not even mentioned in the figure caption, let alone named or described as unknown (Sabloff 1998:72); she is hardly invisible standing there in a halter top! Perhaps this is the kind of obvious insult we need in order to raise the awareness of this invisibility, which has been so typical for women in archaeology.

We can see this historical invisibility often in the Southeast. One summary of New Deal archaeology (Fagette 1996) does not even mention Madeline Kneberg, though the author spends many pages criticizing Tom Lewis's whole operation. In another weird twist, former southeastern archaeologist Jesse Jennings, claiming in his autobiography to be unable to blend the personal and the professional (1994:xx), mentions Madeline as a fellow student at Chicago (58), then, in denigrating the work of Tom Lewis, notes that it was Madeline, Lewis's coauthor, whom he always credited with two of the best monographs in the Southeast (*Hiwassee Island* and *Eva*). Then he notes that Jimmy Griffin credits the quality of these reports to Andrew Whiteford instead! (89–90). (We of course wonder how many pottery tables Griffin himself pasted together line by line for publication, as Madeline did.

We also wonder how these early women's lives might have been different if simple things such as word processors and digital electronic scales had been available earlier. Would they have had more time for generating high-level theory or whatever?)

In writing this book, we have tried not to worry about the "what ifs?" of history. We also were very aware of the difficulties of writing about women who were deceased and could not tell their own stories, as well as the difficulty of writing about professionals who are out there as active as ever, very much alive and not at all retired, and whose bibliographies presented here will soon need updating. We also did not delve deeply into some personal life choice questions in the lives of the women profiled here, mostly out of respect. As with any life history project, there are always limitations and ethical considerations (Sweet 1997). As Parezo (1993a:xvi-xvii) noted in dealing with women scholars in southwestern anthropology, there are topics, such as sexuality, lesbianism, racism, elitism, intellectual rivalries, financial situations, psychological problems, religious prejudice, that are merely skirted but nonetheless have enormous meaning and effects in the course of a career. Friendships, love or hate relationships, cannot fail to influence one's work. Archaeology is known for the ephemeral field (or lab) situation, which often generates special relationships among participants, and creates closer, more relaxed friendships and attractions, as Hester Davis notes, because of the fun of working together on a common goal and not having to worry about more typical social concerns. As the personal is inseparable from the political and the professional, all contribute toward the life and career of an individual archaeologist (Parezo 1993b has a wonderful discussion of these issues). We often find in biographies of important women the tendency to dwell on the personal and the personality, either taking precedence over or intertwined with the professional (Parezo 1993a:15). In this volume we have tried to emphasize these pioneering archaeologists' special contributions, but we felt it important to chronicle some of the personal difficulties they were able to overcome.

The Paths of Change

Things are changing a great deal, of course, and women are lately just as common in archaeology as in many other social and natural sciences—or more so—though we have a long way to go to achieve what might be labeled equality (Zeder 1997; Nelson, Nelson, and Wylie 1994; and why is providing child care at professional meetings such a difficult concept?). Still, a little reform could easily be like a little pregnancy, something that will not continue in the same stage for long (to quote Heilbrun 1995:242). During our interviews for this project there was much discussion of numbers of women in the field and positions they now hold, as well as career styles of past and present. Watson remembered a college catalogue of the 1960s that said women should not go into geology because it is too strenuous. The social movements and intellectual climate of the sixties and seventies have, we hope, changed much of this, just like they have changed archaeology. Also, women may now hold more positions in the field simply because there are more positions, not to mention more women.

The field (and field school) experience remains crucial in the structuring of one's career perceptions of archaeology, including gender considerations. But not only were there lots more women in the field than we expected in the past, there are also increasing numbers today. At the other end of the profession, there are now so many more in professional positions of power and visibility. Pat Galloway and Hester Davis are recent past presidents of the Southeastern Archaeological Conference; both took the stage in November 1995 to present the SEAC Distinguished Service Award to Madeline Kneberg Lewis and Bettye Broyles. There have been many women SEAC officers recently, not to mention those serving similar positions in state and other archaeological societies, but might this be because of the tradition of women in service roles?

Watson recounted an incident about the Society for American Archaeology executive board, on which she served twice. During the second time, in the 1980s, when she was editor of *American Antiquity*, other women on the board were Ruthann Knudson and Leslie Wildesen. They asked her to make a motion to dissolve the Committee on the Status of Women, which had been initiated during a time when there weren't any women in the upper levels of the SAA. Now that this goal had been achieved, it was felt that COSWA's job was accomplished, and it would be a segregating agent if it were continued. Soon after that, Dena Dincauze became president of SAA after serving a stint as editor. The idea was that women had achieved their aims and could blend in with the ranks of men. A few years later, however, Meg Conkey and a number of younger women resurrected the idea. They had been encountering different sorts of problems. Watson and her cohort were far enough along to be unfamiliar with what graduate students and new assistant professors had to put up with. COSWA was reinvigorated with new goals and responsibilities.

There have been many women in the Southeast in leadership positions, especially, as already noted, in historic and CRM archaeology, clearly a case, Watson notes, of all these systems evolving together. She also explores the continuing way the process plays out in academia: three out of four archaeologists in her department at Washington University are women. Recently (and correlated with this fact), most student applicants have been women, as well. There is the thought whether they should worry about representation of male graduate students in archaeology.

The situation of the first typists is now well known. They were all men, since men were more frequently secretaries in that earlier era, and the typewriter was a machine considered far too complex for women to master. After women did master it, the whole job of secretary was of course devalued. Or is the reverse true, that women are only allowed into a profession after it becomes devalued enough to let them in? We have lately heard stories of (usually older male) professors warning young male students about anthropology becoming a feminized field because of the increasing prominence of women in the American Anthropological Association and elsewhere. Or is it simply because archaeology and CRM have expanded so much that there were not enough men around, so women were drafted to the workplace, but as soon as things shrink again, Rosie the Shoveler will go back to her home, kitchen, and children? (Not if she is deeply entrenched or even presiding over the scene.) We like to hope that the intellectual and social climate of archaeology has changed enough that there is room for everybody.

Barriers faced by women in archaeology could be listed differently for every group of women or men discussing them, and many would be common to men as well. In the lives of the women in this book we can see many of the classical problems faced by any archaeologist, but with a woman's overlay: Ashley, Broyles, and Rolingson doing fieldwork in unknown, possibly unsafe, areas and receiving less notice than male co-workers or colleagues; Patterson, Lazarus, and Davis getting the public interested enough to support archaeology with real labor, money, political interest, and official legislation; Kneberg dealing with mountains of data and materials in the lab and never having time or funds to finish some reports; Bullen, Mason, and Wing balancing husbands and children yet delivering tireless labor that often went unrecognized; women of the federal relief programs laboring in the field and lab completely unrecognized.

As we reach the end of the millennium, we can now say that women are no longer marginal in archaeology, including much of the Southeast. They still have enormous hurdles to leap in the quest to become professionals and maintain careers (Spencer-Wood 1992; Nelson, Nelson, and Wylie 1994; Nelson 1997). But now they comprise more than half of recent American archaeology Ph.D.s, a major component of all the primary sectors of archaeological employment, and the majority of the younger cohort of academicians and museum archaeologists (Zeder 1977:31). We hope that documenting the substance and dedication of these southeastern women, who helped pioneer the way for the current more favorable situation, will be just a first step in showing the archaeological heritage of us all. We also hope it will bring more recognition to some whose accomplishments have gone less rewarded and trumpeted. Truly these women were/are made of strong fabric; they surely were/are tempered with grit.

15

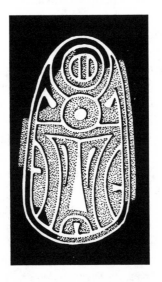

Reflections and Speculations on Putting Women into Southeastern Archaeology

NANCY MARIE WHITE

Archaeology is always rethinking its foundations and coming up with cutting-edge theoretical perspectives incorporating all the best parts of what's new. Just as we now discuss the merits of a combined "cognitive-processual" approach (Renfrew 1994; Preucel and Hodder 1996), for example, it should be possible not only to engender the archaeology we do but also to be aware of the merits of feminist interpretations. There is probably much more hope for feminism in archaeology than in some other natural sciences. Indeed, anthropology in general has been seen as more receptive to feminist concerns not only because there are so many women but also because the field stresses flexibility and adjustment of conceptual frameworks as needed (Imber and Tuana 1988:141) and because anthropologists are supposed to be the experts in understanding the "the other." In addition, a feminist perspective in archaeology is not like a Marshalltown trowel or a Chevy Suburban. There are at least as many brands (type-varieties?) of feminism in archaeology as there are of Marxism or materialism or pocketknives (for example, Little 1994). One can look for agency, domination and resistance, division of labor, kinship, monthly and seasonal cycles, primary and secondary producers, symbol and ceremonial systems, or just change in gender-associated artifacts or biological remains through time with various feminist perspectives.

Furthermore, contrary to Preucel and Hodder (1996:417), who saw "a close connection between postprocessual archaeology and feminist and gender archaeologists," you do not have to dwell in the world of meaning, ideology, contextualism, and cognitive frameworks either to do feminist archaeology or simply to look for gender in the past. It might even be dangerously inaccurate to get too postmodern or postprocessual, as Mascia-Lees, Sharpe, and Cohen (1989) have pointed out, noting how looking for the real voice of the native is often done in an imperialistic, sexist fashion that reinforces elitist perspectives. Hill (1998) demonstrated how existing theoretical frameworks that have already been applied productively to other archaeological questions are fine for addressing gender issues. Positivist science is certainly capable of recognizing women in the archaeological record and understanding gender as the fluid social construct that it was, and the foundation of so many other intertwined social systems. As Friedl (1995:16–17) recently put it: "Since the mid-1970s, anthropological and feminist theories have recognized the limitations inherent in thinking about men and women as essential, eternal types. . . . The variations in race, class, culture and historical circumstance that differentiate men among men, women among women, and men and women from each other make simple studies of so-called women's place obsolete. The political economy of gender is, in my view, still where the main thrust should be found, but the value of studying the richness of symbol, ritual, and literary texts as a source of nuanced understandings of gender and gender relations has become obvious."

Archaeologists are anthropologists; a gendered perspective is possible, even in the Southeast. Certainly some change has already begun, and it will be interesting to see what happens when it is more visible. Researchers are starting to integrate gender into the central questions archaeologists traditionally ask, rather than tacking it on as just another area of study (Wright 1996:3). More overtly feminist, gender-aware, and reflexive treatments of the past are just starting to become important (a good example is Russell 1996). The large number of women in historic archaeology and in cultural resources management have meant lots more "Placing Women in the Past," as a recent publication combining them was entitled (National Park Service 1997). Since the subject is U.S. historic archaeology, this publication has much material on the Southeast. Perhaps historic archaeology has been more successful in seeing women in the past because they are at least documented in the background, if not often the primary spotlights of history.

What about prehistory? Putting women into it is not just sticking on another subheading in the chapter on social reconstruction. Nelson (1997: 27) has suggested thinking of gender studies as a prism that breaks up characteristics of the past into more perceptible details and allows better understanding of the whole social, political, and economic system. Gender is the one set of roles always present, crosscutting or intertwining with all the rest; it is a good place to start, not to add on to the end of the analysis. Nelson also noted (1997:13) how gendered power imbalances among archaeologists obscure parts of the archaeological record.

Some Women Envision the Past

Does looking at prehistory through the eyes of a group of women produce a different kind of science? Such richly debatable premises have long been included in feminist anthropological theorizing. For example, not long ago some primatologists held a conference that did not include men, at first by chance, since there are now so many women primatologists. Men complained about this conference; were the results different than if there had been equal representation or an all-male gathering? Participants noted the uncommon topics, the lack of posturing and filibustering that slow things down, and the absence of competition and attack, victory and defeat in the discussion. Opponents of the idea believed that one's scientific work is not influenced by one's gender or any other personal factors (Dusheck 1990; Morbeck, Galloway, and Zihlman 1997).

What happens when a meeting of archaeologists is held to discuss issues in southeastern prehistory at a specific significant site, and all the participants are women? Are there any differences from what a group of men would do? (I doubt there is any difference in noting the time to break for liquid refreshment.) When asked if she might be able to offer any perspective different from that of a male archaeologist, Martha Rolingson replied face-tiously, "I don't know. I'm not a male archaeologist!" but noted that her perspectives reflect what is current in the field. Thus we get a reduction to the well-known but still important feminist debate (in any field, whether women's art or women in the executive office) over whether women would bring something new or different or distinctive to science, or would do it in the same way it has been done already (for example, Rosser 1987; Schie-binger 1989). Zihlman (1985:375), writing about how early hunter-gather-ers would not have to be monogamous, noted, among other things, that women constructing new views of the past still inherit the issues of the 1960s but draw on events in their own lives and the political climates of the times, whether control of reproduction, choice of work, independence, or the roles of men. Women's anthropological models reflect concerns that are different from each other as well as from those of men, and we cannot expect that women's reconstructions of the past will be inherently more correct. How-ever "[o]ne thing is clear: women [researchers] have broadened the debate," corrected and balanced some past ideas, and redefined issues rather than just reacting to those posed by men. Without trying to repeat what has been said so eloquently by many others (Rosaldo 1980; Moore 1988; Parezo 1993c),

Fig. 15.1. Patty Jo Watson, Hester Davis, Martha Rolingson, and Ann Early envi-sioning prehistoric life, at museum exhibit, Toltec Mounds Archeological State Park, October 1995. (Photo by Nancy White.)

it is worth emphasizing that feminist and feminine views have enormous potential for enhancing or changing our idea base in model construction.

So, picture the interior of the museum at Arkansas's Toltec Mounds Park: cool, refreshing, dark inside compared with glaring sun on the open mounds and plaza. But the exhibits are brightly lit. Chairs lined up in front of the pottery exhibit are occupied by Rolingson, Hester Davis, Patty Jo Watson, and Ann Early, and other women archaeologists stand by (fig. 15.1). They are discussing the intricacies of interpretation at this multi-mound site, but then they get into reconstructing a typical scene from prehistory there; the game is on . . . .

Rolingson notes that she has thought about how we could recognize evidence of women's activities at a site such as Toltec, or any other kind of site, beyond just supposing women gather and men hunt.

Watson is guest instigator. She notes the recent importance of looking for the actual people in the material record after such a long period of dominance in American archaeology of systems approaches, models, and simulations without real people, where the system did this and the perturbation did that (Brumfiel 1992). She suggests that the value in some of the postprocessual or ideational approaches is in getting back to a theme that was present in archaeology before the Binfordian and eco-utilitarian materialist paleosubsistence archaeology, back to looking at the human beings and what they were doing and thinking. She admits being faced with the issue of saying something about this and being given a deadline and calling in a coauthor more familiar with feminist theory in anthropology, and producing a thought piece (Watson and Kennedy 1991) that was, well, fun! The fun is in letting go and imagining the people at the site, without worrying for the moment about hard evidence. She asks that we picture, say, the central area around Mound G at Toltec and dream up a picture of it in its heyday. What might the structure have been? Who built it? Why? Domestic or not? Secular or sacred?

Okay, says Rolingson, it is in the center of the site. It's a sacred building. How big? Six meters diameter, round building.

Post structure? Probably. We have the wall trench nearly three feet deep; it would probably take posts 20 cm in diameter.

So they've gone to some real trouble to dig? Yes. The ground surface on the inside was cleaner than that on the outside, where there is charcoal and other trash, probably the original ground surface before the mound was built. We don't get the posts in the trench, so the structure must have been dismantled before they decided to extend the mound that far or build the mound over it.

Who were "they"? Who made the decisions? Who did the work? Not faceless blobs? Probably some kind of hereditary leadership but not necessarily to the extent of the elite chieftains of the Mississippian period. But people couldn't maintain a center like this without some leadership that says, okay, now it's time to repair these mounds or build this one or enlarge that one or abandon that one. It was not just economics but the ceremonial cycle, and a small group of people living here but so far no evidence of elaborate ceremonialism, so not an extremely ranked (stratified?) society as with Mississippian. And we can view them as matrilineal because southeastern Muskhogeans and Caddoans are matrilineal.

So, there's an important female principle here? Yes, says Davis, but we cannot make these kinds of hypotheses when we haven't dug the mounds, we have so few burials. . . . But, says Rolingson, we know there are burials in Mound C because we put a trench there, but no artifacts have been found with them. Early remarks that it can be misleading to use burials only for social reconstruction. We use them as a crutch to support some ideas but fail to consider alternatives. There could be other ways of disposing of the important deceased.

Watson pauses to reprimand. *You are starting with the data, the virtuoso archaeologist way! You can't help putting a heavy inductivist slant when you want to know so much from those pitifully small remains such as the serious lack of burials here. Just set the data aside for a moment and think about a living group of people here. Pick any time period you want, sketch out a scenario in your mind without worrying about confirming it. You have been immersed in the site for a long time now so anything you say about it is unconsciously, intuitively, going to have a solid data base.*

Rolingson says, okay, I'll pick the time period from 800 to 900 because I know that some mounds were occupied or used then and others were not. Say around 875.

Okay, so what was it like? The beginning of the spring or a summer day?

Rolingson takes up the challenge. Meadowlarks, kids screaming; it's hot, there are trees, not like the golf course it is today, and Mound B is at least halfway up. We've got some sort of structure on it that has trash inside, so it's not strictly a temple.

Is construction under way? People carrying in basketloads of dirt? Who are they? How are they working? Well, it's everybody, not just special people; it's the women, kids, men, old and young. Maybe the women are spending some time getting food ready for the rest of the workers. Maybe it's like an old-fashioned barn raising in which there is a leader, probably male, telling people, okay, we're going to get this soil from here and clean this area here. . . .

Is this male supervisor there all the time? Watching everything? He doesn't pull rank and sit in the shade or go eat his lunch and let the work go on? He probably can because the people know what they're doing, but he needs to be organizing. We can't run an Arkansas Archaeological Society dig without someone organizing everything. But they probably all know what is involved, the older people teaching the younger.

What is their attitude while they are doing it? Is it, oh, well, we have to go out and sweat in the sun again for yet another expansion? No, this is strictly volunteer, something they want to do because they know mound additions are needed or the plaster surfacing needs redoing. It's perhaps like cleaning out the church or a community endeavor, done regularly, for the good of all.

How long would it take to add a stage to the mound? Do you work all day, every day? Experimental construction of mounds shows it does not take as long as we think. And it is more likely to be taking place in the fall after the harvest and in the winter when it's cool instead of when we have projected, since they would have been busy with the crops. They might come and do it for a few weeks then go home, since most actually lived out in farmsteads in the countryside. The model could be the Green Corn ceremony, in which over several days the mounds are plastered and repaired and general renewal of the site takes place. It wasn't a green corn ceremony here though because they did not have that much maize.

Good. That's a great Mound B scene. What else is going on? Well, there is a structure in the center of the site, the pre-Mound G building. I don't know who lived there.

Okay, make up somebody. Did anyone live here full time? I expect we would find more trash around if that were a domestic structure unless they were just keeping it cleaned away from the building.

Now here we come to a good postprocessual point, says Watson. One of the first things Ian Hodder said about Lewis Binford was that we can't generalize what Binford [1981] told us about the Nunamiut and what they do with bones unless we know their attitude towards dirt and trash disposal. Do they think you can just throw it anywhere, or that certain kinds of trash have to be treated differently? Some stuff has to be burned, other things buried? So what would these people's attitudes have been?

Well, says Rolingson, they kept the plazas and plaza sides of the mounds clean; we haven't found much in those areas. So that's a hint toward their attitudes. They were cleaning around the significant central structure.

Well, let's try to get closer to individual people. You feel whoever was in charge would have been a man? How did he get authority? Probably he is someone equivalent to a Big Man with an ascribed rather than an achieved status.

The ideas fly among the participants. Where does he get the status? If these are matrilineal people, through his mother or mother's brother. It may not matter so much who the father was; the key issue was the mother. Might that also suggest some of those women themselves could have had positions of power?

Throw out some ideas. What about labor? Women do most of the physical work in nearly all traditional societies. Farming, toting, carrying basketloads of dirt, building mounds. Maybe your mother or grandmother built your mound.

Rolingson comments that in this environment the heavier work may be digging up the soil, not carrying it, loosening the clay. Maybe the men are digging it up and loading it and the women and children carrying and dumping it. Some of the loads in Mound B stratigraphy are pretty small. There is great variation in basketload size and shape. Maybe they also carry it in skins, or drag it. Maybe people come in with whatever they have from wherever and put it wherever they think it might be okay. Watson mentions at least one North African society where the women go out and do digging for pottery clay, the really heavy work, and bring it to the men, who stay home and make the pots, the reverse of what one would predict. Ethnographically in the Southeast the men helped with the heavy clearing of fields but both men and women farmed. Sometimes the women did most of the heavy farming work on a day-to-day basis.

Early mentions ethnographic data on the Caddo from George Sabo (1987, 1993, 1995a,b), including understanding symbolic information. Construction of the chief's house was a community effort. Everyone pitched in with singing, bringing things, feasting, offering leadership and advice, ceremonial activity and rituals. We need to examine ethnohistoric literature for the specifics on men's and women's roles and changes in them from earlier times through the eighteenth century, when relationships were so transformed. There we could get ideas, Watson notes, about what data to test, in the processual archaeology fashion, but also in the critical theory perspective, to ask questions that a processual archaeologist would not, such as, were the chiefs men or women? How to distinguish them? By different kinds of decoration or badges of office or was a chief a chief in terms of paraphernalia allowed to be worn or handled? Watson says Rolingson is too good an archaeologist, like Davis and the rest of us, trying to stay too close to the data. Let's look at the possibilities of meaning and symbolism.

Early mentions clues of mythology or tradition from powerful representations of women such as those from the Birger and other Cahokia area figurines (and now Galloway [1997] has good suggestions about these artifacts and their contexts in terms of potentially direct female symbolism: vaginas). Watson asks if anyone has made a serious study of all the Hopewellian and other Middle Woodland female figurines and how they look and what they are doing. Weaving and textiles are becoming better understood and are thought to be women's work and indicators of social factors (for example, Kutruff and Kutruff 1996; Kutruff 1993; Barber 1994; Drooker 1992), though in the Southwest, men did the weaving. We know spindle whorls were associated with women's labor in Mesoamerica, and inferences can be made from the distribution of these artifacts (Brumfiel 1991).

Davis points out the need to shed Euro-American bias in reading ethnography. She mentions Sabo's (1993) reinterpretations of the Caddo and Quapaw from their own viewpoint. An incident that comes to mind is the recorded behavior of the chief and chiefly entourage when they come out to meet the Spanish or French: the Indians are crying. The natives are not upset about the strangers; it is a welcoming ceremony, and it occurs often in such contexts (Hall 1997). Rolingson asks if such emotions could be the tear tracks seen as the Southeastern Ceremonial Complex forked eye motif, or if that is just the mark of the falcon.

Early notes that, in the translation of Joutel's (1714) journal of his wanderings through the Caddo area, he described the French going from one village to another; after the greeting and negotiation with the village men, then the French were allowed to approach one of the women and buy their food from her, to exchange beads and other goods for corn. This was repeated all along the route. This did not get into the heavily abbreviated version of the journal. There is something being expressed here about women's roles and the possession and control of processed foods and the relationship between men and women in the community and with outsiders. The men couldn't give food away; they were the first point of contact with the outside world but after that, it was up to the women, the people who owned the goods that the French wanted. Whether it was possession of the processed food or payment for processing in our terminology is not clear. It is an interesting line to pursue; women were not hiding in the huts.

More discussion ensues concerning gender politics. Someone is reminded of the stories of the British negotiating with the Iroquois men, telling them to get rid of the women so they could talk real politics and the Iroquois men replying, whoa, we can't do that! They are the powerful clan mothers and if you want to deal with us you deal with them too; and by the way, they want some blankets and beads, and here is a list of stuff, if you really want to talk with us (Sullivan et al. 1921–65, quoted in Axtell 1981). Iroquois men respected the political power of their women. It had to have been the same, probably even more so, in the South. Has anyone ever resolved whether the

White Woman of the Natchez, the Great Sun's mother, had real political power? Someone was working on it but there is some agreement that the version of the French account commonly used is poorly translated.

Watson points out that even once you work through existing ethnohistoric documents, try to weed out European biases, get the best models possible of the historic aboriginal cultures, even when it's been pummeled and punched and threshed until you have the kernel of the essence of what is reliable, you come to an old/new archaeology/philosophy of science point that even this kind of information is not a ticket straight into prehistory. For the time we are talking about, A.D. 875, this is 600–800 years earlier than ethnohistory; there have been centuries of change. You could make a case for various models, but caution is needed to escape that tyranny of the ethnohistoric and ethnographic record. There have been some radically different things going on in prehistory from anything you could observe or even dream about based on the picture that the Spanish and other Europeans gave us.

Rolingson notes here that this is even more of a problem in the Southeast where there has to be a gap in the ability to carry ethnohistoric knowledge back too far because of the shift into the dependence upon maize and the associated ceremonialism and social change. Shifts in labor patterns indicated by skeletal evidence (for example, Bridges 1989) can give us some hard data to try to characterize those systems before and after maize. Watson thinks this is the kind of synthesis we should aim for, uniting the strengths of both the (old) "new" archaeology and the newer postprocessual archaeology, a cognitive-processual or holistic approach (Renfrew 1994; Marcus and Flannery 1994). We can bring those together, not just fight about which one is better.

Early remembers that in one of the volumes on Great Plains archaeology and ethnohistory, there is an article on women warriors, with historic period drawings, notebook-type artwork, showing women in loincloths and so forth. It is the kind of article that is a revelation. This stuff has not been hidden away; the information has been there and it just needed more people to look at it. Was it overlooked for reasons of bias, just like male or skinny female figurines in the European Upper Paleolithic?

Free-form idea exchange means that one thought triggers another. Davis recalls, from her ethnographic work among the Cherokee thirty years ago, hearing the received anthropological wisdom that three hundred, four hundred years of contact meant that there was nothing left of aboriginal culture, even thought processes, and that anything the researchers did see was actually taken out of Bureau of American Ethnology publications (for example, Mooney 1900, 1975) and taught to the Indians by the BIA school. One fellow student at the time, Paul Kuché, went with Mooney's records of myths and other cultural systems and knew the kinds of questions to ask. He found that there was indeed continuity in certain areas, ways the Cherokee think about and react to things, areas of culture that don't go away or disintegrate so easily. She thinks she saw some of that at a recent meeting about the Native American Graves Protection and Repatriation Act (NAGPRA). The Caddo traditional leader, who did not speak at all during the meeting, commented at the party that evening that there were things he and other Native Americans got from ancestors that are now enabling greater empowerment, things they have not told any outsiders, though they have been there all the time. Watson concurs with this realization and notes that, as a typical American familiar with confrontational styles and outspokenness, it took her a great deal of firsthand contact with Indian peoples before seeing them as more inside themselves, very different from non-native Americans.

The practical item Hester extracted from the story of the NAGPRA meeting was that the Caddo leader said in the course of conversation, I'm the only Caddo in my household. My wife and kids are Delaware. Matrilineality in action may not be that hard to find. Watson narrates an encounter with the female principle during fieldwork on a project in Navajo country in New Mexico. Her husband, Red, was sent to buy a goat and so stopped the first Navajo guy in a pickup truck. The guy said, I don't have any flock. You have to talk to my mother over there.

That was decades ago when she and her husband were graduate students. She thought the notion might be gone by now, but in August 1995 she was surveying with Steve LeBlanc, looking for a site near a Navajo family ranch. As they headed toward it a young guy came running down to stop them, saying they could not go to the site. The family had an agreement with the state that no one could go up there without permission. Did they have an official permit from the state? Watson said no, they did not, but they were both legitimate archaeologists. So he said, okay, but you have to talk to my mother. You can't go up there unless she gives you permission. He went to get his mother, who was anxiously trying to find out where some goats had escaped. They had just bought ten new goats and she was wringing her hands about it and instantly drew Watson and LeBlanc into the crisis. They had just got the goats the day before; they didn't know this area and they had escaped and she didn't know what was going to happen to them. The son had been off trying to find traces of them when he saw the archaeologists. She was so anxious about that problem that she could not focus on the request, but finally she said, if they could show something indicating they were real archaeologists, not looters, she would let them go up to the site, but first they had to go to her other son. She was stage manager of the whole thing, the lost goats, the archaeologists, the adult sons who completely deferred to her, in the manner of the Caddo men mentioned earlier as described by the French. This woman was not an imposing figure but she was in charge and the sons snapped to when she commanded. It was quite remarkable. The son who finally took them to the site was thirty-something, completely generic American in speech patterns, in the way he chugged a soft drink offered by the archaeologists. He said he'd been married to a Hopi, the granddaughter of Frog Woman, who was a famous Hopi potter, then he said, so his kids were Hopi (in the same way as we saw with the Caddo). He said, you know, when I was there I learned to make some pottery and I make it and sell it to trading posts. Steve said ha! Hopi pottery, right? He said, well, no, that wouldn't be right, although I learned some things from the Hopi. I am Navajo and I make the pottery the way I think it ought to be made and it's not really Hopi pottery, it's my pottery.

Rolingson mentions a paper by Pat Galloway (1989a) noting how the French kept talking with the Choctaw in terms of your father this and that, and the French king is your father. It was a totally alien concept to the matrilineal Indians. Their role of father was a casual, informal, familiar one while the mother's role was one of authority.

The discussion turns to Deetz's (1965) classic statistical analysis of Arikara pottery attributes purporting to show matrilineality, if mother trains daughter. This would conflict with some ethnographic evidence, such as Ruth Bunzel's (1929) matrilineal Pueblo potters, who learn the craft and get design ideas from their mothers, yes, but also their aunts, their dreams, and even from prehistoric sherds they pick up! They also say often they would never want to copy another woman's designs. Watson notes that the original problem with the research of Deetz, Longacre (1966), and others trying to show matrilineality was the taking as an assumption of something that has yet to be demonstrated: how the transfer of knowledge works. Other evidence of knowledge passed down the female line might supplement such work: cooking techniques and food residues in vessels, perhaps. Food processing is one of the most conservative cultural systems; when other evidence of ethnicity is gone, traditional foods might remain.

The discussion goes on. What evidence can we find of women in traditional domestic situations and elsewhere? What evidence unmistakably indicates men actors, or children, or third genders? What evidence is there of postmenopausal women, who often constitute a third gender and gain in power as they age (unlike in our own society)? We know so little of the Southeast since *contact was the earliest in the U.S. there and people died out or changed so enormously fast, long before it could be chronicled. A book on women and power in aboriginal America (Klein and Ackerman 1995) chronicles historic cultures so changed that little female power is even evident in the Southeast as compared with other regions. Surely this cannot have been the case. Surely issues of gender, society, and politics must have been crucially important in North America's most complex societies north of Mexico.*

Rolingson notes the theme of expansion and mechanization in socioeconomic systems and what might be applicable to the Southeast. In the reverse of the typewriter-secretary scenario of something being taken over by women and at the same time losing value, does something evolving toward greater importance get co-opted by men from women? There is the theme of the origins of pottery as women's work but when the wheel and industrialization come in, men become the potters. When farming comes in the women may be the innovators because they presumably have the plant knowledge, but when it gets to be big business, mechanized, a large part of the socioeconomic system, then men take over. Perhaps even in the New World, with no mechanization, when maize comes in, at first it is just something you put in the ground with the chenopod and sunflower and amaranth, and the women are doing it. When it becomes crucial to both religious and political-economic systems, perhaps the men take over, as in Mesoamerica. But the Southeast is the exception here. Men are still hunting and women are still farming. Watson asks, is the prehistoric, precontact Southeast the matrilocality, matrilineality, the near-matriarchy that might have been?

There is nothing wrong with storytelling in prehistory (Terrell 1990), especially if it provokes some new lines of thought or awakens old ones into testable possibilities (for example, LeGuin 1986). Fagan (1995:30) entreats us to bring forth the "delicious, provocative experience of the past" in order to understand it better and also bring it to the public. Must we leave it to the novelists (such as Jean Auel, Mary Mackey, or the Gears) not only to visualize prehistoric human life but to have women actors in the scenes (not to mention running things sometimes)? It is not even necessary to plow through every treatise on feminist theory or the ever increasing and often torturous prose of anthropological gender studies and interpretive archaeology to get the message. Especially if we draw from ethnography, ethnohistory, other substantive areas within our own and related disciplines, there should be many avenues of investigation deserving more attention. In the basic context of exploring a single site, a gendered reconstruction can be accomplished (a now classic example is Spector 1993). Nor do we have to be "goddess groupies," doing poor science and misusing archaeological data for present-day empowerment (Gimbutas 1989; Conkey and Tringham 1995), to do feminist archaeology or even just to look for women in the archaeological record.

Engendering Hunters and Gatherers

Many excellent efforts have gone toward hunter-gatherers. For just a few examples, that old stereotype "man the hunter" model hangs on tenaciously, but the evidence is becoming overwhelming that it is as unsupportable as "woman the typist," for so many reasons. "Differential decay of materials over time leads to overrepresentation of large animal bones in the archaeological record and loss of organic material" (Zihlman 1997:99), and most hunter-gatherers have diets dominated by plant foods (which we've known since *Man the Hunter* [Lee and DeVore 1968:4–7]). So let's call them gatherer-hunters and realize that they have enormous flexibility in sociopolitical organization and division of labor by gender, have women who do a tremendous amount of physical labor and long-distance travel away from base camp (often *with* the kids and pregnant with the next one; Zihlman 1981:92), have men who obtain plants and women who get meat (Martin and Voorhies 1975; Goodale 1971; Halperin 1980; Dahlberg 1981; Conkey and Williams 1991; Hager 1997; Wadley 1998), and even may have women who regularly grab large weapons and hunt—even mothers, after coming up with the revolutionary concept known as the babysitter! (Estioko-Griffin and Griffin 1981; Estioko-Griffin 1986; Brumbach and Jarvenpa 1997; Stange 1998; Pringle 1998). Regarding the stereotypes of divisions of labor based on sex or gender, what we really need to ask about is the justification for any division of labor at all other than by age. Bruhns (1991:427–28) reminds us that the only activities universally restricted to a specific sex are insemination and conception.

So it is time to examine anew our assumptions about early American foraging populations, though many old views and usages may die hard. We still must chide colleagues for their continuing reference to male hunters and flintknappers and especially "Early Man." I now believe the only legitimate use of this term is that by Gary Larson; his cartoon captioned "Early Man" shows his typical cave guy in leopard-skin tunic ringing a modern doorbell and a (taller) woman opening the door, her hair still in curlers and the table behind her not totally set for dinner! Assumptions behind common terms can easily be challenged with much of the newest research. For example, Gorman's 1995 study of Andaman Islanders found that all stone tools were made and used by women, and not for hunting. Terminology can change if we heighten awareness of the implications of a single word or phrase. Even Latin American archaeology is lately finding less use of the androcentric term "patrimonio" (patrimony; think of the meaning if we substituted "matrimony"!) and more of "herencia cultural" (cultural heritage).

We now realize that ethnographies of hunter-gatherers or any kind of society are much colored by changes wrought from contact with other cultures by the time they are studied and enormously skewed by the biases of the ethnographers. Leacock (1981) noted that most societies studied by anthropologists "have been influenced by colonization in ways that have destroyed the egalitarian relations between the sexes" (Sanday 1982). Kent (1998:14) lamented perpetuation of Western biases that require rigid divisions of labor cross-culturally. Other Western ethnographic biases are less subtle. Feminist anthropologists (Michard-Marchal and Ribery 1982; Eichler and Lapointe 1985; Wylie 1991:38; Russell 1996:11) love citing the lines from Lévi-Strauss's (1936:283) account of ethnography in the Amazon about how "the entire village" of Indians departed in their thirty canoes, "leaving us alone with the women and children in the abandoned houses." And these were the matrilocal Bororo Indians! (ibid.:272).

Rethinking Assumptions

It is becoming easier to visualize individuals in prehistory as our evidence and attitudes improve. We can see women in the picture with everyone else: they have sex (for example, Taylor 1996), control reproduction (for example, Bentley 1996), make war (for example, Davis-Kimball 1997), and do many other things besides domestic duties. They may have their own physical space in the household, even a matrilocal one (Spain 1992:57–64). They are not always represented by the domestic artifacts we think they used, such as manos and metates, because men used these too (Bruhns 1991). Even domestic situations, food procurement, cooking technologies, birth spacing, menstrual taboos, and other aspects can be examined to see change through time that is then reflected in the social and ceremonial systems (for example, Crown 1997, Claassen 1991).

History from an archaeological perspective can bring fresh insights into categories of work and knowledge of women in the past. My favorite recent examination from the viewpoint of the artifact itself is the case of the failure of the early electric car as a gender issue (Schiffer 1995; women preferred efficient, quiet, clean vehicles for domestic errands while men, economically dominant, wanted speed, power, and distance provided by the gasoline-powered automobile). What other cases, from artifact to system, could be illuminated in the Southeast with an awareness of gender considerations? We must remember to look outside traditional perspectives. For example, the only area of reconstructing past life where women are usually mentioned is reproduction. A view such as Muller's (1997:12), that in Mississippian tribal society, the entire community and older children could help ease women's burden of child care, is therefore not surprising. But Kent (1998:19) reminds us that raising children is not necessarily considered a burden outside Western culture. We use the very Western dichotomy between domestic and public (or extra-domestic) spheres, and forget that, instead of women's work being structured around and accommodated to reproduction, it is the other way around: childbearing and raising are fit in around the rest of women's work (Friedl 1975). Beyond simple reproduction, the "grandmother" hypothesis for understanding forager adaptations is lately gaining ground. This is the idea that natural selection favored the development of menopause so older women could provision grandchildren and daughters with newborns (Gibbons 1997; Hawkes, O'Connell, and Blurton Jones 1997). We must discard the Western notion that a woman's importance declines with age and look for the increase in power and value that is older women's advantage in so many cultures. The data are there to begin remodeling southeastern U.S. prehistory and early history, and the finer details keep coming (Claassen 1997; Galloway 1997). Model construction can be done without postprocessual posturing or great leaps of faith beyond the evidence. And the contributions of women are making a difference.

We have seen how Martha Rolingson studied big (and small) projectile points, so associated with a macho weaponry image recently (for example, Gero 1994). But she noted that the old collections she worked with contained no broken distal points or flakes because they were not saved. This was apparently common archaeological practice in the Southeast, and one wonders when revisiting sites how many artifacts were counted and discarded by earlier workers for later ones to find. Might women be socialized to worry more about such important detail? Would drawers full of chert flakes provide a fuller or different picture of the past? Did men throw the piles of flakes or other tedious stuff away because it was too tiny to worry about or because they wanted to concentrate on the big picture? Would women be more aware of the possibilities for both piecemeal and systematic error in male science that come from misapplied confidence in the objectivity of male science (Wylie 1997:49)?

Walter Taylor's (1948) call for the "conjunctive approach" and Binford's (1962, 1964) pleas for more scientific archaeology, stricter methods, and integration of diverse kinds of information into the big picture have probably been more developed by women since the 1960s. National recognition for scholars in many areas of archaeological research depends on picky detail that may have been more often provided by women than men. The major names are frequently synthesizers who have often, however, not produced their own original data but use new information from the many ethnobotanists, zooarchaeologists, and other specialists, not to mention the lowly lab technicians who have painstakingly sorted, classified, weighed, measured, tabulated, and typed up the list of all the tiny specimens, be they chert flakes, fern spores, mollusk shells, pollen grains, map elevations, or soil samples.

More interesting, in the context of this volume, one wonders whether the early absence of the segregation of women in jobs tediously processing tiny bits of materials was due to the failure to collect such materials until much later in the history of the profession. Once there were enough workers to "ghettoize" into previously unknown specialties such as analysis of lithic debitage or botanical remains, women were not only fully accepted into the lab but also expected to be better at such organization and routinely channeled into such areas since they were so important to the picture. Nonetheless, they were often more like ladies' auxiliaries to the real work going on, being done by men. Many such specialized studies are still confined to appendices, whether zooarchaeology or paleoethnobotany, by men or women, instead of being integral parts such as ceramic analyses.

Pottery and stone tools, the most common artifacts, have been the foundations of southeastern U.S. archaeology. In the earliest work, and up to the present in many sectors, ceramic description and analysis remains paramount. If we do accept the stereotypic division of labor that has women making all the pottery, that leaves us with the amusing picture of many grown men sitting around arguing in mind-numbing detail the specifics of what was everyday women's work, as a presentation by Madeline Kneberg at the 1959 SEAC meeting demonstrated (Williams 1962; see Sullivan 1994:118, Figure 3). However, it is not necessary or even good science to assume that women were the potters throughout prehistory. If that is what the ethnographic record shows, we may be safer in projecting this labor specialty back into late prehistory, but on far shakier ground projecting it back thousands of years to the Late Archaic (Sassaman 1992). There are plenty of ethnographic examples of men as potters, even possibly in the Southeast (noted by Galloway 1995:267). Women could have settled into the specialty much later (as they did with typing). Stone tools are also a complex issue, and it is similarly foolish to assume that women seldom made any. Even if we accept the stereotype that women do most of the domestic drudgery (again, not necessarily a supportable assumption), they certainly would be doing lots of it with sharp edges. Martha Rolingson says "Why are lithics thought of as a male thing when women use stone tools in food processing activities? I'll bet [prehistoric woman] didn't say 'Honey, sharpen my knife' every time a flake knife needed retouching."

Skeletons are a good place to look for women and everyone else (for example, Wilson 1997). Human bone morphology and pathology has traditionally been used to indicate all kinds of activities, conditions, and culture change (Cohen and Bennett 1993; studies noted in Smith 1993:74–75; Borgognini Tarli and Repetto 1997). In the Southeast we can now suggest, for example, shifts in gender divisions of labor moving into the Archaic (Claassen 1991, 1996), or moving from Archaic foragers to Mississippian farmers (Bridges 1989), and even possibly more violence against women and more men in risky behaviors in the shell mound Archaic (Belovich 1994). At the 1996 SEAC symposium on gender organized by J. M. Eastman and C. B. Rodning, discussant Janet Levy pointed out how an engendered archaeology is now well conceptualized as the archaeology of work, though we must be cautious on two methodological fronts, that is, faulty identifications of the sex of skeletons and unreliable ethnohistory written by men observing men. Discussant Pat Watson noted that other human biological data, hormonal evidence in coprolites, so far point to more association of men with caves during prehistory.

Later Prehistory Revisualized

There is a growing literature on the shifts in women's roles with the evolution of greater cultural complexity, especially with the emergence of the state (Moore 1988; Silverblatt 1988, 1991; Brumfiel 1991; Costin 1996; Nelson 1997). Historic archaeology and ethnography can enhance such work. For instance, Kent (1998:17) found that shifting to sedentism by itself does not lead to gender inequality among South African hunter-gatherers, but aggregation, particularly when combined with sedentism, is more significant.

Especially in later prehistory and ethnohistory in the eastern United

States, there is a wealth of iconographic material and symbol systems in which to seek women and female meaning (Koehler 1997). A perusal of the literature shows Mississippian Southeastern Ceremonial Complex paraphernalia with both male and female elite burials (for example, Galloway 1989), and plenty of ethnography that includes women's religious, ceremonial, artistic, elite, and supernatural activities. Why are bird-people (birdmen, eagle or falcon warriors, winged beings, bird dancers) depictions, especially the ones with protruding chests, automatically considered men (Brown 1982; Strong 1989)? Rolingson recounts that she remembers the meeting at which Brown's presentation suggested that some of these personages looked female; men in the audience snickered and shook their heads, saying the figures were not out of line with male anatomy. But Thomas (1995:1) noted the stretches of imagination needed to see some of these figures as male, opining that the two Spiro images described as beer-bellied, slightly grotesque individuals looked to her like pregnant dancers. Why consider male to be the default character?

Figure 15.2 might be a realistic contribution to this argument (and compare with fig. 11.9), suggesting a shaman dancing with a trophy head (our reluctance to deal with anything unacceptable in modern Western culture eliminates not only women but also other prehistoric realities; the severed head is often squeamishly portrayed as a wooden artifact or other symbolic item, though there are plenty of real trophy skulls). Once we get into the symbolic realm, lack of direct or overwhelming evidence should not tether the imagination. Are women really so absent from both southeastern native art and ethnohistory (Emerson 1989:61–62)? Would women archaeologists be less unwilling to see the obvious character of a symbol consisting of a long thin rod flanked by two circular or semicircular forms at its base? To their credit, some have seen the Southeastern Ceremonial Complex bi-lobed arrow motif as a male symbol (Waring 1968), intertwined with general virility and shooting or projecting. Is this more believable to our American imaginations than considering it a symbol of trachea and lungs, or an atlatl and dart? Hall (1989) suggests the bi-lobed arrow and the long-nosed god could be related motifs, possibly symbolizing male generative power; this would not be the first time these two projecting male body parts were considered important and analogous. In a matrilineal society, why would there not be images signifying female power as well? Whether the power of reproduction, blood, fertility/renewal and harvest, political control over the family, or any other kind, we should start thinking (and reading ethnographic accounts) of what sorts of symbols to look for.

Fig. 15.2. Reinterpretation of the Southeastern Ceremonial Complex bird dancer motif. (Drawing by Scott Mitchell.) Cf. fig. 11.9, p. 252.

Beyond all this, it is time to start dealing with issues of inequality (or equality and complementarity) and control that hinge on gender in the Southeast, as is being done elsewhere so well (for example, many papers in Walde and Willows 1991; in Gero and Conkey 1991; in Claassen 1992; in Claassen and Joyce 1997; Robb 1994). We must compare culture processes, such as gender transformations that may come with horticulture and agriculture, especially if the Southeast is an exception to the pattern of agricultural intensification leading to male dominance (Boserup 1970; Martin and Voorhies 1975; Ember 1983). The anthropological debate has now shifted from explaining why men rule in all human cultures to exploring what is meant by dominance and a demonstrating that male dominance is not universal (Higgins 1989; Mukhopadhyay and Higgins 1988; Leacock 1981). We have ethnographies of horticultural societies that are matrilineal and egalitarian (for example, Lepowsky 1993).

Southeastern archaeology must contribute to this anthropological inquiry and document different kinds of power and prestige systems interacting with gender. Southeastern native women were not oppressed or relegated to low status. They were heads of families, controllers of production and reproduction; many may have been chiefs (Troccoli 1993). Though the idea of female leadership is becoming acknowledged, its implications remain largely unexplored. What, for example, is the revision in inference about a Middle Woodland society where the mound's "Big Man" burial is later found to be a woman (Milanich et al. 1997:xvi)? Why are many radical feminists trying to find women in prehistory by looking for the traditional domestic, plant- and pot-related things of the stereotyped role? Even if that division of labor is supported ethnographically, which is debatable, can we push it back many millennia, before agriculture and chiefdoms? Even before we get to heavy theorizing, we must keep in mind the real human beings of the past that we study. A good method of putting women specifically into the past is to rethink our value-laden museum displays, artists' reconstructions (Gifford-Gonzales 1995; Conkey 1997; Wiber 1997), and images of daily life at our sites. We might look, to paraphrase Mae West, not for the women in prehistoric life but for the life in our prehistoric women (and men)!

What would look different in our pictures of the past if women, or anyone with women more in mind, envisioned the Southeast? There might be many subtle differences, swirls of color in unexpected places, or graceful shading and imperceptible shifts where things used to be clearly black and white, but some sharp angles where things were assumed to be smooth and colorless or not even thought about. There would be menstrual huts in the artist's reconstructions of villages, with women sitting around them taking a break, not working but maybe sleeping or stretching or painting or playing. There would be women chiefs wearing stunning outfits or at least tattoos and accessories, berdaches (wearing more utilitarian or more outrageous outfits?), people dancing, lots more children, perhaps working hard, playing, or even fighting. Clan mothers might be pictured running the show, or perhaps a young girl at her menarche ceremony. Men might be bending over doing tedious work or holding babies, as well as bringing home the deer or the trophy head. There might be women dirty and covered with blood from one thing or another; insects and things that would have smelled bad lying around; women catching netloads of fish and traveling by canoe; women and men playing games, people gambling, even people hugging or showing some affection; old, injured, or sick folks being cared for by the rest but able to tell good stories as they hunch closer to the fire. There might be lovers' glances among the facial expressions, or how about two women holding hands, mouths open, singing, as they return home with a passel of fish? Or even a lustful look from the adorned chief sitting on her litter gazing at the muscular young men carrying it around? It wouldn't be hard to come up with real human life, and the evidence will not only continue to improve but inspire alternative views perhaps shut out or overlooked in the past.

Many have suggested (for example, Wylie 1997:50–51) that in a field such as archaeology, where interpretation is so desperately important to both science and public education, a greater diversity of voices can only result in better thinking, improved research, more creativity, more possibility. It is also important that the romanticism that drew us all into this profession should not be denied: the lure of the past, the excitement of the outdoors, the thrill of the find, the ancient objects, the reflection on what it all means for humanity. Then and now, when we step onto an archaeological site or lay out its materials in the lab, we should recognize also the seductive voices we hear from the past, a dozen, a thousand voices, half of them female.

REFERENCES CITED

Allen, Glover M.
1920   Dogs of the American Aborigines. *Bulletin of the Museum of Comparative Zoology* 63(9):431–517.

Allsebrook, Mary
1992   *Born to Rebel: The Life of Harriet Boyd Hawes.* Oxbow Books, David Brown Book Company, Bloomington, Indiana.

Anonymous
1969   *Harvard Class of 1919: Fiftieth Anniversary Report.* Harvard University, Cambridge.

Aptheker, Bettina
1982   *Woman's Legacy: Essays on Race, Sex, and Class in American History.* University of Massachusetts Press, Amherst.

Armelagos, George J., David S. Carlson, and Dennis P. Van Gerven
1982   The Theoretical Foundations and Development of Skeletal Biology. In *A History of American Physical Anthropology, 1930–1980,* edited by Frank Spencer, pp. 305–28. Academic Press, New York.

Armelagos, George J., and M. Cassandra Hill
1990   An Evaluation of the Biocultural Consequences of the Mississippian Transformation. In *Towns and Temples along the Mississippi,* edited by D. Dye and C. Cox, pp. 16–37. University of Alabama Press, Tuscaloosa.

Ashley, Margaret E. *See bibliography at end of chapter 2.*

Auel, Jean
1980   *Clan of the Cave Bear.* Crown Publishers, New York.
1982   *The Valley of Horses.* Crown Publishers, New York.
1985   *The Mammoth Hunters.* Crown Publishers, New York.

Axtell, James, editor
1981   *The Indian Peoples of Eastern America: A Documentary History of the Sexes.* Oxford University Press, New York.

Babcock, Barbara A., and Nancy J. Parezo
1988   *Daughters of the Desert: Women Anthropologists and the Native American Southwest, 1880–1980, an Illustrated Catalog.* University of New Mexico Press, Albuquerque.

Bachofen, Johann
1861   *Das Mutterrecht* [The Mother-Right]. Benno Schwabe, Basel, Switzerland.

Bacus, Elisabeth A., Alex W. Barker, Jeffrey D. Bonevich, Sandra L. Dunavan, J. Benjamin Fitzhugh, Debra L. Gold, Nurit S. Goldman-Finn, William Griffin, and Karen Mudar, editors
1993   *A Gendered Past: A Critical Bibliography of Gender in Archaeology.* University of Michigan Museum of Anthropology Technical Report 25. Ann Arbor.

Balme, Jane, and Wendy Beck, editors
1995   *Gendered Archaeology: The Second Australian Women in Archaeology Conference*. ANH Publications, RSPAS, Australian National University, Canberra.

Barber, Elizabeth Wayland
1994   *Women's Work, the First 20,000 Years: Women, Cloth, and Society in Early Times*. W. W. Norton, New York.

Barker, Alex W., and Timothy R. Pauketat, editors
1992   *Lords of the Southeast: Social Inequality and the Native Elites of Southeastern North America*. Archaeological Papers of the American Anthropological Association No. 3.

Belovich, Stephanie J.
1994   Fractures in the Carlston Annis Shell Mound (Bt-5) Late Archaic Skeletal Population. Paper presented at the annual (joint) meeting of the Southeastern Archaeological Conference and Midwest Archaeological Conference, Lexington, Kentucky.

Bender, Susan J.
1994   Marian E. White: Pioneer in New York. Archaeology. In *Women in Archaeology*, edited by Cheryl Claassen, pp. 84–95. University of Pennsylvania Press, Philadelphia.

Bender, Susan J., and Nancy J. Parezo
1994   On the Periphery: Women and the Pursuit of Archaeological Science in the Americas, 1914–1960. Manuscript on file, Department of Sociology, Anthropology, and Social Work, Skidmore College, Saratoga Springs, New York.

Bender, Susan J., and George S. Smith
1998   SAA's Workshop on Teaching Archaeology in the 21st Century. *Society for American Archaeology Bulletin* 16(5):11–13.

Bentley, Gillian R.
1996   How Did Prehistoric Women Bear "Man the Hunter"? Reconstructing Fertility from the Archaeological Record. In *Gender and Archaeology*, edited by R. Wright, pp. 23–51. University of Pennsylvania Press, Philadelphia.

Berenbaum, Max
1995   Review of *Brethren of the Net: American Entomology, 1840–1880* by W. C. Sorensen. *Science* 270:2035–36.

Binford, Louis R.
1962   Archaeology as Anthropology. *American Antiquity* 28:217–25.
1964   A Consideration of Archaeological Research Design. *American Antiquity* 29:425–41.
1981   *Bones: Ancient Men and Modern Myths*. Academic Press, New York.

Blakely, Robert L., editor
1988   *The King Site: Continuity and Contact in Sixteenth-Century Georgia*. University of Georgia Press, Athens.

Bleier, Ruth
1984   *Science and Gender: A Critique of Biology and Its Theories*. Pergamon Press, New York.

Boaz, Noel T.
1995   Somatotyping, the W. H. Sheldon Collection, and the "Ivy League Posture Photo Scandal." *Physical Anthropology News* 14(1):1–3.

Bonta, Marcia Myers
1991 *Women in the Field: America's Pioneering Women Naturalists.* Texas A&M University Press, College Station.

Borgognini Tarli, Silvana M., and Elena Repetto
1997 Sex Differences in Human Populations: Change through Time. In *The Evolving Female: A Life History Perspective,* edited by M. Morbeck, A. Galloway, and A. Zihlman, pp. 198–219. Princeton University Press, Princeton, New Jersey.

Boserup, Esther
1970 *Women's Role in Economic Development.* St. Martin's Press, New York.

Braidwood, Linda
1959 *Digging beyond the Tigris: A Woman Archaeologist's Story of Life on a Dig in the Kurdish Hills of Iraq.* Abelard-Schuman, London.

Braley, Chad O., and W. Dean Wood
1982 *Cultural Resources Survey of the IFV Ranges, Fort Benning, Georgia.* Southeastern Wildlife Services, Athens.

Brannon, Peter A.
1909 Aboriginal Remains in the Middle Chattahoochee Valley of Alabama and Georgia. *American Anthropologist* 9:186–98.

Bridges, Patricia S.
1989 Changes in Activities with the Shift to Agriculture in the Southeastern United States. *Current Anthropology* 30(3):385–94.

Briuer, Frederick L., Janet E. Simms, and Lawson M. Smith
1997 Site Mapping, Geophysical Investigation, and Geomorphic Reconnaissance at Site 9 ME 395: Upatoi Town, Fort Benning, Georgia. *Miscellaneous Paper EL–97–3.* June. CD-ROM. U.S. Army Corps of Engineers Waterways Experiment Station.

Browman, David L., and Douglas R. Givens
1996 Stratigraphic Excavation: The First "New Archaeology." *American Anthropologist* 98:80–95.

Brown, Catherine
1982 On the Gender of the Winged Being on Mississippian Period Copper Plates. *Tennessee Anthropologist* 7(1):1–8.

Broyles, Bettye J. *See bibliography at end of chapter 6.*

Brucker, Roger W., and Richard A. Watson
1976 *The Longest Cave.* Knopf, New York.

Bruhns, Karen O.
1991 Sexual Activities: Some Thoughts on the Sexual Division of Labor and Archaeological Interpretation. In *The Archaeology of Gender,* edited by D. Walde and N. Willows, pp. 420–29. Chacmool 1991, Archaeological Association of the University of Calgary.

Brumbach, Hetty Jo, and Robert Jarvenpa
1997 Woman the Hunter: Ethnoarchaeological Lessons from Chipewayan Life-Cycle Dynamics. In *Women in Prehistory: North America and Mesoamerica,* edited by C. Claassen and R. Joyce, pp. 17–32. University of Pennsylvania Press, Philadelphia.

Brumfiel, Elizabeth
1991   Weaving and Cooking: Women's Production in Aztec Mexico. In *Engendering Archaeology: Women and Prehistory,* edited by J. Gero and M. Conkey, pp. 224–54. Basil Blackwell, Cambridge, Massachusetts.
1992   Distinguished Lecture in Archaeology: Breaking and Entering the Ecosystem—Gender, Class and Faction Steal the Show. *American Anthropologist* 94:551–67.
Brush, Stephen G.
1991   Women in Science and Engineering. *American Scientist* 79:404–19.
Buckley, Thomas
1988   Menstruation and the Power of Yurok Women. In *Blood Magic: The Anthropology of Menstruation,* edited by T. Buckley and A. Gottlieb, pp. 188–209. University of California Press, Berkeley.
Buckley, Thomas, and Alma Gottlieb, editors
1988   *Blood Magic: The Anthropology of Menstruation.* University of California Press, Berkeley.
Bullen, Adelaide K. *See bibliography at end of chapter 7.*
Bullen, Ripley P.
1975   *A Guide to the Identification of Florida Projectile Points.* Kendall Books, Gainesville.
Bullen, Ripley P., and Adelaide K. Bullen. *See bibliography at end of chapter 7.*
Bunzel, Ruth L.
1929   The Pueblo Potter: A Study of Creative Imagination in Primitive Art. AMS Press, New York.
1960   Introduction to Part 6, New Horizons. In *The Golden Age of American Anthropology,* selected and edited with an introduction and notes by Margaret Mead and Ruth L. Bunzel, pp. 574–76. G. Braziller, New York.
Caldwell, Joseph R.
1958   *Trend and Tradition in the Prehistory of Eastern United States.* Illinois State Museum Scientific Papers, vol. 10, and the American Anthropological Association, Memoir Number 88. Springfield and Menasha.
Caldwell, Joseph R., and Catherine McCann
1941   *Irene Mound Site, Chatham County, Georgia.* University of Georgia Press, Athens.
Callender, Charles, and Lee M. Kochems
1983   The Native American Berdache. *Current Anthropology* 24:443–70.
Ceram, C. W.
1951   *Gods, Graves and Scholars: The Story of Archaeology.* Knopf, New York.
Chapman, Jefferson
1977   *Archaic Period Research in the Lower Little Tennessee River Valley—1975: Icehouse Bottom, Harrison Branch, Thirty Acre Island, Calloway Island.* Report of Investigations No. 18. Department of Anthropology, University of Tennessee, Knoxville. Publications in Anthropology No. 13, Tennessee Valley Authority.
1978   *The Bacon Farm Site and a Buried Site Reconnaissance.* Report of Investigations No. 23, Department of Anthropology, University of Tennessee, Knoxville. Publications in Anthropology No. 23, Tennessee Valley Authority.

1984   *A Buried Site Reconnaissance in the Tellico Reservoir, Eastern Tennessee.* National Geographic Society Research Reports 17:273–80.

1988   The Federal Archaeological Program in Tennessee, 1966–1986: An Archeological Second Coming. In *Advances in Southeastern Archeology 1966–1986: Contributions of the Federal Archaeological Program,* edited by B. C. Keel, pp. 46–49. Southeastern Archeological Conference Special Publication No. 6.

Christenson, Andrew L., editor

1989   *Tracing Archaeology's Past: The Historiography of Archaeology.* Southern Illinois University Press, Carbondale.

Claassen, Cheryl P.

1991   Gender, Shellfishing, and the Shell Mound Archaic. In *Engendering Archaeology: Women and Prehistory,* edited by J. Gero and M. Conkey, pp. 276–300. Basil Blackwell, Oxford.

1996   A Consideration of the Social Organization of the Shell Mound Archaic. In *Archaeology of the Mid-Holocene Southeast,* edited by K. Sassaman and D. Anderson, pp. 336–60. University Press of Florida, Gainesville.

1997   Changing Venue: Women's Lives in Prehistoric North America. In *Women in Prehistory: North America and Mesoamerica,* edited by C. Claassen and R. Joyce, pp. 65–87. University of Pennsylvania Press, Philadelphia.

Claassen, Cheryl P., editor

1992   *Exploring Gender through Archaeology.* Selected papers from the 1991 Boone Conference. Monographs in World Archaeology 11. Prehistory Press, Madison, Wisconsin.

1994   *Women in Archaeology.* University of Pennsylvania Press, Philadelphia.

Claassen, Cheryl, and Rosemary A. Joyce, editors

1997   *Women in Prehistory: North America and Mesoamerica.* University of Pennsylvania Press, Philadelphia.

Clayton, Lawrence A., Vernon James Knight, Jr., and Edward C. Moore, editors

1993   *The DeSoto Chronicles: The Expedition of Hernando de Soto to North America in 1539–1543.* 2 vols. University of Alabama Press, Tuscaloosa.

Cleere, Henry F., editor

1984   *Approaches to the Archaeological Heritage.* Cambridge University Press, Cambridge, England.

1989   *Archaeological Heritage Management in the Modern World.* Unwin Hyman, London.

Coe, Joffre L.

1964   *The Formative Cultures of the Carolina Piedmont.* Transactions, American Philosophical Society, vol. 54, pt. 5. Philadelphia.

1995   *Town Creek Indian Mound.* University of North Carolina Press, Chapel Hill.

Cohen, Mark Nathan, and Sharon Bennett

1993   Skeletal Evidence for Sex Roles and Gender Hierarchies in Prehistory. *Sex and Gender Hierarchies,* edited by M. di Leonardo, pp. 102–39. University of California Press, Berkeley. Reprinted in *Reader in Gender Archaeology,* edited by K. Harp-Gilpin and D. S. Whitley, pp. 297–317. Routledge, New York, 1998.

Cole, Fay-Cooper, and Thorne Deuel

1937   *Rediscovering Illinois: Archaeological Explorations in and around Fulton County.* University of Chicago Press, Chicago.

Cole, Jonathan R., and Burton Singer
1991   A Theory of Limited Differences: Explaining the Productivity Puzzle in Science. In *The Outer Circle*, edited by H. Zuckerman, J. Cole, and J. Bruer, pp. 277–310. W. W. Norton, New York.

Cole, Stephan, and Robert Fiorentine
1991   Discrimination against Women in Science: The Confusion of Outcome with Process. In *The Outer Circle*, edited by H. Zuckerman, J. Cole, and J. Bruer, pp. 205–26. W. W. Norton, New York.

Collins, Patricia Hill
1990   *Black Feminist Thought: Knowledge, Consciousness, and the Politics of Empowerment*. Routledge, New York.

Columbus (Georgia) Enquirer
1987   Obituary of H. Wayne Patterson. April 2, p. B-2.

Columbus (Georgia) Ledger
1940   DeSoto Trail Marked. Mrs. Patterson to Present Work to National Group. May 1.
1955   Obituary of Mrs. H. W. Patterson. Jan. 7, p. 1.

Conkey, Margaret W.
1997   Mobilizing Ideologies: Paleolithic "Art," Gender Trouble, and Thinking about Alternatives. In *Women in Human Evolution*, edited by L. Hager. Routledge, New York.

Conkey, Margaret W., and Joan M. Gero
1997   Programme to Practice: Gender and Feminism in Archaeology. *Annual Review of Anthropology* 26:411–37.

Conkey, Margaret W., and Janet Spector
1984   Archaeology and the Study of Gender. In *Advances in Archaeological Method and Theory*, vol. 7, edited by M. Schiffer, pp. 1–38. Academic Press, New York. Reprinted in *Reader in Gender Archaeology*, edited by K. Hays-Gilpin and D. S. Whitley, pp. 11–45. Routledge, New York, 1998.

Conkey, Margaret W., and Ruth E. Tringham
1995   Archaeology and the Goddess: Exploring the Contours of Feminist Archaeology. In *Feminisms in the Academy*, edited by D. C. Stanton and A. J. Stewart, pp. 199–247. University of Michigan Press, Ann Arbor.

Conkey, Margaret W., with Sarah H. Williams
1991   Original Narratives: The Political Economy of Gender in Archaeology. In *Gender at the Crossroads of Knowledge: Feminist Anthropology in the Postmodern Era*, edited by M. di Leonardo, pp. 102–39. University of California Press, Berkeley.

Cope, Oliver
1977   *The Breast: Its Problems, Benign and Malignant, and How to Deal with Them*. Houghton Mifflin, Boston.

Cordell, Linda S.
1993   Women Archaeologists in the Southwest. In *Hidden Scholars: Women Anthropologists and the Native American Southwest*, edited by N. Parezo, pp. 202–20. University of New Mexico Press, Albuquerque.

Costin, Cathy Lynne
1996   Exploring the Relationship between Gender and Craft in Complex Societies: Methodological and Theoretical Issues of Gender Attribution. In *Gender and*

Archaeology, edited by R. P. Wright, pp. 79–110. University of Pennsylvania Press, Philadelphia.

Cotter, John L.
1993   Kentucky Memoir: Digging in the Depression. *Archaeology* 46(1):30–35.

Cox, P. E.
1926   Pre-Historic Man in Tennessee. *Journal of the Tennessee Academy of Science* 1(3):22–30.

Crown, Patricia L.
1997   Prehistoric Food Processing, Preparation and Gender in the Greater American Southwest. Paper presented at the symposium "Sex Roles and Gender Hierarchies in Southwestern Prehistory," annual meeting of the Society for American Archaeology, Nashville.

Crown, Patricia L., and Suzanne K. Fish
1996   Gender and Status in the Hohokam Pre-Classic to Classic Transition. *American Anthropologist* 98:803–17.

Cutler, Hugh
1962   Review of *The Ethnobotany of Pre-Columbian Peru. American Antiquity* 28:256–57.

Dahlberg, Frances, editor
1981   *Woman the Gatherer.* Yale University Press, New Haven.

Davis, Angela
1971   Reflections on the Black Woman's Role in the Community of Slaves. *The Black Scholar* 3(4):2–15.

Davis, Cinda-Sue, et al.
1996   *The Equity Equation: Fostering the Advancement of Women in the Sciences, Mathematics, and Engineering.* Jossey-Bass, San Francisco.

Davis, E. Mott
1996   Excavations in 1940 at the Palmer-Taylor Mound, Seminole County, Florida. *Florida Anthropologist* 49(2):95–99.

Davis, Hester A. *See bibliography at end of chapter 10.*

Davis-Kimball, Jeannine
1997   Warrior Women of the Eurasian Steppes. *Archaeology* 50(1):44–48.

Deetz, James
1965   *The Dynamics of Stylistic Change in Arikara Ceramics.* University of Illinois Press, Urbana.

Diaz-Andreu, Margarita, and Marie Louise Stig Sorens
1998   *Excavating Women: A History of Women in European Archaeology.* Routledge, New York.

di Leonardo, Micaela, editor
1991   *Gender at the Crossroads of Knowledge: Feminist Anthropology in the Postmodern Era.* University of California Press, Berkeley.

Dick, Herbert W.
1965   *Bat Cave.* School of American Research Monograph No. 27. Santa Fe.

Dickens, Roy S., Jr.
1982   *Of Sky and Earth: Art of the Early Southeastern Indians.* High Museum of Art, Atlanta, and Georgia Department of Archives and History, Office of the Secretary of State, Atlanta.

Dincauze, Dena
1992 Exploring Career Styles in Archaeology. In *Rediscovering Our Past: Essays on the History of American Archaeology,* edited by J. Reyman, pp. 131–36. Avebury/Ashgate Publishing Co., Brookfield, Vermont.

Drooker, Penelope Ballard
1992 *Mississippian Village Textiles at Wickliffe.* University of Alabama Press, Tuscaloosa.

duCros, Hilary, and Laurajane Smith, editors
1993 *Women in Archaeology: A Feminist Critique.* Australian National University Occasional Papers in Prehistory No. 23. Canberra.

Dunkerley, Jean
1992 Harriet Minola Smith: In Memoriam. *Illinois Antiquity* 27(3):5.

Dunnell, Robert C.
1990 The Role of the Southeast in American Archaeology. *Southeastern Archaeology* 9:11–22.

Dusheck, Jennie
1990 Female Primatologists Confer—Without Men. *Science* 249:1494–95.

Dye, David H., and Cheryl Anne Cox, editors
1990 *Towns and Temples along the Mississippi.* University of Alabama Press, Tuscaloosa.

Eichler, Margrit, and Jeanne Lapointe
1985 *On the Treatment of the Sexes in Research.* Social Sciences and Humanities Research Council of Canada, Ottawa.

Eisenhart, Margaret A., and Elizabeth Finkel
1998 *Women's Science: Learning and Succeeding from the Margins.* University of Chicago Press, Chicago.

Elliott, Daniel T., Karen G. Wood, Rita Folse Elliott, and W. Dean Wood
1996 Up on the Upatoi: Cultural Resources Survey and Testing of Compartments K-6 and K-7, Fort Benning Military Reservation, Georgia. Southern Research, Ellerslie, Georgia.

Ember, Carol R.
1983 The Relative Decline in Women's Contribution to Agriculture with Intensification. *American Anthropologist* 85:285–304.

Emerson, Thomas E.
1989 Water, Serpents and the Underworld: An Exploration into Cahokian Symbolism. In *The Southeastern Ceremonial Complex: Artifacts and Analysis,* edited by P. Galloway, pp. 45–92. University of Nebraska Press, Lincoln.

Engelstad, Ericka
1991 Images of Power and Contradiction: Feminist Theory and Post-processual Archaeology. *Antiquity* 65:502–14.

Estioko-Griffin, Agnes
1986 Daughters of the Forest. *Natural History,* May.

Estioko-Griffin, Agnes, and P. Bion Griffin
1981 Woman the Hunter: The Agta. In *Woman the Gatherer,* edited by F. Dahlberg, pp. 121–52. Yale University Press, New Haven.

Ewen, Charles R., and John H. Hann
1988 *Hernando deSoto among the Apalachee: The Archaeology of the First Winter Encampment.* Univerity Press of Florida, Gainesville.

Fagan, Brian
1994   Perhaps We May Hear Voices. In *Save the Past for the Future II: Report of the Working Conference,* Breckenridge, Colorado, September 19–22, pp. 25–30. Society for American Archaeology, Washington, D.C.
1996   Archaeology's Dirty Secret. In *Archaeological Ethics,* edited by K. Vitelli, pp. 247–52. Alta Mira Press, Walnut Creek, California. Originally published in *Archaeology* 48:4, 14–17, July/August 1995.

Fagette, Paul
1996   *Digging for Dollars: American Archaeology and the New Deal.* University of New Mexico Press, Albuquerque.

Fairbanks, Charles H.
1965   Excavations at the Fort Walton Temple Mound, 1960. *Florida Anthropologist* 18(4).
1970   What Do We Know Now That We Did Not Know in 1938? *Southeastern Archaeological Conference Bulletin* 13:40–45.

Fausto-Sterling, Anne
1985   *Myths of Gender: Biological Theories about Women and Men.* Basic Books, New York.

Fedigan, Linda Marie
1986   The Changing Role of Women in Models of Human Evolution. *Annual Review of Anthropology* 15:25–66.

Finger, John R.
1991   *Cherokee Americans: The Eastern Band of Cherokees in the Twentieth Century.* University of Nebraska Press, Lincoln.

Fischman, Joshua
1992   Hard Evidence. *Discover* 13(2):44–51.

Fitz
1928   Woman Digging for Creeks and Their Relics. *Columbus Ledger Magazine* 4(27):1. Columbus, Georgia.

Flannery, Kent V., Joyce Marcus, and Robert G. Reynolds
1989   *The Flocks of the Wamani: A Study of Llama Herders on the Punas of Ayacucho, Peru.* Academic Press, San Diego.

Flannery, Regina
1943   Some Notes on a Few Sites in Beaufort County, South Carolina. Anthropological Papers No. 21, *Bureau of American Ethnology Bulletin* 133(1):143–53.

Floyd, Dolores B.
1936   *New Yamacraw and the Indian Mound Irene.* Published by the author, Savannah, Georgia.

Folmsbee, Stanley J., and Madeline Kneberg Lewis, editors
1965   *Journals of the Juan Pardo Expeditions, 1566–1567,* translated by Gerald W. Wade, pp. 106–21. East Tennessee Historical Society's Publications, No. 37.

Ford, James A.
1935a   *Ceramic Decoration Sequence at an Old Indian Village Site near Sicily Island, Louisiana.* Department of Conservation, Louisiana Geological Survey, Anthropological Study 1.
1935b   Outline of Louisiana and Mississippi Pottery Horizons. *Louisiana Conservation Review,* April, pp. 33–38.

1936a   Archaeological Methods Applicable to Louisiana. *Proceedings of the Louisiana Academy of Sciences* 3:102–5.

1936b   *An Analysis of Indian Village Site Collections from Louisiana and Mississippi.* Department of Conservation, Louisiana Geological Survey, Anthropological Study 2.

Ford, Janet L., and Martha A. Rolingson

1972   Investigation of Destruction to Prehistoric Sites Due to Agricultural Practices in Southeast Arkansas. In *Site Destruction Due to Agricultural Practices,* by J. L. Ford, M. A. Rolingson, and L. D. Medford. Arkansas Archeological Survey Research Series 3, Fayetteville.

Fowler, Melvin L.

1959   Modoc Rock Shelter Report: An Early Archaic Site in Southern Illinois. *American Antiquity* 24(3):257–70.

1985   A Brief History of Illinois Archaeology. *Illinois Archaeology, Bulletin* 1, revised, pp. 3–11. Illinois Archaeological Survey.

1997   *The Cahokia Atlas: A Historical Atlas of Cahokia Archaeology, Revised Edition.* University of Illinois, Illinois Transportation Archaeology Research Program, Studies in Archaeology Number 2, University of Illinois at Urbana-Champaign.

French, Laurence

1977   Tourism and Indian Exploitation: A Social Indictment. *Indian Historian,* vol. 10.

Friedl, Ernestine

1975   *Women and Men: An Anthropologist's View.* Holt Rinehart and Winston, New York.

1995   The Life of an Academic: A Personal Record of a Teacher, Administrator, and Anthropologist. *Annual Review of Anthropology* 24:1–19.

Frisbie, Theodore R.

1974   A Biography of Florence Hawley Ellis. In *Collected Papers in Honor of Florence Hawley Ellis,* edited by T. R. Frisbie, pp. 1–11. Papers of the Archaeological Society of New Mexico, 2.

Fritz, Gayle J.

1990   Multiple Pathways to Farming in Precontact Eastern North America. In *Journal of World Prehistory,* vol. 4, edited by F. Wendorf and A. Close, pp. 387–435. Plenum Publishing, New York.

Gacs, Ute, et al., editors

1989   *Women Anthropologists: Selected Biographies.* University of Illinois Press, Urbana.

Galloway, Patricia

1989a   "The Chief Who Is Your Father": Choctaw and French Views of the Diplomatic Relation. In *Powhatan's Mantle: Indians of the Colonial Southeast,* edited by P. H. Wood, G. A. Waselkov, and M. T. Hatley, pp. 254–78. University of Nebraska Press, Lincoln.

1995   *Choctaw Genesis 1500–1700.* University of Nebraska Press, Lincoln.

1997   Where Have All the Menstrual Huts Gone? The Invisibility of Menstrual Seclusion in the Late Prehistoric Southeast. In *Women in Prehistory: North America and Mesoamerica,* edited by C. Claassen and R. A. Joyce, pp. 47–64. University of Pennsylvania Press, Philadelphia. Reprinted in *Reader in Gender*

Archaeology, edited by K. Hays-Gilpin and D. S. Whitley, pp. 197–211. Routledge, New York, 1998.

Galloway, Patricia, editor
1989b   *The Southeastern Ceremonial Complex: Artifacts and Analysis.* University of Nebraska Press, Lincoln.

Garland, Elizabeth B.
1992   The Obion Site: An Early Mississippian Center in Western Tennessee. *Report of Investigations* 7. Cobb Institute of Archaeology, Mississippi State University.

Gear, Kathleen O'Neal, and W. Michael Gear
1995   *People of the Lightning.* Tom Doherty Associates, New York.

Gear, W. Michael, and Kathleen O'Neal Gear
1992   *People of the River.* Tom Doherty Associates, New York.

Gero, Joan M.
1985   Socio-politics of Archaeology and the Woman-at-Home Ideology. *American Antiquity* 50:342–50.
1991   Genderlithics: Women's Roles in Stone Tool Production. In *Engendering Archaeology: Women and Prehistory,* edited by J. M. Gero and M. Conkey, pp. 163–93. Basil Blackwell, Cambridge, Massachusetts.
1994   Gender Divisions of Labor in the Construction of Archaeological Knowledge in the United States. In *Social Construction of the Past,* edited by George Bond and Angela Gilliam, pp. 144–53. One World Archaeology Series, Routledge, London.

Gero, Joan M., and Margaret W. Conkey, editors
1991   *Engendering Archaeology: Women and Prehistory.* Basil Blackwell, Cambridge, Massachusetts.

Gibbons, Ann
1997   Why Life After Menopause? *Science* 276:536.

Gifford-Gonzalez, Diane
1995   The Real Flintstones? What Are Artists' Depictions of Human Ancestors Telling Us? *Anthro Notes: National Museum of Natural History Bulletin for Teachers* 17(3):1–6. Smithsonian Institution, Washington, D.C.

Gimbutas, Marija
1989   *The Language of the Goddess.* Harper and Row, San Francisco.

Givens, Douglas R.
1992   The Role of Biography in Writing the History of Archaeology. In *Rediscovering Our Past: Essays on the History of American Archaeology,* edited by J. Reyman, pp. 51–68. Avebury/Ashgate Publishing Co., Brookfield, Vermont.

Goodale, Jane
1971   *Tiwi Wives.* University of Washington Press, Seattle.

Gorman, Alice
1995   Gender, Labour and Resources: The Female Knappers of the Andaman Islands. In *Gendered Archaeology: The Second Australian Women in Archaeology Conference,* edited by J. Balme and W. Beck, pp. 87–91. ANH Publications, RSPAS, Australian National University, Canberra.

Gould, Stephen Jay
1993   The Invisible Woman. *Natural History* 102(6):14–23. Reprinted in *Natural Eloquence: Women Reinscribe Science,* edited by B. T. Gates and A. B. Shteir, pp. 27–39. University of Wisconsin Press, Madison, 1997.

Gradwohl, David M.
1997   Pioneer Woman in Iowa Archaeology and Prairie-Plains Ethnohistory: Mildred Mott Wedel. *Journal of the Iowa Archeological Society* 44:1–6.

Graham-Bryce, Isabel, Adelaide K. Bullen, and W. H. Forbes
1945   Effect of Pregnenolone on the Ability to Perform Prolonged Psychomotor Tests. *Psychosomatic Medicine* 7(6):352–58.

Grayson, Donald K.
1997   Review of *Case Studies in Environmental Archaeology,* edited by Elizabeth J. Reitz, Lee A. Newsom, and Sylvia J. Scudder. *American Scientist* 85:577.

Griffin, James B.
1992   Women in Archaeology: A Point of Clarification. *Illinois Antiquity* 27(4):7–9.
1994   Early and Later Archaeology of the Ocmulgee National Monument Area. In *Ocmulgee Archaeology 1936–1986,* edited by D. J. Hally, pp. 51–54. University of Georgia Press, Athens.

Griffin, John W.
1949a   The Historic Archaeology of Florida. In *The Florida Indian and His Neighbors,* edited by John W. Griffin, pp. 45–54. Inter-American Center, Rollins College, Winter Park.

Griffin, John W., editor
1949b   The Florida Indian and His Neighbors. Rollins College Inter-American Center, Winter Park, Florida.

Guthe, Carl E.
1936   Report of the Secretary. *American Antiquity* 1:310–11.

Haag, William G.
1948   An Osteometric Analysis of Some Aboriginal Dogs. *University of Kentucky Reports in Anthropology* 7(3):107–264.

Hager, Lori D., editor
1997   *Women in Human Evolution.* Routledge, New York.

Hall, Robert L.
1989   The Cultural Background of Mississippian Symbolism. In *The Southeastern Ceremonial Complex: Artifacts and Analysis,* edited by P. Galloway, pp. 239–78. University of Nebraska Press, Lincoln.
1997   *An Archaeology of the Soul: North American Indian Belief and Ritual.* University of Illinois Press, Urbana.

Halperin, Rhoda H.
1980   Ecology and Mode of Production: Seasonal Variation and the Division of Labor by Sex among Hunter-gatherers. *Journal of Anthropological Research* 36:379–400.

Haraway, Donna
1989   *Primate Visions: Gender, Race, and Nature in the World of Modern Science.* Routledge, New York.

Harding, Sandra, and Jean F. O'Barr, editors
1987   *Sex and Scientific Inquiry.* University of Chicago Press, Chicago.

Hart, John P., and Nancy Asch Sidell
1997   Additional Evidence for Early Cucurbit Use in the Northern Eastern Woodlands East of the Allegheny Front. *American Antiquity* 62:523–37.

Hawkes, Kristen, J. F. O'Connell, and N. G. Blurton Jones
1997   Hazda Women's Time Allocation, Offspring Provisioning, and the Evolution of Long Postmenopausal Life Spans. *Current Anthropology* 38:551–77.

Hawkins, Benjamin
1938   *A Sketch of the Creek Country in the Years 1798 and 1799.* Americus Book Company, Americus, Georgia.

Hays-Gilpin, Kelley, and Davis S. Whitley, editors
1998   *Reader in Gender Archaeology.* Routledge, New York.

Heilbrun, Carolyn G.
1995   *The Education of a Woman: The Life of Gloria Steinem.* Dial Press, New York.

Heimlich, Marion Dunlevy
1952   *Guntersville Basin Pottery.* Geological Survey of Alabama Museum Paper 32, University, Alabama.

Hemmings, E. Thomas, and Kathleen A. Deagan
1973   Excavations on Amelia Island in Northeast Florida. *Contributions of the Florida State Museum, Anthropology and History* 18. Gainesville.

Herdt, Gilbert, editor
1994   *Third Sex, Third Gender: Beyond Sexual Dimorphism in Culture and History.* Zone Books, New York.

Higgins, Carol
1989   New Gender Perspectives in Anthropology. *Anthro Notes: National Museum of Natural History Bulletin for Teachers* 11(3):13–15. Smithsonian Institution, Washington, D.C.

Hill, Erica
1998   Gender-Informed Archaeology: The Priority of Definition, the Use of Analogy, and the Multivariate Approach. *Journal of Archaeological Method and Theory* 5:99–128.

Hillyer, Elinor
1927   Indians' Gambling Rock. *Atlanta Journal Magazine,* December 27, p. 23.

Hollimon, Sandra E.
1997   The Third Gender in Native California: Two Spirit Undertakers among the Chumash and Their Neighbors. In *Women in Prehistory: North America and Mesoamerica,* edited by C. Claassen and R. A. Joyce, pp. 173–88. University of Pennsylvania Press, Philadelphia.

Holmes, William H.
1905   Contributions of American Archaeology to American History. *Annual Report of the Smithsonian Institution for 1904,* p. 558. Washington, D.C.

hooks, bell
1981   *Ain't I a Woman: Black Women and Feminism.* South End Press, Boston.

Hooton, E. A.
1930   *The Indians of Pecos Pueblo: A Study of Their Skeletal Remains.* Yale University Press, New Haven.

Howell, Nancy
1990   *Surviving Fieldwork.* A Report of the Advisory Panel on Health and Safety in Fieldwork. American Anthropological Association Special Publication No. 26, Washington, D.C.

Hubbard, Ruth
1988   Science, Facts and Feminism. *Hypatia* 3(1):5–18. Special Issue: Feminism and Science 2.
Hudson, Charles
1976   *The Southeastern Indians.* University of Tennessee Press, Knoxville.
1996   The Early Days of the SAS. *Southern Anthropologist* 23(2):8–17.
Hudson, Charles M., and Joyce Rockwood Hudson
1989   Tracking the Elusive De Soto. *Archaeology* 42(3):32–36.
Hudson, Joyce Rockwood
1993   *Looking for DeSoto: A Search through the South for the Spaniard's Trail.* University of Georgia Press, Athens.
Huntsville (Alabama) Times (HT)
1938   150,145 in State without Work. January 3, p. 4.
1938   Billion Dollar Deficit for Next U.S. Fiscal Year Predicted. January 4, p. 2.
1938   WPA Rolls Keep Growing as Idle Situation Worse. May 23, p. 8.
1938   No Aid in View to 600 Families in Dire Straits. July 3, p. 2.
1939   WPA Projects. April 2.
1940   Chairman Says Charge Untrue. April 15.
Hurston, Zora Neale
1942   *Dust Tracks on a Road.* HarperCollins Publishers, New York.
Hutchinson, Leonard Patrick
1961   *History of the Playground Area.* Great Outdoors Publishing Co., St. Petersburg, Florida.
Imber, Barbara, and Nancy Tuana
1988   Feminist Perspectives on Science. *Hypatia* 3(1):139–44.
Irwin-Williams, Cynthia
1990   Women in the Field: The Role of Women in Archaeology before 1960. In *Women of Science, Righting the Record,* edited by G. Kass-Simon and Patricia Farnes, pp. 1–41. Indiana University Press, Bloomington.
Ivins, Molly
1991   *Molly Ivins Can't Say That, Can She?* Vintage Books, New York.
Jacobs, Sue-Ellen, Wesley Thomas, and Sabine Lang, editors
1998   *Two-Spirit People: Native American Gender Identity, Sexuality and Spirituality.* University of Illinois Press, Urbana.
Jahoda, Gloria
1967   *The Other Florida.* Scribner's, New York.
Jameson, John H., Jr., editor
1997   *Presenting Archaeology to the Public: Digging for Truths.* Alta Mira Press, Walnut Creek, California.
Jennings, Jesse D.
1994   *Accidental Archaeologist.* Foreword by C. Melvin Aikens. University of Utah Press, Salt Lake City.
Johnson, Jay K., editor
1993   Conclusion. In *The Development of Southeastern Archaeology,* edited by J. Johnson, pp. 207–13. University of Alabama Press, Tuscaloosa.

Johnson, Jay K., and Bettye J. Broyles
1985   Cultural Resources Survey and Testing in Colbert Ferry Park, Alabama. *University of Mississippi Center for Archaeological Research, Archaeological Papers* 6.

Jones, Charles C., Jr.
1873   *Antiquities of the Southern Indians, Particularly of the Georgia Tribes.* D. Appleton and Company, New York.

Jones, Sian, and Sharon Pay
1990   The Legacy of Eve. In *The Politics of the Past,* edited by P. Gathercole and D. Lowenthal, pp. 160–71. Unwin Hyman, London.

Joutel, Henri
1714   *A Journal of the Last Voyage Performed by Monsr. De la Salle to the Gulph of Mexico to Find Out the Mouth of the Mississippi River.* A. BeB. Lintott, J. Baker, London.

Kass-Simon, G., and Patricia Farnes, editors
1990   *Women of Science: Righting the Record.* Indiana University Press, Bloomington.

Kastner, Joseph
1993   At Home in Nature. *Natural History* (December) 106:78–82.

Kehoe, Alice Beck
1995   Review of *Hidden Scholars,* edited by N. Parezo. *Science* 269:1600–1601.
1998   Appropriate Terms. *SAA Bulletin* 16(2):23, 34.

Kellar, James H., A. R. Kelly, and Edward McMichael
1962   The Mandeville Site in Southwest Georgia. *American Antiquity* 27:336–55.

Keller, Evelyn Fox
1983   *A Feeling for the Organism: The Life and Work of Barbara McClintock.* W. H. Freeman, New York.

Kelley, Jane H.
1992   Being and Becoming. In *Rediscovering Our Past: Essays on the History of American Archaeology,* edited by J. Reyman, pp. 81–90. Avebury/Ashgate Publishing Co., Brookfield, Vermont.

Kelly, A. R.
1938   A Preliminary Report on Archaeological Explorations at Macon, Georgia. Anthropological Papers No. 1. *Bureau of American Ethnology Bulletin* 119:25–31. Smithsonian Institution, New York.

Kelly, A. R., and Lewis H. Larson, Jr.
1957   Explorations at Etowah, Georgia 1954–1956. *Georgia Mineral Newsletter* 10(2):60–67.

Kelly, A. R., and Betty A. Smith
1975   *The Swift Creek Site, 9Bi3, Macon, Georgia.* Manuscript on file, Department of Anthropology, University of Georgia, Athens.

Kent, Susan
1998   Gender and Prehistory in Africa. In *Gender in African Prehistory,* edited by S. Kent, pp. 9–21. Alta Mira Press, Walnut Creek, California.

Kessler, Evelyn S.
1976   *Woman: An Anthropological View.* Holt, Rinehart and Winston, New York.

King, Florence
1976   *Southern Ladies and Gentlemen.* Bantam Books, New York.
Kirby, Jack Temple
1995   *The Counter Cultural South.* Mercer University Lamar Memorial Lectures No. 38. University of Georgia Press, Athens.
Klein, Laura F., and Lillian A. Ackerman, editors
1995   *Women and Power in Native North America.* University of Oklahoma Press, Norman.
Kneberg, Madeline D. *See bibliography at end of chapter 4.*
Knight, Chris
1991   *Blood Relations: Menstruation and the Origins of Culture.* Yale University Press, New Haven.
Knight, Lucian Lamar
1917   *A Standard History of Georgia and Georgians.* The Lewis Publishing Company, New York.
Koehler, Lyle
1997   Earth Mothers, Warriors, Horticulturalists, Artists, and Chiefs: Women among the Mississippian and Mississippian-Oneota Peoples. In *Women in Prehistory: North America and Mesoamerica,* edited by C. Claassen and R. Joyce, pp. 211–26. University of Pennsylvania Press, Philadelphia.
Kramer, Carol, and Miriam Stark
1988   The Status of Women in Archaeology. *Anthropology Newsletter* 29(1):11–12. American Anthropological Association, Washington, D.C.
Kroeber, Alfred L.
1940   Statistical Classification. *American Antiquity* 6(1):40.
1942   On "An Interpretation of the Prehistory of the Eastern United States." *American Antiquity* 7:326.
Krogman, Wilton M.
1962   *The Human Skeleton in Forensic Medicine.* Charles C. Thomas, Springfield, Illinois. (Updated as Wilton M. Krogman and M. Y. Iscan, C. C. Thomas, Springfield, Illinois, 1986.)
Kuttruff, Carl, and Jenna Tedrick Kuttruff
1996   Mississippian Textile Evidence on Fabric-Impressed Ceramics from Mound Bottom, Tennessee. In *A Most Indispensable Art: Native Fiber Industries from Eastern North America,* edited by J. B. Peterson, pp. 160–73. University of Tennessee Press, Knoxville.
Kuttruff, Jenna Tedrick
1993   Mississippian Period Status Differentiation through Textile Analysis: A Caddoan Example. *American Antiquity* 58:125–45.
Kyle, F. Clason
1986   *Images: A Pictorial History of Columbus, Georgia.* The Donning Company Publishers, Norfolk, Virginia.
Lamphere, Louise, Helena Ragone, and Patricia Zavella, editors
1997   *Situated Lives: Gender and Culture in Everyday Life.* Routledge, New York.
Lazarus, William C.
1961   The Morrison Spring Site (8Wl43), Florida. *Florida Anthropologist* 14:17–20.
1962   Ten Middens on the Navy Liveoak Reservation. *Florida Anthropologist* 14:49–64.

1964   The Postl's Lake II Site, Eglin Air Force Base, Florida (8Ok71) *Florida Anthropologist* 17:1–16.

1965   Alligator Lake: A Ceramic Horizon Site on the Northwest Florida Coast. *Florida Anthropologist* 28:83–124.

Lazarus, Yulee W. *See bibliography at end of chapter 8.*

Leacock, Eleanor Burke
1981   *Myths of Male Dominance: Collected Articles on Women Cross-Culturally.* Monthly Review Press, New York.

Leakey, Mary Douglas
1984   *Disclosing the Past.* Doubleday, Garden City, New York.

Ledbetter, R. Jerald
1995   *Dear Isabel: Archeological Correspondence of A. R. Kelly and Isabel Patterson, 1934–1953.* LAMAR Institute Publication 33, Watkinsville, Georgia.

1997   *The Bull Creek Site, 9ME1, Muscogee County, Georgia.* Georgia Department of Transportation Occasional Papers in Cultural Resource Management 9. Atlanta.

Lee, Richard B., and I. DeVore, editors
1968   *Man the Hunter.* Aldine, Chicago.

LeGuin, Ursula
1986   The Carrier Bag Theory of Fiction. In *Dancing at the Edge of the World: Thoughts on Words, Women, Places,* by U. K. LeGuin, pp. 165–70. Grove Press, New York, 1989.

Lepowsky, Maria
1994   *Fruit of the Motherland.* Columbia University Press, New York.

Leslie, Vernon
1949   Let's Put Some Meat on the Bones. *Pennsylvania Archaeologist* 19:2.

Lester, F.
1938   Preliminary Report of Excavation at Bull Creek Village Site, Muscogee County, Georgia. Unpublished manuscript on file Columbus Museum, Columbus, Georgia.

Levine, Mary Ann
1991   An Historic Overview of Research on Women in Anthropology. In *The Archaeology of Gender.* Proceedings of the 22nd Annual Chacmool Conference, edited by D. Walde and N. Willows, pp. 177–86. Archaeological Association of the University of Calgary.

Lévi-Strauss, Claude
1936   Contribution à l'étude de l'organisation sociale des indiens Bororo. *Journal de la Société des Américanistes* 27:269–308.

Lewis, Madeline Kneberg. *See bibliography at end of chapter 4.*

Lewis, Thomas M. N.
1935   The Lure of Prehistoric Tennessee. *Journal of the Tennessee Academy of Science* 10(3):153–59.

1937   Annotations Pertaining to Prehistoric Research in Tennessee. *University of Tennessee Record.* University of Tennessee Press, Knoxville.

1942   Early Chapters of Tennessee. *Tennessee Folklore Society Bulletin* 8(2):27–53.

Lewis, Thomas M. N., and Madeline Kneberg (Lewis). *See bibliography at end of chapter 4.*

Lewis, Thomas M. N., Madeline Kneberg Lewis, and Lynne P. Sullivan, editor and compiler
1995 *The Prehistory of the Chickamauga Basin in Tennessee,* by T. M. N. Lewis, Madeline Kneberg, and others. 2 vols. University of Tennessee Press, Knoxville.

Lipe, William D., and A. J. Lindsay, editors
1974 *Proceedings of the 1974 Cultural Resource Management Conference, Denver, Colorado.* Museum of Northern Arizona, Technical Series No. 14. Flagstaff.

Lister, Florence C.
1997 *Pot Luck: Adventures in Archaeology.* University of New Mexico Press, Albuquerque.

Little, Barbara J.
1994 Consider the Hermaphroditic Mind: Comment on "The Interplay of Evidential Constraints and Political Interests: Recent Archaeological Research on Gender." *American Antiquity* 59:539–44.

Longacre, William A.
1966 Changing Patterns of Social Integration: A Prehistoric Example from the American Southwest. *American Anthropologist* 68:94–102.

Lyon, Edwin A.
1996 *A New Deal for Southeastern Archaeology.* University of Alabama Press, Tuscaloosa.

MacArthur, R. H., and J. W. MacArthur
1961 On Bird Species Diversity. *Ecology* 42:595–98.

Mackey, Mary
1983 *The Last Warrior Queen.* Berkeley Books, New York.
1993 *The Year the Horses Came.* Penguin Books, New York.
1995 *The Horses at the Gate.* Penguin Books, New York.

Marable, Manning
1983 *How Capitalism Underdeveloped Black America.* South End Press, Boston.

Marcus, Joyce, and Kent V. Flannery
1994 Ancient Zapotec Ritual and Religion: An Application of the Direct Historical Approach. In *The Ancient Mind,* edited by C. Renfrew and E. Zubrow, pp. 55–74. Cambridge University Press, New York.

Marrinan, Rochelle A., and Elizabeth S. Wing
1980 Prehistoric Fishing. In *Florida's Maritime Heritage,* edited by B. A. Purdy, pp. 8–10. Florida State Museum, Gainesville.

Martin, M. K., and Barbara Voorhies
1975 *Female of the Species.* Columbia University Press, New York.

Martin, R.
1914 *Lehrbuch der Anthropologie,* Jena.

Mascia-Lees, Frances E., Patricia Sharpe, and Colleen Ballerino Cohen
1989 The Postmodernist Turn in Anthropology: Cautions from a Feminist Perspective. *Signs* 15:7–33.

Mason, Carol I. *See bibliography at end of chapter 9.*

Mathews, Holly F.
1989 Introduction: What Does It Mean to Be a Woman in the South Today? In *Women in the South: An Anthropological Perspective,* edited by H. F.

Mathews, pp. 1–8. Southern Anthropological Society Proceedings, No. 22. University of Georgia Press, Athens.

McCann, Catherine
1939a   Faunal Remains at Irene Mound: Abstract. *Southeastern Archaeological Conference Newsletter* 2(1).
1939b   Faunal Remains at Irene Mound, Savannah. *Society for Georgia Archaeology Proceedings* 2(2):37–40.
1941   The Development of Cord Marked Pottery in Chatham County. *Society for Georgia Archaeology Proceedings* 3(1).

McGimsey, Charles R., III
1972   *Public Archaeology.* Seminar Press, New York.
1980   *Mariana Mesa: Seven Prehistoric Settlements in West Central New Mexico.* Peabody Museum of Archaeology and Ethnology Papers 72. Harvard University, Cambridge.

McGimsey, Charles R., III, Carl Chapman, and Hester A. Davis
1970   *Stewards of the Past.* University of Missouri, Columbia. Reprinted in *Melanges* 4, May 15, 1972.

McGimsey, Charles R., III, and Hester A. Davis, editors
n.d.   *A Handbook for Arkansas Archeologists.* Arkansas Archeological Society.
1968   Modern Land Use Practices and the Archeology of the Lower Mississippi Alluvial Valley. *Arkansas Archaeologist* 9:28–36.
1977   *The Management of Archaeological Resources: The Airlie House Report.* Society for American Archaeology, Washington, D.C.
1984   The United States of America. In *Approaches to Archaeological Heritage,* edited by H. Cleere, pp. 116–24. Cambridge University Press, Cambridge, England.

McGrayne, Sharon B.
1993   *Nobel Prize Women in Science.* Birch Lane Press, New York.

McGuire, Jeanie L., and David Allerton
1982   An Interview with Elizabeth S. Wing. *Florida Anthropologist* 35:65–75.

Mead, Margaret
1928   *Coming of Age in Samoa.* William Morrow and Company, New York.
1972   *Blackberry Winter: My Earlier Years.* William Morrow and Company, New York.

Meyer, Kathleen
1989   *How to Shit in the Woods: An Environmentally Sound Approach to a Lost Art.* Ten Speed Press, Berkeley, California.

Michard-Marchal, Claire, and Claudine Ribery
1982   *Sexisme et sciences humaines.* Presses Universitaires de Lille, Lille, France.

Milanich, Jerald T.
1994   *Archaeology of Precolumbian Florida.* University Press of Florida, Gainesville.

Milanich, Jerald T., and Charles H. Fairbanks
1980   *Florida Archaeology.* Academic Press, New York.

Milanich, Jerald T., and Charles Hudson
1993   *Hernando de Soto and the Indians of Florida.* University Press of Florida, Gainesville.

Milanich, Jerald T., Ann S. Cordell, Vernon J. Knight, Jr., Timothy A. Kohler, and
Brenda J. Sigler-Lavelle
1997   *Archaeology of Northern Florida*, A.D. *200–900: The McKeithen Weeden Island Culture*. University Press of Florida, Gainesville.

Milanich, Jerald T., and Susan Milbrath, editors
1989   *First Encounters: Spanish Explorations in the Caribbean and the United States, 1492–1570*. University of Florida Press, Gainesville.

Miller, John E. III
1982   Construction of Site Features: Tests of Mounds C, D, E, B and the Embankment. In *Emerging Patterns of Plum Bayou Culture*, edited by M. A. Rolingson, pp. 30–43. Arkansas Archaeological Survey Research Series 18.

Mitchem, Jeffrey M.
1987   Obituary: Adelaide Kendall Bullen. *Florida Anthropologist* 40:169.

Mooney, James
1900   *Myths of the Cherokees*. Bureau of American Ethnology Nineteenth Annual Report, Smithsonian Institution, Washington, D.C.
1975   *Historical Sketch of the Cherokee*. Aldine, Chicago.

Moore, Clarence Bloomfield
1901   Certain Aboriginal Remains of the Northwest Florida Coast. *Journal of the Academy of Natural Sciences* 11, Part 1, pp. 456–72. Philadelphia.
1918   The Northwestern Florida Coast Revisited. *Journal of the Academy of Natural Sciences* (second series) 16:514–81. Philadelphia.

Moore, Henrietta L.
1988   *Feminism and Anthropology*. University of Minnesota Press, Minneapolis.

Moorehead, Warren King
1929   Georgia. In Reports, *American Anthropologist*, n.s. 31:343.
1931   Phillips Academy. In Anthropological Notes and News, *American Anthropologist*, n.s. 33(2):299.
1932   Acknowledgments. In *Etowah Papers*, edited by W. K. Moorehead et al., pp. v–vi. Yale University Press, New Haven.

Moorehead, Warren King, Charles C. Willoughby, Margaret E. Ashley, Zelia Nuttall, and Frank Collins Baker
1932   *Etowah Papers*. Yale University Press, New Haven.

Morbeck, Mary Ellen, Alison Galloway, and Adrienne L. Zihlman, editors
1997   *The Evolving Female: A Life History Perspective*. Princeton University Press, Princeton, New Jersey.

Morgan, Ann Haven
1930   *Fieldbook of Ponds and Streams*. Putnam and Company, New York.
1955   *Kinship of Animals and Man*. McGraw-Hill Book Company, New York.

Morgan, Lewis Henry
1877   *Ancient Society*. World Publishing, New York.

Morgen, Sandra, editor
1989   *Gender and Anthropology*. Critical Reviews for Research and Teaching. American Anthropological Association, Washington, D.C.

Morris, Ann Axtell
1933   *Digging in the Southwest*. Doubleday, Doran and Company, New York.

Morse, Mary
1995   *Women Changing Science: Voices from a Field in Transition.* Insight Books, Plenum Press, New York.
Mozans, H. J. [pseudonym for John Augustine Zahm]
1913   *Woman in Science.* D. Appleton and Company, New York. Reprinted 1974 by MIT Press, Cambridge, Massachusetts.
Mukhopadhyay, Carol C., and Patricia J. Higgins
1988   Anthropological Studies of Women's Status Revisited: 1977–1987. *Annual Review of Anthropology* 17:461–95.
Muller, Jon
1997   *Mississippian Political Economy.* Plenum Press, New York.
Mulvihill, Frank J.
1925   Some Indications of Indian Occupancy along Bull Creek, Near Columbus, Georgia. *Arrow Point.* Montgomery, Alabama.
Nassaney, Michael S.
1992   Communal Societies and the Emergence of Elites in the Prehistoric American Southeast. In *Lords of the Southeast: Social Inequality and the Native Elites of Southeastern North America,* edited by A. W. Barker and T. R. Pauketat, pp. 111–43. Archaeological Papers of the American Anthropological Association No. 3.
National Park Service
1997   *Placing Women in the Past. CRM* 20(3) [whole volume]. U.S. Department of the Interior, National Park Service, Cultural Resources, Washington, D.C.
Nelson, Margaret C., Sarah M. Nelson, and Alison Wylie, editors
1994   *Equity Issues for Women in Archaeology.* Archaeological Papers of the American Anthropological Association Number 5.
Nelson, Sarah Milledge
1997   *Gender in Archaeology: Analyzing Power and Prestige.* Altamira Press, Walnut Creek, California.
Norwood, Vera
1993   *Made from This Earth: American Women and Nature.* University of North Carolina Press, Chapel Hill.
Nyman, Lynette
1994   Madeline Kneberg Lewis: A Southeastern Archaeologist and Educator. Paper prepared for class directed by I. Brown, University of Alabama. Manuscript in possession of author.
O'Reilly, Jane
1972   The Housewife's Moment of Truth. *Ms.* 1:55–58.
Ortner, Sherry B.
1974   Is Female to Male as Nature Is to Culture? In *Woman, Culture and Society,* edited by M. Z. Rosaldo and L. Lamphere, pp. 67–88. Stanford University Press, Stanford, California.
1996   *Making Gender: The Politics and Erotics of Culture.* Beacon Press, Boston.
Parezo, Nancy J.
1993a   Preface and Anthropology: The Welcoming Science. In *Hidden Scholars: Women Anthropologists and the Native American Southwest,* edited by N. Parezo, pp. xi–37. University of New Mexico Press, Albuquerque.

1993b   Conclusion: The Beginning of the Quest. In *Hidden Scholars: Women Anthropologists and the Native American Southwest,* edited by N. Parezo, pp. 334–67. University of New Mexico Press, Albuquerque.

Parezo, Nancy J., editor
1993c   *Hidden Scholars: Women Anthropologists and the Native American Southwest.* University of New Mexico Press, Albuquerque.

Patterson, Isabel Garrard. *See bibliography at end of chapter 3.*

Patterson, Thomas C.
1995   *Toward a Social History of Archaeology in the United States.* Harcourt Brace College Publishers, New York.

Pauketat, Timothy R.
1994   *The Ascent of Chiefs: Cahokia and Mississippian Politics in Native North America.* University of Alabama Press, Tuscaloosa.

Peebles, Christopher S.
1990   From History to Hermeneutics: The Place of Theory in the Later Prehistory of the Southeast. *Southeastern Archaeology* 9:23–34.

Petersen, James B., and Nancy Asch Sidell
1996   Mid-Holocene Evidence of *Cucurbita* Sp. from Central Maine. *American Antiquity* 61:685–98.

Phillips, Philip, James A. Ford, and James B. Griffin
1951   *Archaeological Survey in the Lower Mississippi Alluvial Valley, 1940–1947.* Peabody Museum Papers 25. Harvard University, Cambridge.

Pickering, Robert
1992   Harriet Minola Smith, 1911–1992. *Illinois Antiquity* 27(3):4.

Poewe, Karla
1991   Ship without a Rudder? (correspondence). *Anthropology Newsletter* 32(9):3.

Preucel, Robert, and Ian Hodder
1996   Understanding Sex and Gender. In *Contemporary Archaeology in Theory: A Reader,* edited by R. Preucel and I. Hodder, pp. 415–30. Blackwell, Cambridge, Massachusetts.

Preucel, Robert, and Rosemary Joyce
1994   Feminism, Fieldwork, and the Practice of Archaeology. Paper presented at the 93rd annual meeting of the American Anthropological Association, Atlanta.

Pringle, Heather
1998   New Women of the Ice Age. *Discover,* 19(4):62–70.

Professional Geographer
1994   Women in the Field: Critical Feminist Methodologies and Theoretical Perspectives. *Professional Geographer* 46(1):54–66.

Pycior, Helena M., et al., editors
1996   *Creative Couples in the Sciences.* Rutgers University Press, New Brunswick, New Jersey.

Quimby, George I., and Charles E. Cleland
1976   James Bennett Griffin: Appreciation and Reminiscences. In *Cultural Change and Continuity: Essays in Honor of James Bennett Griffin,* edited by C. E. Cleland, pp. xxi–xxxvi. Academic Press, New York.

Quitmyer, Irvy R., H. Stephen Hale, and Douglas S. Jones
1985   Seasonality Study Based on the Incremental Growth Data from the Quahog Clam *Mercenaria mercenaria.* In *Aboriginal Subsistence and Settlement Ar-*

chaeology of the Kings Bay Locality, vol. 2: *Zooarchaeology*, edited by William H. Adams, pp. 59–71. University of Florida, Department of Anthropology, Reports of Investigations 2. Gainesville.

Quitmyer, Irvy R., E. S. Wing, H. S. Hale, D. S. Jones, and S. J. Scudder
1985 Zooarchaeology. In *Aboriginal Subsistence and Settlement Archaeology of the King's Bay Locality*, edited by William H. Adams, pp. 1–112. University of Florida, Department of Anthropology, Report of Investigations 2. Gainesville.

Rathje, William L., and Michael B. Schiffer
1982 *Archaeology*. Harcourt Brace Jovanovich, Inc., New York.

Reitz, Elizabeth J., and Elizabeth S. Wing
1999 *Zooarchaeology*. Cambridge University Press, Cambridge.

Reitz, E. J., I. R. Quitmyer, H. S. Hale, S. J. Scudder, and E. S. Wing
1987 Applications of Allometry to Zooarchaeology. *American Antiquity* 52:304–17.

Reitz, Elizabeth J., Lee A. Newsom, and Sylvia J. Scudder, editors
1996 *Case Studies in Environmental Archaeology*. Plenum Press, New York.

Renfrew, Colin
1994 Toward a Cognitive Archaeology. In *The Ancient Mind*, edited by C. Renfrew and E. Zubrow, pp. 3–12. Cambridge University Press, New York.

Reyman, Jonathan
1992 *Rediscovering Our Past: Essays on the History of American Archaeology*. Avebury/Ashgate Publishing Co., Brookfield, Vermont.

Riley, Carroll L.
1998 Review of *Pot Luck: Adventures in Archaeology*, by F. Lister. *American Antiquity* 63:189–90.

Robb, John
1994 Gender Contradictions, Moral Coalitions, and Inequality in Prehistoric Italy. *Journal of European Archaeology* 2(1):20–49.

Robinson, Brian S.
1995 *The Overlock Site: A Late Moorehead Burial Tradition Site in Warren, Maine*. Report to the Maine Historic Preservation Commission.

Rolingson, Martha Ann. *See bibliography at end of chapter 11.*

Rosaldo, Michelle Z.
1980 The Use and Abuse of Anthropology: Reflections on Feminism and Cross-Cultural Understanding. *Signs* 5:389–417.

Rosaldo, Michelle Z., and Louise Lamphere, editors
1974 *Women, Culture, and Society*. Stanford University Press, Stanford, California.

Roscoe, Will
1991 *The Zuni Man-Woman*. University of New Mexico Press, Albuquerque.

Rosser, Sue V.
1987 Feminist Scholarship in the Sciences: Where Are We Now and When Can We Expect a Theoretical Breakthrough? *Hypatia* 2(3):5–18.

Rossiter, Margaret W.
1982 *Women Scientists in America: Struggles and Strategies to 1940*. Johns Hopkins University Press, Baltimore.
1995 *Women Scientists in America: Before Affirmative Action, 1940–1972*. Johns Hopkins University Press, Baltimore.

Rothschild, Bruce M., and Christine Rothschild
1996 Treponemal Disease in the New World. *Current Anthropology* 37:555–61.

Russell, Sharman Apt
1996   *When the Land Was Young: Reflections on American Archaeology.* Addison-Wesley Publishing Company, Reading, Massachusetts.

Sabloff, Jeremy
1992   Visions of Archaeology's Future: Some Comments. In *Quandaries and Quests: Visions of Archaeology's Future,* edited by L. Wandsnider, pp. 266–72. Occasional Paper No. 20. Center for Archaeological Investigations, Southern Illinois University, Carbondale.
1996   The Past and Future of American Archaeology. Distinguished Lecture in Archeology, American Anthropological Association annual meeting, San Francisco, December 1996. Excerpted as Communication and the Future of American Archaeology. *AnthroNotes* 20(1):6–7, Smithsonian Institution, Washington, D.C. Also *American Anthropologist* 100:869–75.

Sabloff, Paula L. W.
1998   *Conversations with Lew Binford.* University of Oklahoma Press, Norman.

Sabo, George, III
1987   Reordering Their World: A Caddoan Ethnohistory. In *Visions and Revisions, Ethnohistoric Perspectives on Southern Cultures,* edited by G. Sabo III and W. M. Schneider, pp. 25–47. Southern Anthropological Society Proceedings No. 20. University of Georgia Press, Athens.
1993   Indians and Spaniards in Arkansas: Symbolic Action in the Sixteenth Century. In *The Expedition of Hernando de Soto West of the Mississippi, 1541–1543,* edited by G. A. Young and M. P. Hoffman, pp. 192–209. University of Arkansas Press, Fayetteville.
1995a Images and Encounters: European Contact and the Caddo Indians. *Historical Reflections* 21(2):217–42.
1995b Rituals of Encounter: Interpreting Native American Views of European Explorers. In *Cultural Encounters in Early America: Native Americans and Europeans in Arkansas,* edited by J. M. Whayne, pp. 76–87. University of Arkansas Press, Fayetteville.

Sanday, Peggy Reeves
1982   Review of *Myths of Male Dominance* by Eleanor B. Leacock. *American Anthropologist* 84:930–31.

Sandweiss, Daniel H., and Elizabeth S. Wing
1997   Ritual Rodents: The Guinea Pigs of Chicha, Peru. *Journal of Field Archaeology* 24(1):47–58.

Sassaman, Kenneth E.
1992   *Early Pottery in the Southeast: Tradition and Innovation in Cooking Technology.* University of Alabama Press, Tuscaloosa.

Savannah (Georgia) Evening Press (SEP)
1938   Student Typists Do Mound Work. March 16.
1938   Irene Mound Is Subject of Poem. March 24.
1938   Remarkable Ancient Sites in Georgia Valuable Asset. March 30.
1938   Praises Work at Irene Mound. April 20.
1938   M'Intosh Indian Sites Are Visited. April 21.
1938   Special Loans Add to Archaeological Exhibit. May 5.
1938   Expert to Make Study Economy of Indians Here. July 25.

Savannah (Georgia) Morning News (SMN)
1937   Excavating at Irene Mound. October 9.
1938   Ground Changes at Irene Mound. April 6.
1938   Art Students Are Sketching Irene. April 8
1938   Dr. Lucy Wenhold to Visit Irene. April 14.
1938   Miss M'Cann Is on Irene Staff. July 26.
Savannah (Georgia) Tribune (ST)
1937   Force Women to Dig Ditches. October 14.
1937   Editorial. October 21.
1938   Housekeeping Aids a Major WPA Project in Savannah. April 14.
1939   New Deal a Threat to the Negro. April 6.
Scarry, John F., editor
1996   *Political Structure and Change in the Prehistoric Southeastern United States.* University Press of Florida, Gainesville.
Schiebinger, Londa
1989   *The Mind Has No Sex? Women in the Origins of Modern Science.* Harvard University Press, Cambridge.
Schiffer, Michael
1995   Social Theory and History in Behavioral Archaeology. In *Expanding Archaeology,* edited by J. Skibo, W. Walker, and A. Nielsen, pp. 22–35. University of Utah Press, Salt Lake City.
Schnell, Frank T., Jr.
1990   Phase Characteristics for the Middle Chattahoochee River. In *Lamar Archaeology, Mississippian Chiefdoms in the Deep South,* edited by M. Williams and G. Shapiro, pp. 67–69. University of Alabama Press, Tuscaloosa.
Schwartz, Douglas W.
1963   An Archaeological Survey of Nankoweap Canyon, Grand Canyon National Park. *American Antiquity* 28(3):289–302.
Schwartz, Douglas W., and Martha A. Rolingson
1966   *Late Paleo-Indian and Early Archaic Manifestations in Western Kentucky.* Studies in Anthropology No. 3, University of Kentucky Press, Lexington.
Science
1992   Women in Science. 25:1363–88 (March 13 issue) and the response, 256:1610–15 (June 19 issue).
1993   Women in Science 93, Gender and Culture. 260:383–432.
Shapiro, Judith
1981   Anthropology and the Study of Gender. *Soundings* 64(4)446–65.
1982   "Women's Studies": A Note on the Perils of Markedness. *Signs* 7:717–20.
Sheldon, Andrew L.
1969   Equitability Indices: Dependence on the Species Count. *Ecology* 50:466–67.
Sherratt, A.
1981   Plough and Pastorialism: Aspects of the Secondary Products Revolution. In *Pattern of the Past,* edited by I. Hodder, G. Isaac, and N. Hammond, pp. 261–305. Cambridge University Press, New York.
Sherrod, P. Clay, and Martha A. Rolingson
1987   *Surveyors of the Ancient Mississippi Valley.* Arkansas Archeological Survey Research Series 28.

Shipman, Pat
1995   One Woman's Life in Science. *American Scientist* 83:300–302.
Shreeve, James
1995   *The Neanderthal Enigma: Solving the Mystery of Modern Human Origins.* Avon Books, New York.
Siefert, Donna J., editor
1991   Gender in Historical Archaeology. *Historical Archaeology* 25(4).
Silverblatt, Irene
1988   Women in States. *Annual Review of Anthropology* 17:427–60.
1991   Interpreting Women in States: New Feminist Ethnohistories. In *Gender at the Crossroads of Knowledge: Feminist Anthropology in the Postmodern Era,* edited by M. di Leonardo, pp. 140–74. University of California Press, Berkeley.
Simson, Rennie
1983   The Afro-American Female: The Historical Context of the Construction of Sexual Identity. In *Powers of Desire: The Politics of Sexuality,* edited by Ann Snitow, Christine Stansell, and Sharon Thompson, pp. 229–35. Monthly Review Press, New York.
Smith, Bruce D.
1987   The Independent Domestication of the Indigenous Seed-Bearing Plants in Eastern North America. In *Emergent Horticultural Economies of the Eastern Woodlands,* edited by W. Keegan, pp. 3–47. Occasional Paper No. 7. Center for Archaeological Investigations, Southern Illinois University, Carbondale.
1992   *Rivers of Change: Essays on Early Agriculture in Eastern North America.* Smithsonian Institution Press, Washington D.C.
Smith, George S., and John E. Ehrenhard, editors
1991   *Protecting the Past.* CRC Press, Boca Raton, Florida.
Smith, Maria O.
1993   Physical Anthropology. In *The Development of Southeastern Archaeology,* edited by J. K. Johnson, pp. 53–77. University of Alabama Press, Tuscaloosa.
Sobolik, Kristin D.
1996   Direct Evidence for Prehistoric Sex Differences. *Anthropology Newsletter* 3(9):7–8 (December 1996). American Anthropological Association, Washington, D.C.
Sobolik, Kristin D., Kristen J. Gremillion, Patricia L. Whitten, and Patty Jo Watson
1996   Technical Note: Sex Determination of Prehistoric Human Paleofeces. *American Journal of Physical Anthropology* 101:283–90.
Sonnert, Gerhard
1995   *Gender Differences in Science Careers.* Rutgers University Press, New Brunswick, New Jersey.
Spain, Daphne
1992   *Gendered Spaces.* University of North Carolina Press, Chapel Hill.
Spector, Janet C.
1993   *What This Awl Means: Feminist Archaeology in a Wahpeton Dakota Village.* Minnesota Historical Society, Minneapolis.
Spector, Janet C., and Mary K. Whelan
1989   Incorporating Gender into Archaeology Courses. In *Gender and Anthropology: Critical Reviews for Research and Teaching,* edited by S. Morgen, pp. 65–94. American Anthropological Association, Washington, D.C.

Spencer, Frank
1982   Introduction. In *A History of American Physical Anthropology, 1930–1980*, edited by Frank Spencer, pp. 1–10. Academic Press, New York.

Spencer-Wood, Suzanne M.
1992   A Feminist Program for Nonsexist Archaeology. In *Quandaries and Quests: Visions of Archaeology's Future*, edited by LuAnn Wandsnider, pp. 98–114. Center for Archaeological Investigations, Southern Illinois University, Carbondale.

Stange, Mary Zeiss
1998   *Woman the Hunter*. Beacon Press, Boston.

Stark, Miriam
1991   A Perspective on Women's Status in American Archaeology. In *The Archaeology of Gender*. Proceedings of the 22nd Annual Chacmool Conference, edited by D. Walde and N. Willows, pp. 187–94. University of Calgary Archaeological Association.
1992   Where the Money Goes: Current Trends in Archaeological Funding. In *Quandaries and Quests: Visions of Archaeology's Future*, edited by L. Wandsnider, pp. 41–58. Occasional Paper No. 20. Center for Archaeological Investigations, Southern Illinois University, Carbondale.

Stephens, Autumn
1993   *Untamed Tongues: Wild Words from Wild Women*. Conari Press, Berkeley, California.

Stolte-Heiskanen, Veronica
1991   *Women in Science: Token Women or Gender Equality?* Berg, Oxford, and St. Martin's Press, New York.

Stone, Linda
1997   *Kinship and Gender*. Westview Press, Boulder, Colorado.

Strong, John A.
1989   The Mississippian Bird-Man Theme in Cross-Cultural Perspective. In *The Southeastern Ceremonial Complex: Artifacts and Analysis*, edited by P. Galloway, pp. 210–37. University of Nebraska Press, Lincoln.

Sullivan, James, et al., editors
1921–65 *The Papers of Sir William Johnston*. 14 vols. University of the State of New York, Albany.

Sullivan, Lynne P.
1994   Madeline Kneberg Lewis: An Original Southeastern Archaeologist. In *Women in Archaeology*, edited by C. Claassen, pp. 110–19. University of Pennsylvania Press, Philadelphia.

Swanton, John R., chairman
1939   *Final Report of the United States DeSoto Expedition Commission*. U.S. Government Printing Office, Washington, D.C. Reprinted in 1985 by Smithsonian Institution Press, Washington, D.C.

Sweet, Jill
1997   Ethical Considerations in an Intergenerational Life History Project. *Anthropology Newsletter* 38(4):11, 17 (April 1997). American Anthropological Association.

Swift, Camm, and Elizabeth S. Wing
1968   Fossil Bony Fishes from Florida. *Plaster Jacket* 7. Florida State Museum, Gainesville.

Syfers, Judy
1972   I Want a Wife. *Ms.*, vol. 1 (inaugural issue), Spring 1972:56.
1973   Why I Want a Wife. In *Radical Feminism*, edited by A. Koedt, E. Levine, and A. Rapone, pp. 60–62. Times Books, New York.

Taylor, Timothy
1996   *The Prehistory of Sex: Four Million Years of Human Sexual Culture.* Bantam Books, New York.

Taylor, Walter W.
1948   *A Study of Archeology.* Originally published as Memoir 69, *American Anthropologist,* vol. 50, no. 3, pt. 2. Reprinted by the Center for Archaeological Investigations, with foreword by Patty Jo Watson, Southern Illinois University, Carbondale, 1983.

Tebeau, Charlton W.
1971   *A History of Florida.* (Revised 1980). University of Miami Press, Coral Gables.

Terrell, J.
1990   Storytelling and Prehistory. In *Archaeological Method and Theory,* vol. 2, edited by M. Schiffer, pp. 1–30. University of Arizona Press, Tucson.

Thomas, Cyrus
1887   The Cherokee Probably Mound-Builders. In Burial Mounds of the Northern Sections of the United States, pp. 87–107. *Fifth Annual Report of the Bureau of Ethnology to the Secretary of the Smithsonian Institution: 1883–84.* Smithsonian Institution, Washington, D.C.

Thomas, Julian
1992   Gender, Politics, and American Archaeology. *Anthropology Today* 8(3):12–13.

Thomas, Larissa A.
1995   Images of Women in Mississippian Iconography. Paper presented at the Southeastern Archaeological Conference, Knoxville, Tennessee.

Thompson, David D.
1982   Forensic Anthropology. In *A History of American Physical Anthropology, 1930–1980,* edited by Frank Spencer, pp. 357–69. Academic Press, New York.

Thorne, Robert, Bettye J. Broyles, and Jay K. Johnson
1981   Lithic Procurement and Utilization Trajectories: Archaeological Survey and Excavations, Yellow Creek Nuclear Power Plant Site, Tishomingo County, Mississippi, volume 1. *University of Mississippi Center for Archaeological Research, Archaeological Papers* 1.

Thorne, Robert, Harry Owens, and Bettye J. Broyles
1982   A Cultural Resources Reconnaissance of the Four Corps Owned Lakes in Mississippi: Grenada Lake, Enid Lake, Sardis Lake, and Arkabutla Lake. *University of Mississippi, Center for Archaeological Research, Archaeological Papers.*

Towle, Margaret Ashley. *See bibliography at end of chapter 2.*

Trinkaus, Erik
1982   A History of *Homo Erectus* and *Homo Sapiens* Paleontology in America. In *A History of American Physical Anthropology, 1930–1980,* edited by Frank Spencer, pp. 261–80. Academic Press, New York.

Troccoli, Ruth
1993   Women as Chiefs in the Southeast: A Reexamination of the Data. Paper presented at the annual meeting of the Southeastern Archaeological Conference, Raleigh, North Carolina.

Ubelaker, Douglas H.
1982   The Development of American Paleopathology. In *A History of American Physical Anthropology, 1930–1980,* edited by Frank Spencer, pp. 337–56. Academic Press, New York.

Vitamin Research Products, Inc.
1997   Pregnenolone and Mental Function. VRP Home Page http://www.vrp.com (8/1/97).

Wadley, Lyn
1998   The Invisible Meat Providers: Women in the Stone Age of South Africa. In *Gender in African Archaeology,* edited by Susan Kent. Alta Mira Press, Walnut Creek, California.

Walcher, D., N. Kretchmer, and H. L. Barnett, editors
1976   *Food, Man, and Society.* Plenum Press, New York.

Walde, D., and N. Willows, editors
1991   *The Archaeology of Gender.* Chacmool 1991, Archaeological Association of the University of Calgary, Alberta, Canada.

Walker, John W.
1994   A Brief History of Ocmulgee Archaeology. In *Ocmulgee Archaeology 1936–1986,* edited by D. J. Hally, pp. 15–35. University of Georgia Press, Athens, Georgia.

Walker, Laurence C.
1991   *The Southern Forest: A Chronicle.* University of Texas Press, Austin.

Ware, Susan
1981   *Beyond Suffrage: Women in the New Deal.* Harvard University Press, Cambridge.

Waring, Antonio J.
1940   The Bilbo Site—Chatham County, Georgia. Paper Number 10. In *The Waring Papers,* edited by S. Williams, Papers of the Peabody Museum of Archaeology and Ethnology No. 58, pp. 152–97. Harvard University, Cambridge, 1968.
1945   The Southern Cult and Muskogean Ceremonial. In *The Waring Papers,* edited by S. Williams, Papers of the Peabody Museum of Archaeology and Ethnology No. 58, pp. 30–69. Harvard University, Cambridge, 1968.

Watson, Patty Jo
1986   Archaeological Interpretation, 1985. In *American Archaeology Past and Future: A Celebration of the Society for American Archaeology 1935–1985,* edited by D. J. Meltzer, D. D. Fowler, and J. A. Sabloff, pp. 439–58. Smithsonian Institution Press, Washington, D.C.
1991   A Parochial Primer: The New Dissonance as Seen from the Midcontinental United States. In *Processual and Postprocessual Archaeologies: Multiple Ways of Knowing the Past,* edited by R. Preucel, pp. 265–74. Occasional Paper No. 10. Center for Archaeological Investigations, Southern Illinois University, Carbondale.

Watson, Patty Jo, editor
1985   *American Antiquity* 50(2) (50th anniversary issue devoted to history of archaeology).
See also bibliography at end of chapter 13.
Wauchope, Robert
1948   The Ceramic Sequence in the Etowah Drainage, Northwest Georgia. *American Antiquity* 13: 201–9.
Webb, William S., and David L. DeJarnette
1948   *The Whitesburg Bridge Site Ma^v10.* Museum Paper 24. Alabama Museum of Natural History, University, Alabama.
Wells, Brian W. P.
1983   *Body and Personality.* Longman, New York.
Welty, Eudora
1980   *The Collected Stories of Eudora Welty.* Harcourt Brace Jovanovich, New York (1936–80).
Whalen, Gail, and Michael E. Price
1998   Georgia History in Pictures. The Elusive Women of Irene: The WPA Excavation of a Savannah Indian Mound. *Georgia Historical Quarterly* 82 (3):608–26.
White, Nancy Marie
1982   The Curlee Site (8Ja7) and Fort Walton Development in the Upper Apalachicola–Lower Chattahoochee Valley. Ph.D. dissertation, Case Western Reserve University. Photocopy, University Microfilms, Ann Arbor, Michigan.
1995   Review of *The Development of Southeastern Archaeology,* edited by J. Johnson. *Journal of Field Archaeology* 22:121–28.
White, Nancy Marie, and Patricia S. Essenpreis
1989   Letter on women in field archaeology. *Anthropology Newsletter* 30(8):3. American Anthropological Association, Washington, D.C.
White, Nancy Marie, Rochelle A. Marrinan, and Hester A. Davis
1994   Early Women in Southeastern Archaeology: A Preliminary Report on Ongoing Research. In *Women In Archaeology,* edited by C. Claassen, pp. 96–109. University of Pennsylvania Press, Philadelphia.
White, Theodore E.
1953   A Method of Calculating the Dietary Percentage of Various Food Animals Utilized by Aboriginal Peoples. *American Antiquity* (4):396–98.
Wiber, Melanie G.
1997   *Erect Men, Undulating Women: The Visual Imagery of Gender, "Race," and Progress in Reconstructive Illustrations of Human Evolution.* Wilfrid Laurier University Press, Waterloo, Ontario.
Widmer, Randolph J.
1994   The Structure of Southeastern Chiefdoms. In *The Forgotten Centuries: Indians and Europeans in the American South,* edited by C. Hudson, pp. 125–55. University of Georgia Press, Athens.
Willey, Gordon R.
1939   Ceramic Stratigraphy in a Georgia Village Site. *American Antiquity* 5:140–47.
1949   Archaeology of the Florida Gulf Coast. *Smithsonian Miscellaneous Collections* 113.

1961   Foreword. In *The Ethnobotany of Pre-Columbian Peru,* by Margaret A. Towle. Viking Fund Publications in Anthropology, No. 30. Wenner-Gren Foundation.

1988   *Portraits in American Archaeology: Remembrances of Some Distinguished Americanists.* University of New Mexico Press, Albuquerque.

1994   Macon, Georgia: A Fifty-Year Retrospect. In *Ocmulgee Archaeology 1936–1986,* edited by D. J. Hally, pp. 36–46. University of Georgia Press, Athens, Georgia.

Willey, Gordon R., and Jeremy A. Sabloff

1977   *A History of American Archaeology.* 3d ed., W. H. Freeman, San Francisco, 1993.

Willey, Gordon R., and William Sears

1952   The Kasita Site. *Southern Indian Studies* 4:3–18. Chapel Hill, North Carolina.

Williams, Barbara

1981   *Breakthrough: Women in Archaeology.* Walker and Company, New York.

Williams, Stephen, editor

1962   *Proceedings of the Sixteenth Southeastern Archaeological Conference* (Macon, Georgia, 1959), Newsletter, 8:33–40.

1968   *The Waring Papers.* Papers of the Peabody Museum of Archaeology and Ethnology No. 58. Harvard University, Cambridge.

Williams, Walter

1986   *The Spirit and the Flesh: A Study of the North American Indian Berdache.* Beacon Press, Boston.

Wills, W. H.

1988   *Early Prehistoric Agriculture in the American Southwest.* School of American Research Press, Santa Fe.

Wilson, Diane

1997   Gender, Diet, Health and Social Status in the Mississippian Powers Phase Turner Cemetery Population. In *Women in Prehistory, North America and Mesoamerica,* edited by C. Claassen and R. Joyce, pp. 119–35. University of Pennsylvania Press, Philadelphia.

Wimberly, Christine Adcock

1960   The Geographic and Historic Background. In *Indian Pottery from Clarke County and Mobile County, Southern Alabama,* by S. B. Wimberly. Geological Survey of Alabama, Museum Paper 36.

Woodbury, Nathalie F. S.

1991   In the Shadow of Man, or Just the Shade of the Lab Tent? Women in the History of American Archaeology. *SAA Bulletin* 9(1):6–7.

Woodbury, Nathalie F. S., editor

1987   Deaths: Adelaide Kendall Bullen. *Anthropology Newsletter,* October.

Wormington, Marie

1957   *Ancient Man in North America.* Denver Museum of Natural History, Denver.

Wright, C. E.

1967   Gulf Coast Shows Its Age. *New York Times,* December 4.

Wright, Rita P., editor

1996   *Gender and Archaeology.* University of Pennsylvania Press, Philadelphia.

Wurtzburg, Susan J.
1994   Women in the Field: A Historical Perspective on the Role of Women in Louisiana Archaeology. In *Women in Archaeology*, edited by Cheryl Claassen, pp. 120–37. University of Pennsylvania Press, Philadelphia.

Wylie, Alison
1991   Gender Theory and the Archaeological Record: Why Is There No Archaeology of Gender? In *Engendering Archaeology: Women and Prehistory*, edited by J. M. Gero and M. W. Conkey, pp. 31–54. Basil Blackwell, Cambridge, Massachusetts.
1997   Good Science, Bad Science, or Science as Usual? Feminist Critiques of Science. In *Women in Human Evolution*, edited by L. Hager, pp. 29–55. Routledge, New York.

Xie, Yu
1996   Review of *The Equity Equation*. *Science* 273:443–44.

Yarnell, Richard A.
1969   Contents of Human Paleofeces. In *The Prehistory of Salts Cave, Kentucky*, edited by P. J. Watson. Illinois State Museum, Reports of Investigations No. 16. Springfield, Illinois.
1974   Plant Food and Cultivation of the Salts Cavers. In *Archaeology of the Mammoth Cave Area*, edited by P. J. Watson, pp. 113–22. Academic Press, New York.

Yentsch, Clarice M., and Carl J. Sinderman
1992   *The Woman Scientist*. Meeting the Challenges for a Successful Career. Plenum Press, New York.

Zeder, Melinda A.
1997   *The American Archaeologist: A Profile*. Alta Mira Press, Walnut Creek, California.

Zihlman, Adrienne L.
1981   Women as Shapers of the Human Adaptation. In *Woman the Gatherer*, edited by F. Dahlberg, pp. 75–120. Yale University Press, New Haven.
1985   Gathering Stories for Hunting Human Nature. Review Essay. *Feminist Studies* 11(2):365–77.
1997   The Paleolithic Glass Ceiling: Women in Human Evolution. In *Women in Human Evolution*, edited by L. Hager. Routledge, New York.

Zuckerman, Harriet
1991   The Careers of Men and Women Scientists: A Review of Current Research. In *The Outer Circle*, edited by H. Zuckerman, J. Cole, and J. Bruer, pp. 27–56. W. W. Norton, New York.

Zuckerman, Harriet, Jonathan R. Cole, and John T. Bruer, editors
1991   *The Outer Circle*. W. W. Norton, New York.

CONTRIBUTORS

Cheryl Claassen, professor, Department of Anthropology, Appalachian State University, Boone, North Carolina 28608

Hester A. Davis, state archeologist, retired, and professor emerita, Arkansas Archeological Survey, 2475 N. Hatch Ave., Fayetteville, Arkansas 72704-1249

R. Jerald Ledbetter, staff archaeologist, Southeastern Archaeological Services, Inc., 565 N. Milledge Ave., Athens, Georgia 30601

Rochelle A. Marrinan, associate professor, Department of Anthropology, Florida State University, Tallahassee, Florida 32306

Carol I. Mason, professor emerita, University of Wisconsin Colleges—Fox Valley, and adjunct professor of anthropology, Lawrence University, Appleton, Wisconsin 54912

Frank T. Schnell, Jr., archaeologist/historian, The Columbus Museum, 1251 Wynnton Road, Columbus, Georgia 31906-2898

Lynne P. Sullivan, curator of archaeology, Frank H. McClung Museum, Knoxville, Tennessee 37996

Patty Jo Watson, professor, Department of Anthropology, CB1114, Washington University, St. Louis, Missouri 63130-4899

Nancy Marie White, associate professor, Department of Anthropology, University of South Florida, 4202 E. Fowler Ave., SOC 107, Tampa, Florida 33620

INDEX

Ripley P. Bullen Series
Florida Museum of Natural History
Edited by Jerald T. Milanich

Tacachale: Essays on the Indians of Florida and Southeastern Georgia during the Historic Period, edited by Jerald T. Milanich and Samuel Proctor (1978); first paperback edition, 1994
Aboriginal Subsistence Technology on the Southeastern Coastal Plain during the Late Prehistoric Period, by Lewis H. Larson (1980)
Cemochechobee: Archaeology of a Mississippian Ceremonial Center on the Chattahoochee River, by Frank T. Schnell, Vernon J. Knight, Jr., and Gail S. Schnell (1981)
Fort Center: An Archaeological Site in the Lake Okeechobee Basin, by William H. Sears, with contributions by Elsie O'R. Sears and Karl T. Steinen (1982); first paperback edition, 1994
Perspectives on Gulf Coast Prehistory, edited by Dave D. Davis (1984)
Archaeology of Aboriginal Culture Change in the Interior Southeast: Depopulation during the Early Historic Period, by Marvin T. Smith (1987); first paperback edition, 1992
Apalachee: The Land between the Rivers, by John H. Hann (1988)
Key Marco's Buried Treasure: Archaeology and Adventure in the Nineteenth Century, by Marion Spjut Gilliland (1989)
First Encounters: Spanish Explorations in the Caribbean and the United States, 1492–1570, edited by Jerald T. Milanich and Susan Milbrath (1989)
Missions to the Calusa, edited and translated by John H. Hann, with an Introduction by William H. Marquardt (1991)
Excavations on the Franciscan Frontier: Archaeology at the Fig Springs Mission, by Brent Richards Weisman (1992)
The People Who Discovered Columbus: The Prehistory of the Bahamas, by William F. Keegan (1992)
Hernando de Soto and the Indians of Florida, by Jerald T. Milanich and Charles Hudson (1993)
Foraging and Farming in the Eastern Woodlands, edited by C. Margaret Scarry (1993)
Puerto Real: The Archaeology of a Sixteenth-Century Spanish Town in Hispaniola, edited by Kathleen Deagan (1995)
Political Structure and Change in the Prehistoric Southeastern United States, edited by John F. Scarry (1996)
A History of the Timucua Indians and Missions, by John H. Hann (1996)

Archaeology of the Mid-Holocene Southeast, edited by Kenneth E. Sassaman and David G. Anderson (1996)

Bioarchaeology of Native American Adaptation in the Spanish Borderlands, edited by Brenda J. Baker and Lisa Kealhofer (1996)

The Indigenous People of the Caribbean, edited by Samuel M. Wilson (1997); first paperback printing, 1999

Hernando de Soto among the Apalachee: The Archaeology of the First Winter Encampment, by Charles R. Ewen and John H. Hann (1998)

The Timucuan Chiefdoms of Spanish Florida: vol. 1, *Assimilation*; vol. 2, *Resistance and Destruction,* by John E. Worth (1998)

Ancient Earthern Enclosures of the Eastern Woodlands, edited by Robert C. Mainfort, Jr., and Lynne P. Sullivan (1998)

An Environmental History of Northeast Florida, by James J. Miller (1998)

Precolumbian Architecture in Eastern North America, by William N. Morgan (1999)

Archaeology of Colonial Pensacola, edited by Judith A. Bense (1999)

Grit-Tempered: Early Women Archaeologists in the Southeastern United States, edited by Nancy Marie White, Lynne P. Sullivan, and Rochelle A. Marrinan (1999)